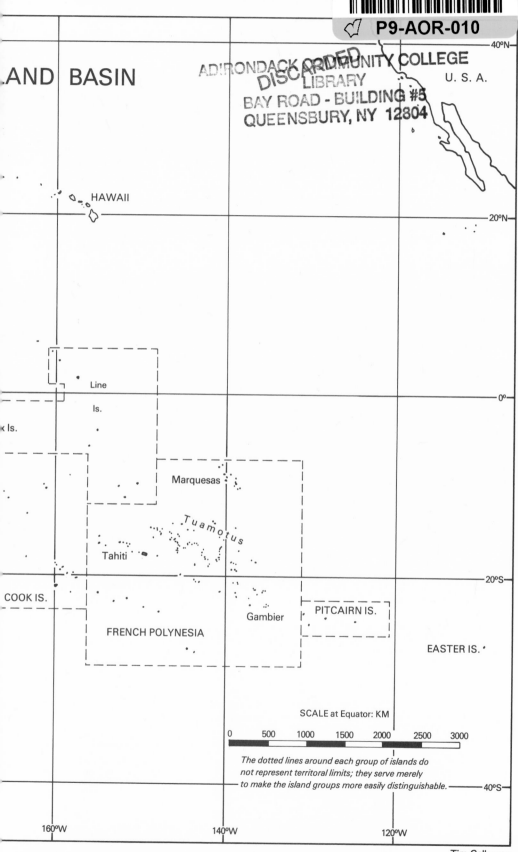

P9-AOR-010

ADIRONDACK COMMUNITY COLLEGE
DISCARDED
LIBRARY
BAY ROAD - BUILDING #5
QUEENSBURY, NY 12804

LAND BASIN

U. S. A.

40°N

HAWAII

20°N

Line

Is.

0°

Is.

Marquesas

Tuamotus

Tahiti

20°S

COOK IS.

Gambier

PITCAIRN IS.

FRENCH POLYNESIA

EASTER IS.

SCALE at Equator: KM

| 0 | 500 | 1000 | 1500 | 2000 | 2500 | 3000 |

*The dotted lines around each group of islands do
not represent territorial limits; they serve merely
to make the island groups more easily distinguishable.*

40°S

160°W

140°W

120°W

Tim Galloway

These Roots Remain

These Roots Remain

Food Habits in Islands of the Central and Eastern Pacific since Western Contact

Nancy J. Pollock

PUBLISHED BY
THE INSTITUTE FOR POLYNESIAN STUDIES
LAIE, HAWAI'I

FUNDED BY THE
POLYNESIAN CULTURAL CENTER
BRIGHAM YOUNG UNIVERSITY–HAWAI'I

Copyright © 1992 Nancy J. Pollock
All rights reserved
Manufactured in the United States of America

Library of Congress Cataloging in Publication Data

Pollock, Nancy J.
    These roots remain : food habits in islands of the central and
eastern Pacific since western contact / Nancy J. Pollock.
        p.   cm.
    Includes bibliographical references and index.
    ISBN 0–939154–51–X
    1. Nutritional anthropology—Polynesia.   2. Nutritional
anthropology—Micronesia.   3. Food habits—Polynesia.   4. Food
habits—Micronesia.   5. Food—Symbolic aspects.   6. Polynesia—
Social life and customs.   7. Micronesia—Social life and customs.
I. Title.
GN670.P59   1992
394.1'2'0996—dc20   92–12250

This book is printed on acid-free paper and meets the guidelines for
permanence and durability of the Council on Library Sources

Distributed for The Institute for Polynesian Studies
by the University of Hawaii Press:

Order Department
University of Hawaii Press
2840 Kolowalu Street
Honolulu, Hawaii 96822

Frontispiece: Colocasia taro roots with stems at Talamahu market,
Tonga, 1990. Photo by Nancy J. Pollock

Not Quite Paradise

You'd say a hurricane would swamp these islands
Doughnut rings of coral, green with palms;
But life goes on, checked, yes, but not extinguished
When storms fling spume that kills the leaf,
For, roots remain.

With an air of omnipotence, loud with technology
The western gales invade this little world,
Jarring tradition, breaking down memory,
Bringing fresh airs, new sights to dazzle young eyes.

But on our islands the church bells ring,
The frangipani will go on blooming,
Scattering golden stars. With reverence
The milk of the nut is poured, the bread is broken;
These roots are wings.

Brother Thorogood, 1966
(courtesy of Cook Islands Library)

Contents

Figures

Tables

Preface

LIVING on an atoll such as Namu in the mid-Pacific on a narrow strip of land with the sea all around, one becomes very conscious of dimensions of life that had not been previously considered. Food looms large; I knew that my small supply of canned and packet foods would last for only three months maximum if I used the items sparingly—a can of soup or fruit per day. I also became very quickly aware that for the two hundred people of Majkin islet food was extremely significant. But there was a subtle difference between their views of food and mine.

The supply of local produce was very limited and the arrival of ships that brought basic items such as sacks of rice, flour, and sugar was very irregular. I was worried that I would not be able to replenish my meager stores and I would become a burden on the people whose local supplies were already severely stretched. I was worried about food to keep me healthy, while they were more concerned about having something to share with others; whatever the supply, it belonged to everyone, not to any one individual. They considered my food supply as an addition to their general pool, to be shared with those who shared food with me.

It became very apparent to me that food greased the wheels of that society—a phenomenon I have experienced in many parts of the Pacific. We can argue that it does so in our own society, but there is a subtle difference. For the Namu people food was a means of expressing social relationships, and was the receptacle of many symbolic representations. It was talked about openly and was a key feature of any event, however large or small. This contrasted with my own view of food as something I took for granted as being always available, and not of as high value as more elevated considerations of Christian life.

The only foods available on Namu throughout the 1968–1969 period of fieldwork were rice, breadfruit, coconuts, pandanus, fish, and bread made from imported flour; and that flour rapidly became full of weevils, and breadfruit and pandanus were seasonal. The occasional can of corned beef or fish and cooking fat to make doughnuts and pancakes were luxuries available only when a ship had just delivered supplies. And ships were few and far between—only five in the fifteen months I was on Namu.

In my proposed research I intended to assess the relative importance of imported food to local food in various aspects of life on an atoll. The topic was not considered a very valid one for a Ph.D. dissertation at that time. I was encouraged to consider food as an economic good, and thus to fit it into the arguments sustaining economic anthropology at the time —the formalist versus substantivist debate. I found myself agreeing with Polanyi that the economy was embedded in a wider social framework, and with Raymond Firth (1939) who had difficulty applying either model to his Tikopia data. Food was not an anthropological topic in its own right at that time. It was not until the ICAES meetings in Chicago in 1972 that led to the publication of a group of papers entitled *Gastronomy,* edited by M. Arnott (1975), that a number of anthropologists identified their interests in food in anthropology.

My own interest in anthropology grew out of an interest in history; I was frustrated with the concentration on winning battles and constitutional changes, with little interest shown in social history. My undergraduate program at Colorado College exposed me to the riches of the American Southwest, and also gave me my first chance at fieldwork in Jamaica for my B.A. honors thesis. The background to the arrival of Africans in the Caribbean was a stimulus to my interest in the effects of past events on current social organization.

Upon completion of my dissertation, "Breadfruit or Breadwinning on Namu," I chose to pursue the theme of persistence of traditional food habits in a number of different Pacific Island societies, rather than monitoring changes happening over time on Namu. I considered the widely held view that all Pacific Islanders would soon be eating nothing but rice and corned beef to be founded on Western pre-judgments with very little factual basis. Most of the dietary surveys of Pacific Island societies had been conducted in small urban populations where imported food was available and prestigious, and where the subjects were easier to survey. I chose to go to a Tuamotuan atoll, Niue, a small isolated island, to a village in the Sigatoka valley of Fiji (as part of an ongoing study of rural dietary change), and to Wallis and Futuna,where the people are still heavily reliant on their subsistence foods.

These dietary studies led me to focus on concepts of food as viewed locally and on the social contexts of food use in Pacific Island societies. I was concerned that a Western medical model of food use was inadequate in considering the wide social implications of food use in Pacific societies.

Moreover, I was concerned that a lot of money and energy was being poured into nutrition education in Pacific societies to help those people avoid the health problems associated with dietary change. But the starting point for these programs was Western concepts of food, based on Western-type eating habits; the aim was to alleviate health problems that were seen to result from so-called poor nutrition. The recommendation that foods from the three food groups be included in three meals a day has achieved little success because it does not start from the people's own beliefs and criteria for selecting and using food. It misses entirely the social context of food while focusing on the physical health aspects.

In this book, most of which was completed in 1987, I have set out some of those beliefs and values and social contexts in which food is important in a range of Pacific societies with three goals in mind. First, I wanted to make available in one place all the material on food use over time in a range of Pacific societies so that the people of those societies may be able to draw on that evidence in arguments supporting the use of local foods and their efficacies. Second, I wanted to pull together this material for anthropologists in order to provide a base for further considerations of the place of food in Pacific societies. And third, I hope that nutrition educators can use these ideas as a base for building their programs for better health, and agriculturists and development agents can draw on this information to guide their thinking in new directions that draw Western and local concepts closer together.

Acknowledgments

I WELCOME the assistance of Victoria University of Wellington in providing me with leave from teaching in order to conduct the research in the field and in libraries. I also thank The Institute for Polynesian Studies for its support in data gathering and preparation for the book. I also wish to thank the librarians around the Pacific who suffered with my requests for assistance, particularly Mlle. Renée Heyum and Karen Peacock of the Pacific Collection, Hamilton Library, at the University of Hawaii, and Bess Flores, then at the South Pacific Commission Library in Noumea.

Tim Galloway provided the illustrations. The Fiji Museum, National Archives of Fiji, and the Bishop Museum were most kind in providing copies of photographs in their collections. For assistance with conversion between word-processing systems, I am grateful to Alex Heatley and staff at the VUW Computing Services Centre.

The book would not have been possible without the kindness and assistance of many people around the Pacific. In particular, I would like to thank the late Lejolan Kabua and the people of Namu in the Marshalls; the people of Takapoto, Tuamotus; the people of Niue; the people of Naduri in the Sigatoka valley in Fiji; and the people of Wallis and Futuna. The Finau family of Tonga and the Guineas in Rarotonga also provided me with much support. The Commission for the Rehabilitation of Nauru enabled me to visit that island in order to talk with a number of Nauruans. They all share in the production of this book, but the responsibility for the presentation is my own.

I gratefully acknowledge the inspiration Dr. Katharine Luomala provided through my graduate school years and later, and regret the book was not published before she died (1992). I am most grateful to Andrew Branson and Susan Parkinson for their support throughout its long production.

These Roots Remain

1

Introduction

Taro and yams piled in slices alongside sweet potatoes and boiled green leaves with a covering of coconut cream, a crayfish, a whole baked fish, and some shellfish; perhaps also some dishes of taro leaves cooked in coconut cream, or cassava starch cooked with papaya and coconut cream—all these are laid out on coconut mats, perhaps under some temporary shelter in case it rains. Several ladies are busily engaged in fanning the food to keep away flies. Here we have a typical Pacific Island feast.

All these enticing foods set before us stimulate our senses. We can see and smell some of them and will taste them once the guests are all assembled, and grace has been said. We may have heard the sounds of preparation going on long before this moment when the feast is ready. Yet what are we really seeing? Are we to consider these delicacies food because we have been invited to "come and share a little food with us?" Many of the foods may be familiar to our eye, but perhaps there is a dish that requires some explanation. "What is this?" we ask. "Oh, that's *palolo*—you know, sea worms that come out once a year."

Such an unfamiliar dish may cause us to stop and consider. Is this really a food? Can we eat it? What of the taro in coconut cream and its leaf wrapping? Can the wrapping be eaten too? And what of the head of the fish? Is it edible? How do you eat it?

Such experiences raise questions, some of which may be put to the hosts and receive an appropriate answer. But understanding a food event requires a much wider range of inquiry. Who are the hosts, who are the guests, and why have these items been placed here? Why are they cooked in this particular way? Are we expected to eat everything in front of us? Must one make loud sucking noises with the fish head? What if we don't like the taste of something? Why are these women standing around not eating? Who provided this food? Who caught the fish? Is this event common? How different is it from a normal household meal?

In these pages I will explore some of these lines of inquiry. The ultimate aim is twofold. First, as an anthropologist, I want to try to understand the meaning of food in the Pacific Island context; that is, what are the different kinds of food and in what contexts they are appropriate. By careful comparison of various societies, I aim to clarify the ways in which food is important in social life in order to better understand its place in the thinking of Pacific Island peoples and in their world view.

Food is a term that is culturally specific. I use it here to draw a contrast between the Western view of food as primarily a substance that all human beings need to maintain their biological existence, and the Pacific Island view of food as a symbol that binds social groups together. At another level of contrast, to the Westerner the protein content of food is of greater value than other nutrients (Sahlins 1976:171). In Pacific Island societies, however, the starchy foods are of major importance, especially in day-to-day living, while fish, pig, and chicken are accompanying food items, especially important at feasts. These and several other categories of food items used by Pacific Island people in their own societies are discussed in detail in Chapter 2.

I will use the term *edibles* to encompass the broad view of food in Western thinking. In Pacific societies, edibles include tree and root crop starches, fish and other marine life, birds, pork, some greens and fruits, as well as recently introduced foods such as rice and bread. In former times, fish featured at ceremonial occasions, as did pig and dog. Birds, including some chicken, were also eaten on some important occasions. But for the most part these animal foods were used in small amounts to accompany the starchy foods; though significant, they are not the main focus of this study. Similarly, coconut in various forms has always been an important foodstuff, and its place in the food system will be discussed; fruits too were eaten, but on a casual basis. The importance of all of these was their use as items to accompany the starchy food(s). But the starchy foods predominated.

Edibles are a separate cultural category from drinkables in many Pacific societies. My focus here is on the edible starches, but sometimes these are almost drinkables, as in the case of breadfruit soup, which in the Marshalls was considered a food rather than a drink. Similarly, the coconut yields both food and drink, but in this case the two are clearly distinguished.

The uses of food and its strong symbolic messages will be considered across a range of societies in the Pacific. For the anthropologist, "it is through culture patterns, ordered clusters of significant symbols, that man makes sense of the events through which he lives" (Geertz 1973: 363). In this study I have looked for a number of generally accepted and frequently used culture patterns related to food and the events at which it is used that may be found in a number of the societies in this area. These patterns are in part unique to each society, or some section of it, but some are also shared among different societies, indicating links in times past and an overall pattern of Pacific Island societal integration. There, food use is symbolic as well as pragmatic.

These "significant symbols" both persist and change. So does the cultural patterning of food use. I am more concerned here with the persistence of the perceived values of foods and their place in the world view of these societies than with the changes. Why has the predominant use of starchy foods, in particular, persisted despite Westernization and other outside influences?

Second, my aim is to consider some practical implications to be gained from an understanding of the values the people of the Pacific place on food, so that these values may play a more integral part in modern food policy. For too long we have imposed our own (Western) ideas, either nutritional or agricultural, with the intention of improving the way of life of societies we saw as different from our own. We have barely stopped to see what attributes already existed before striving to change them. For example, we introduced bread and meat to island societies and made them high-status foods, thus beginning the importation of flour and beef. In the 1980s and 1990s, we tried to rectify the health and agricultural problems these ideas have created. By looking at the contrasts between Pacific Island peoples' ways of seeing food and our own, we can see the implications involved in attempts to change particular meanings in those social systems. I offer here a detailed consideration of Pacific Islanders' values regarding local foods and ways those values can be reestablished positively in today's world.

Food, as we are using the term here, has two dimensions, one biological and one social. The biological dimension has been heavily emphasized in the Western world; food is considered essential to provide the fuel by which the human body operates and regenerates itself. The need for energy input to match energy output is a basic nutritional message (Davidson et al. 1975). On the other hand, in its social dimension food plays a wider role in Pacific Island societies. It is given by one social group to another and received, not because the recipients are hungry, but as a message to indicate good relations and the strength of feeling and empathy between the groups. In Pacific societies those symbolic attributes are strong.

The uses and symbols associated with food are by no means static; they change over time. But Westerners have chosen to draw a marked contrast between the ways in which food was used at the time when they first viewed these societies and in more recent times. In the earlier period, people were considered to be deriving their diet from their own produce;

this has been labeled a subsistence-based diet, or the "traditional diet" (Ferrando 1981). In an overview of the effects of urbanization and Western diet on the health of Pacific Island populations, Coyne, Badcock, and Taylor view "some of the existing data on the health of the Pacific island populations as it is, or was in traditional-living island groups, compared with people presently living a 'western' way of life in towns and cities in the Pacific" (1984:3). These authors start from what they call a traditional base in order to endorse the commonly held view that contact with the Western world and increased urbanization have brought about rapid and dramatic changes in food habits. These changes, they claim, result in increased rates of chronic diseases, such as diabetes, hypertension, obesity, ischaemic heart disease, and gout. In particular they associate these diseases with increases in intake of energy (calories)—sugar, salt, fats of animal origin, and alcohol—and a decrease in fiber intake (Coyne, Badcock, and Taylor 1984:3, 11, 17). However, their assessments of the content of the traditional diet need closer examination before we can "blame" the process of Westernization for the associated ills. It is just such a clarification of the picture of the traditional diet that I hope to provide here as a base for directing modern food policy.

In looking at Pacific Islanders' traditional diet, we need to ask a number of questions, such as: What, to them, does "food" include? What is non-food? Where does food fit into a society's social activities? What wider values incorporate food and its meanings, and what are some of the indicators of these values? To find the answers to these questions, we need to disregard for the time our own categories and values and follow pathways through Pacific Islanders' modes of thinking, their categories, and how those categories are brought to bear when certain decisions are made. In this way we can begin to understand where food fits in their general scheme of things and why certain food habits have persisted in spite of Western intrusions. We can then go on to examine the consequences of these intrusions, such as high imports of foreign foods and increased incidence of obesity and diseases.

FOOD AND WORLD VIEW

By approaching the concept of food as the carrier of symbolic messages that are shared among a wide group of people, thus transmitting values, I aim to demonstrate that food is a very important part of the world view of societies in the Pacific. As a general concept, world view encompasses both ideology and practice. In its broadest sense, for any group of people, "Their world view is their picture of the way things in sheer actuality are, their concept of nature, of self, of society. It contains their most comprehensive ideas of order" (Geertz 1973:12). A world view is a set of images, assumptions, and beliefs that influence social behavior. It includes the composite package of principles and meanings that are accepted as ordering procedures, for example, in selecting foods for particular occasions. These idea systems are an integral part of the culture that has been forming and is being transformed over time. "The primary forces shaping ideas are the external social and environmental realities that the perceiving mind responds to" (Kearney 1984:5). Indications of those forces and how they affect the concept of food and its application are the subject of my quest for the role of food in the world view of Pacific societies.

As both a cultural and a biological necessity, food shapes one of the basic assumptions underlying a way of thinking about the world. It may be even more dominant than that, since assumptions are ordered and have meaning in the form of concepts. "No doubt food is, anthropologically speaking (though very much in the abstract), the first need; but ever since man has ceased living off wild berries this need has been highly structured. Substances, techniques of preparation, habits, all become part of a system of differences in signification" (Barthes 1975:50–55). Associations of order and of meaning are expressed in ideas and action. Together they are part of the communication system. If we can receive some of those messages, we have a powerful tool with which to build up an understanding of food in local terms. The images that people hold about a particular item such as food are part of the content of a wider set of categories that are fixed as fundamental categories of human thought (Kearney 1984:44). Food comprises one set of symbols, carefully categorized, that help determine thought and action in Pacific societies. As Hipsley and Kirk concluded from their studies of diet and energy in two New Guinea societies:

> It seems important to study in greater detail the inter-relationships between the environment, diet and culture, and the way in which the physiological mechanisms of the New Guineans have adapted to these factors. The demonstration of relevant associations in these inter-relationships could help greatly to predict future trends that could have harmful consequences to the people concerned, and which could be prevented by more soundly based policies. In addition, by offering contrasts with Western ecologies such studies could lead to a deeper understanding of them. (1965:128)

The value of food has been noted by Margaret Titcomb (1967) for Hawai'i and by several anthropologists working in Pacific societies (e.g., Raymond Firth 1936, 1939; Young 1971; Meigs 1984; McArthur 1977; Sahlins 1957; Finney 1965). It can be summed up under what Firth has termed "the alimentary approach" (1936:104). The values are expressed in what I will call here *food events*. These include all occasions when edibles are present, such as household gatherings, community celebrations, and rituals, as well as individual consumptions. Behind those expressions lie cultural values. Young notes, "It is a truism that Melanesian peoples in general value food in ways which transcend its value for them as a necessity of life" (1971:146).

To find the meanings expressed through particular uses of foods, we will examine the way people of various Pacific societies use different types of food for particular food events. This will show us some of the ways in which different food classifications express different sets of cultural values, what Schwartz (1984) has termed "cultural totemism." Such classifications may be expressed in terms of rules or in terms of action.

Some of those categories provide very strong guidelines (e.g., for or against eating a certain food), while others are ambiguous. The guidelines are formulated on the basis of certain shared values that a society uses in thinking about and serving up food. Some of those values may be expressed verbally and be apparent; others may be only implied. Meigs has differentiated absolute rules from relative rules in her study of Hua food (1984:17). For her, the absolute rules define a relation between the consumer and a certain kind of food, while the relative rules define a relationship among a consumer, a food, and a source. I want to go beyond rules here to find the "social and environmental realities that the perceiving mind responds to" (Kearney 1984:5).

Thus I am concerned with both the explicit and implicit expressions of food habits as these form part of the socially accepted pattern of behavior. By eating certain foods, values are expressed that are part of the symbolic attributes of those foods; those values are also closely tied to other values in society, such as health and social status. On these values, meanings are based. Among the ways by which the meanings of food may be conveyed are repetitive use of a food in particular circumstances or statements about people conforming or not conforming.

STUDIES OF FOOD IN SOCIAL LIFE

Until recently, the role of food in social life has been mentioned only in passing in much of the general scholarly literature. In the political concerns of Lester Brown (1970), Susan George (1976), George and Paige (1982), and Lappe and Collins (1979), the distinctions between production, consumption, and distribution become blurred, as they merge with the neo-Malthusian arguments. Only a few social scientists have considered food as a key issue with meaning in a social system. Nor have many writers considered it a subject in its own right until recently. Messer (1984a, 1984b) has furnished us with an excellent overview of this rapidly developing sector of anthropological study.

Ethnographers have described food habits in varying detail, but usually in a section on economics (e.g., Raymond Firth 1939; Finney 1973), or with passing references to the food elements in rituals (e.g., Firth 1967). Rappaport's study (1967) of the contribution of pig sacrifices in New Guinea Highland rituals to the dietary needs of the people has taken its place in the classic ethnographies of New Guinea, but his argument regarding the nutritional importance of the protein thus provided has come under considerable criticism (McArthur 1977). The emphasis has been mostly on the production of food and its role in the "economy"— that is, as one product of labor, or output from agricultural or fishing systems. What happens after food crops are harvested and are about to be consumed has largely been ignored. Their place within the social context needs further consideration.

One exception to this general statement is Audrey Richards's classic work, *Hunger and Work amongst the Bemba of Northern Rhodesia* (1939). This followed in the wake of Malinowski's two-volume work *Coral Gardens and Their Magic* (1935), which has given us some good insights into the ritual associated with the production of food. Richards's study is broader and does look at food as an aspect of world view. While examining the diversity of social relations among the various sectors of that society and explaining why the Bemba did not work harder, she described the local food categories and how they influenced people's perceptions of the social effects of eating millet and other grains plus relishes. She showed how these perceptions changed over time and in context; for example, eating at a ceremony had a different meaning from that of eating in the household, or from drinking beer made from millet. The social dimensions of food sharing, from production through to social and political events, are all described based on her own observations and those of botanists, nutritionists, and biochemists. Thus she includes the formal characteristics of food use from several perspectives along with descriptions of various food-related activities.

Richards's study, with its balanced approach, has not been as widely replicated for other societies as it deserves. Rosemary Firth's study of housekeeping among Malay peasants (1939) provides a broad view of how a fishing community managed its resources at the household level, but does not give a detailed discussion of food categories. Young's study (1971) of the use of food as a political tool by Goodenough Islanders provides a good description of command over food exchanges for social ends, but gives no comprehensive picture of these Melanesians' food categories and use of food by various social groups.

Douglas (1972, 1978, 1984) too has contributed to the debate on the place of food in cultural systems by examining relations between food sharing and social integration. In her study of food habits in three U.S. communities, she "seeks to present an expanded and humanist approach to food" (1984:2). She too starts from food choice but approaches these choices through structural rules and through information theory. Her central idea is that of culinary complexity and the way it is structured—that is, the rules that govern food events, which she uses to establish a calendrical ordering of food uses (Douglas 1984:21).

Lévi-Strauss pioneered the structural approach by drawing on food analogies to provide a framework for building elaborate abstract theories. He started from sets of paired oppositions based on empirical categories, such as raw and cooked, moistened and burned, fresh and decayed, as drawn from his own culture. His aim was to find principles that had universal application. Mythologies of the New World provided the substantive data that resulted in publication of a trilogy, subtitled *Introduction to a Science of Mythology,* that includes *The Raw and the Cooked* (1970), *From Honey to Ashes* (1973), and *The Origin of Table Manners* (1978). Throughout these works he develops the contrast between myths involved in the origins of the cooking of food and those involved in the origin of meat as a foodstuff (Lévi-Strauss 1973:21). The myths are the means of access to a matrix of meanings that can be arranged in lines or columns that highlight the oppositional nature of the structure.

Both Douglas and Lévi-Strauss were chiefly concerned with the common structural elements in Western and non-Western societies. My emphasis, in contrast, is on attributes of food use in Pacific societies that differ from those of the West.

Jerome, Kandel, and Pelto (1980) also reject a focus on rules of food use, preferring to draw attention to the non-nutritional meanings of food. Their study is important because it shows the role of social networks in changing dietary models.

Margaret Mead has contributed to the study of food in society both in her guidelines for dietary surveys and in her ethnographic works. Her paper entitled "How the Papuan Plans His Dinner" shows how the Mountain Arapesh ritual system emphasizes the principles of generosity and exchange commitment. A good person is one who feeds his visitors well (Mead 1934).

Meigs's account (1984) of food symbolism in Papua New Guinea has led the way in rectifying the general banishment of food to a subsection of the chapter on economics in most ethnographies. Her study of food, sex, and pollution among the Hua relies heavily on the concept of an accumulating life force to which food and the rules surrounding its consumption make a major contribution. "Eating and sex are two versions of the same behavior and both are subject to pollution, which is merely the transfer of body substance under negative social conditions" (Meigs 1984:124). In a skillful interpretation of Hua rituals, she assesses the importance of food in their world view. However, like Douglas and Lévi-

Strauss, she is more concerned with the rules by which food is an important part of their ideology than with factors of food selection and the social variables surrounding the uses of food. Her study follows Douglas (1966, 1975) in developing the dual concepts of purity and pollution as key factors in what Meigs calls "a religion of the body" (1984:125–136).

Since studies of food in cultural systems are a product of the last twenty years, our knowledge of how those systems have changed over time is limited. We can only reconstruct the early forms, using data from modern ethnographies together with archeological and biological data on plant remains and cooking structures. The work of Wing and Brown (1980) and of Gilbert and Mielke (1985) on the analysis of prehistoric diets follow on from the work of Isaacs (1978) and the symposia of prehistorians published in the Ucko and Dimbleby volume (1969). Since Pacific societies do not fit neatly into the hunter/gatherer versus agriculture dichotomy, the diets in island communities have been only partially reconstructed, and then mainly from the view of production of the food items, not their consumption. But the buzz of activity among Pacific prehistorians, particularly those concerned with establishing the subsistence patterns associated with the Lapita culture complex, is providing a wealth of information on plant materials used and modes of production for the last three to four thousand years (Golson 1977; Bellwood 1978; White and O'Connell 1982; Kirch 1984; Spriggs 1982; Yen 1980a). The emphasis to date has been focused on the production of food items rather than on prehistoric diets in the Pacific. Some concerns I want to raise here, such as the degree of dependence on plant material, have strong implications for the ways that plant production has been interpreted.

Social historians are also now turning more attention to changing food habits. Much of the focus is on Europe. A volume of the *Journal of Interdisciplinary History* that devoted an entire issue to the topic "Food and Hunger" is but one example of this new focus. For years, Tannahill's study (1975) and that of Drummond and Wilbraham (1939), as well as the work of Rowntree (1902) with Lancashire factory workers, have been the main sources of written information about diets in times past. Now Mennell (1985) and others are reexamining the texts of social histories to extract more detail about variation in diet in sixteenth- and seventeenth-century England and Europe.

In addition, interdisciplinary articles are beginning to appear in such journals as *Ecology of Food and Nutrition* and *Foodways*. These range from studies of diets and food habits to articles on nutritional anthropology. Messer (1984a) has cogently summarized the field as it stands. She too shows that the bulk of work on perspectives on diet has been focused on the material dimensions of food systems, such as energy exchange, gatherer-hunters, and biocultural concerns. The evolution of diets from various subsistence categories through to modern-day commercialism has loomed large in many of these studies. New approaches are, however, being taken, particularly in the study of sensory, cognitive, and symbolic aspects of food habits. A combination of psychological, biological, and cultural approaches is leading to examination of such properties of foods as taste, texture, smell, and visual appeal. In summary, Messer states: "Anthropologists, like economists, must keep in mind that people choose foods, not energy or other nutrients, in their dietary selections. The manner in which these dietary preferences influence and in some cases enhance caloric returns, nutritional complementarity, or both, are material dimensions that need further explanation" (1984a:224). She also deals with ways people's inclination to "follow the rules" may change as they move away from local communities that give support and meaning to careful observance of the rules (Messer 1984a:224). Food as a central concern in the way people organize their lives and think about their world needs more direct consideration.

CLASSIFICATION OF FOOD

Anthropologists, social psychologists, and others have looked at systems of classification in many areas of social activity. Classifications are summaries of information that assist our memories and allow us to manipulate objects within systems. But above all they aim to describe the relationships of the constituent objects to each other and to similar objects within boundaries (Sokal 1974:1116). Using classifications as a tool we can describe what is known as the natural system, that is, to describe objects in such a way that their "true" relationships are displayed. We can use those findings to generate hypotheses and thus question how the perceived order has arisen and how it is being maintained, an approach to classification as natural structure which contrasts with one that imposes an external constraint by fitting the data to a fixed number of classes, as in the case of some biological taxonomies (Sokal 1974:1117). By using a classification as natural structure, we have a system closer to local criteria, as distinct from Western or scientific classifications (Ellen 1979:5). Applying this natural structure model to food will enable us to see new dimensions of food in its social context.

In Western thinking, food is derived from the land and the sea, that is, from agricultural crops or by hunting/gathering, and thus is considered a part of "a natural system." But other societies may not perceive food production in the same manner. We have yet to understand fully how other societies establish the link between the mode of production and the environment. Thus we can accept man's intuitive natural classificatory ability (Lakoff 1987) but maintain that the purposes for which any classification is used are culturally specific. Here we will take classification in its generally used sense as indicating a process rather than an end in itself so that we can use that process both as an indication of how particular classes of food have persisted over time and as an indication of the place of food in the social system.

People of Pacific Island societies put food into categories that differ considerably from those used in the English-speaking world. Foremost of the differences are the Islanders' emphasis on starchy food, such as taro or yam, as "real food"; their lack of a term for a meal; and the use of a specific noun class for edibles in some languages. By drawing out these distinctive patterns we can not only appreciate a different way of thinking about food but also use that understanding to assist professionals in the development of food programs that are consistent with locally held cultural values. Understanding a different way of thinking about food may also enable us to improve our own images of food.

My two aims—gaining an understanding of the place of food in the world view of a number of Pacific Island societies and establishing the implications for current and future patterns of food use—can best be achieved if we begin by looking at the various categories used for food by peoples of the Pacific. To find a particular island society's way of conceptualizing food, we must start from observations of food events, that is, occasions on which food is actually eaten, exchanged, or features as part of some social interaction. Since such events involve some ordering, we must seek out the food categories appropriate to those occasions. We can then look at how those categories are used when deciding what to eat at any given time or what food to give at a feast.

Some information on these indigenous categories of food in the Pacific and their social associations is buried in ethnographies, such as *We the Tikopia* (Firth 1936). Bell (1948–1949), Massal and Barrau (1956), and Wolff (1966) warned of the gulf between English categorizations of food and those used in Pacific societies, warnings that for years were largely unheeded. More recently, Shimizu's careful exploration of the place of food in Pohnpeian culture (1982) and Akimichi's explicit study of Palauan food categories (1980) provide us with both data and careful analyses of local categorization of food use. These are welcome adjuncts to the material on island societies farther east, such as the work of LeMaitre (1972) for Tahiti, Pollock (1985a) for Fijian concepts, and Pollock (1986c), which compared Fijian concepts with those of Hawai'i and Tahiti. These studies all point to similar features of the diet, even though different foods are used to convey the same social messages.

Food may be a crop of wheat, or a breadfruit, or a herd of beef cattle, or a whale, or *coq au vin,* or a vitamin-enriched food, or *kakana dina* (starchy food, to a Fijian). It is classified differently by agriculturists, nutritionists, *cordon bleu* cooks, and Fijians. And members of each group would probably not agree as to a single means of ordering foods.

Yet another contrast in approaches is that between monothetic and polythetic classifications. Monothetic classifications are those in which the classes differ by at least one property that is uniform among the members of that class, whereas polythetic classifications are based on a number of factors with similar weightings (Sokal 1974:1116). For my analysis, I prefer the second type because it allows me to use several features rather than selecting any single one as predominant. Thus edibility may be a predominant characteristic, though several factors, such as taste, smell, and degree of cooking, are also incorporated in this concept. Yet edibility is only one element; exchange value and social acceptability to the recipients may be equally or more important.

Using a classification system that stresses similar weightings for several factors, we can, for example, examine the argument that yam storage as practiced in the Trobriands is irrational because the amounts placed in the storage houses are far more than necessary to feed the population. In that society yams are primarily an exchange item (and a highly rated one), rather than a food item. The link between the two characteristics, then, is the fact that this root was planted and raised as a crop for use on the basis of certain shared values that activated certain social relationships to meet obligations in exchange. Such an example points up the dangers of transferring our Western rules of classification to other societies. One society may give a particular weighting and interpretation to food, while another may give it a different weighting.

Whether we classify food as a crop or as a component of a particular dish depends on what we want to know and the purpose for which we want to use that information. My purpose in seeking the local classifications of food is to see, not only how food fits into social life, but also how that pattern of food use has been adapted over time to changing lifestyles. If the current pressure to bring about a replacement of imported foods with local foods is to succeed, we must understand the local classification of food and the total social value of food. In this study I shall highlight some of the practical considerations as well as the symbolic attributes with which food is associated to help broaden our vision of Pacific Island food as more than just something to eat and to see its place in a view of reality, a world view.

FOOD IN THE PACIFIC

My focus in this book is on Pacific societies inhabiting the smaller islands of the northwest, central, and eastern Pacific basin, that is, basically Micronesia and Polynesia. These islands cover a vast expanse of ocean that extends over half the world's circumference at the equator. The land area of many of the islands is small. The density of population on those small pieces of land is very high; Nauru (a single island) and Tuvalu (nine islands), for example, have 400 persons and 331 persons per square kilo-meter, respectively. The food supply is thus a major problem. Also, populations are increasing very rapidly; on six of these islands the rate is over 3 percent per annum, with Wallis and Futuna having the highest, at 4.9 percent per annum. On the other hand, Niue and the Cook Islands show an annual decrease in population due to outmigration. For details of areas and population size, see Table 1.

This study covers food habits in various parts of this geographic area from Guam to Easter Island, and from the Marianas and Hawai'i to New Zealand, drawing particularly on my own fieldwork in Namu in the Marshall Islands, Takapoto in the Tuamotus, Niue, Fiji, and Wallis and Futuna. However, examples from other areas are used for comparative

TABLE 1. Land and Sea Areas and Population of Pacific Islands

Island(s)	Land Area (sq km)	Sea Area (sq km)	Est. Population 1985		
			Total	Density (persons/ sq km)	Annual Growth Rate (%) 1980– 1985
American Samoa	197	390	35,500	180	1.8
Cook Islands	240	1,830	17,600	73	−0.3
Federated States of Micronesia	701	2,978	91,300	130	3.5
Fiji	18,272	1,290	700,500	38	2.0
French Polynesia	3,265	5,030	172,800	53	3.1
Guam	541	218	114,700	212	1.6
Kiribati	690	3,550	64,000	93	2.0
Marshall Islands	181	2,131	35,700	197	2.9
Nauru	21	320	8,400	400	1.2
New Caledonia	19,103	1,740	151,300	8	1.7
Niue	259	390	2,900	11	−2.6
Northern Mariana Islands	471	1,823	19,900	42	3.3
Palau	494	629	13,800	28	0.7
Papua New Guinea	462,243	3,120	3,320,700	7	2.1
Pitcairn	5	800	100	20	0.0
Solomon Islands	27,556	1,340	272,500	10	3.5
Tokelau	10	290	1,600	160	0.0
Tonga	699	700	94,400	135	0.3
Tuvalu	26	900	8,600	331	2.8
Vanuatu	11,880	680	135,600	11	3.3
Wallis and Futuna	255	300	13,700	54	4.9
Western Samoa	2,935	120	160,000	55	0.6

Source: Extracted from SPC 1987:4.

purposes. New Guinea and the islands of the southwest Pacific are not considered in detail here, as they are well covered elsewhere (e.g., Kahn 1986; May 1984; Mead 1934; Oomen and Malcolm 1961; Hipsley and Kirk 1965; Bailey 1968; Malcolm 1975; Sinnett 1977; Heywood 1987; Denoon and Snowdon 1982; Powell 1982; and Gregory 1982). Small island societies that are culturally Polynesian but are geographically located in Melanesia (known as Polynesian outliers)—for example, Tikopia and Sikaiana—are, however, included.

Consideration of food as an important aspect of social life across Pacific societies is not new, though general interest in food studies in this area has developed only recently. Linton (1939), Williamson (1924), Raymond Firth (1939), Bell (1948–1949), and Sahlins (1957) collated the material then available on various Pacific societies. For the Tikopia, "Food is not merely an object of satisfying appetite or of providing hospitality; it is a means of expressing obligations to kinsfolk and chiefs, of paying for a variety of services, and of making religious offerings" (Raymond Firth 1939:33). Finney (1965) provided an important comparison of food use between a rural and a peri-urban community in French Polynesia.

One study that did bring out the difference between local and Western systems of classifying food is that of Hipsley and Kirk (1965), whose examination of food intake and energy expenditure in two New Guinea societies reinforced the findings of Oomen and Malcolm (1958) that energy values in these diets were low by Western standards. However, they saw no evidence to suggest that the peoples' well-being suffered (Hipsley and Kirk 1965:127). Looking at food patterns in terms of subsistence commodities, luxury commodities, and valuables, they categorized the place in the diet of some twenty-five items for each village. Sweet potato was considered the only staple; the rest of the foods were classed either as supplementary or complementary to the staple (Hipsley and Kirk 1965:61–67). Their study begins to show some of the discrepancies between Western thinking and local thinking. We can use it as a basis for our assessment of the distinction between staples and supplementary foods.

There are three major differences between previous studies of food habits and this one. First, in those works food was usually a secondary or lesser consideration, particularly to kinship or nutrition, and presented as a minor aspect of social and political systems. Second, most of those authors were not concerned with local categories of food and applied their own categorizations, thus reflecting the author's values rather than local values. A third characteristic that has pervaded existing studies is an emphasis on food production without closely examining how the products were used and how that usage was built into the social system.

The abundance of foodstuffs in the Pacific world was noted by some of the first European visitors to the area, such as Cook, Banks, and Samwell (see Beaglehole 1962, 1967). As Banks so cogently stated:

> In the article of food these happy people may almost be said to be exempt from the curse of our forefathers; scarcely can it be said that they earn their bread by the sweat of their brows, when their chief sustenance, bread-fruit, is procured with no more trouble than that of climbing a tree and pulling it down. Not that the trees grew here spontaneously, but, if a man in the course of his life planted ten such trees (which, if well done, might take the labour of an hour or thereabouts) he would as completely fulfil his duty to his own as well as future generations, as we natives of less temperate climates can do by toiling in the cold of winter to sow, and in the heat of summer to reap, the annual produce of our soil. . . . Besides the bread-fruit the earth almost spontaneously produces cocoanuts; bananas of thirteen sorts . . . plantains, but indifferent; a fruit not unlike an apple . . . ; sweet potatoes; yams; cocos, a kind of arum. . . . (1769:134–136)

Banks's rosy picture of life and the ease of food getting in the Pacific Islands has been both quoted and questioned.

When missionaries and government officials took up long-term residence, they found the local foods not to their liking, so they began importing the wheat flour and salt beef they felt they needed to fit their own concept of food (Pollock 1989). The disparity in the consumption of local food and imported food has increased markedly in the intervening one hundred years or so. Now island governments are seeking ways to reduce dependence on imports and increase the use of local foodstuffs (McGee 1975; Coyne, Badcock, and Taylor 1984).

That all these island societies shared a similar food inventory is clear from the literature. The variety of foods used was greater on high islands than on atolls and also greater in the western part of the Pacific basin than the eastern. Also, some societies developed more varieties of a particular food plant than did others. Barrau, the ethnobotanist, has provided us with a useful survey of food plants in different parts of the South Pacific (Massal and Barrau 1956; Barrau 1961), and the work on nutritional analyses of certain Pacific Island foodstuffs by Murai, Pen, and Miller (1958) has yet to be superseded. Starchy foods predominated in the diet throughout the islands of the Pacific (Massal and Barrau 1956).

I will focus here on eleven starchy foods that have been the predominant contributors to the diet throughout the area during the period for which we have historical data: four "taros," yams, breadfruit, bananas, pandanus, sweet potatoes, cassava, and arrowroot.

The four taros (or aroids) are the species *Colocasia esculenta, Alocasia macrorrhiza, Cyrtosperma chamissonis,* and *Xanthosoma sagittifolium.* These will be referred to as *Colocasia* taro, *Alocasia* taro, *Cyrtosperma* taro, and *Xanthosoma* taro to avoid confusion in the English labels. Of these, *Colocasia* taro has been the most widely used (see Figure 1 and, for a map of its distribution, Appendix C1). Less important was *Alocasia* taro, though it too has been in use for a long time. *Cyrtosperma* taro is used mainly on atolls, where it grows in swampy areas. *Xanthosoma* taro is a fairly recent introduction. The four taros are shown in Figure 2. (For a detailed discussion of worldwide uses of the different forms of taro see Petterson 1977; also Standal 1982; and Plucknett 1976.)

Some five species of yams (genus *Dioscorea*) were widely distributed in the islands; two were cultivated while the others were generally found growing wild. The cultivated ones were preferred as food; the wild forms were generally used only in time of emergency. Breadfruit trees, *Artocarpus altilis*, bear a profuse supply of fruit in season that made a major con-

TABLE 2. Main Starch Foods Grown and Eaten in Pacific Island Societies

Common English Name	Common Local Names*	Latin Name	Source
Taro	*talo, dalo, taro, kalo*	*Colocasia esculenta*	Lambert 1982
Giant taro	*kape, 'ape, ta'amu*	*Alocasia macrorrhiza*	Lambert 1982
Swamp taro	*pulaka, via kana, lak, babai*	*Cyrtosperma chamissonis*	Lambert 1982
Tannia or cocoyam, kong kong taro American taro	*taro tarua, talo tonga, dalo ni tanna*	*Xanthosoma sagittifolium*	Lambert 1982
Yam	*ufi, uhi*	*Dioscorea esculenta, D. alata,* etc.	Coursey 1972
Breadfruit	*mei, uru, ulu*	*Artocarpus altilis*	Stone 1967
Cassava	*tavioka, manioka, pia*	*Manihot esculenta*	Moran 1975
Sweet potato	*kumara, 'umala, kumala*	*Ipomoea batatas*	Yen 1974
Banana	*mei'a, fusi, futi*	*Musa paradaisica (Eumusa)*	Simmonds 1976
Plantain	*fe'i, fehi*	*Musa troglodytarum (Australimusa)*	Simmonds 1976
Pandanus	*bub, fala, hala*	*Pandanus odoratissimus*	Stone 1967
Polynesian arrowroot	*pia, masoa, mahoa'a*	*Tacca leontopetaloides*	Pollock 1991

*For additional local names, see Appendix A and, for breadfruit, Appendix D.

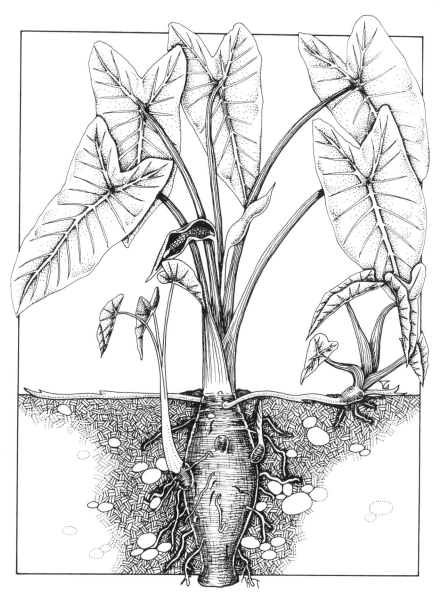

Figure 1. *Colocasia* taro plant, showing edible corm and leaves. Drawing by Tim Galloway

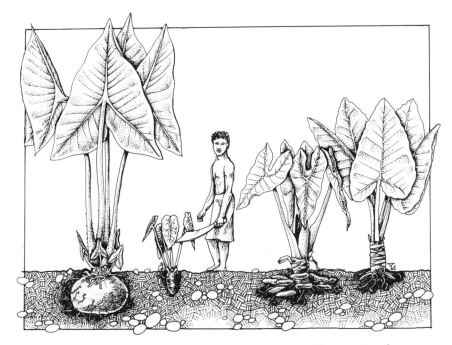

Figure 2. Four types of taro. From left: *Cyrtosperma, Colocasia, Xanthosoma, Alocasia.* Drawing by Tim Galloway

tribution to the local diet (see Figure 3). The trees are found throughout the Pacific, on both high and low islands (see Appendix C2). The fruits of pandanus, *Pandanus odoratissimus,* were used as food, but only on atolls. Bananas (*Musa* spp.) also made a significant contribution to the diet. Polynesian arrowroot, *Tacca leontopetaloides,* was used on both atolls and high islands in season, but mainly in grated form, as an ingredient in puddings. Its place as a starch flour has largely been replaced by cassava flour. In the relatively recent past this basic plant inventory has been increased by the addition of sweet potatoes, *Ipomoea batatas,* and cassava, *Manihot esculenta,* along with the *Xanthosoma* taro. The sweet potato was introduced probably in the last three hundred years, though just when is open to considerable debate (Yen 1974). Its use is now widespread throughout the Pacific Islands, though seldom as a ritual food. Cassava and *Xanthosoma* taro are even more recent introductions, arriving in about the 1840s, but were little used until the 1960s.

The people of the various Pacific Island societies used similar food processing techniques. Food was cooked in an earth oven, both on a daily basis and for feasts. Certain foods were preserved. Great feast displays were a significant part of the social life of all these societies. And food was used as an expression of mutual aid and support, as well as for

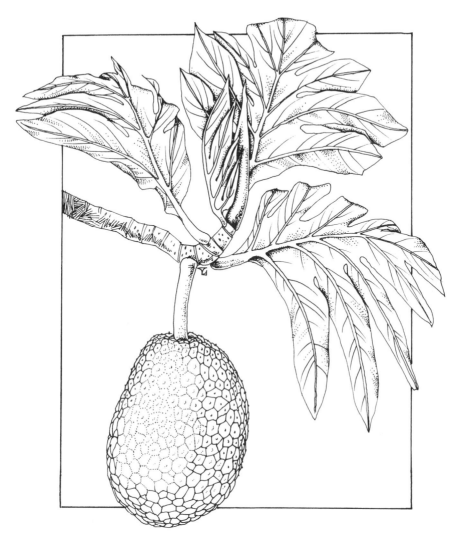

Figure 3. Breadfruit, from district of Papara, Tahiti. Drawing by Tim Galloway, after Wilder 1928

more symbolic expressions of generosity. These similarities are the main concern of my study.

The written records on which we rely to establish the continuities in food habits over time go back only as far as the time of first Western contact, that is, the 1520s for Guam and the 1700s for most of the rest of the Pacific. For earlier times, we have a growing body of literature from prehistorians who have been examining archeological evidence in order to reconstruct subsistence patterns (Green 1979; Bellwood 1978; Jennings

1979; Kirch 1979; Spriggs 1982; Ayres and Haun 1981; Cordy 1984; Takayama 1981/1984). They have been assisted in this work by ethnobotanists Massal and Barrau (1956) and Yen (1971, 1973a, 1980a). All these studies are based on the investigators' own interpretations (e.g., Yen and Gordon 1973, for Anuta; Kirch and Yen 1982, for Tikopia). Their concerns, however, have focused on production systems for foodstuffs rather than on how those foodstuffs fitted into the social system.

METHODOLOGY

Three sources of data have been used in this study—my own fieldwork, written historical accounts by Westerners, and ethnographic material.

In the course of two periods of my own fieldwork on Namu atoll in the Marshalls (1967–1969), as well as during fieldwork on Niue (1975–1976), on Takapoto atoll in French Polynesia (1976), in Fiji (1976, 1981, 1983, 1986), Tonga, Western Samoa, and the Cook Islands (1983), and Wallis and Futuna (1987, 1991), I was impressed with the importance placed on breadfruit, taro, and other starches by the households in which I was working and living. The predominance of starches was evident not only for daily consumption, but also for feasts and community events, which occurred frequently. It became clear that maintaining availability of these foodstuffs took precedence in some aspects of social life but was less significant in others. From this base I began to seek further clarification of what were the important things to know about food and its uses, what was available, the importance of the different items, and the ways they were prepared—in fact the whole basis on which decisions were made by households about how food resources should be used. The local classification of foods suitable for particular occasions became a major clue to understanding food use. This was a major focus of my work in the Sigatoka valley of Fiji in 1982. I sought similar data in 1982 in villages on Tongatapu, Tonga; Upolu and Savai'i, Western Samoa; and Mauke and Rarotonga in the Cook Islands by talking to older people and asking them to reminisce about food in times past.

By consulting the early written accounts by visitors to the Pacific—travelers, missionaries, whalers, and expatriate government officials—and noting all references to food, cooking, agriculture, feasts, and social parameters, I was able to see more clearly how a European (including American) view of food differed from the local view. Captain Cook recorded his feelings about the food he was offered, along with much other detail about its use (Beaglehole 1955, 1962, 1967). Other writers were not as clear in discriminating between their personal reactions and the peoples' own views about food. Reports of amounts available, for example, in most cases were based on the writer's view of an adequate food supply rather than on the local view. To these writers there was only one set of values of food.

Only by reading numerous works by different authors about each island or island group have I been able to draw together the significant details for understanding the place of food in that society's world view. These details can be formulated thus: (1) Certain similarities in the use of food by various Pacific societies can be identified. (2) Certain foods are more highly valued than others. (3) Food sharing is a highly significant part of social relationships in Pacific Island societies; as such it is a part of a mutual support system. (4) Food is viewed as a powerful symbol, used to convey a set of meanings beyond just its edibility, and therefore is a means of communication. (5) This importance of food as a symbol is shared by societies of the island Pacific. (6) Food with all its wider symbolic implications is a major aspect of world view in Pacific societies.

The level of understanding of these symbols is, however, still as an outsider—the anthropologist uses her/his tools of comparison and knowledge of other cultures in order to highlight differences between Western and Pacific conceptualizations of food habits. Overall, such cross-cultural study helps us to understand world views that differ from our own.

The overall question is, What are the cultural mechanisms that have allowed these distinctive factors about food to persist in the face of many intrusions into Pacific societies? I am not implying that food habits and their cultural implications have been unchanging. Rather, I am challenging the philosophy that asserts that traditional food habits in Pacific Island cultures have undergone major changes with Westernization (Coyne, Badcock, a..d Taylor 1984). Observing how food habits have changed has been the usual approach. Here I will stress the continuities by asking the alternative questions: In what ways have food habits persisted, and why? Do "traditional" food habits have a place in the Pacific Islands of the 1980s and 1990s?

2

Food Classification

IN EVERYDAY life people order their thoughts and actions and the world around them. Food comprises one set of categories that are part of that ordering process. Here I will examine the relations between how those food categories form part of a society's consciousness for ordering, and how they are used when selecting food for particular occasions. Examining the ways in which people of South Pacific societies classify their food will help us to understand what food means in their society and how people use food to express meaning. This is an alternative approach to one that looks at the rules and techniques of classification per se (Ellen 1979:5; Douglas 1975).

The term "food" is used in several societies, including English-speaking ones, at different levels. In Fijian, for example, there is a general term for "things eaten" *(kakana)* and a more exclusive one, "real food" *(kakana dina)*, applied only to the starches such as taro, breadfruit, and yams. This qualification makes it advisable to use the English term "edibles" to refer to the broader category of everything that is eaten. Within that broad term different categories can be identified (for details for Fiji, see Pollock 1985a). Also, edibles are differentiated from drinkables; for example, sugar cane is considered a drinkable in Fiji.

In many islands of the eastern Pacific, as in Fiji, only the starchy foods are considered "real food." For the food event we call a meal in English, Pacific Island informants stated that "real food" must be accompanied by a dish of coconut or fish or some small item that is considered appropriate. This combination of starch and accompaniment is the main category of edibles in many Pacific societies (see Table 3). It is also the main basis of a feast, though for that occasion many kinds of starch and accompanying dishes in large amounts will abound. A gift of food to a foreign visitor is more appropriate if it consists of local food such as breadfruit rather than introduced or imported foods. Factors such as taste, texture,

TABLE 3. Terms for Starchy Food and Accompanying Dish
in Selected Pacific Island Societies

Society	Starchy Food	Accompaniment	Source
Fiji	*kakana dina*	*i coi*	Pollock 1985a
Futuna	*magiti*	*kina*	Pollock and Tafili 1988
Hawai'i	*'ai*	*'ina'i*	Pollock 1986c
Marshalls	*manga*	*jelele*	Pollock 1970
Palau	*ongraol*	*odoim*	McCutcheon 1985a
Pohnpei	*kisin mwoange*	*sali*	Shimizu 1985
Rapa	nd	*ma'a*	Hanson 1970
Samoa	nd	*'ina'i*	Buck 1930
Samoa	*mea 'a'ano*	*mea lelei*	Shore 1982
Satawal	*mwongo woot*	*saniyeniy*	Akimichi 1987
Tahiti	*ma Tahiti*	*'ina'i, miti*	Pollock 1986c
Tonga	*haka*	*kiki*	Maude 1971
Truk	*mwenge*	*seni*	Goodenough and Sugita 1980
Uvea / Wallis	*magisi*	*kina*	Pollock and Tafiki 1988
Yap	*gagan*	*niq*	Lingenfelter 1975

nd = No data, in this and following tables.

and whether or not the edible should be cooked are all taken into consideration when deciding what is appropriate to the occasion.

Other types of food such as fruits, or snacks, or foods eaten occasionally by oneself are considered edibles but may also be seen as separate categories in various Pacific Island societies.

CATEGORIES

General Concepts

Through examination of the local ordering process that classifies edibles we can begin to understand the meaning of food in local contexts. Food encompasses only one set of concepts within a society's total ordering system, but clarification of this set can help us see links to other concepts through noting the social uses of foods. As Geertz has suggested, "Once we have uncovered the conceptual structures that inform our subjects' acts we can construct a system of analysis in whose terms what is generic to those structures, what belongs to them because they are what they are, will stand out against the other determinants of human behavior" (1973:27).

Traditionally in anthropology, food has been discussed most usually in the section of an ethnography that is headed "economics." Or else it has been included in discussions of agriculture or the botanical system or the health system. For example, Tikopian food is discussed under the chapter on economics in *We the Tikopia* (Firth 1936) and in *Primitive Polynesian Economy* (Raymond Firth 1939). Chinese humoral theory has been applied to food in various Southeast Asian societies (e.g., Wu 1979 and Manderson 1981). Ethnobotanists have added a different dimension with their examination of the various uses of plants in many societies; food comprises just one subset of useful plants (Massal and Barrau 1956; Bellwood 1980; Yen 1980a). Yet another line of approach has been taken by anthropologists who have developed ideas from zoology in applying an optimal diet model to explain the food-gathering behavior of hunting and foraging societies (e.g., Hawkes and O'Connell 1985:404). While these approaches all add scope to our inquiry as to what we know about food and its role in society, they are not adequate because they relegate food to a secondary role. Furthermore, they apply Western concepts a priori, without consideration of the local form of classification.

I am more concerned about food as part of a local view of the world and as a social category in its own right. When people select things to eat they do so on the basis of some local knowledge, not only about what items are available, but also the wider social consequences of that eating. I shall examine some aspects of the meaning of food in various Pacific societies by looking at how people group foods for particular social contexts in order to assess the relationship of the different items considered as foods to one another and also the relationships with which they are associated.

A system of classification of foods includes several categories that may or may not be labeled, but are marked by certain common factors. All have a place within the total picture that people in that society share, based on a common set of values. The total food classification system is then one indicator of values within the social system of which it is a part.

I am seeking to present here what might be called a "folk classification" of food. It differs in four ways from the color classification of Berlin and Kay (1969), which is often cited as the classic in ethnosemantics. First, I focus on the total experience of a food event instead of just the words used to describe that event. Thus I am looking for concepts underlying the semantic domain and the cognitive domain (Mathiot 1970) with a particular focus on food. Second, I am not looking for the universals that ethnographic semanticists are seeking (Schweder and Levine 1984). Rather I am striving to point out significant cultural differences between the Western and the local concepts of food. Third, this exercise differs from others in folk classification as it seeks to present a set of underlying concepts that are shared by several societies in the Pacific, rather than terms pertaining to just one society. And fourth, I am less concerned with the rules of classification of food use than with examining how these concepts are used to guide decisions about food (see Chapter 3).

By means of this alternative approach to folk classification, I aim to draw together the material on food in various societies of the Pacific to show variations on a common theme. No rigid set of rules which one society or another adheres to or deviates from will be presented. Rather the intent is to show how people choose certain foods for particular reasons, and how those foods convey the right messages in the contexts in which they are used.

Since my approach is as an English-speaking visitor to the Pacific, I cannot present the inside view (Helu 1981; Hau'ofa 1982). My thinking can yield only themes that strike me as drawing together or distinguishing certain aspects of food habits in a number of societies in the hope that individuals from within those societies will in turn present their evidence. Inevitably, some of my own ordering principles intrude.

Thus the approach used here is to present a form of classification of food events consisting of several categories. From my own experience I have found categories used in the English-speaking world to be inadequate in Pacific contexts. Categories such as food or meal cannot simply be translated into Fijian or Samoan without some explanation of how starchy food features in the dietary patterns. For this reason, dictionaries ideally must list several terms for "food," each term reflecting the event in which that food will be used (see Goodenough and Sugita's Trukese dictionary [1980] for a good example of such a broad listing). Similarly the word "meal" has no close corresponding term in Fijian or Samoan. In English the term refers to eating a number of foods at a particular time of day and this concept has been translated back into the Pacific languages —e.g., *manga in jibon, manga in raelik* in Marshallese. Translated literally, these are "food in the morning," "food at midday." This absence of a term for meal has not stopped writers from describing such in many accounts of the Pacific. Instead of approaching the concept of meal as related to the time of day, I will discuss how certain combinations of foods should be eaten at least once a day and how that event contributes to people's feeling well fed and generally satisfied. Not only the food items themselves, but also the processing techniques and the mutual sharing of that processed food with other persons impart the meaning associated with that social event. I will refer to this and other occasions on which food is used under the broad heading of "food event," derived from the widely used Polynesian term *me'a 'ai* (a food thing).

Starchy Foods

The predominant use of starchy foods and thus the mainly vegetable content of Pacific Islanders' diet was noted by several early European visitors to the Pacific, perhaps because this diet differed from their own. Banks, writing about Cook's expeditions, observed:

This indeed must be said in their favour, that they live entirely on vegetables. . . . Though they seem to esteem flesh very highly, yet in all the islands I have seen the quantity they have of it is very unequal to the number of their people; it is therefore seldom used among them, even the principal chiefs do not have it every day or even every week, though some of them had pigs. . . . When any of these chiefs kills a hog, it seems to be divided almost equally among all his dependents, he himself taking little more than the rest. Vegetables are their chief food, and of these they eat a large quantity. (1769:136)

Similarly, another expedition leader, Wilkes, in the 1840s noted of Pacific Islanders that "their food seems to be mainly of the vegetable kind" (1845, 2:350). Buck, as an ethnographer, noted that vegetarian foods formed the larger part of the Samoan diet (1930:127). And the ethnobotanist Barrau noted of the Pacific in general that "85 per cent of the quantity of food consumed was of vegetal origin" (1960:3).

Living for a total of seventeen months in two separate periods on two different atolls in the Marshall Islands, I too lived on starchy food (NJP fieldnotes 1967, 1968–1969). My own dietary needs cried out for green vegetables and fruit and more meat. I learned to survive without meat, but I missed the fruit and green vegetables. Breadfruit (either fresh or preserved), pandanus, or rice were the major items of diet there for 365 days of the year. That starch should be accompanied by some grated coconut or fish, or *ramen* (Japanese noodle soup) if the supply ship had just called. The accompaniment was referred to as *jelele* (relish) to the *manga* (starch food).

In the Tuamotus, in Niue, in the Sigatoka valley of Fiji, and in Tonga (Ha'apai) I was again struck by the preponderance of the starchy foods (NJP fieldnotes 1975, 1983). The starchy food was obviously the main item on the menu. On Niue I was served taro, yams, and cassava or white potatoes at each meal in the Niuean household in which I was a guest. These were served together with some canned beef or stewed meat (NJP fieldnotes 1975). My daily inquiries into what people were eating in one Niue village during a one-week period showed that the common denominator for every household was the starchy food—either taro, or yam, or breadfruit if it was in season. This was served "with" some fish or coconut, or canned fish or canned meat if the household could afford it.

On Takapoto in French Polynesia, when I asked about the mangoes, or pawpaws (papaya), or 'ava (lychee) I was told that they were foods that children ate occasionally, like snacks. Adults rarely ate those fruits.

In Palau *kall* is a general term for food, consisting of four major food groups: *ongraol, odoim, kliou,* and *ilumel.*

Ongraol is the term used for crops such as taro, breadfruit, cassava, sweet potato, and imported rice. It is distinguished from the other three categories of food; *odoim* consists of animal foodstuffs such as shellfish, pig, bird, egg, crab, trepang, other marine invertebrates, and even tinned meat like corned beef. . . . *Kliou* is possibly analogous to the western concept of dessert, and includes varieties of fruits; papaya, mango, jackfruits, orange and banana. . . . *Ilumel* is a general term for beverages such as coconut juice, imported whisky, or canned juice. (Akimichi 1980:598, 600)

Foods from the *odoim* or *ongraol* groups are usually paired to make up a meal.

A mode of classification of food in various parts of the Pacific now begins to take form. The dominant category of edibles is what would be labeled starches in English, including all the species of taros, yams, bananas, breadfruit, cassava, and sweet potatoes. They are dominant not only in terms of amount consumed but also in terms of the importance local people place on consuming a goodly portion of at least one of these during the day. All these starchy foods are included under the local term which we can gloss in English as "real food." Thus I treat them here as a distinct category.

Accompanying Dish

In many Pacific Island societies the starch food has to have an accompanying dish if those eating are to feel properly satisfied. In Fiji the starchy component, known as *kakana dina,* is the main element in Fijians' food events. It may consist of some taro or breadfruit or sweet potatoes—whatever is available. Each of these must be cooked and served in slices and in abundance for daily household consumption. But it must be served together with some other edible that is acceptable as an accompanying dish *(i coi)* in order that the food event will make the eaters feel satisfied. Thus in the Sigatoka valley in November 1982, sweet potatoes were served with some river *kai* (shellfish), which were in season. A few households had breadfruit or yams in place of the sweet potatoes (NJP fieldnotes 1982).

In Hawai'i, *'ai* is the term used for the main starchy foods. The term applies to any cultivated food plant but primarily to *Colocasia* taro or sweet potato. The *Colocasia* taro is usually used in its pounded fermented form, known as *poi*. This forms the main item of diet. It too should have an accompaniment *(i'a),* which consists of meat or fleshy food (Pukui and Elbert 1965). In fact the Hawaiian diet has been built around *poi* and fish (Handy and Pukui 1972:3–4; Titcomb 1967). This is the regular fare.

In Tahiti, *ma'a* is the term used for food. *Ma'a Tahiti* is most commonly eaten in the form of breadfruit, although *Colocasia* taro, sweet potatoes, and green bananas also serve as the starchy element (Oliver 1983:58; O'Reilly 1982). It should be accompanied by some *i'a* or *'ina'i* —that is, fish or flesh such as chicken or dog; alternatively another accompanying food, coconut cream *(miti)*, or fermented coconut might be served with the starch (LeMaitre 1972:67).

The serving of a main starch with an accompaniment is a pattern found in other Pacific Island societies (see Table 3 for a list of the local terms for these two categories). As Churchill generalized from his work on Easter Island, "In Polynesian gastronomy it is repugnant to the taste to make a meal of one dish; food from the sea must be accompanied by food from the shore, meat with vegetable, each of which may stand to the other in the *inaki* relation" (1912:211).

In Futuna the starchy food is known as *magiti,* which should be accompanied by some *kina* (Kirch 1975; Pollock and Tafili 1988). In Samoa, Buck tells us of *ina'i* of fish (1930), while Shore offers an alternative classification, that of *mea a'ano* for starchy heavy foods and *mea lelei* for "good foods," that is, European foods (1982:249). For Tonga, Gill noted that "the native while he has many dishes of which he eats with zest yet is well served if he has an abundance of but one good food" (1902:110). But that starch must have an accompanying dish. Pulu gives no Tongan terms, but under the heading "Tongan food plants," she includes only plants that have tubers and plants that have fruits (1981: 60). In Tikopia, Firth noted that the ordinary household fare was one kind of pudding and a single bulk food (1936:97).

The distinction in Micronesia is more widely recorded. In Yap the vegetable part *(gagan)* was accompanied by some fish *(niq)* and ripe coconuts *(mareum)* (Lingenfelter 1979). On Palau the starchy food *(ongraol)* was accompanied by some *odoim* (Aoyagi 1982:24). As McCutcheon puts it, "A meal is technically complete as long as there is *odoim* and *ongraol*" (1985a:3). On Ulithi plant foods *(mogoi)* were distinguished from fish and coconuts (Ushijima 1985:20). And on Puluwat in Truk district, and on Truk itself, the cooked vegetable staple was distinguished from the side dish or snack (Steager 1971:67; Hall and Pelzer 1946:32). Without a side dish or two, a Trukese meal would not be complete (Gladwin and Sarason 1963:53). For Pohnpei Bascom refers to the starchy fruit or vegetable, such as breadfruit or taro, as constituting "the bulk of each meal, but a meal is not considered complete without *sali,* a term used for a protein dish of meat, fowl or other kinds of seafood. When none of these proteins are available, a sauce of chili pepper and salt may be used as *sali*" (1965:38). In Futuna and Wallis the people refer to eating a starch without an accompaniment as *omaki*. It is a rather deplorable state in their terms, but may happen after a cyclone when no coconut or fish is available (Pollock and Tafili 1988).

Thus across the Pacific from Easter Island to Palau, though the starchy food, drawn from an inventory of locally grown crops, was the predominant feature of the daily intake in households, it was considered satisfying (like a Western "meal") only if it was served with one of a number of accompanying dishes. Together these closely linked food items were the basis on which a person would say that she/he had eaten that day.

The emphasis on the starchy food as distinct from its accompaniment is not confined to the central Pacific. In the Philippines the Hanunóo distinguished "real food" from its accompaniment. Real food, known as *karan unun,* formed the cooked starch staple; it included preripe (green) bananas, cereals, and root crops, accompanied by meats and most vegetables, but "the primacy of the starch staple is obvious" (Conklin 1957: 30). Similarly, for Malays fish and rice are necessary parts of a meal (Laderman 1984:547). Dentan noted that the Semai distinguished the starchy food, including rice and taro, from the other small dishes that accompanied it (1968).

Wolff (1966) assessed these meanings of food for Malays in terms of five categories: rice for survival, accompanied by meat, fish, and chicken for strength, and vegetables—plus red peppers for taste. Fruit and special foods such as cakes were for special occasions. We also have references to similar modes of classification in Indonesia (Kuipers 1984). Many writers have noted that rice is the main food in Southeast Asia. Errington (1984) and Provencher (1979) have taken this observation a step further. Provencher remarked that "it is the intensity, the thoroughness of Malay interest in food that attracts notice, just as Malays notice the intensity of Western interest in sex" (1979:45).

The accompanying dish may be raw if it is a piece of coconut, or cooked if it is fish or pork. Or it may consist of a sauce such as coconut cream or sea water into which the pieces of starch are dipped. The amount may be very small. It is the combination of that relish (as some have termed it) with the starchy food that is satisfying, according to informants.

Main Food Event

On Namu during my fieldwork in 1968–1969, a household meal was cooked by one of the many adult women in the household. A household consisted of several nuclear families linked by sisters who share rights in the house site through their matrilineage. Cooking was rostered each day among the adult women, so that no woman cooked two days in a row. One food was selected, usually a local one if available. Most of the daily food was cooked over a fire of coconut husks. Breadfruit were baked whole in the coals. Rice was boiled in a large pot. Fermented breadfruit paste had to be baked in an oven; the gasoline tin oven was usually used rather than the earth oven because it was quicker and required less fuel. The earth oven was still used every Sunday and for special occasions. The household food was cooked communally in the cook house, but each of the nuclear families was served with its own utensils and ate as a unit, though usually in close proximity to other family units. Groups ate either inside the cook house or outside sitting on mats. Food was taken either in individual portions in half a coconut shell or by the handful from the central family pot. Breadfruit or taro was served in slices. Grated coconut was served in a half coconut shell for all to share.

Everyone gathered for this food event and sat down together. All shared in the main starch, but if there were fish, the parts were allocated to individuals. The head of a fish was a particular delicacy, saved for the eldest sister of the household. If a man was off fishing, some food would be set aside for him. If someone was passing by or was visiting in the house, he/she was offered food from the family unit's supply.

Children and adults would eat to their satisfaction, but the amounts varied depending on how much food was available. Children and the men had first priority. Satisfaction was derived from having a portion of breadfruit, accompanied by *jelele*—some grated coconut or fish. The complementarity of these two types of food was more important than the amount consumed. Particularly high levels of satisfaction were expressed after a Sunday meal when baked ripe breadfruit stuffed with coconut cream was served with plenty of fish. But this dish was available for only about two weeks of the year because breadfruit is a seasonal crop.

Dissatisfaction at a household meal, however meager, was never expressed openly. It would have reflected on everyone because all members of the household had joined in the effort to make sure there were plenty of breadfruit trees, or that copra had been made in sufficient quantity to buy enough rice to feed everyone.

Leftovers were set aside by the family to be eaten as snacks whenever someone felt hungry. They were used most frequently in the early morning; a child might eat a piece of breadfruit before going to school, as the first "meal" was not likely to be cooked by then. A leftover was eaten without any accompanying dish (NJP fieldnotes 1968–1969).

Time and shortage of fuel were two reasons for making only one fire per day on Namu. The main aim of cooking was to render the starchy food edible, rather than to serve it hot. In fact, it was often cool by the time everyone had assembled. The earth oven was the main means of cooking throughout the islands of the Pacific, as all the starchy foods that had to be cooked could be placed in the one oven. Its use has persisted to the present day, particularly in many rural areas (for a full discussion of cooking, see Chapter 4). In all societies of the Pacific, cooking is a necessary part of the main food event since none of the starchy foods can be eaten raw. Some, such as *Colocasia* taro and cassava, require very careful, long cooking to rid the food of its toxic substances. And since no freshly harvested food keeps in the tropics for much more than a day, at least one fire had to be made each day—and enough food cooked to last for a second meal.

The structural resemblance between the Pacific food event and the English meal can be found in the essential components and the core of people involved (Douglas 1975). But in Pacific food events, amounts are not carefully calculated. Rather, the expectation is only that there should be enough to feed anyone who happened to be present when the food was served. Informants have explained that the food itself is more a symbol of mutual obligation and respect than a substance whose main purpose is to make the eaters feel full, though that was an important secondary consideration.

But within the structure of the food event there is considerable variation as to which starchy food is served, or what is used as the accompaniment. Informants stated that what brings a feeling of satisfaction is that the two parts be served together. The social nature of the occasion also contributes to the feeling of well-being. Cultural satisfaction is derived from the structure of the event, the taste of the foods, and the social occa-

Figure 4. Food table. Wallis Island, 1988. Photo by Nancy J. Pollock

sion, rather than from amounts available or any inherent quality of the foods themselves. Eating was a social rather than a biological event.

Other Edibles

The main food events each day were highly structured, but edibles of various kinds were consumed at other times of the day, when the occasion arose. These edibles generally required more elaborate processing than the staple foods and were much more varied in constituents and flavor. They might be eaten by an individual alone, such as when a man was out fishing. There was no group label for these items other than an equivalent of *mea 'ai* (a food thing).

As these events were less dominant in daily life, they were less visible to the casual observer and likely to be forgotten by informants. Nevertheless, in a discussion of use of resources or of total nutrients consumed, and a total overview of food events and edibles, they are important. I have designated four broad types.

First are puddings, complex dishes made from one or more starches cooked, cut into cubes or grated, and mixed with some form of coconut cream and some banana, pumpkin, or pawpaw. Small amounts of this mixture were wrapped in banana, *ti,* or breadfruit leaves and baked in the earth oven (see Grattan 1948 and Sua 1987 for detailed constituents of the various kinds of puddings in Samoa; see Pulu 1981 for Tongan puddings).

Several types of pudding were made. Each was designated by a general term and then a specific indicating the starch from which it was made. For example, a popular pudding known as *faikakai* was made in Tonga by boiling cut-up *kape* (*Alocasia* taro), then pounding it until soft and sticky, placing it in coconut syrup, and cutting it into bite-size pieces, which were then wrapped ready to be eaten. Other versions made with a different starch were known as *faikakai talo tonga* (made with *Xanthosoma* taro) and *faikakai mei* (made with breadfruit). These versions are also found in Samoa and Fiji, Wallis and Futuna.

Such packets of food might be made as a gift to another household as a return for a specific gift or a favor, or simply on a whim because the women felt like making some. In the Marshalls, Namu people made several complex dishes, but not on a regular basis. Some, such as *jokwob* and *benben* and *jaibo,* were souplike, boiled dishes, no doubt more recently introduced than the leaf-packet foods cooked in the earth oven.

In Fiji *i vakalau* or *vakalomavinaka* was the general term used to refer to these puddings. A main ingredient was grated cassava. They were wrapped, baked separately from the main foods, and were usually eaten apart from the main event. Thus they were not puddings in the English sense because they were not part of a meal. They were snacks or refreshments, similar to cake or a cookie that some English-speaking person might eat if she/he felt slightly hungry.

In Hawai'i such wrapped edibles were known as *laulau,* in reference to the leaves in which they were wrapped. *Laulau* were made from pieces of taro covered in coconut cream, and together with a piece of fish or pork, wrapped in *ti* or banana leaves (Titcomb 1967:23). For Tahiti, LeMaitre lists six of these complex dishes (1972:68, table 6). Packets of *po'e* are the most widely known, probably because they appealed to European taste buds. *Poke* in Rarotonga and the southern Cooks is a similar co-mestible. The basic ingredient of both is a grated starch mixed with coconut cream and some sweet banana or pawpaw.

The main structural features of puddings were that they were wrapped in leaves, that they consisted usually of a root or tree starch and coconut cream; also they were eaten apart from the daily food event or were presented at feasts. They were a complex processed food in contrast with the simple cooked pieces of taro or breadfruit and coconut.

Fijians identified a second category of these non-meal foods as *gunu ti.* This consisted of "tea drunk with buns or scones." This was not a meal but rather a snack, where the emphasis was on the drinkable part; the starchy component was the accompanying item in this case (P. Geraghty and T. Navadra, pers. comm. 1983). Whether this category occurs in other Pacific societies is not known. It may be an adaptation to European influence and is interesting because it emphasizes the introduced component.

A third category of non-meal foods, widely identified in the Pacific, consisted of raw fruits or raw fish that could be eaten at any time of day, whenever someone felt like it. These were products of the environment that came from the land or the sea to which, according to myth, the ancestors had granted these people access (see Chapter 7). They were considered part of the communal heritage, to be used and shared, but not abused. Fijians specifically included raw fruits *(vuata)* and raw fish *(kokoda)* in this subcategory (Pollock 1985a). Pawpaw was one type of *vuata,* something a child might pick for his/her self but not a "real food." In Palau this category was known as *kliou* and included varieties of fruits such as papaya, mango, jackfruits, oranges, and bananas (Akimichi 1980:598). They were not considered real food because a starch was not the main component. Thus the suggestion by English-speaking nutritionists that pawpaw should be incorporated in Fijian breakfasts to ensure a good intake of vitamin A violated several Fijian food concepts. In fact pawpaw was generally considered food for pigs, not for humans. Also, Fijians did not have the concept of breakfast per se. Such discrepancies in key concepts between English and Fijian lead to miscommunications.

Raw fish is a delicacy served in many societies of the Pacific. It may be marinated in lime juice or coconut cream, in which case some informants considered it to be "cooked." Or it may be served alone. This has become popular with visitors to the Pacific and so is often served in restaurants as a starter dish.

A fourth category that Pulu, for Tonga, calls fruit soups consisted of ripe fruits chopped and baked or boiled in coconut cream (1981:72). On Namu such a soup was made from breadfruit. It was "eaten" because it consisted of a starch food, rather than "drunk," as is indicated by the linguistic form of possessive used with this dish (see below for discussion of possessives).

The range of edibles in addition to those of the main food event was very wide in scope. The packet foods, fruits, and so forth not only added significant variation to the diet but were important items of exchange between households. They also featured prominently at any big feast. As products of the land and sea, these foods were a means of expressing ties to the land and social status; they were also used for reinforcing social ties in the community. Because they were eaten on such an irregular basis they were not so readily observed by visitors and might certainly be missed by those assessing food intake based only on what they called meals. These edibles may also have been easily forgotten by those who had eaten them, because they were important for social reasons, not as food.

FEAST FOODS

Besides household food events that could be either structured or unstructured, feasts also could be closely or loosely structured. Above all, feasts were communal events involving several households; all members of those households were involved in preparing the food, as well as the feast itself. The food content of a feast was highly structured in that the main constituents were the real food and the accompanying dish, but with a much greater variety of each of these than in household fare. Taro and breadfruit and yams were served in slices, together with several kinds of accompanying dishes, including taro leaves or *bele* leaves in coconut cream, fish, pig, and shellfish, and possibly some turtle. In addition puddings, such as *vakalolo* in Fiji or *faikai* in Wallis and Futuna or *poke* in Rarotonga, were part of the content of a feast. The foods should be of the highest quality, superior to those used for daily fare in the household. Mode of presentation was important.

Certain foods were not acceptable at feasts. Boiled bananas in parts of Fiji (Quain 1948) and elsewhere, plain cassava root, and sweet potato were not considered of high enough standing, though cassava flour might be used in complex dishes.

The quantity and variety of food at a feast varied greatly with the nature of the occasion. Special foods were featured at household feasts, feasts for a chief's wedding or investiture, and feasts associated with tribute presentation and large community celebrations, such as first fruits presentations (see Chapter 6).

Thus the principal constituents of this feast food category were drawn from the best of both daily fare and the irregularly eaten edibles. A variety of foods was also highly desirable. Highly ranked foods were more acceptable than low-ranked foods. These principles guided those giving food and, when properly fulfilled, were sources of great satisfaction for those sharing a feast. Food might be the centerpiece of the social occasion or just part of a stream of social events. But it was rare to find a social event at which food did not feature in some small way.

RESTRICTED ACCESS TO CERTAIN FOODS

Special food rules include those in which certain foods are proscribed or prescribed for a particular situation, such as for a lactating mother or before a man goes fishing; also rules exist for who should eat apart from others and what foods should be eaten to make a person well. The distinctions in access to food have been dealt with by most researchers as mainly sexual—that women's food differed from men's food, or that women were not allowed to eat certain foods that men ate, and so on. However, the picture is not that simple. For several different groups of people, such as chiefs, old men, men, women, young girls, and special-status persons such as warriors, priests, and navigators, there were special rules of access to food that addressed not only the food itself, but also the fires on which it was cooked and the utensils used (see Chapter 4).

Restrictions on women handling food when menstruating appear to have been the most commonly stated proscriptions. However, the interpretation needs further consideration because it has not warranted much serious appraisal in the modern literature, except for Labby (1976) and Lingenfelter (1975). The gender interpretation also needs to be examined from a female point of view.

Women's access to certain foods did differ from men's in some societies. In two societies on opposite sides of the Pacific, namely Yap and Tahiti, a clear distinction was made between men's food and women's food, as well as other distinctions having to do with food. In Yap this was institutionalized in what have become known as eating classes.

Yapese, according to ethnographic studies in the 1960s and 1970s, distinguished several aspects of food use: where the foods were cooked, who cooked them, and who could have access to them. Men's food was clearly distinguished from women's and children's food and from the food of menstruating daughters. A man took his food from land designated specifically for him according to his rank in the community, while a woman and her children took theirs from land specifically designated for them. Each had his/her own taro *(Cyrtosperma)* patch, garden, food-bearing trees, and water supply; and as soon as a catch of fish was brought to shore, it would be divided into those fish that would be eaten by the man and those that would be eaten by the woman and her children. The one could not eat or drink what was designated for the other; they could not eat out of the same pot; nor could the same pot or cooking fire be used in preparing their food. Each would become ill eating food from the others' land. The land produced sustenance specifically for particular estate members—the ranked subunits could be used only by the appropriate persons (Labby 1976:70; Lingenfelter 1975:95). Thus these eating classes affected not only who ate together but the whole organization of daily life.

Also in Yap, old men ate in a separate part of the house from the women and children, and menstruating girls ate and cooked in a separate house. Male children over ten years old lived in the village young men's house. Each of these groups had its own separate cook house apart from the main house, one for the head of household with his own cooking utensils, another for the mother and young children, and another for a daughter who had reached puberty. Who did the cooking is not clear, though Hunt, an ethnographer who worked in Yap just after World War II, indicates that the women did much of it: "The source of evil is that a woman must go to each grade plot separately for food, carry it home, return to another graded plot for another's food, carry it home and finally cook it in several pots. . . . She must serve it to several people who may want to eat at widely different times" (1949:62). When one woman was menstruating, presumably another took over the cooking tasks. This account depicts the woman doing the cultivating and the cooking of the man's food, but not eating with him.

Lingenfelter implies that the reason for the eating classes lies in the polluting aspects of menstruation, not just the physical signs, but more powerfully the symbolic values: "Young girls and people [sic] of childbearing age are befouled by menstruation. These people should not go near the table for distributing fish to chiefs, taro patches for old men, meeting places for old men, cooking places for old men, and other taboo places" (1975:85). But nowhere does he give any evidence that this association between the so-called polluting aspects of women and the eating classes was part of Yapese reasoning. Nor does he tell us how the eating classes affected women's work habits, other than that middle-aged women were the most industrious workers and led in the affairs of women in the village (Lingenfelter 1975:96).

There are many more questions that need to be answered about these eating classes. We do not get a clear picture of how this formalized structure operated in everyday life. How did these distinctions affect the running of the households? How did the people manage in times of sickness, or when food was short? What rules prevailed when sharing food at communal feasts?

In a wider context we are told that "the eating class is a social and religious grouping of men with express reference to religious ritual, obtaining and eating of food, and the concomitant taboos accompanying rank and ages" (Lingenfelter 1975:97). Perhaps just as Schneider's rethinking of his Yapese data has indicated a new importance of the *tabinaw,* or Yapese household group in kinship (Schneider 1984), so further focus on the importance of food may shed light on the social relationships that apparently governed access to food in Yap. I feel that to label this as an example of a tabu on women's food is an inadequate representation of the complexities of Yapese eating classes.

Such eating classes were but one form of controlled access to food that operated in some Pacific societies but not in others. Ethnographers have labeled them eating classes, but the distinctions were made for activities such as planting and cooking, not just for eating. Exactly which aspect applies to which group needs to be examined systematically. Each affected a person's status in the community and many other dimensions of social life.

The label "food tabus" is often used for these and other forms of restricted access to food by particular groups. But since the term includes a multiplicity of types of prohibitions, I will not use it here.

If we examine which foods were restricted, we find no instances cited whereby the special groups of people could not touch the starch foods. In fact, in Hawai'i a very positive value has become associated with *poi;* it has become an important baby food, and indeed since 1906 has been made available commercially to non-Hawaiians because of its easy digestibility and lack of allergenic properties (Begley, Spielmann, and Vieth 1981). Weaning foods included the starches in grated, pounded, or premasticated forms, together with the sprout of the coconut. Given the psychological satisfaction derived from the starch and its accompaniment, it is unlikely that this combination would be denied to anyone, particularly the sick or elderly.

Restrictions on women handling food when menstruating or lactating appear in records of a wide range of societies in the Pacific. In particular, a woman in those conditions was not allowed to handle the food that her husband would eat, either harvesting it or cooking it. Nor were women allowed to eat with their husbands. In Tahiti and Yap, among other societies, men and women were not allowed to eat together at any time, not just when a woman was menstruating. This was as much a class factor as a pollution factor, as discussed above. In addition, some foods such as pork were not eaten by women, and in many societies, certain foods such as turtles were reserved only for chiefs.

Not only were certain foods proscribed and prescribed differently between the sexes, but there were distinct rules about men's fires and women's fires, as well as utensils used in cooking. Men could cook for both sexes but on different fires. Also, they should not touch foods destined for women. These different customs have been described in detail for eastern Polynesia, drawing on the old accounts (Orliac and Orliac 1980:66). Similar rules applied in Yap, across the Pacific (Lingenfelter 1975). But for many societies we lack detailed descriptions of the terms and nature of these restrictions; we need more information on how such special rules applied in other societies at the time of Western contact.

These special uses of foods based on class or gender served to underline certain aspects of the social system. In some cases they were used as a means of distinguishing certain classes and in others they were used to honor certain ranks. Knowledge of these special uses formed part of the general social system.

LINGUISTIC MARKERS OF EDIBLES

Another mode of classification can be found in the structure of the language of certain Pacific Island societies. Food forms a separate noun class in several central Pacific languages and each language has its own distinctive form of the possessive. People of those societies distinguish several classes of food or edibles from one another and from drinkables and other objects possessed. As early as 1839, the missionary Cargill noted: "The last peculiarity which I shall mention as distinguishing Feejeean from the other Polynesian dialects exists in the pronouns which are applicable only to eatables and drinkables. . . . For instance one pronoun is used when speaking of a liquid and a different one when speaking of a solid article of food; and neither of these pronouns is applicable to other things. This is a very striking peculiarity in the Feejeean language" (Schütz and Geraghty 1980).

This system of a separate possessive class of edibles as distinct from other classes of possession is found only in the central Pacific. Each of some eight languages in Fiji had a separate edible class (Geraghty 1983), as did the languages of Motu and Lenakel in Tanna, Vanuatu (Lynch 1982:244). Also northeast Santo, North Malekula, Ambrym and Epi, South Malekula, Efate, and the Shepherd Islands, all in the Vanuatu area, shared this feature of having a separate edible class of nouns (Tryon 1976:313). Tryon tabulates fourteen noun classes for these Vanuatu languages, but no one language group has more than seven. Food is one class for each of these language groups.

In languages of eastern Micronesia there are also several classes of possession. In the Marshalls the edible class is one of seven classes of nouns, each of which takes a different form of possessive (Bender 1969: 18). In Kusaie (now Kosrae) Kee Dong Lee (1975) identified food as one of eight major categories of possessive classifiers; within the food class he distinguished a drinkable from raw uncooked, from chewable and edible. Similarly, Rehg identified four possessive classifiers for Pohnpei: edible things, drinkable things, catch, share food at a feast (1981:179). In Truk, too, there are many possessive classifiers, including separate ones for eating and for drinking (Goodenough and Sugita 1980). In both the Marshalls and Truk chewing and sucking take the drinkable possessive classifier. Smoking is considered eating and thus takes the edibles classifier: In the Marshalls they say, *"Letok kijam jikka"* (Give him a cigarette [to eat]).

The absence of this noun class for edibles in Hawaiian, Tahitian, and other languages of the eastern Pacific is a noteworthy break from the languages of Fiji, the Marshalls, etc. In Hawai'i and Tahiti only two noun classes exist, one (including edibles) marked by the "a" form of the possessive and the other by the "o" form. In Easter Island Rapanui language, the two-form possessive system was also distinguished by the use of a-form and o-form. Work, tools, food, and craft products fall into a-form, while land, houses, and canoes fall into o-form. Thus "my food" in Rapanui is *ta'aku kai* (Mulloy and Rapu 1977:12–13.) "Things, actions and persons for which the possessor is responsible, that are dependent on him, are a-class possessives. Things or persons which protect, shelter, care for the possessor, that he is dependent upon, are o-class possessives," suggest Mulloy and Rapu (1977:17–18).

Amidst the many attempts to account for this major difference in the languages of the central and eastern Pacific, Pawley leads us back in time:

> In the marking of possessive relations Proto-Oceanic showed a three-way contrast where PAN [Proto-Austronesian] had only one way of marking possession: a relation controlled by the possessor was marked by *na-* plus person-marker before the possessed pronoun; one not controlled was marked by *ka-;* while inalienable relationships (kin terms and body parts) were marked by directly suffixing the person-marker to the possessed noun. . . . In some Oceanic languages (chiefly those of Fiji, northern New Hebrides and Micronesia) the POC [Proto-Oceanic] system was elaborated by adding a distinction between edible and drinkable possession. In the Polynesian group, this possessive system was simplified to a two-way contrast between controlled and non-controlled possession (marked by a and o respectively) with only vestiges of the earlier drinkable category. (1981:20)

Clark (1979) also considers that there has been a reduction of categories in Polynesian languages. He suggests that the system of four categories of possession in Fijian (inalienable, edible, drinkable, and neutral) has been reduced over time and geographical spread to two categories in Maori (dominant and subordinate).

The major question for our consideration here is whether that "reduction" has likewise affected the importance of food in those cultures. From the data available this does not appear to be the case, so we must look beyond the use of food for reasons for this change in language structure.

What is not clear is what are the defining limits of edibles. Lynch, in his paper on the origin of Oceanic possessive constructions (1982), suggests that it is the intention of eating, not the edibility of the object, that is the distinguishing point. He suggests that in earlier times when Proto-Oceanic (POC) was the language of the island Pacific "the possessive constructions in POC derive in some way from verb-object relationships" (Lynch 1982:246). Thus the use of the particular form of the possessive marker for "your (sing.) taro," as in Fijian *na ke-mu dalo,* is an indication that that person will eat that taro, not give it away or do something else with it. The item possessed is clearly intended for eating. Lynch distinguishes this type of active eating possession from direct possession, active manipulative possession, passive possession, and active drinking possession (1982:246).

We can further extend Lynch's ideas to suggest that the existence of active classes of possession is an indication of the importance of human control over certain resources needed for the maintenance of life. Where food resources were all very similar, based on the same tree and root starches everywhere and no way of distinguishing "my" taros from "their" taros existed, the use of the particular possessive form for an edible indicated just what disposition was intended for that article. The purpose for which the possessor intended to use that article was verbalized, and became a part of his social commitment to the others participating in that conversation. It was thus a subtle but strong way of indicating how a particular object would be used. Such a communication depended as much on the implicit meanings as on the explicit words used.

Then again, Lynch's paper can lead us to believe that edible items were so regarded only if they were clearly designated for eating purposes. Thus yams or breadfruit set aside in storage may have taken a different form of possessive, such as active manipulative possession, if it was recognized that they were to be given as a gift and not to be eaten. Similarly, an item such as a mango being sold would take the property possessive, not the edible possessive. This makes the concept of eating a pragmatic choice as well as an abstract mode of thinking. Food and edibles are thus very concretely imbedded in the knowledge system.

Edibles are a structurally marked class, clearly set apart from other objects in certain societies of the Pacific by means of this structural fea-

ture. The particular form of possession is distinct from that for drinkables and other items possessed. This feature of certain Pacific languages
seems to indicate that either the activity of eating or use of the goods
themselves involved in eating and drinking were two social activities of
major importance. The most adequate explanation might be that since
edibles (and drinkables) played such a pervasive role in social relations
within and between communities, a distinction was drawn between eating and other uses of these foods, such as exchange. The disposition of
edibles was distinct from other important areas of activity, such as voyaging (another possessive marker in Marshallese) and kin relations (yet
another possessive marker in several languages). Food was used to express particular social messages such as status differences. Also, the various uses to which a coconut tree could be put were clearly designated.
Use for food was distinct from its use for house building or a canoe.
More especially its use as food was clearly expressed.

However, the main reasons for structurally marking these distinctions
are lost in the mists of time. They may be seen as an example of what
Sapir termed "the tyrannical hold that linguistic form has upon our orien-
tation in the world." These possession markers specifically for edibles
may be regarded as "words as symbols of detached cultural elements but
we may suppose the grammatical categories and processes themselves to
symbolize corresponding types of thought and activity of cultural significance" (Sapir, quoted in Durbin 1973:455, 454). Without bowing to
Sapir's linguistic determinism, we can still use the existence of these possessive markers, and thus of edibles as a distinct class of nouns, as a
strong indication of the significance of food in these societies. But this
linguistic evidence must be taken along with the non-verbal evidence.

SUMMARY

The categories I have described here are both verbal and contextual. We
cannot rely on verbal categories alone. Rather we must see the classification process growing out of the interplay between verbal and non-verbal
communication that is an integral part of everyday life. In addition, the
rules for food use apply as much for social reasons as for biological satisfaction.

The main categories discussed here are not discrete in the sense that
they are always clearly labeled. They are derived from observation and
questioning. They are also based on a range of determining factors such
as local knowledge, social acceptability, and mutual obligations—that is,
culturally specific criteria. Some of those meanings are implicit in the situation. For example, time, which is such an ordering factor in connection with food in Western society, especially where meals are concerned,
is not a dominant factor here. Rather the important factors are the right

ingredients and the social gathering. The categories, then, are a guideline to the ways in which food can be used.

Identifying the main principles by which food is categorized highlights certain aspects of food use in the Pacific societies. One is the importance of the starchy component, whether a root or tree starch, and another is the importance of having an accompanying dish. Together these two elements comprise the main eating event. These principles and the processes of cooking and eating, which also make up a food event, are carried over to the wider social setting where they operate alongside additional principles, such as amounts, particular foods, preferences, and particular modes of processing.

The correspondence between the classification of food concepts as used by English speakers and those used by Pacific Island speakers is far from direct. Much care is needed when translating from English, French, or any non-Austronesian language because food, in one sense, in Pacific societies refers only to starches. But in another sense it is more than just an edible; it has a strong social context. From examining both social events as well as linguistic aspects, it becomes apparent that a similar form of classification is pervasive throughout the social system of any one Pacific Island society.

While the general principles apply widely across Pacific Island societies, there is still considerable cultural variation in the way these principles are interpreted in particular contexts. These unspoken rules are a guideline for acceptable and proper performance when using food. They are a baseline on which decisions are made.

3

Food Choices

Food choice is based on general principles by which food is classified as food, as well as the specific categories that are applied locally. But choice is guided by other idiosyncratic factors, such as local preferences, availability, taste, and so forth, that apply to a particular community or household. They, as much as the principles, determine what is eaten when. By observing food events in a particular society we can abstract certain common features.

People in Pacific households make decisions every day as to which of the several starchy foods available they wish to use and which dish will accompany that starch. In addition to deciding what to cook, they decide how to cook the starch, when to start cooking, and how much to cook. Here I will examine how those decisions are made and acted upon, some of the practical constraints, and the wider social implications, especially in regard to work.

Let us first spend a day in a village household on Namu, a Marshall Islands atoll, to see the context in which food decisions were made.

FOOD EVENTS ON NAMU, 1968

The day on Namu began at dawn, about 6:00 A.M., when everyone from the household arose, rolled up their sleeping mats and pillows and put them away, and went outside to clear away leaves and other debris around the house site. Children going off to school might search their family food container for a piece of leftover breadfruit or some rice. The cook for the day might start preparing a fire by gathering coconut husks or having someone else bring them. A pot of rice with coconut cream, or some breadfruit roasted in the coals, would be ready by about 10:30, together with a pot of tea. Children would come back from school at mid-morning break—or they might not. Some children found food in another household where they had relatives, especially if they smelled pancakes (made from flour and water) frying. A group of men might have gathered at a house where the resident provided a cup of coffee, a real luxury.

The very young children of the household were fed sweet tea and a breadfruit, flour, or rice soup, both prepared specially for them about noon. If the household was making copra on the house site, the young children would be fed any sprouted coconut on hand; occasionally someone might drink a coconut, but these were precious and therefore the supply was conserved. About 4:00 P.M. the cook for the day would start making a fire again, either in the cook house or outside if the weather was suitable, to roast some breadfruit in the coals. Or the gasoline tin oven might be used to bake some small loaves of fermented breadfruit paste or flour. If one of the men in the household had been successful fishing during the day or the night before, the fish would be grilled over the coals. Otherwise a piece of coconut would suffice as relish to go with the breadfruit, rice, or bread. A cup of sweet tea was served with the evening meal. Such was the pattern of daily food events on an outer island in the Marshalls twenty years ago.

This pattern was broken by the weekends. Saturdays were spent preparing a big earth oven and also special foods to be baked in the oven, such as bread with yeast, or breadfruit stuffed with coconut cream tied up in leaves, or fermented breadfruit paste *(bwiru)* kneaded for an hour or more and made into loaves. One or more of the men made a special effort to get some fish, going out in a canoe or a power-boat (if one was working and had some gasoline). If it was not a good time for fishing, a couple of women might search on the oceanside for small crabs. Even the young boys liked to contribute a fish or two to the Saturday food preparation.

Once the food was cooked on Saturday evening, some would be eaten by the household that night. But a goodly portion of both starchy food and the accompanying fish or shellfish and drinking coconuts would be held back for Sunday. That food was then eaten after church, at midday on Sunday. Any leftovers would be eaten Sunday evening. Thus no cooking took place on Sunday except for a pot of tea in the evening, in order to conform with local religious custom that forbade any work between dawn and dusk on Sundays.

Feasts and celebrations served to break up this pattern. They happened irregularly—for example, in conjunction with a child's first birthday celebration, a funeral, the arrival of a chief or important person, or the launching of a canoe. The notable difference was that a chicken or occasionally a pig might be killed and cooked for such a special occasion. For any feast all households in the community contributed a share and then received a redistribution from the central pool. A small amount would be eaten at the feast and the rest taken home to be eaten later. If Lejolan, one of the paramount chiefs, was visiting, he called for a *kamlo* (party) on his first day in Namu. Each household paraded past bearing two or three coconuts or a roasted breadfruit on a coconut leaf tray, which were presented to Lejolan. When deciding what to contribute, each household knew the range of acceptable foods and what it had available, and each was expected to give some local food. After the parade everyone sat down to receive a tray of rice with coconut cream and a portion of canned beef provided by the paramount chief. Throughout his visit each household made sure it made at least one major presentation of food to Lejolan; included would be a chicken or a large fish and some coconuts. The presenters would be given some food in return, of which they would eat a little there with him, but would carry most back to their household. Lejolan's kitchen was piled high each day with these contributions, but most was redistributed and little was wasted. The people of the village welcomed such diversions from the normal routine. They sang and danced and made merry, and talked about the events afterward.

If a child felt hungry she/he would seek food at the home of one relative or another, and thus could be sure of not being hungry for long. Because each household cooked at different times during the morning, it was fairly likely that one household would have some food on hand that a child could have on the way to or from school, or going through the village. An adult who felt hungry would probably have to wait until the next food was cooked in his or her own household, though if passing by another household when others were eating she/he would be invited to join them.

Because the arrival of ships at Namu was very irregular, the rice and flour supply was as precious as the breadfruit and coconuts; therefore decisions about which foods should be used and in what amounts had to be made carefully. There were no stores on the island, and so the rice, flour, tea, and sugar had to be purchased from the supply ship, using money realized from selling copra. Supplies had to last until the next ship appeared, and this was a very unpredictable event. The population of Namu and throughout the Marshalls has grown rapidly in the last fifteen years, exacerbating this situation.

The pattern of daily food events on Namu was similar to those in which I have participated in Niue (1975), Ha'apai, Tonga (1975), and Naduri, Fiji (1982), though in all these places the food supply was more varied and abundant than in the Marshalls. Moreover there were local stores from which food could be purchased daily, though shortage of cash was a restriction. In Fiji and the Polynesian islands, slices of taro or yam or cassava were the mainstay food. The accompanying dish was generally more substantial than in Namu—for example, a can of fish or corned beef, or river *kai* (shellfish) in Fiji. And biscuits, Twisties, and other processed commercial snack foods were bought for preschool children. Adults too had access to more snack-type foods. The special meal on Sunday and the numerous feasts at which food was both given and received were as common in Polynesia as in Namu, in Micronesia. The choice on all these islands was between locally grown and purchased foods.

SELECTION OF FOODS AND DECISION MAKING

On Namu in extended family households where there were several adult women, the woman rostered as the cook for the day decided which starch food and accompaniment would be served to all families. This roster system allowed them to arrange cooking activities around the menstrual patterns of the women; a woman was not allowed to prepare food for her husband or other males for the five days or so that she was menstruating. The woman who was the cook for the day prepared, cooked, and served whatever food was available in sufficient quantity for all the family units within that household.

In households I have observed in Fiji and Niue the selection of food is a joint decision among the adult members of the household, as it involves some work commitment by several of the adults and young people. The men dig or pick the starchy food, while the women and young men decide what and how much of what has been harvested should be cooked. The decision is made with minimal discussion.

Harvesting the food, preparing it, and cooking it are tasks likely to be undertaken by different members of the household. Only in small households consisting of a nuclear family does one person carry the onus of the work. In most Pacific societies in earlier times when the earth oven was made every day, making the oven and tending the food were considered men's work. The decision whether or not to have an oven was largely contingent upon what foods were to be cooked. The selection of foods to be cooked therefore had to be coordinated between those harvesting the foods and those doing the cooking. In some societies, such as Samoa, all men harvested while the young untitled men were responsible for the

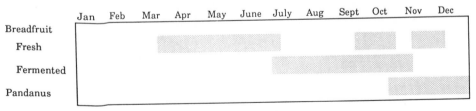

Figure 5. Availability of foods on Namu during one year.

FOOD PREFERENCES

Selection is also based on a preference for one crop over another. This is an important guideline for those providing food for a household and for a community event. Those making the decisions know without discussion what foods the people of their household and community prefer. Their selection is based on knowledge of the ranking order of particular foods for particular occasions.

In Africa, Lee found that the Dobe !Kung did not value all plant foods equally: "Some are prized and eaten daily; others are despised and rarely eaten. Complex criteria are applied by the !Kung to arrange their plant foods into a hierarchy of classes of desirability" (1984:40). A number of factors affected preferences, including taste and the desire for variety.

In the Pacific, Tongans strongly prefer yams over *Colocasia* taro and breadfruit (Hau'ofa 1979). Yams are also important as the main item to be given at an '*inasi* (community feast), though, so that factor may influence harvesting. Similarly, in Pohnpei yams were found to have high priority (Bascom 1965). In Western Samoa breadfruit and *Colocasia* taro were the preferred foods (Turner 1841), and in Tahiti breadfruit was the number-one food (Ellis 1831). In the Marquesas breadfruit was also the preferred food but it was eaten in the form of *popoi,* a mixture of fresh breadfruit with the fermented breadfruit (Handy and Handy 1923). Ukese also preferred their *kon* of pounded breadfruit over other foods. Hawaiians *poi* made of fermented *Colocasia* taro was the daily fare (Kui 1967; Handy and Handy 1972; Titcomb 1967). For a full list of preferred foods for the different island societies see Table 4.

These foods were not only preferred for household consumption but also the main element expected to be contributed at feasts. This was particularly true of yams in Tonga and Pohnpei, and of *Cyrtosperma* taro (*babai*) in the Gilberts (Luomala 1974). For each society of the Pacific, one of the starchy foods was ranked more highly than all the other starchy foods available. This predominance seems to have continued over time, especially in rural areas, despite the introduction of new foods such as cassava or sweet potatoes (Pollock 1984a). The Japanese tried to introduce sweet potatoes to Truk during the World War II occupation, but the Trukese found them unacceptable (LeBar 1963); breadfruit has remained their preferred food.

Across the Pacific either breadfruit or *Colocasia* taro or yams was preferred over the other starches (see Table 5 for the geographical distribution and the uses of the eleven main starch foods). The less favored starches can be ranked as either secondary or fall-back foods (Pollock 1983). Secondary foods usually include bananas (eaten green), *Alocasia* and *Xanthosoma* taro, and others (see Table 4). These foods were also

cooking. Now that boiling and frying have been accepted through(
Pacific as quicker means of cooking, women tend to do more of
to day cooking; men must still prepare the earth oven when it (
usually for a festive occasion such as Sundays or a community e
a fuller discussion of cooking, see Chapter 4.

To keep a steady supply of food available for selection, tho
ing a particular food item must make sure that the supply of (
ensured for the future. For *Colocasia* taro, the tops are rer
harvesting and planted almost immediately to provide a
some eight to nine months. Since *Colocasia* taro reproduce(
selecting taro for dinner one night also provides planting n
next crop.

Those digging the *Colocasia* taro or picking the br(
household are guided by local knowledge about the
means of reproduction. They know what has been plan
ous pieces of land. They know when it was planted a(
mature (see Appendix A). And they know what can l
what must be eaten immediately to avoid spoilage
know is when they may suddenly need to provide so(
a large feast, perhaps a funeral, or to entertain a
know just when a hurricane or drought will damag(
supply. So, based on past experiences, they must
and how much, leaving some margin for the unex(

What a household can provide either for its m
nity event is dependent in large part on what th(
land. How land is used is discussed fully in Ch(
in the central and eastern Pacific have breadfr
rainfall. They also will probably have some
yams if the soil and moisture are right. Banan
And today some cassava is usually planted (
vested as it is not the most favored starch.
soma taro may also be available.

For daily use only one main starch foo(
which to harvest of these various food pl
on what is in season. Breadfruit and y(
may be used when mature in preferen
Colocasia taro takes some nine months
ity depends on whether the household
of the crop, to be available when need

An accompanying food item also
either grated coconut, sea water, or
coconut was the easiest and most re
cially on atolls such as Namu.

TABLE 4. Importance Rating of Starch Foods by Island

Island(s)	Primary	Secondary	Fall-Back
Central and Eastern Pacific			
Australs/Gambiers	taro	breadfruit	yams, bananas, *ivi*
Rapa	taro	*'ape,* breadfruit	nd
Cook Islands			
Rarotonga	taro, breadfruit	*taro tarua, kumala,* arrowroot	plantain, bananas, *tavioka*
Aitutaki	breadfruit	arrowroot, taro	nd
Mauke, Atiu, Mangaia	taro, breadfruit	nd	nd
Ellice/Tuvalu	taro, *'ape*	breadfruit, *Cyrtosperma*	nd
Fiji			
East side	taro, *tavioka*	breadfruit, *kumala,* yam	wild yams
Rewa	taro, *Cyrtosperma*	breadfruit, *kumala,* yam	nd
West side	sweet potato, *tavioka*	*Alocasia*	nd
Lau	yams	nd	nd
Kadavu	taro	nd	nd
Vanua Levu	taro, bananas	nd	nd
Futuna	taro, *kape*	breadfruit, yams	bananas, wild yams
Hawai'i	taro (as *poi* with fish)	breadfruit, sweet potato	nd
Kiribati	*babai,* pandanus	breadfruit	nd
Marquesas	breadfruit	bananas, coconut	taro, yams
Nauru	pandanus, coconut	none	none
Niue	taro	*kumala,* yams, *tavioka, ufi lei*	breadfruit
Ocean	pandanus, coconut	none	none
Samoa, Western			
Upolu	taro, breadfruit	*ta'amu,* green banana, yam	yams, sweet potato, *tavioka*
Savaii	taro, *ta'amu,* breadfruit	nd	nd
Tahiti	breadfruit, taro	bananas, plantains	sweet potato, wild yams, *ivi, 'ape*

TABLE 4 (continued)

Island(s)	Primary	Secondary	Fall-Back
Tokelau	coconut, fish	breadfruit	nd
Tonga	yam, *kape*	*talo tonga, talo futuna,* breadfruit	other yams, *ivi,* manioc
Tuamotus	pandanus	taro, *fakea (Cyrtosperma)*	purslane
Wallis/Uvea	*kape,* breadfruit	taro, yam, *kumala, tavioka*	yams
Northwest Pacific			
Carolines, W.	breadfruit	*Cyrtosperma,* taro	taro, bananas
Guam	taro, yams	rice, breadfruit	*fadang,* bananas
Kapingamarangi	taro	breadfruit, pandanus	nd
Kosrae	breadfruit, taro	bananas	nd
Marshalls	breadfruit, pandanus	*Cyrtosperma*	arrowroot, bananas
Namoluk	breadfruit	taro, *Cyrtosperma*	nd
Palau	taro	*Cyrtosperma, Alocasia, Xanthosoma*	breadfruit, yams
Pohnpei	yams	breadfruit, *Cyrtosperma,* taro	nd
Ngatik	*Cyrtosperma*	pandanus	nd
Mokil	*Cyrtosperma*	pandanus, breadfruit	nd
Pingelap	*Cyrtosperma*	pandanus	nd
Puluwat	breadfruit	*Cyrtosperma*	taro
Saipan, Marianas	taro, yams	breadfruit	nd
Satawal	breadfruit	taro, *Cyrtosperma, Alocasia*	nd
Truk	breadfruit	taro, bananas	nd
Yap	*Cyrtosperma*	taro, yams, breadfruit, bananas	sweet potato, *Xanthosoma,* cassava

taro = *Colocasia esculenta.* See Table 2 for local names.

TABLE 5. Geographical Distribution of Uses of the Eleven Main Starch Foods

Starch Food	Household Use	Ritual Use
Colocasia taro		
Fresh	Fiji, Samoa, Niue, So. Cooks, Wallis, Futuna	Fiji, Samoa, Niue, Wallis, Futuna
Fermented	Hawai'i, Rapa, Tubuai	nd
Alocasia taro	Samoa, Tonga, Wallis, Futuna	nd
Cyrtosperma taro	Yap, Kapingamarangi, Tuamotus, Fiji (Rewa)	Kiribati
Xanthosoma taro	Tonga, Fiji	not used
Yams	Tonga, Niue, Pohnpei, Samoa, Wallis, Futuna	Tonga, Wallis, Futuna, Niue, Pohnpei
Sweet potato	Tonga, Cook Is., Fiji (western side)	not used
Cassava	Fiji, Tonga, Cook Is.	not used, except in puddings
Breadfruit		
Fresh	Truk, Pohnpei, Kosrae, Marshalls, Tahiti, Marquesas	Truk, Pohnpei, Kosrae, Marshalls, Tahiti, Marquesas
Fermented	Truk, Marshalls, Kosrae, Pohnpei, Tahiti, Marquesas	Truk, Kosrae, Pohnpei, Marquesas
Banana	Samoa, Fiji, Tonga, Cook Is., Tahiti, Fiji, Wallis, Futuna, Truk	Samoa, Tonga, Fiji, Cook Is., Wallis, Futuna
Pandanus	Marshalls, Tuamotus, Nauru, Tuvalu, Kapingamarangi	same societies in processed form
Arrowroot	Palau, Yap, W. Carolines, E. Carolines, Marshalls, Kiribati, Tuvalu, Cook Is., Fiji, Niue, W. Samoa, Tonga, Societies, Tuamotus	Fiji, Tonga, W. Samoa, Cook Is.

cultivated but as a backup for use when the primary foods were unavailable or needed to be saved for a ceremonial occasion. A *rahui*, the Polynesian term for proscription against harvesting, may be placed on primary foods, but seldom on secondary foods. Secondary foods are thus mainly household foods; for example, in Vanua Levu, Fiji, and in Samoa bananas are purely household fare and should never be served to visitors or given at a community event (Quain 1948; Grattan 1948).

Fall-back foods are non-cultivated foods, or food plants that were once cultivated but not harvested before use of the cultivation plot was discontinued; so they were left in the ground. They may be found amongst secondary growth or in the forest. Wild yams *(Dioscorea bulbifera; D. pentaphylla)* are most frequently cited (e.g., Morrison 1790, for Tahiti). All these foods may be sought out in times of stress; some villagers on Tongatapu contemplated using wild foods after Hurricane Wally in 1982 (NJP fieldnotes 1982). In earlier times wild foods were sought after cultivated crops were destroyed in war (Gill 1876). Many of these foods are very acrid and thus require a great deal of careful preparation before they can be eaten.

Taste

Taste is a special base for preferring one food over another. Little has been recorded about Pacific Islanders' tastes for different foods, but Grattan has recorded that some Samoans preferred breadfruit underripe because they did not like it too sweet, and they did not like sweet potato for the same reason (Grattan 1948). Firth noted of Tikopians: "These natives have a definite food aesthetic, a theory of taste which holds that taro alone, though satisfying, needs coconut cream to make it really appetizing" (Raymond Firth 1939:51–52).

The taste for sour foods, such as fermented breadfruit paste or fermented taro, was also peculiar to certain island groups (see Table 7 and discussion in Chapter 5). On Truk fermented breadfruit was a delicacy (Lebar 1963), and Marquesans liked their *popoi* (fermented breadfruit) but could vary its acidity by adding more or less fresh breadfruit to the fermented paste (Handy and Handy 1923). On Namu the acidity of *bwiru* was cut by both kneading and adding coconut cream. Similarly, in Hawai'i *poi* could be made less acid by adding more water (Pukui 1967).

The authors note that in all these societies the fermented product was used on a daily basis and was prepared according to preferred taste. It seems likely that fermentation served at least a dual purpose—to add a sharp acid taste to the diet and also, at the end of the season, as a means of preserving some *Colocasia* taro or breadfruit. This line of argument will help to clarify why Fijians and Tikopians processed some eight different starches by fermenting them in pits and even mixing several different starches in the same pit. If foods were fermented only for times of shortage, one food would have sufficed. But by fermenting several different foods, they were able to have several different tastes available.

In my opinion the use of fermentation of foods is an indication, not that these societies were short of food, but that they liked the different flavors of the fermented foods that came out of the pits. Therefore it seems preferable to consider these fermented foods as part of the society's aesthetic values, as Raymond Firth (1939:51–52) and Huntsman (1978) have pointed out for Tikopia and Tokelau, respectively, and not simply as a means of storage, as so many Westerners have argued (Yen 1975; Barrau and Peeters 1972; Testart 1982). This form of processing should be seen as part of the general picture of food usage, the different taste of the end product being more significant than the processing per se (Pollock 1984b).

How these distinctive tastes have developed is a matter of speculation. We know that fermented foods, such as *tempeh* and *miso,* have been used for a considerable time in Southeast Asia. And since that is the major point of origin of migration into the Pacific, a link is possible between tastes developed theré and those for fermented breadfruit and taro in the Pacific (Pollock 1984b). Moreover, some societies have developed these tastes even further by mixing fresh and fermented breadfruit or mixing different fermented foods, as in Fiji. These have all met a level of acceptability. We don't know about those tastes that have been tried and dropped.

Anthropological discussions of taste among various peoples of the world are sadly missing. We understand little of this complex area, as Kuipers (1984) has noted for an Indonesian society. We can be guided in understanding what tastes other people express only by our own categories of sweet, sour, bitter, pungent. But we should be reaching out to find categories expressed in other societies (Bourdieu 1984). For example, "salty" has been generally used as the translation of the Polynesian *masi,* which is the term widely associated with food fermented in pits (Chowning, pers. comm. 1984). However, this translation may need rethinking when we better understand factors determining local taste discriminations. Sour taste may be a separate category of taste, or it may be the equivalent of salty in Pacific Island categories of taste.

Selecting foods that had some pungency, such as fermented ones, may have had a specific purpose—to complement the bland taste of the starchy foods. Use of salt water in which to dip the breadfruit or taro, or the accompanying grated coconut or fish, would have added some astringency as well as a different texture. But we need more data on taste factors governing the choices of particular foods.

Variety

Pacific Island peoples, like many others, enjoy a wide variety of food. They plant as many different starch food plants as they can in order to have a range from which to select one for each day's household use. In those societies of the Pacific that have a limited range of food, such as on atolls and in the eastern Pacific, variety is an especially desirable feature. Cook noted that Tahitians ate the same food day after day, with breadfruit, taro, and fish as their daily fare (Beaglehole 1955). This went against Cook's own preference for different foods each day. He led the way in attempts to increase the variety of foods on many of the islands, leaving seeds of garden crops and grains that could produce trade items. Only the pumpkins, melons, and pineapples were successful; other visitors also tried to introduce new foods by bringing seeds (see Leach 1983).

Pacific people welcomed any variety in their diet, though any new food item was likely to be ranked as secondary food. Seasonal foods such as breadfruit provide a welcome change of diet because they are available only at certain times. Namu people anticipated with pleasure the times when breadfruit could be harvested to provide a change from rice. But when they had been eating breadfruit every day for about three weeks, they longed to eat some rice.

A family or household was considered well cared for if it had a number of different crops growing from which it could select one for the day. Another way to add variety within the starchy category is to obtain some new planting material that has characteristics different from those cultivars generally found in that particular island. That has led to a number of significant exchanges of planting stock among the various islands of the Pacific (Barrau 1979). As a result, there are large numbers of varie-

Figure 6. Selecting food in the market. Fiji, 1985. Photo by Nancy J. Pollock

ties of the main food plants, many of which have not been identified in Western botanical systems of classification. For example, at the time of contact Hawai'i was noted as having seventy-two varieties of taro growing, for each of which the locals had a name (Handy and Handy 1972). On Namu the people had obtained several varieties of breadfruit and pandanus over the years, each distinguished by its local name and particular characteristics. They had twenty-four varieties of pandanus, some of which matured early in the season and some late; some had to be cooked, others were sweet enough to be eaten raw. Similarly, cassava and *Xanthosoma* taro, two late arrivals in the Pacific root crop inventory, have been welcomed as additions providing variety. They fit well into the local conception of food—more so than cabbage and tomatoes. However, they have not yet become substitutes for the traditional starches as primary foods.

This varied inventory can be considered an important form of insurance as it serves to reduce the risks of food shortage after a hurricane or storm. For that reason imported rice and wheat flour have been welcomed, not as substitutes for the other starches, but as alternatives (Pollock 1975).

Yet another way to add variety to the starch food was through the accompanying dish. As already mentioned, the flavor of the taro or breadfruit can be changed by dipping a piece in sea water at the time of eating, or eating it with a piece of coconut. On Namu, when one ship brought several cases of *saimin* (Japanese noodle soup), it was added to the rice, the only starchy food we had at the time. Similarly, spaghetti (canned) was served over rice, as the accompaniment.

Different ways of cooking have also added variation in flavor and texture. Cooking in the earth oven gives a very distinctive flavor and softens the starchy foods considerably. Breadfruit roasted in the coals becomes harder and drier. The metal pots now available for boiling foods have added a new taste—less acceptable for *Colocasia* taro, as Handy and Handy (1972) note, but still a change. Frying provides yet another flavor; the taste for fat was noted by Anderson on Cook's expedition (Beaglehole 1967). This was also observed during my own fieldwork; Namu children, large and small, made a feast out of doughnuts when the ship had visited with a new batch of flour, yeast, and cooking fat. Similarly, fat pork was considered more flavorful than lean; mutton flaps *(sipi)* are greatly desired in Tonga to accompany yams or cassava.

EATING TIMES

In Pacific societies, when to eat was not a major decision. It happened. The oven was made usually around midday, and people ate at the day's end. In a few societies, such as the Marquesas, the main meal was at midday. Any food left from the main cooking was set aside for later that day or the next morning, or enough was made to last for two days, as in Tikopia (Firth 1936). The process of heating leftovers (e.g., *tihana* in Tahiti) was designed to prevent spoilage, not to render food hot.

Many European observers have noted with some concern that people of the Pacific ate when food was available and did not follow any regular schedule (e.g., Wilkes 1845, 2:78 for Samoa; Krämer 1935 for Truk; Ellis 1831:130 for Tahiti). In reporting the times of eating, they tried to impose their own measures of frequency. For example, Wilson noted in Tahiti (1799) that "they have not always regular meals, but usually eat as soon as they rise at daybreak. Some are voracious, especially the chiefs." Ellis added that the Tahitians arranged their meals, in a great measure, according to their avocations or the supply of provisions (1831:130). Similarly, Mariner reports that during his stay in Tonga there were "no fixed times for meals though it generally happens to be in the morning, about noon, and again in the evening" (1831:342). And in Samoa they ate as a group once before noon and again about dusk (Turner 1841; Brown 1910). In the Marquesas Forster noted that "about noon a meal was baked by hot stones under ground. And in the evening there was another slight repast" (1777:405). This pattern of the main meal being taken at midday contrasted with that in Samoa where it was taken in the evening (Turner 1841:1990), though we are not told whether it was amount or content that was used as the basis on which these reporters distinguished a "main" meal. One advantage of eating in the evening was that the flies were less troublesome; this was particularly significant if fish was on the menu. Suffice it to say that these visitors found the irregular eating habits noteworthy, perhaps because a deep-rooted principle in their own culture was being violated.

The number of times of day that people ate also varied, according to the availability of food, status of the individual, and other factors. Ellis noted a difference between eating patterns of chiefs and commoners: "Breadfruit is dressed two or three times a day for chiefs; but the peasantry etc. seldom prepare more than one oven, during the same period; and frequently Tihana or bake it again on the second day" (1831:41). This implies that freshly cooked food was available more frequently for high-status persons than for low-status persons. This difference may have been due to several factors, perhaps relating more to the number of visitors who shared a chief's food and who received what according to distribution patterns than to any European values about hot food and its freshness.

On Namu times for eating were not set for any particular times of day, but happened as work allowed, when the cook got around to preparing the food, and when people felt like eating. People would gather to eat together when food was being served out, and would eat as much as they wanted or was available to them. Preschool weaned children were fed more frequently than adults. Breast-fed children were fed to meet both the mother's comfort and the baby's demands.

Care must be taken in considering these eating events as meals. That term has specific connotations in English (Douglas 1972). The rigidity of Western culture where the clock regulates eating habits is missing in Pacific societies. So also is the principle that food that has been cooked should be consumed immediately. The temperature of the food was unimportant. The main concerns were that food was available and that it was cooked so as to be edible.

It is clear that the Western concept of meal is not synonymous with the kind of eating patterns discussed here, either in terms of content and the need for hot food, frequency, or regularity. In the Pacific other, local principles governed when people would eat. A food event consisted of two parts, the cooking process and the eating; each was a social activity.

AMOUNTS OF FOOD EATEN

If food was freely available, it was eaten. If there was little food, people went hungry. This appears to have been a general pattern across the Pacific, and is well summed up in the Samoan saying: *Le polo e nanea mea mata, ae le nanea mea vela,* "Eat while you see it."

The large amounts eaten were noted by several missionaries and other European visitors. For example, Banks has left us a vivid description of the amounts eaten in Tahiti by what he terms "their principal people," presumably chiefs: "It may be thought that I have given rather too large a quantity of provision to my eater, when I say that he has eaten three bread-fruits, each bigger than two fists, two or three fish, fourteen or fifteen plantains or bananas, . . . and concluded his dinner with about a quart of a food as substantial as the thickest unbaked custard. But this I do affirm, that it is but few of the many I was acquainted with that eat less, while many eat a good deal more" (1769:141).

Similarly chiefs in Tonga ate at least double the amount commoners ate, according to some early observers. Samwell, a young seaman on Cook's third voyage, noted:

> In the morning they drink Kava and eat baked yams or breadfruit. They dine about noon generally upon baked yams and breadfruit with puddings made of Plantains and sometimes the better sort have Pork but more commonly fish, drinking water with it which they seem to prefer to coconut milk. The Chiefs are served at their meals with much parade; a single yam being often brought on a pole between 2 men so that a dinner consisting of

a dozen or two of yams, some parcels of baked Fish, Plantains, cocoanuts
and shells of water and Plantain leaves . . . will employ 30 or 40 people.
(Quoted in Beaglehole 1967)

Large amounts of foods were prepared for a Tongan chief, and a lot of
work was required to feed him. Such commitments indicate the high
value placed on a well-fed person, as shown in his body structure. A fat
chief was a mark of a prosperous society (Ellis 1831). Leanness was a
sign of hard work and was deplored. Even in the 1960s the Namu people
were most concerned that I should eat well so that I would be fat when I
returned to Hawai'i; that would indicate to Americans, they said, that I
had been well looked after in the Marshalls (NJP fieldnotes 1968–1969).
This high value placed on fattening up a person was institutionalized in
Tahiti in a custom known as *ha'apori* (Oliver 1974:222).

The eating of large amounts at one time has been labeled "gorging" by
Oliver (1974:222), who claims that this was an adjustment in Tahiti to
seasonal variation. The missionary Ellis noted of the ordinary Tahitian
people: "The natives take a much larger quantity of refreshment than
European labourers but their food is less solid and nutritive. They have
however the power of enduring fatigue and hunger in a greater degree
than those by whom they are visited. A native will sometimes travel 30 or

Figure 7. "Good foods" at Talamahu market (breadfruit, *kape,* green bananas,
coconuts, and taro leaves). Tonga, 1990. Photo by Nancy J. Pollock

40 miles over mountain and ravine without taking any refreshment except the juice from a piece of sugar cane and apparently experience but little inconvenience from his excursion" (1831:99). Tati recorded that when a church was dedicated, he and his fellow Tahitians ate for three days. "We Polynesians were always that way, Gargantuan eaters at times but able to go fifty miles at top speed on a coconut in war" (quoted in O'Brien 1921:201).

Similarly, Freycinet noted of Hawaiians that a "prodigious quantity of food is devoured, rather than eaten by these people" (1960:520). And Miller adds that 5 pounds of *poi* per day was an average amount for a man or woman, but that old Hawaiians might eat 10 or 15 pounds a day, depending on the work they were doing and abundance of supply (1927: 17). Thomson tells us that "the Fijians require a heavy weight of food per head to satisfy them, from 5 to 10 lbs. weight of yams or other roots being the normal daily food of a full-grown man" (1908:23). In contrast, for Tonga, the missionary Gill reported that "one large yam will provide sufficient food for a native family for two weeks" (1902:109–110).

Such marathon eating events have not been described in such detail for Micronesia, but that does not mean they did not occur. We do have descriptions of the mounds of food at feasts, as discussed in Chapter 6.

Daily household consumption comprised only one starch, together with its accompaniment. If there was plenty this might amount to 5 or 10 pounds of taro for one adult, male or female. If less was available, they cut back accordingly. In lean times there might be little left over from the one oven. Then there might be only one eating event in the day. As Buck noted for Samoa, "there is a tendency to overeat and to encroach on what was cooked for two meals" (1930:138). Thus eating was not only irregular, but varied in the amounts consumed.

Casual eating, or snacks as we call them, was only a pastime. A fisherman might eat a fish raw while out fishing, or someone making copra might find the spongy fruit inside a coconut that has started to sprout. Young people might chew on a sweet coconut husk or lick some salt. When biscuits and sweets became more readily available they took the place of these snacks. The puddings that were part of the non-meal foods were prepared mainly for guests and ceremonial occasions and were not a part of the regular daily intake, but after a feast a household might receive some from a food division. Perhaps only in recent times has food been plentiful enough that women make these puddings for each other (NJP fieldnotes, Fiji/Naduri 1982).

SUMMARY

In this chapter I have discussed some of the factors affecting food use. Decisions are based on the general principles examined in association with the classification of food. But a whole range of other factors at the level of both household and community must be taken into account. Choices about which food is to be consumed are complex in any society. Certain constraints operate, but the options allow a certain amount of flexibility (Dwyer 1985). Social as well as biological factors are involved in food selection. A food event is accomplished satisfactorily only when these factors are considered, albeit at a very low level of consciousness.

4

Cooking

IN THE Pacific cooked food was generally considered synonymous with the concept of food (see Bascom 1965 for Pohnpei). That is, an earth oven of food contained the two main elements of household fare, the starchy food and the accompaniment in the form of fish or taro leaves.

All the starchy foods that were so important in Pacific societies' life-styles had to be cooked. This was necessary to rid them of the toxic substances that lay just under the skin. Even breadfruit and the fermented paste made from it had to be cooked before they could be eaten. Thus starchy foods were synonymous with cooked foods because the "real food" must always be cooked. In contrast the accompanying dish could be cooked or raw (for Samoa, see Grattan 1948; for Tikopia, see Firth 1936).

However, the cooked/raw distinction does not seem to have been as important in the Pacific as the distinction between starchy foods and their accompaniment. Rather there is a three-way distinction between what must be cooked, what may be cooked, and what may be cooked or left uncooked. The starches had to be cooked, the accompaniment such as fish might be cooked, and other edibles such as puddings or fruit might be cooked or uncooked. This three-way contrast is a significant departure from the binary opposition of the "raw" and the "cooked" that Lévi-Strauss has bequeathed to the anthropological literature in order to equate the raw with nature and the cooked with culture (1970).

The main mode of cooking was either baking in the earth oven or broiling in the coals of a fire. "Broiling and baking are the only two modes of applying fire to their cookery. Capt. Wallis observes that having no vessel in which water could be subjected to the action of fire, they had no more idea that it could be made hot than that it could be made solid" (Bligh, quoted in Barrow 1980:28). The *umu* (the word for earth oven in many Polynesian and some Micronesian languages) was the most frequently used mode of cooking because it cooked the food well, added a good taste to the food, saved on firewood, and involved a pleasant, sociable activity (see Table 6).

Using the earth oven to cook the starch foods was a process that involved several people's commitment; other edibles could be processed by only one person. Consider the term *kainga,* widespread in Polynesian and some Micronesian languages, referring to the extended family (Marshall 1979); its etymological base suggests the idea of eating together. Cooking thus was a strongly symbolic action, converting the product of the land into socially sustaining food. It epitomized the essence of social life in which people shared the products of their land.

It is clear that at a very early stage in the domestication of taro and yams for use as foodstuffs, the processes for rendering these edible had to be worked out. By both experimentation and by chance, a process of heat treatment of these root starches was developed and formed part of what Barrau and Peeters call "des premieres transformations que l'homme fit subir aux ressources naturelles pour les rendre conformés à ses besoins" (1972:142; NJP translation: "those first transformations which man applied to the natural resources in order to make them fit his needs"). Once this initial hurdle of rendering these roots less toxic was overcome in pre-contact times, the preparation of these foodstuffs has changed little right up to present times, and the processes have been prevalent across a wide geographical area.

The question of whether Pacific Islanders used any other methods of cooking prior to the earth oven is under considerable debate (Irwin 1981; Leach 1983; Davidson 1984; Pollock n.d.*a;* Guiart 1982; Takayama 1981/1984). The missionary Cargill, who landed in Tonga in the 1830s, certainly got the impression that "Tongans before they received pots from Fiji were obliged either to cook all their food on stones, or wrap it in leaves. They of consequence experience great difficulty in cooking liquids" (Schütz and Geraghty 1980:xiv). Cargill is referring to either grilling or baking in the earth oven.

Evidence of these ovens has been found from Guam in the west to Easter Island in the east, though Takayama (1981/1984) believes the earth oven may be a late introduction in Micronesia. At the time of European contact certainly, the *umu* was in widespread use. As Banks noted in the eighteenth century: "Cookery seems to have been but little studied here, they have only two methods of applying fire. Broiling or baking, as we called it, is done thus" and he proceeded to describe in great detail the making of the earth oven, which must have struck him and many other Europeans as a novel way to cook (1769:136–137). This reliance on the earth oven and baking in the coals contrasted with the four ways in which Europeans could cook their food (Maurisio in Barrau and Peeters

TABLE 6. Cooking Methods in Pacific Island Societies at Time of Western Contact

Island(s)	Main Method	Secondary Method	Source
Easter	earth oven	nd	Routledge 1919
Fiji			
Eastern	earth oven	pots	Williams 1858
Lau Is.	earth oven	bamboo	Thompson 1945
Western	earth oven	bamboo	NJP fieldnotes 1983
No. Div.	earth oven	nd	Quain 1948
Futuna	earth oven	roasting	Burrows 1936
Hawai'i	earth oven	boiling	Handy and Handy 1972
Guam	concrete (chahan) stove, earth oven	pottery	Pollock 1986a
Kapingamarangi	earth oven	roasting on stones	Buck 1950
Kiribati	earth oven	roasting	Grimble 1933
Kosrae	earth oven	roasting on hot stones	Sarfert 1919/1920
Mangareva	earth oven	roasting on stones	Laval 1938
Marianas	earth oven	pots, cassis shells	Navy Handbook 1949
Marquesas	earth oven	nd	Linton 1939
Marshalls	earth oven	roasting in coals	Krämer and Nevermann 1938
Nauru	earth oven	nd	Kayser 1934
Niue	earth oven	nd	Loeb 1926
Nukuoro	earth oven	none	Someki 1938
Ocean	earth oven	nd	Ellis 1936
Palau	earth oven	pots	Owen ca. 1965
Pitcairn	earth oven	nd	Shapiro 1929
Pohnpei	earth oven	roasting in coals	Bascom 1965
Ra'ivavae	earth oven	nd	Marshall 1961
Rapa	baking in coals	nd	Hanson 1970
Rarotonga and			
So. Cooks	earth oven	roasting in coals	Buck 1927
Rotuma	earth oven	nd	Gardiner 1898
Samoa	earth oven (shallow)	roasting on stones	Buck 1930
Tahiti/			
Mo'orea	earth oven	roasting on stones	Morrison 1790
Tokelau	earth oven	nd	Williamson 1924
Tonga	earth oven	nd	West 1865
Tongareva	earth oven	nd	Buck 1927
Truk and atolls	earth oven	stone boiling, roasting	Alkire 1965
Tuamotus	earth oven	nd	Danielsson 1956
Tubuai	earth oven	nd	Aitken 1930
Tuvalu	earth oven	nd	David 1899
Wallis	earth oven	roasting	Burrows 1937
Yap	roasting, baking	earth pots	Someki 1938

1972), and so it is not surprising that missionaries and others considered societies that had only two ways of cooking food to be backward.

So why has the earth oven been both so prevalent and so persistent a form of cooking? Was the process particularly suited to the root and tree starches? Was it the best way of cooking these in bulk? Did it save firewood, or save time? Did it have wider social implications than just as a method of cooking food?

CASE STUDY: NAMU

People on Namu atoll in 1967 made an earth oven *(um)* at least once a week and sometimes more frequently. Watching them prepare food, particularly on a Saturday when a large *um* was made for the Sunday feast, I learned that their considerations differed markedly from my own ideas of preparing a meal. First, all members of the household were involved—men, women, children, and the elderly. At least one man from the household, and often two or three, would take off to fish early in the morning if the weather was right. Each had his own one-man canoe. Meanwhile other men of the household picked the breadfruit (in season) and brought it back to the house site to be prepared by the women. If fermented breadfruit was used, one of the men assisted a woman with the kneading

Figure 8. Making coconut cream. Kapingamarangi, 1947. Photo by K. P. Emory, courtesy Bishop Museum

of the paste, a task that took a couple of hours. The other women of the house might be cooking other foodstuffs, or preparing coconut cream, or collecting breadfruit leaves with which to cover the *um*. A couple of the men and boys scraped out an old *um* pit on the sandy shore at the lagoon's edge, and replaced the stones at the bottom. Meanwhile any extra personnel gathered old coconut husks and other firewood and left it at the side of the oven pit. The fire was usually lit after noon on Saturday, so that a big feed was available Saturday evening, and the abundant leftovers set aside for after church on Sunday.

Thus everyone except the smallest and most infirm was involved in the preparation of this Sunday feast. No major chore fell to any one person. And everyone knew what had to be done with minimal overt allocation of tasks. If a task was not done, someone did it. And jobs like digging the oven and kneading breadfruit paste were occasions for discussion and socializing with others standing around. Such a group activity had none of the overtones of drudgery but was part of the social life of the community. The nature of the activity was evident from the sounds: people working and people talking—a general buzz of enjoyment.

During the rest of the week an oven might be made, or rice was boiled in a metal pot over the open fire, or breadfruit was roasted in the coals. Loaves of breadfruit paste or of wheat flour were baked in the *um in gajolin,* an adaptation of the earth oven using a gasoline drum on its side in the sand. Fish was grilled over the coals (Figure 9). Thus it was not necessary to make the oven every day, now that they had metal pots. Conserving the firewood supply was an important concern.

If we consider this example of cooking on one atoll and other observers' accounts of cooking activity in the Pacific, we can distinguish between the technical process and the wider social interaction of which it is a part. The technical process of cooking must fit the products to be cooked.

TOXICITY OF ROOT FOODS

In their raw state taro, yams, and cassava are mildly toxic due to oxalic acid crystals lying just under the skin. For a discussion of toxicity of each starchy root, see Appendix A. If these roots are not properly cooked they will leave an itchy feeling around the mouth—a sensation that has long been associated by Pacific Islanders with improper cooking. The chemistry of these toxic substances is still to be determined, but it is known that the calcium oxalate crystals in taro and hydrocyanogens in cassava are responsible for the unpleasant sensation. Some varieties are more toxic than others, and environmental variables may be a cause. But work is continuing to gain a fuller understanding of this acridity (Tang and Sakai 1983:148–163).

The symptoms are unpleasant rather than of long-term significance.

Figure 9. Cooking a meal on hot stones. Tahiti, 1930s. Photo by G. Spitz, courtesy Bishop Museum

However, oxalic acid does have the ability to bind calcium, and thus it could have a serious affect on health if large amounts were ingested over a long period of time; "but it would require a rather impossible combination of circumstances, a very high intake of oxalate-containing food plus a simultaneous low calcium and vitamin D intake over a prolonged period for chronic effects to be noted" (Liener 1969:430). Such a combination of circumstances would be highly unlikely in the sunny Pacific where vitamin D is readily synthesized. Nevertheless, those serving taro endeavor to ensure that it has been well cooked and so avoid causing this itchiness.

FIRE FOR COOKING

The application of heat to these foods was, of course, an essential step in processing them to be eaten. Besides baking in the earth oven and grilling in the coals, a third, more limited, mode of cooking was the use of pots for steaming food. All presuppose access to fire.

In their careful examination of what they call "structures of combustion," the Orliacs offer some ideas on how we can fit uses of fire together with the structures that archeologists have unearthed. They suggest that most of the structures of combustion had a culinary function. These fires might have been made on the surface or in a pit, with or without a stone lining (Orliac and Orliac 1980:64). But this is only one kind of evidence for types of cooking practiced in pre-European times. Another is myth.

The early association of food and fire is clearly recorded in myths. Missionaries and other visitors have left us records of myths that indicate two stages in the development of food practices. During the first stage, island people say their ancestors ate everything raw, including red earth. Grimble offers one explanation for this in the Gilberts by linking it to betel chewing as evidence of an evolutionary connection to Indonesia (1933:55–59). In the second stage, the ancestors obtained fire from the underworld. As Turner, a missionary in various parts of Polynesia in the 1840s, noted: "The Samoans say that there was a time when their forefathers ate everything raw; and that they owe the luxury of cooked food to one Ti'iti'i the son of a person called Talanga. . . . He went back to his father with some cinders and the two set to work to bake some taro. They kindled a fire, and were preparing the taro to put on the hot stones when suddenly the god Mafuie blew up the oven. . . . Go said Mafuie, you will find the fire in every wood you cut" (1841:252–254).

Versions of this myth were recorded for Samoa, Niue, and other societies. Mafuike, an old blind lady, was said to bring fire to Tokelau (Turner 1841:280), while Mahike brought fire to the Tuamotus (Emory 1975:180). On Niue fire was caused by Maui motua and Maui tane (Grimshaw 1907b:194). In those times before there was fire, coconuts and fish were the prevailing foods of the people; there were no fowls or pigs, only swarms of rats. In Samoa Talanga went down to Mafuie in the lower regions and asked her to give him some fire. She obstinately refused until he threatened to kill her, and then she yielded. He made her say what fish were to be cooked with the fire and what were still to be eaten raw; and then began the time of cooking food (Turner 1841:528). Buck obtained a similar myth in Samoa almost a hundred years later (1930) in which fire was obtained by Tiitii. The rocks opened to a region where Mafuie tended a fire. Tiitii broke one of Mafuie's arms and brought a lighted brand to the earth. Before this, say the Samoans, man ate raw food ('ai mata) but afterwards by kindling the fire he was enabled to eat cooked food ('ai vela). Perhaps Tiitii is a character similar to Maui Tikitiki (Luomala 1949:123).

The Niuean story, obtained from Lupo but told by an old Samoan chief, tells how the first mortals got their food. These first inhabitants of Niue were Fao and Huanaki, who came from Tulia below. There was little food, no coconuts or yams or breadfruit to furnish food for man. No pleasant foods grew here. And man increased. And the land was hungry. Fao and Huanaki put to sea in a canoe to seek food for their starving people. They wandered to and fro over the ocean. At last they reached the island of Tutuila in Samoa. There the people gave them coconuts (niu) to plant, and they returned. Then people arrived on Niue from Tonga; after a major confrontation the god ruled that the invaders should be spared.

Maui motua and Maui tama first caused fire to be kindled on the land so that the people might have fire forever after (Cowan 1923b:239).

The Tongan version of obtaining fire is similar to the Samoan one. There, Maui is credited with providing the most useful tree, the *toa* (ironwood), commonly known as casuarina. Maui had two sons; the elder was called Maui Atalanga and the younger, Kisikisi. Kisikisi obtained some fire from the earth and taught the people to cook their food, which they found was good, and from that day food has been cooked that before was eaten raw (Wilkes 1845, 3:23).

Fijians at first had no cooked food, according to Waterhouse's version of the myth about the origins of fire (1866). In New Zealand a similar myth existed (Orbell 1985).

The widespread similarity of characters and themes in these myths may be an indication of similar beliefs in the powers of cooked food over uncooked food. Since the main foods must be cooked, accounting for fire was a significant step in discriminating good foods (cooked foods) from raw foods such as coconut and fish. However, in places such as atolls where the roots would not grow and where there were no breadfruit, the people had to rely on coconut and fish, as was the case in Tokelau (Huntsman 1978).

The fact that fire was essential to the manufacture of voyaging craft and thus must have been known to the first arrivals (Bellwood 1978) casts some doubt on the relation between these myths of a period before fire was known and the development of cooking. We cannot take them as historical accounts, as Orbell has discussed for the historicity of myths in New Zealand (1985). On the other hand we cannot dismiss them entirely. We may need to reconsider, in association with the archeological evidence, whether early voyagers may have brought myths referring to an earlier time without fire.

Cooking hearths on board canoes were still being used in the 1880s by voyagers; Cumming (1885) both painted and described in words those used by Fijians. This type of canoe hearth, known as *miga,* was used to cook yams and pigs. It was clearly used "to bake food" (Clunie 1984: 105), and also to cook food in earthenware firepots. These consisted of a pot about 20 inches in diameter set on four supports and on which rested a smaller cooking pot about 10 inches deep (Cumming in Clunie 1984: 110). (See Figure 10.) It is evident that at least these nineteenth-century Fijian seafarers relished cooked food as much as did their more land-oriented counterparts, and that they used the same cooking methods as they would on shore (Clunie 1984:102). The fire itself must have been carried aboard, or at least the right woods for use as fire-ploughs. In this way, during a long voyage Fijian seafarers and perhaps others could cook their taro and yams and did not have to subsist on raw fish and coconuts or

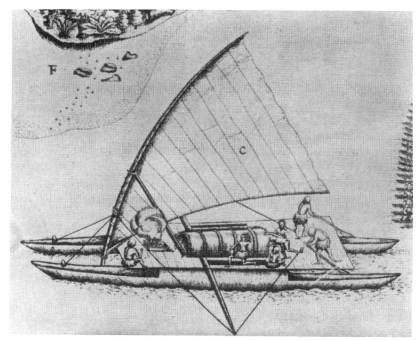

Figure 10. Cooking on board a sailing canoe. Courtesy Fiji Museum and National Archives of Fiji, Suva

rain water. They may also have carried arrowroot starch in pots (Seemann 1862) and packets of fermented breadfruit, which would have to be cooked, as well as pandanus conserve that could be eaten as it was.

The process of making fire by the fire-plough method is carefully described for many of the islands, particularly in the various Bishop Museum Bulletin reports; see, for example, Buck (1930) for Samoa, and Handy and Handy (1923) for the Marquesas. Fire making must have been one of the time-consuming factors in food preparation that contrasted with the ease of procuring foods such as breadfruit.

The recent introduction of matches is a welcome aid in the cooking process, though they are not always readily available, particularly on outer islands. Even in the late 1960s I quickly discovered during fieldwork that matches were a very precious possession on Namu atoll where there was no store at which to replenish depleted supplies. Matches were coveted by persons of all ages, but only the women who needed them for lighting fires seemed to attempt to conserve their stocks. When a supply ship was overdue and supplies were low, fire brands were carried from one household to another in a folded sheath from a coconut; the lucky donor had a cigarette lighter that was working. Alternatively, a fire was kept smoldering. We tried the fire-plough method in desperation at one stage, but it took about half an hour to get a flame, probably because of our inexperience (NJP fieldnotes, Namu atoll 1969).

Knowledge of the special woods best suited for use as fire-ploughs was one important factor associated with cooking and thus with the process of gaining food. Bougainville even suggested that the fires of upper-class Tahitians were made from different woods from those of the lower classes (Orliac and Orliac 1980:62). The fire-plough was apparently not known in the Marquesas; there they may have started fire by use of stones (Orliac and Orliac 1980:61).

The evidence for controlled uses of fire is of major significance to archeologists and prehistorians who welcome finds of charcoal, both to indicate how fire was used and as a means of dating other material found in sites. (In addition to Orliac and Orliac 1980:64, see McCoy 1978 for a useful discussion of different kinds of fires on Easter Island). To this archeological evidence and the myths, we can add such information about uses of fire at the time of first contact as the early visitors recorded.

THE EARTH OVEN

Throughout the Pacific baking in the earth oven was the major way of applying fire to food, and it was used for all foods. There were two types, household ovens and communal ovens, which differed not only in size and the amount and types of food cooked in them, but also in the social groups involved in their use.

Household Ovens

Households usually made an oven once a day, though in Tikopia and elsewhere an oven might be made every second day (Firth 1936). Once missionaries became installed, they discouraged cooking on Sundays, and so a major ovenful of food was made on Saturdays to last for the two days.

Cooking in the earth oven either baked the food or steamed it, depending upon whether water was added. Societies varied in their preferences, perhaps because the mode of cooking altered the taste. Many descriptions of the process were recorded by early commentators on the Pacific. For example:

> Hawaiians, cooking in the old style, steam the taro corms in the cooking pit *(imu* or *imu lua)*. In a hole in the ground about 18 inches deep is laid fuel that will burn long enough to heat the cooking stones to almost the temperature of red-hot charcoal. On the fuel are laid the cooking stones, which are roundish stream or beach boulders of porous lava that will not explode or crumble under intense heat. These stones are called *'eho*. When the fire is burned out, the unburned wood and embers are prodded out

with a stick and the stones are leveled. Ti or banana leaves, grass or sea-
weed is laid on the hot stones, and on this are placed the unpeeled but
washed corms as they come from the patch. Other foods, sweet potatoes,
yams, arrowroot, fish, pig, chicken and so forth, wrapped in ti leaves with
or without accompanying greens—may be laid in with the taro. Over the
food to be cooked are laid coarsely woven mats and banana and ti leaves to
keep in the heat. Sometimes a little water is poured on the food. (Handy
and Handy 1972:111)

The whole oven was then covered with earth and left to steam for two to
six hours. As the Handys also note, wild taro, the corms of which contain much calcium oxalate crystal, must be steamed long to dissolve the
little prickly spikes that are responsible for the "itch" *(mane'o)* caused in
the throat by coarse taros; mild taros like Lauloa need be cooked only a
couple of hours (1972:111). Such local knowledge was important in the
total food preparation process.

From the many similar accounts, we can identify certain main elements of earth ovens common to all Pacific societies: (1) A hole was dug
to varying depths, either near the house compound or within the house
itself; (2) the hole was lined with big stones or other material; (3) suitable
firewoods were placed on these stones; (4) a fire was lit on these stones;
(5) when stones were hot, the ashes were moved to one side and some of
the hot stones picked out of the fire with tongs; (6) a bed of green leaves
was placed over the hot stones; (7) the foods to be cooked were placed on
this bed; (8) hot rocks were returned on top of food; (9) the whole was
covered with leaves of breadfruit, ti, banana, heliconia or coconut
fronds, or an old mat (in modern times, sacks) to provide a thick layer,
then earth placed on top; (10) the making of the *umu* itself was usually
men's work.

Variations on these general principles can be found in terms of detail
such as the size of the pit, the depth of the pit, the location of the earth
oven, addition of water to produce moist heat, and the materials used for
lining (Orliac and Orliac 1980). In Pohnpei (Bascom 1965:40), Samoa
(Grattan 1948:69), and Tokelau (Macgregor 1937:46), the pit was no
longer dug, but "baking on hot stones is done in a small depression, previously used as a fire; by placing the food on a bed of hot stones and covered with large leaves and more hot stones, it is left to cook in its own
juice, and steam from the heat of the stones above it, beneath it and at
the sides. This takes up to two or three hours of a man's time each day"
(Bascom 1965:40).

Where pits for the earth oven were dug, they were usually located in a
cook house, or in a structure separate from the sleeping house, or in the
open air. One must wonder whether the location varied in parts of Fiji
according to climate and cultural traditions (see Figure 12). Certainly

Naduri people in the Sigatoka valley said that they liked to have a covered place in which to cook in bad weather in addition to their open-air fireplace; they cooked mainly on small wood fires inside a fairly flimsy cook house. There the earth oven *(lovo)* was seldom used except for ceremonial feasts (NJP fieldnotes, Fiji 1982).

In a few societies like Pohnpei and parts of Fiji, an area of the sleeping house was set aside for their form of oven. Nowadays, according to Roth, cooking in the living house is carried out only in an emergency of overcrowded conditions (1953; Quain 1948:73). In other places the cooking fire was located either at one end of the cook house, or at the end of the main house for the commoners, or in the center for a chief in Fiji (Williams 1858:88, 138). In the Ellice Islands (Tuvalu), Mrs. David noted that cooking was carried out in the oven end of the house (1899), though on other atolls such as the Marshalls, ovens *(um)* were located on the sandy beach shore adjacent to the residential site. In settlements in the Cooks, Buck reported that the *umu* was located in the rounded open end of the cooking house (1927:52).

Making the earth oven was mainly men's work throughout most of Oceania. Women prepared the foods for the oven and also roasted any food in the coals (see Figure 11). In Samoa the ovens were the daily work of untitled men (Grattan 1948:69). The notable exception to this division of labor was in Niue where the women did the cooking aided by the men (Loeb 1926:82). Was this evidence of a more equally shared lifestyle in that island society? Or was it a result of missionary influence?

In various parts of the Pacific this division of labor went even further, to the extent that separate fires and ovens were made for men as distinct from women's (for Fiji, see Quain 1948:73; for Tahiti, Ellis 1831:129; and Cook's account in Orliac and Orliac 1980:65). This separation of fires was practiced most notably in Yap (see Lingenfelter 1975).

The amount of food cooked in a household earth oven depended on whether the food was to feed people for one or two days. For a household of six to ten people some fifteen medium-size taro might be cooked and some fish, if the fishermen had been successful; this might be sufficient for two days. In some parts of the Pacific an oven was made every day, while elsewhere, only one every other day. Moerenhout tells us that in Tahiti two fires a day were the rule (see Orliac and Orliac 1980:68).

The cooking time was determined by the amount of food in the oven (Morrison 1790:176), and perhaps by the type of wood used. In general throughout the Pacific, food would be left in the oven for about two hours, that is, until certain associated tasks were completed (Firth 1959: 98). The time, of course, was not monitored, but years of experience had taught people when they should open the oven so that the food would be neither overcooked nor undercooked. For certain foods, such as the *ti*

Figure 11. Women preparing food. Pohnpei, 1951. Photo by Raymond Sato, courtesy Honolulu Academy of Arts

and the *opi'o* bake of breadfruit, the oven was left for twenty-four to thirty-six hours; but these were usually communal ovens (see below).

Whether the food was to be steamed or roasted in the earth oven is another point of difference throughout the Pacific. Some societies preferred their food moist and succulent, while others preferred their food dry. The presence of leaves, either as a lining over the hot stones or as wrapping for pounded and processed foods, introduced a certain amount of moisture additional to that of the foods themselves. In addition, sometimes a little water was sprinkled over the food before the oven was sealed with the layers of leaves. In the Gilberts four kinds of ovens were distinguished on the basis of whether the food was to be steamed or dry roasted (Grimble 1933:7–11). Most frequently, even where the leaves were not added to the stones in the oven, the roots, fruits, and meat and fish were converted into acceptable foods by a process combining steaming and roasting.

Several kinds of pits for cooking have been found by archeologists excavating Easter Island. The stone-lined pit, *umu pae,* contrasts with the open-sided pits, *umu keri oka oka* and *umu ava.* McCoy recorded some five hundred *umu pae* and speculates that they may indicate permanent residence (1978:211). Englert had noted constructional differences between the stone-lined *umu pae* and the open-sided pit ovens, excavated with a digging stick. The *umu ava* was larger than the *umu pae* and used for communal feasts *(koro)* (quoted in McCoy 1978:270).

A modern adaptation of the earth oven for household cooking is called *um in gajolin* by the Marshallese. They use a 50-gallon drum set in the sand on its side as the container for the fire. A portion of the long side, about 2½ feet by 1 foot, is cut out and kept to use as a lid. Rocks and the fire are placed inside the drum, and the "lid" replaced once the fire is lit, to form an enclosed cooking place. This produces a drier heat, such as is needed for making bread with European white flour. It is not suitable for foods that need moist heat, though breadfruit paste loaves wrapped in breadfruit leaves were also cooked in the *um in gajolin.* There were no taros on Namu with which to try this method of cooking. This kind of oven was also made in the Ellice Islands (Roberts 1955:228). Namu people claimed explicitly that it saved fuel.

The earth oven was probably a fairly economical use of the firewood supply, which was limited, particularly on low islands. Some reports specify the woods for use in the earth oven (e.g., in Rapa, Hanson 1970: 55; in Tahiti, Moerenhout 1837). On Tahiti only breadfruit trees grew on the strand, so the people had to go into the mountains for wood. On Easter Island, where all wood was in short supply or non-existent at the time of Cook's visit, the ovens were made with grass or the head of sugar cane or plantains (Orliac and Orliac 1980:63). On atolls the most commonly used combustible material was the coconut husk, a material that has become more readily available since copra has become a commercial commodity (Pollock 1970).

Communal Ovens

Large communal ovens were a feature of most societies of the island Pacific. In contrast to the household ovens, they were not used regularly —only when a large feast was to be prepared. A group of households linked by kinship, or a village, might have a communal oven. Nowadays there may be an oven specially set aside for church feasts. Three kinds of communal ovens have been discussed in the literature: large ovens for communal feasts, *opi'o* bakes, and *ti* ovens; the latter two were specialized uses of the first.

The very large ovens were used less frequently than the regular household ones. In some societies these special ovens were set aside for feast occasions, whereas in other societies the food for communal events was cooked in the household ovens and brought together later. It is hard to separate the sociality of these occasions from the pragmatics of cooking. Certainly Namu people in the 1960s expressed the joy of those occasions when a large central oven was lit and the women came together to prepare the food while the men joined together to fish and prepare the pig. As in household cooking, the organization of such a community-wide event was done with minimal overt assignment of tasks. The range of goods available to choose from was so limited that knowledge of the day on which the feast would be held was sufficient. Each person did whatever his/her household's role necessitated. Kinship relations were important as the determinant of whose pig was contributed and who got what from the communal bake, but all households in the community were expected to contribute to the pool of labor. This was not onerous; it was pleasurable. Much jocularity and banter accompanied the tasks.

The amounts of food cooked at these communal bakes was a matter worthy of remark by some early European visitors to the islands. Several implied that the food was excessive to need, as they saw it. They were judging them from their own moral standards rather than from the local values of generosity and respect shown through providing a large display of food at such communal events. This issue will be discussed further in Chapter 6.

The large ovens were made in exactly the same way as the smaller ones for the most part, the significant difference being the sociality of the occasion. It is possible, however, that in some societies such as Tahiti a distinction was made between two kinds of oven pits for big feasts, the *taupiti* and the *oroa,* the first for the vegetables, the other for the pigs, dogs, birds, and fish (Moerenhout 1837, quoted in Orliac and Orliac 1980:68). This is another example of the distinction between the vegetable part of the diet and the accompaniments.

Large earth ovens for special community feasts were (and are) the work of men of the community. Not only must they go fishing the day before the feast in order to have plenty of fish, but on the day of the feast they must clear the pit, build a fire sufficient to cook all the different kinds of foods, and close the fire up and open it at the appropriate time. And today on Namu, it is the men who make all the bread that is cooked in these ovens for feasts.

It is hard to tell whether restrictions on men cooking for women were relaxed through these communal events. Today the big feast ovens supply everyone. They have become part of the churches' celebrations, they are a showpiece for tourists, and they are still an integral part of community life. They are one of the major symbols of life in the Pacific and are thus a tangible marker of Pacific identity.

The two special uses of communal ovens that we know about from the records of early visitors were used for particular foodstuffs. Both have been dropped from practice, due in large part to the objections of missionaries. One, the *opi'o* bake, was used in the Society Islands to cook extensive quantities of breadfruit at the end of the breadfruit season, while the other, the *ti* bake, was used to cook large quantities of this sugary root, again for communal occasions. The main characteristics were the same for both foodstuffs—the ovens were large, and the foodstuff was left in for two to three days. After that time it could be taken out as required. The actual cooking of the breadfruit and *ti* involved large groups of people and thus was a very sociable occasion.

Morrison suggests the *opi'o* bake could accommodate 750 to 1,000 kilograms (1790:177). The oven measured some 20 feet or more in circumference and required much cooperative labor. Ellis, among other early visitors, has left us a direct account: "The large oven was left for two or three days. When it was opened food was taken from the side. Breadfruit cooked in this manner could be kept for several weeks" (1831: 51–52). This kind of oven has been documented in use for Tahiti, as Ellis described, and also for Tonga and Rarotonga, where it was known as *hopiko* and *opito,* respectively. In the latter two islands, the making of these ovens appears to have been less of an event than in Tahiti, partly because there were fewer breadfruit than in Tahiti. However, wherever they were made, social occasions on a big scale accompanied them. Ellis moralizes about them: "The general or district ovens of opio . . . were usually attended with debauchery and excess, highly injurious to the health and debasing to the morals of the people, who frequently relinquished their ordinary employment, and devoted their nights and days to mere animal existence, of the lowest kind—rioting, feasting, and sleeping until the opio was consumed" (1831:42).

A similar large oven was made for baking *ti* roots throughout eastern Oceania, including southern New Zealand. The *umu ti,* as it was called in Maori, was used specifically for baking the sweet roots of *Cordyline terminalis* (formerly *Dracaena terminalis;* see Neal 1965 and Fankhauser 1986 for clarification of these botanical identifications).

In Samoa large ovens for cooking *ti* have been noted in the literature and have been found by archeologists. Informants gave Davidson details of their participation in the construction and use of such *umu ti* in times past, thus indicating their continued use within the last twenty-five years in parts of Samoa (Davidson 1984:236). These ovens were always made in the bush, never in settlements (Krämer 1902–1903:155). They consisted of large circular pits (as contrasted with the oblong pits in Tahiti) and had a raised rim. It was this rim which marked the sites for investigation and also which distinguishes them from the more generally used household ovens.

Pits of large dimensions were also found in Rarotonga; Buck (1927) thinks these probably were *ti* ovens. He also noted pits for ripening bananas.

Several New Zealand South Island pits have been excavated and their contents examined in detail by Fankhauser (1986). Here, the plant used was the New Zealand cabbage tree *(Cordyline australis)*. It differs slightly from the *Cordyline terminalis* of tropical Oceania, but the same parts of the plant were used to yield a substance high in fructose. The whole process of the *ti* oven was carefully analyzed by Fankhauser for his doctoral dissertation; he brought a combination of analytical skills from both chemistry and archeology to shed new light on a Polynesian activity not practiced for some time. He suggests that the *ti* root was used seasonally together with the fern root as part of the New Zealand Maori early diet. It was cooked in the large pits for about two days before the syrup was available.

The nature of the social occasions for which both these large special pits were used is not clear. Perhaps making them was part of an activity that provided a welcome break in the monotony of daily life. Or perhaps they had a more ritualistic purpose. It did require a great deal of work to dig the pit and to dig up the large *ti* roots or gather in all those breadfruit. Both men and women gathered the large amount of firewood needed to keep the fire going for at least two days. We do know that these occasions were accompanied by much singing, dancing, and lively entertainment, according to Miss Teuira Henry for Raiatea (1893). There the ceremony of the *ti* ovens was conducted by the heathen priests of Raiatea, limited at the time she wrote to only two individuals, both descendants of those early priests. Part of this ceremony involved people walking in procession through the hot oven barefoot or shod, and on their emergence not even smelling of fire (Henry 1893:107). Unfortunately, further detail of the ritual meaning of these *ti* bakes has not been followed up.

It is possible that one by-product of the long-term baking process was some form of alcohol. Cuzent, a medical visitor in Tahiti in 1860, found that some alcohol could be derived from breadfruit through fermentation of the starch, and it could also be derived from the product of the *ti* ovens (1860). In Hawai'i this by-product of *ti* is now sold commercially as 'okolehao. But since these ovens of *opi'o* and *ti* have not been made for some 150 years, except perhaps in Samoa, it is difficult to assess just what were some of the "delights" associated with them and the ritual functions of which they formed a part.

Some confusion exists in reconstructing the prehistory of residence in the various islands from the archeological record because of these special types of oven pits and the pits used for fermenting breadfruit and other foodstuffs. Depressions, either shallow or deep, together with the presence of stones for lining the sides and to act as a cover, may be interpreted either as storage pits for breadfruit or as places for ripening bananas, or (in the case of the Marquesas) as places for making a form of conserve, or for storing *kumara* (in the case of New Zealand). Or if some charcoal is associated with them, they may be either household or communal ovens. Nevertheless, Davidson claims that "the bases of Samoan settlement and economy have been firmly established with indications of earth-ovens, and hearths, food pits and probably round-ended or oval houses" (1979:101).

In Tonga the word generally translated into English as "work" *(ngaue)* literally means "an oven of food" (Gifford 1929:125). This serves to underline my main line of argument here, that in the Pacific food refers in the first place to starch food, that is, cooked food—food cooked mainly in the earth oven. This seems to indicate that preparing food was considered the main form of work. Similarly, in Tikopia the work of the oven was more important than planting and other activities associated with village life (Firth 1959:36). Making the earth oven was a major social event. Other occupations, such as fishing and planting, may have been considered secondary to the all-important task of making the food from the land fit for consumption.

To accomplish this end involved the handiwork of both men and women. It was thus a communal and cooperative endeavor. One derivation of the Tongan term *kainga* was that of a group *(nga)* that makes food *(kai)* together, thus an extended family household. That this term has come to mean the extended family, again with the implied focus on the oven, is significant for my argument for the social importance of food.

OTHER TRADITIONAL METHODS OF COOKING

Several other methods of cooking were in use at the time the first European visitors began to write about the area, but they differed widely from island group to island group, and they were not as widely used as the earth oven. The use of pottery for cooking has received considerable attention, particularly from prehistorians. Cooking in bamboo stems and in cassis shells, as well as stone boiling, were other cooking techniques, used mainly for small quantities of food and for the accompanying dish rather than the "real food."

Use of Pots

Before contact, the use of pots for cooking was more common in Melanesia (Irwin 1981) than in Polynesia or Micronesia, although pottery was still being used for cooking in Fiji in the early missionary period (Lawry 1850:151; Williams 1858:69) (see Figure 12). Pots were still being

Figure 12. Preparing food in a cook house, 1850s. (From *James Calvert, or Dark to Dawn in Fiji,* by Richard Vernon.) Courtesy Fiji Museum

traded to Tonga from Fiji in the 1840s, as Cargill noted (Schütz and Geraghty 1980). However, most early European reports focus on the earth oven as the main method of cooking in Tonga (Mariner 1831).

Pots were also in use in Guam and the Marianas, though to what extent we can only speculate (Pollock 1986a; Kurashina et al. 1981/ 1984). Pottery has been found on both high islands and atolls of Micronesia and is more widespread than was first thought (Takayama 1981/1984:2). The finding of pottery on Pohnpei (Ayres 1983), on Truk (Parker and King 1981/1984:19), and on Kapingamarangi (Cordy 1984; Takayama 1981/1984:2), where previously none had been known, has changed the picture of pottery use in the Pacific. It has narrowed the cultural gap between the Marianas and Fiji, and perhaps is an important link connecting these northern and central islands into a Lapita cultural system (Takayama 1981/1984).

Our knowledge of cooking in clay pots is limited, as few societies in the Pacific area considered here still used pots at the time of contact. However, Fiji was one such place, and we have some useful observations from the missionaries Cargill and Williams and from Miss Constance Gordon Cumming, as well as from women today in some parts of Fiji who still use clay pots. The Fijian kitchen pots *(kuro)* were of various sizes, from a quart up to 20 gallons, and various shapes, such as a turtle and a double canoe (Schütz and Geraghty 1980:xiv). They were prized possessions of most, usually mature, women and were rarely used except by the owner. To avoid damage, they were seldom removed from the kitchen (Ravuvu 1983:25).

We do know that food was steamed in these pots rather than boiled. The more acrid taro and wild yams, such as the *kaile* (Fijian term for the wild yam), were soaked in water before boiling in order to remove some of the acridity (Seemann 1862:302, 304, 305–306). The accompanying foods, such as Fijian *bele* or *rourou* leaves, were placed next to the lid and steamed just before the main food was fully cooked. Water had to be added now and then (Ravuvu 1983:27). The pots were placed on their sides over the fire resting on three clay support stones (Williams 1858).

There are several difficulties in the argument about how these pots were used for cooking. The amounts that could be cooked in them were small compared to the earth oven's capacity, so steaming or boiling in pots would have had to be done more often, thereby using more fuel and time, especially when cooking for large groups such as for feasts. But more important, one of the principles of good food would have been violated—perhaps it could be called an aesthetic principle of taste and presentation. Taro and yams were properly served as whole slices, but to get them into all but the very widest-necked pot, they would have to be cut into small pieces. This might have been acceptable for day-to-day household fare but would not have been acceptable for feasts, where presentation protocols are so important. In addition, as Handy and Handy (1972) noted for Hawai'i, boiling (in this case in tin containers) changed the flavor of taro. Thus it is likely that cooking in pots was acceptable only for household use and in emergencies.

But cooking in pots has other connotations. Missionary Cargill felt that Fijians in the 1830s were "on an elevation above all the other South Sea Islanders" because they could cook liquids. He contrasted them with the people of the Friendly Isles (Tonga) who were obliged to cook all their food on stones or wrap it in leaves. So Fijian pots were welcome in trade with Tonga (Schütz and Geraghty 1980:xiv). This view of the use of pots for cooking as more civilized than cooking in the earth oven was shared by others writing accounts of life in the Pacific at that time, who made concerted efforts to change habits to what they considered were improved household ways (see Pollock 1989 for a discussion of housekeeping in Fiji in the mid-nineteenth century).

Guiart has questioned the view that those Pacific societies that used pots were somehow "more developed" than those without pots. In his long acquaintance with peoples of New Caledonia, Isle of Pines, and the Loyalties, he came to believe that they are not much different from peoples of Tonga and Fiji, even though they do not have pots. He puts forward the idea that in Fiji pottery underwent specialized evolution toward larger pots to allow steam cooking. This reduced cooking time (over that of earth ovens) and allowed an easier life for smaller families, but did not make those societies necessarily more advanced (Guiart 1982:141).

Guiart's line of argument is part of a larger concern, namely, that technology is one measure of development. However, I prefer to use other indicators to distinguish societies. And I disagree that life was easier when people cooked in pots, for three reasons: first, less food could be cooked at one time; second, the pots were fragile and would have had to be handled carefully; and third, the special flavor that the leaves added in the earth oven was lost in boiling. Moreover, cooking in pots does not appear to have been a favored way to prepare food for a chief; if it had been we would expect to find more pots traded specifically for use by those of high status. Only in special circumstances such as on a voyaging canoe do we learn of pots being used, perhaps out of convenience. Thus we need to look more closely at the issue that prehistorians are facing in the particular instance of "How Lapita Lost Its Pots" (Irwin 1981; Y. Marshall 1985; Pollock n.d.*a*).

Pottery has been used in Pacific societies for some three to four thousand years. The form and technique of pottery manufacture are both key features of the history of the Pacific and of food habits in the area. Lapita pottery represents a particular trend that has been used for linking the prehistoric developments of societies in the western Pacific and beyond (Green 1979; Spriggs 1984). It penetrated eastward to Samoa about three thousand years ago, but no evidence of it has yet become available in islands farther east. In the northern Pacific, Marianas pottery has been known for some considerable time (Spoehr 1957), but more recent archeological work has found pottery in Palau, Yap, and Guam (Takayama 1981/1984). None of this appears to be Lapita pottery. However, the recent discovery of pottery on Truk and Pohnpei has led Athens to conclude that this Late Lapita pottery continued to be made in these islands until its use for cooking was not essential and it was entirely dispensed with (1987:14). Why people stopped using pottery is still unknown.

We cannot be sure any of these pots were used for cooking or for food storage since they were no longer in use at the times of first European contact, except in Fiji. Green (1979) has left the question of use open. Irwin has studied methods of current pottery-making techniques and uses of pots in the Milne Bay, d'Entrecasteaux, area off eastern New Guinea. This has enabled him as an archeologist to suggest that Lapita pottery making, which flourished in the southwestern Pacific, may have been impractical in areas lacking suitable clay or tempers; alternatively the small amount of pottery that may have been made may await discovery or be already destroyed (Irwin 1981:6).

Archeologists and prehistorians are also concerned with the sequence of appearance of wooden vessels and pottery vessels. Irwin's discussion of whether wooden vessels replaced pots in the eastern Pacific raises the question of the importance of boiled food in the overall diet of Pacific Islanders. It has become clear from reports of societies when they were first seen by Europeans that baking in the earth oven *(umu)* was the main mode of cooking food for most peoples, with some foods such as bread-fruit and fish being roasted in the coals. Stone boiling to caramelize coco-nut cream was the extent of boiling.

Fijian pots *(kuro)* are larger than those reconstructed for Lapita ware and may represent a specialized evolution (Guiart 1982:141). Cooking with steam, Guiart argues, simplified cooking, allowing an easier life for smaller families, and reduced the cost in energy used obtaining firewood. However, a small earth oven is a more efficient use of firewood than an open fire. In the Sigatoka valley, Fiji, in 1982 I weighed several bundles of firewood brought from the bush to estimate the rate of use; a 15-pound bundle was sufficient for about four or five fires, each one to boil one (metal) pot of some liquid, whereas a similar weight of wood fired two earth ovens in which a whole array of foodstuffs could be cooked (NJP fieldnotes 1982). Thus Guiart's argument for "reduced cost of energy" using pots for steaming would be true only for small families of five or six people who were content to eat only one starchy food (perhaps cooking the fish over the coals). Yet we know that some families ate two or more starchy foods at a meal (see Chapter 3), so that enough was usu-ally cooked for at least two food events, sometimes three, using one batch of firewood. Nowadays the custom is to cook (using metal pots) three times a day, and in Fiji there is considerable concern about the rapid depletion of firewood resources (Siwatibau 1981).

Furthermore, baking in the earth oven was men's work, whereas boil-ing was women's work; thus there would need to be rethinking of social organization to incorporate boiling as a major means of food prepara-tion. The specialized nature of pottery production, which is part of Irwin's discussion of the possible reasons for the demise of Lapita pots, is also an important consideration regarding the use of pots for cooking. In Fiji alone, pots would have had to be obtained in trade over quite long distances, making them a luxury item that was perhaps not very durable and not easily replaced. For these reasons, I argue that pottery in Fiji, and perhaps in the Marianas, was probably a fairly peripheral aid to cooking the starch foods. Perhaps its use was limited to a few families for a few cooking occasions. The large pots to which Guiart draws attention were probably of greater use for holding water than for cooking, at least to people on a high island who lived some distance from their water sources.

Preparing Puddings (Leaf-wrapped Foods)

The term "puddings" is used here to refer to all forms of composite cooking using one or more starches as the base. They are sometimes referred to in the literature as leaf-wrapped or packaged foods (Figure 13). Puddings are made from several ingredients variously processed. Most frequently the starch root or fruit was cooked first, then grated or pounded and mixed with coconut cream, wrapped in *ti,* banana, or breadfruit leaves, and baked in the earth oven. There was variation on these "ways of dressing food," as the early European reports referred to the practice. Some reports recorded in great detail the ways to make favorite dishes, such as Samoan *fai'ai* and *pia sua* (Krämer 1902–1903; Buck 1930; Grattan 1948), Fijian *vakalolo* (Horne 1881:76; Deane 1921:214), Tahitian *popoi* (Morrison (1790:176, 177), and Rarotongan *poke* (Buck 1927).

Even where only one food was the major item eaten, as in the case of breadfruit in the Marquesas, variation was introduced by adding some fermented breadfruit to pounded fresh breadfruit (see Figure 14). By

Figure 13. Food bundle. Austral Islands, 1920s. Photo by John Stokes, courtesy Bishop Museum

Figure 14. Making *ma* for puddings. Marquesas, 1930s. Photo by R. Linton, courtesy Bishop Museum

mixing the foods in this way the needs of children and sick persons could be accommodated. In Truk also, the main dish, *kon,* was made from a mixture of fresh and fermented breadfruit. The main starch component was pounded in the case of breadfruit, or grated in the case of the taros, yam, and cassava. Cassava had to be washed thoroughly to remove the hydrocyanic acid before the flour could be used in puddings. Mixing the starch with coconut cream in various ways also added variety. Susan Parkinson's collection of traditional recipes now being compiled for several island groups in the South Pacific under the Food and Agriculture Organization Root Crops Project will help to fill a gap, though many of the recipes remembered today may be adaptations over time of those that were used earlier.

The artistry behind these productions, particularly in the balance of color and taste, is discussed for Tokelau cookery in the modern day as art form (Huntsman 1978). To appreciate the significance of these finer details of local culinary works, the previous experiences of the European beholder may not be adequate; rather they must be assessed according to local criteria, as Huntsman suggests. What is pleasing to the taste, to the eye, and to the cook's own feeling of creativity varies from society to society and culture to culture. Some Pacific societies did pay more attention to culinary creations by putting together several possible combinations of the foodstuffs available to them. The Chamorro people of

Guam, for example, seem to have relied more and more on their Philippine connections to bring variety to the diet than on developing the range of dishes for taro, yams, and breadfruit (Pollock 1986a).

In contrast, a considerable variety of puddings or combinations of breadfruit and coconut has been developed on Truk, where the breadfruit is the most highly prized food. On Tikopia these puddings were a part of the daily consumption; in fact, Raymond Firth records these "mushy puddings" as being the main form in which the starchy food was served (1939). Neither is it the case that low islands had less variety of complex foods than high islands (see Murai, Pen, and Miller 1958 for the Marshalls and eastern Carolines; Pollock 1970 for Namu, Marshall Islands; Huntsman 1978 for Tokelau).

Roasting in the Coals

Roasting in the coals was a process of cooking that was best suited to breadfruit and smaller fish and occasionally bananas. Food to be reheated from an earlier oven might also be roasted on this kind of fire. This form of cooking was known as *sinikarrol* in the Marshalls and as *rotika* in the Tuamotus (Emory 1975:53). Generally considered women's work, it was often done in the cook house, though it could be done outside.

Figure 15. Grating manioc for puddings. Rapa, 1930s. Photo by John Stokes, courtesy Bishop Museum

Other Traditional Techniques

Cooking in a bamboo stem was another alternative form of cooking. It was suitable only for such foods as small fish and shellfish, particularly shrimp. Pritchard (1866) has discussed this form of cooking in Samoa. In Fiji freshwater shrimp are still cooked by steaming them in a hollow bamboo tube, and the whole tube sold at the roadside (NJP fieldnotes 1982).

Cooking by dropping hot stones into a substance, most usually coconut cream, was also important in the process of making some complex dishes. Labillardiere (1800:135) described this process in Tonga. Caramelizing coconut cream by the hot stone method is still an important step in producing some favorite Tongan dishes such as *tafolo:*

> Grate some ripe coconuts and squeeze out the milk. It is all right to dilute it a bit with a green coconut, or just leave alone in its concentrated form. Heat up rocks until they are white hot. As soon as the rocks are white hot, take one out with tongs and put it into two coconut shells. Then shake it in the shells until the dirt and the ashes are gone. As soon as it is clean, it is placed into the bowl of coconut milk where it is stirred back and forth with a specially shaped coconut stalk spatula. As soon as the rock hits the bowl of coconut milk, the milk boils. When the rock that is in the milk cools off, it is replaced by another hot rock. This is kept up until the coconut milk begins to get cooked. (Pulu 1981:67–68)

Meanwhile breadfruit has been cooked and pounded until soft. Then the pounded breadfruit is cut into smaller pieces and placed with coconut-milk sauce. Its tastiness is irresistible, according to Pulu. Many other dishes are made throughout the Pacific using coconut, either heated with hot stones or grated.

Yet another form of cooking was in cassis-shell cooking pots. This was practiced on the atolls of the western Carolines, mainly for small amounts, usually for the accompanying dish rather than the main starch food.

MODERN COOKING METHODS

Boiling the root and tree starches was not generally practiced until metal pots became available, either through missionary influence or the whalers in the early 1800s, judging by the early accounts at the time of contact. Handy and Handy (1972) describe boiling taro in cans in Hawai'i, a process that had been introduced by missionaries and others. It was quicker, but according to Hawaiian tastes the taro was too soft and they did not like the flavor. On Pohnpei, Bascom contrasts boiling *(inim ainpot)* and frying *(inim pirain),* as the introduced methods of cooking, with

baking *(umun nan um)* and roasting *(inim nan pas),* as the former traditional Pohnpeian methods of cooking. He suggests that boiling and frying were introduced during the Spanish period, when pottery and iron
cooking utensils first became available from Europeans in the early and
mid-nineteenth century (Bascom 1965:40). Confirmation of this point
can be deduced from the localized form of English names for the process
and the utensils. In the Marshalls and Carolines *ainbat* is the term used
for boiling (NJP fieldnotes 1968–1969; Murai, Pen, and Miller
1958:15).

Frying is used mainly for flour products such as pancakes and doughnuts, luxury foods that are made when the cook feels like providing a
treat. Frying breadfruit to make chips is done mainly for European
tastes; it takes a lot of (imported) cooking oil. Fish might also be fried,
particularly smaller reef fish. Fondness for the taste of fat has been noted
(e.g., Hau'ofa 1979).

The earth oven is still the most pervasive means of cooking, especially
in rural areas, though it is used less when people have gas or electric
cookers. Nevertheless, I was told that in the 1980s many Samoan families, even those with modern cooking appliances living in the main urban
area, Apia, still make their earth oven early every Sunday morning—
ready to be opened when they return from church (NJP fieldnotes 1982).
Also, I found that in Rarotonga food for parties and large gatherings, as
at Christmastime, is cooked in the earth oven (NJP fieldnotes 1982).
Thus, despite all the new-fangled cooking conveniences, use of the earth
oven has persisted.

One concern about the earth oven and other means of cooking is the
firewood supply. This has been expressed in a general report on the
future energy needs of Fiji (Siwatibau 1981), but it is also a concern in
other Pacific Island nations, particularly on atolls. Fuel-saving stoves
have been produced in Fiji for F$2.50 and have sold well to villagers. A
larger communal wood-burning oven, designed to be built at a residential school at a cost of F$27, was supported by the Fijian Ministry of
Energy to help reduce the amount of firewood being used in cooking,
particularly for institutions (*New Zealand Woman's Weekly,* 22 Feb.
1982). Subsequently, however, the government had a change of heart
and preferred to back electricity as the main fuel supply even to the villages, instead of ensuring the supply and the more efficient use of wood
for cooking purposes.

TECHNOLOGY USED IN FOOD PROCESSING

It is clear that cooking depended very little on technological aids to render the food edible until European processes of boiling and frying were
introduced. Traditionally cooks relied on disposable aids, such as tongs

made from a bent coconut midrib to remove hot coals, stones that would hold the heat (see Danielsson 1956 for stone brought to the atoll of Raroia in the Tuamotus), and leaves to cover the earth oven and to wrap foodstuffs for cooking. The main tools were digging sticks to harvest the roots, long poles to pick breadfruit, breadfruit and *poi* pounders made of basalt or wood, wooden or pottery dishes known in many Polynesian languages as *kumete* for holding pounded foodstuffs, and long wooden troughs in which fermented foodstuffs were kneaded. Rough coral was used to grate cassava or taro; today a piece of tin, with holes roughly punched in it, is used. Low tables, presumably for pounding breadfruit, have been found by archeologists in Mangareva (Laval 1938). Low tables were used also for the chief's food in Yap (Lingenfelter 1975). Several sets of cooking utensils were also necessary there to meet the needs of the different eating classes. Use of breadfruit splitters and pegs of guava wood for ripening breadfruit artificially was confined to the Societies and eastern islands of the Pacific (Linton 1939).

The food pounders for mashing cooked breadfruit or taro range in degree of manufacture from simply another breadfruit in Samoa to the many styles of "ring" and "stirrup" pounders, which have delighted collectors in Hawai'i, Tahiti, and the Marquesas (see Figure 16). Sinoto has questioned the sequence of shapes over time, suggesting that the stirrup pounder was a recent elaboration, particularly on Kaua'i in the Hawaiian islands (1979:122–123). Some of these manufactured pounders were made of coral, some of basalt, and some of wood (see Soderstrom 1937 for details of use).

Figure 16. Breadfruit poun-
der. National Museum of
Wellington. Photo courtesy
Photography Dept., Victoria
University of Wellington

SUMMARY

Taro, yams, and breadfruit all needed to be cooked. Thus "starch food" is synonymous with "cooked food." The predominant mode of cooking was the earth oven, which was widely in use at the time of contact. Other modes of cooking in the Pacific, such as pots and bamboo stems, were more suited to smaller amounts of particular foods. The advantage of the earth oven was that its size could be adjusted to meet needs. It enabled all the food to be cooked over one fire once a day, thus saving firewood. And it was suitable for both household and communal cooking.

The earth oven was more than just a means of rendering taros and yams edible. It was also a social occasion. The cooking process required the cooperative endeavors of several people, both male and female. And it served as a focus of communication. While standing around waiting for the fire to burn down, pleasantries and ribaldries may be exchanged (today accompanied by beer) and people can keep in touch with one another across household boundaries.

This important role of the earth oven has undoubtedly contributed to its continuation up to the present day, even in urban areas where electricity and gas are used for everyday cooking. In a Pacific Island context no other method of cooking is as satisfactory both materially or socially. The earth oven produces good food that tastes right and helps to satisfy both physical and spiritual needs.

5

Preservation and Storage of Foods

THE ROLE of food storage in Pacific societies is problematic. The question is whether to consider all instances of holding food for later consumption as storage. The common line of argument is that food was stored for times of shortage in the future on the basis of the "providential ethic" (see Testart 1982:533–534 for a theoretical discussion of storage). However, I have argued that the people of these societies encouraged fermentation as much as a means of adding variety of taste as a means of setting aside an abundance of a seasonal resource (Pollock 1985b). For example, in the Marquesas even today the daily dish consists of some fermented breadfruit mixed with fresh breadfruit to make the preferred dish, *popoi*. Similarly in Hawai'i, *poi,* the fermented form of taro, is preferred to fresh taro for daily consumption.

Preparing food for delayed consumption in a tropical climate such as the Pacific requires some treatment of harvested crops. Neither the root nor the tree crops will keep more than five days from time of harvesting unless processed by cooking, by fermenting, by grinding into flour, or by drying. Alternatively, consumption can be delayed by leaving crops in the ground or by not eating much when there is little food and eating a lot when there is plenty—that is, storing food as fat.

Many missionaries, travelers, and others reasoned that breadfruit was fermented only as a safeguard against famine or times of shortage (Ellis 1831; Forster 1777; Morrison 1790; Loeb 1926). But this reasoning was not based on local ideas. Rather, I suggest that it was a reflection of their outsiders' views. Concern about future shortages may have been one factor leading to these forms of processing, but others such as taste and the conviviality of a large breadfruit or *ti* bake were equally important, but not recorded by Europeans.

Thus the categories of processed food are not as clear-cut as those for edibles as examined in Chapter 2. Breadfruit was the food crop most

TABLE 7. Foods Preserved and/or Stored, by Island Society

Island(s)	Main Type	Secondary Type	Source
Cooks, So.	nd	arrowroot; *ivi*	Buck 1927
Easter	none	arrowroot	McCoy 1978
Fiji	11 foods, fermented	arrowroot	Williams 1858
Futuna	breadfruit; taro	nd	Burrows 1936
Gilberts/ Kiribati	*babai (Cyrtosperma)*	*te bero*	Luomala 1953
Guam	dried breadfruit	arrowroot; cycad	Pollock 1986a
Hawai'i	taro *(poi)*	taro, dried	Handy and Handy 1972
Kapingama-rangi	breadfruit; pandanus	none	Buck 1950
Kosrae	breadfruit	nd	Sarfert 1919/1920
Mangareva	breadfruit	*ti;* cassava; sweet potato	Laval 1938
Marianas	nd	arrowroot	Sproat 1968
Marquesas	breadfruit	taro *(poi);* arrowroot	Linton 1939
Marshalls	breadfruit	pandanus; arrowroot	Pollock 1970
Nauru	pandanus	none	Kayser 1934
Niue	nd	arrowroot; *ti; kape*	Loeb 1926
Nukuoro	pandanus	none	Buck 1950
Ocean/Banaba	pandanus	none	Ellis 1936
Palau	none	none	Sproat 1968
Pohnpei	breadfruit; yams	arrowroot	Bascom 1965
Ra'ivavae	taro, fermented	manioc; *poe* of watermelon; *'ape*	Marshall 1961
Rapa	taro, fermented	nd	Hanson 1970
Rurutu	taro, fermented; breadfruit	nd	Verin 1969
Samoa	breadfruit	banana; arrowroot	Krämer 1906
Tahiti/ Mo'orea	breadfruit	arrowroot; *ti;* banana; *mape* (Polynesian chestnut)	Ellis 1831
Tokelau	nd	arrowroot	Macgregor 1937
Tonga	yams; breadfruit	arrowroot	West 1865
Truk and atolls	breadfruit	none	Hall and Pelzer 1946
Tuamotus	*Cyrtosperma*	pandanus; arrowroot	Danielsson 1956
Tubuai	taro; manioc	"sundry fruits"	Aitken 1930
Tuvalu/Ellice	pandanus	arrowroot	David 1899
Wallis/Uvea	breadfruit; taro	arrowroot	Burrows 1937
Yap	none	none	Sproat 1968

extensively processed (see Table 7). The Samoan term *masi* for fermented breadfruit has cognates across the Pacific (see Pollock 1984b; Appendix D). It has also been reconstructed for Proto-Oceanic (Biggs, Walsh, and Waqa 1972) with a meaning of "salty" (Chowning, pers. comm. 1983). The general forms of processing are also similar among Pacific societies (Table 8). Fermentation of taro was much less widespread and other modes of processing seem to have been used only on a minor scale.

To alleviate periods of shortage due to drought or cyclone damage or warfare, each society had several means of ensuring a food supply. Reliance on a range of starch food crops, knowledge of wild fall-back foods, some unharvested crops, as well as exchange partners who could be called on in times of need—all these served as buffers against possible times of hunger. These were both technical and social means of overcoming food shortages.

For example, Cox (1980) sought to reconstruct the techniques of breadfruit and banana preservation in Samoa to show that these were former means of preserving crops. If he had assessed the role of bread-

TABLE 8. Methods of Food Preservation, by Island Society

Method of Preservation	Island(s)
Fermentation	
taro	Hawai'i, Rapa, Marquesas, Rurutu, Ra'ivavae, Wallis/Uvea, Futuna
breadfruit (in pits)	Truk, Pohnpei, Kosrae, Marshalls, Mangareva, Samoa, Tonga, Fiji, Tahiti, Wallis/Uvea, Futuna, Marquesas
other foods in pits	Fiji (11 kinds), Anuta (5), Tikopia, Samoa (1)
Holding in pits	
other foods than above	New Zealand *(kumara);* Futuna, Samoa, Tahiti, Rarotonga (banana)
As flour	
pandanus (dried in cakes)	Marshalls, Nauru, Gilberts, Nukuoro, Kapinga-marangi, Tuamotus
arrowroot	Guam, Marianas, Easter, Marquesas, Tahiti, Cooks, Samoa, Tonga, Niue, Wallis/Uvea, Futuna, Tokelau, Marshalls, Pohnpei, Kosrae, Truk
Long baking	
ti	Tonga, Niue, Rotuma, Marquesas, Tahiti, Cooks
other foods	Marquesas (breadfruit), Niue *(kape talo, he luku* fern root, *tau* [banana tree root])
Leaving in ground	Gilberts *(babai),* Pohnpei (yams), Tuamotus *(pulaka)*
Drying: taro slices	Hawai'i, Guam

fruit and *masi* in the food consumption patterns in Samoa, he would have had a clearer picture of all the other means they had for coping with shortages, and a different perspective from his own set of values for evaluating them.

A strong argument has been made that the peoples of the Pacific developed particular techniques for preparing and storing foodstuffs before they developed techniques of production for the root crops (Barrau and Peeters 1972:147–149). Barrau and Peeters suggest that in Australasia the development of food preparation processes was absolutely essential to the use of the root crop starches and was thus more essential to the survival of the population than the development of new production techniques. Detoxification, fermentation, and long baking in the earth oven were all processes to render edible the early plant forms that were used as foodstuffs in this part of the world. A way to remove the acridity of taro and other roots had to be found before they were worth cultivating in large quantity as subsistence crops. Similarly, processing breadfruit or taro by fermentation was not worthwhile if the very acid product was not to the liking of the people who would have to eat it. So I am adding the factor of a taste for the preserved product to Barrau and Peeters's argument that processing was an important precursor to widespread use of the starches and their storage. If storage techniques have not been carefully tried and tested to assess the palatability of their products, then the effort spent in preserving those foodstuffs will be wasted.

Undoubtedly Pacific Islanders were concerned about the possibility of future food shortages. We have already seen that food intake varied from week to week and that people could go several days on a very meager intake. Some societies, such as the Marquesas and Yap, were deeply concerned about the effects of famine (Linton 1939; Lingenfelter 1975). It can be argued that by setting aside some foodstuffs in various ways, these populations had a means of overcoming natural hazards to meet their needs, both physical and social. Food storage was just another piece of local knowledge put to use for the good of the community.

Such resilience can be built into either the food production system or the mode of consuming food. In having a wide inventory of root and tree starches on which to draw, the supply side in the Pacific has a certain degree of flexibility. The cultural sorting of the starchy foods into those most desirable and those to be drawn on in emergencies adds resilience by taking pressure off any one particular resource. Processing techniques such as fermentation add a further resilience factor to the food supply.

FERMENTATION OF BREADFRUIT

The most widely practiced form of preservation at the time of Western contact was fermentation of breadfruit (see Figures 17, 18, 19). The ripe fruits were harvested and fermentation was started by steeping them in

Figure 17. Preparing breadfruit for making paste. Tahiti, 1930s. Photo courtesy
Bishop Museum

sea water before placing them in pits to complete the process. The paste
that resulted could be left there for one month, one year, or ten years,
depending upon tastes and demand.

The seasonal and bountiful nature of the breadfruit crop (Dampier
1697) were two important factors leading to the storage of the paste.
Making the paste was an activity in which the whole community participated. The task of turning the fast-ripening breadfruit into paste was an
annual one in most places, though in a few two lots were made in the
year. Usually only the main crop of breadfruit was used for this purpose.
However, in the Marquesas and Truk, where breadfruit was so important a foodstuff, two distinct batches of paste were named, one made
from the main crop (Marq. *mei nui*) and one made from the lesser crop
(Marq. *mei momo*) (Handy and Handy 1923). In the Marquesas the
main crop was stored in enormous communal pits, while the second crop
was stored in household pits (Linton 1939:139) (see Figure 19). The
lesser crop in Truk was said not to produce such good-tasting paste
(Lebar 1963).

Figure 18. Making breadfruit cake. Majuro, Marshall Islands, 1950. Photo by Raymond Sato, courtesy Honolulu Academy of Arts

Usually not all pits were emptied every year, though with increasing populations, this happened more and more often; on Namu in 1968–1969, pits lasted only three or four months because of the rapidly growing population, but informants remembered years when there were pits left over at the time the new crop of breadfruit was ready (Pollock 1970). Since in some places pits were not distinctively marked and their location subject to the memories of those making the paste, the pits were sometimes lost or forgotten if not needed for several years; one such pit found by archeologists in the Ha'apai group in Tonga was reputed to be some one hundred years old (NJP fieldnotes 1982).

The main steps in fermenting breadfruit were: (1) gathering up the fruit in one place; (2) peeling and/or cutting up the fruit after the stem was removed; (3) steeping the fruit in sea water for twelve to twenty-four hours; (4) digging the pit(s) and lining with *ti,* banana, or heliconia leaves; (5) mashing the fruit; (6) placing the mashed fruit in the pits in the form of paste; (7) covering the pits carefully to keep out dirt; and (8) taking out the paste to be prepared for eating and baking. This whole process could take five to seven days, depending on how long the fruits were left above ground to begin fermenting. The paste remained edible in the pits for about fifty years, though its flavor changed (Bascom 1965). The

Figure 19. Fermented breadfruit paste. Hivaoa, Marquesas, 1920s. Photo by
R. Linton, courtesy Bishop Museum

timing of when the paste was taken from the pits was largely a matter of
local tastes together with need. Large amounts of breadfruit were preserved in this way, particularly in the Marquesas, Tahiti, Truk, and
Manu'a (Crocombe 1968:142). In the first three places, the fermented
paste was mixed with some fresh breadfruit to make the favorite daily
dish, *popoi mei* or *kon* (Handy and Handy 1923:151; Lebar 1963). Fermented paste, called *mahi,* was made also on Rurutu as a means of conserving this crop, second to taro in preference (Verin 1969:232).

The paste was eaten at various stages of fermentation depending on
the taste preference of the society concerned. The acidity was high for
about ten days after the mashed breadfruit was first placed in the pit;
thereafter it declined somewhat, but the paste acquired other flavors.
The Namu people informed me that these acquired flavors could be controlled by changing the leaves lining the pit at monthly intervals, though I
observed that not many pits were changed.

Wherever breadfruit was fermented, control of acidity was in the
hands of the household or community that made the pits. However,
sometimes the paste was needed before the preferred level of acidity was
achieved. In the Marquesas some *popoi* was made with two packages of
paste to one of fresh fruit; when it was desired very sweet or for children,
one package of paste was added to two of fresh fruit (Handy and Handy
1923:190–191). The pounding or kneading of the paste was also an
important step in rendering the paste digestible (NJP fieldnotes, Namu
1968–1969) These alternative ways of controlling the taste are not docu-

mented adequately to indicate the detailed local knowledge involved in meeting preferences of taste.

The chemical composition of the paste as a foodstuff also awaits further analysis. Murai, Pen, and Miller (1958) analyzed one sample gathered in Micronesia, but it was made from breadfruit with seeds, which is not usually used in the eastern Pacific. Furthermore, the product was dried and pounded rather than being fermented. Parker's thesis (1967) reports on his investigation of the fermentation process in breadfruit; but he used breadfruit on O'ahu and relied on Micronesian informants to recall a process they had used on their home islands, thereby leaving some doubts about the reliability of his findings. Breadfruit on O'ahu was not often fermented, as Pukui noted (1967). However, Parker's limited analysis showed an increase in acidity, development of anaerobic conditions, and a marked decline in bacterial growth (1967:107). Analysis of a more recent experimental pit in Suva has shown a similar rapid drop in pH, so that the paste had become quite acidic after eight days (Aarlsberg et al. 1981).

Another experimental pit was put down in the grounds of the Musée des Îles in Tahiti, in order to reconstruct old Marquesan methods (*Les Nouvelles,* March 1984). And an experimental reconstruction of a pit in Samoa was conducted by Cox with the help of a male Samoan informant, but no analysis was made of the contents of that pit or the changes in composition of the paste (1980). He claimed this process was anaerobic, but this question remains to be settled. In the eastern Pacific it is common practice to open the pit and add layers of newly processed paste to the contents. In the northwestern Pacific it is more common to leave pits closed except for regularly changing the leaves lining them.

How long people have been fermenting breadfruit is a matter of conjecture. The practice was certainly widely reported by the early visitors to the Pacific, such as Cook (Beaglehole 1967). Since the practice was more prevalent in the eastern Pacific, it seems likely that it may have been developed in that general area rather than farther west, as Kirch (1979) suggests. We can speculate that this process was a development subsequent to the introduction of the root crop plants from Southeast Asia. However, we must note that the practice of fermentation of soy beans and fish products was well developed in Southeast Asia, as was the taste for these acidic foods in the form of miso, soy sauce, and tempeh. I am suggesting that the taste for fermented foods was known to the ancestors of the settlers of the eastern Pacific. It may be that settlers leaving island Southeast Asia brought with them the idea of the process, which was then tried on breadfruit and *Colocasia* taro, as these were favorite foods in the eastern Pacific and available in sufficient quantities for fermentation to be tried experimentally without depleting the day-to-day household supply of food.

FERMENTATION OF *COLOCASIA* TARO

The practice of fermenting *Colocasia* taro is perhaps the best known example of fermentation of food in the Pacific, though it was practiced on a less wide scale than fermenting breadfruit. *Poi* was made from *Colocasia* taro in Hawai'i and also in Rurutu (Verin 1969:232), Tubuai (Aitken 1930:43), Ra'ivavae (Marshall 1961), and Rapa (Hanson 1970: 73–76).

Poi was made in Hawai'i by peeling and cooking the *Colocasia* taro corms, then mashing them with a stone pounder with a little water added; this begins the fermentation process (Figure 20). This firm mass, termed *'ai pa'i*, could be wrapped in *ti* leaf packages and left until needed. *Poi* was made from this *'ai pa'i* base by mixing it with water to the desired consistency, kneading the paste, and then straining it. "Thin poi is likely to ferment rapidly, hence it is kept thick, except when actually prepared for eating" (Pukui 1967:429; Handy and Handy 1972:112). Pukui has described the process of *poi* making in Hawai'i as she learned it as an eight-year-old from her grandmother. Her recollections are an extremely

Figure 20. Making *poi*, Hawai'i. Photo courtesy Bishop Museum

valuable record of the details of *poi* making in the past (Handy and Handy 1972:111–115).

In the Hawaiian diet, *poi* was the preferred main food, accompanied where possible by fish, and was eaten every day. It and sweet potato were the staff of life, and constituted *'ai* (translated simply as "food"). *Poi* was eaten by each person dipping one or two fingers into a common bowl (Soderstrom 1937). Soft taros of different varieties could be combined, or hard taros of different varieties, but the soft and hard varieties were not mixed in the same *poi.* Hawaiians could tell from the taste and appearance which varieties had been used. Since 1906 *poi* has been made commercially by machine (Begley, Vieth, and de la Pena n.d.), making the hand-made product all but obsolete (Pukui 1967).

Taro paste was also made into a kind of pudding called *poi* in Rurutu, where taro was again the main foodstuff; cooking and pounding were the main processes (Verin 1969:232). In Tubuai, Ra'ivavae, and Rapa, taro was eaten in the form of *popoi,* where it was a part of most meals. In Rapa a woman would make enough *popoi* for about three bundles, which were wrapped in leaves with the maker's name scratched on each and hung in a tree while the *popoi* fermented. There was a competitive spirit among women to make the best *popoi* for feasts. Well-made *popoi* maintained its shape, a glistening white mound filled with tiny air holes. It should be eaten within about four days of its preparation; older *popoi* became so badly fermented that it was fit only for pigs. Hanson reports that it "is a light food, large quantities of it are easily digestible, and the fermentation gives it a tangy taste faintly reminiscent of beer" (1970:76). He does not tell us whether that same taste was reported by the Rapans themselves.

Many kinds of *poi* were made on Tubuai. There, *popoi* was made by pounding cooked taro and adding a small amount of water and crushed ripe banana. This mixture kept for weeks (Aitken 1930:42). Their food known as *poi* was made of manioc starch combined with papaya, bananas, cooked pumpkin, or *fe'i* bananas cut into small pieces, and wrapped in leaves; the packets were cooked in the earth oven and served with a sauce of fresh coconut milk (Aitken 1930:40). Breadfruit was formerly important on Tubuai, but by the 1920s the number of trees had decreased, as had the number of pits of fermented breadfruit paste *(mahi)* (Aitken 1930:14).

The terms *poi* and *popoi* can be very confusing. Either can refer to the simple pounded paste of taro, breadfruit, or other starches that have begun to ferment. If mixed with a very small amount of water, the paste would keep in hard form for weeks without further fermentation; in this form in Hawai'i it was wrapped in *ti* or other leaves and stored in the rafters of the living house. In contrast, *popoi* required more processing, using fermented paste as a base, mixed with other foodstuffs including unfermented breadfruit and/or coconut, and baking it in the earth oven. Such a mixture formed a sort of pudding for immediate consumption, whether by the household or a larger group.

An analysis of the Hawaiian *poi* paste conducted by Carey Miller (1927) showed that the acidity increased rapidly in the first four days and then leveled off by the tenth day to pH 3.5. Miller commented that the vitamin A and C content did not change markedly. She did not comment on B12, which Taylor (1982) shows is an important nutrient in fermented foods.

Occasionally foods other than breadfruit and *Colocasia* taro were preserved in pits or fermented slightly in puddings. Seemann lists eleven foodstuffs so stored as *madrai* in Fiji (1862:305–306). In Tonga *ma kape* (made from *Alocasia* taro), *ma hopa,* and *ma manioke* were made, in addition to *ma mei* (breadfruit) (Pulu 1981:64). It is worth noting also that in Tonga po'opo'oi is a Tongan pudding *(malolo).* In Samoan *poipoi* means to cut up or to carve (Krämer 1906:271, 153–154). Bananas were also preserved in pits in Samoa, Wallis and Futuna, Tahiti, and Rarotonga.

The technology associated with fermentation of these foodstuffs was fairly simple. Breadfruit was peeled with a cowrie shell from which a portion of the dome was cut away. Both breadfruit and taro were pounded in some societies at some stage before the paste was left to ferment; pounders of basalt became stylized in Hawai'i and Tahiti, whereas in Samoa and Tonga another breadfruit was the common pounder. On Namu the ripe, peeled breadfruit were trodden in order to mash them to a paste, reminiscent of wine making. Wooden receptacles, known in Polynesia as *kumete,* were used to hold the paste during kneading or mixing with coconut cream. The pits in which the breadfruit was stored have been frequently described by early visitors such as Cook and Banks, and in ethnographic accounts such as that of Grattan (1948) for Samoa. Graters for the coconut that was an integral part of the final food product have also been widely described. In Hawai'i the fermented *poi* was stored in coconut leaf baskets, sealed against the damp weather (Pukui 1967). Wherever fermentation was practiced, the technology was less important than the knowledge of how to encourage the fermentation process.

Strong interest is being shown in these indigenous processing techniques as one means of diversifying the world's food supply and drawing on existing knowledge rather than applying only Western knowledge. Steinkraus (1983) and others are drawing attention to these indigenous processes with a view to understanding their scientific bases and perhaps incorporating them in modern-day technology. With so much breadfruit being left where it falls in Tahiti and Samoa, this revived interest could help to give breadfruit paste a new image and make it acceptable once again. Reducing the labor necessary for processing will be an essential factor in that endeavor.

FLOUR FROM ARROWROOT AND CASSAVA

A flourlike product made from Polynesian arrowroot *(Tacca leontopetaloides),* and later cassava (or manioc, *Manihot esculenta*), was the basis of several forms of puddings throughout the Pacific. The flour was seldom eaten alone but was mixed with other starches such as banana or pandanus and coconut cream to make delicacies, particularly for a chief or for a special occasion.

The main steps in making starch from either arrowroot or cassava were grating, leaching with many pourings of water over the grated material, and drying the leached product (Pollock 1991). The leached product was hung in a piece of net for several days until the starch formed a solid lump that could then be wrapped in leaves and left in a dry place. In Fiji the starch was stored in pots (Seemann 1862), but this practice is not recorded for any other Pacific islands.

Leaching was the most important step in the process, as the *Tacca* root is extremely toxic. Stories are told of chickens dying from drinking the runoff (NJP fieldnotes, Rarotonga 1982). The toxic factor is hydrogen cyanide (prussic acid), which can be present in cassava in varying amounts. The stem when cut produces cyanogenetic glucoside, which is very soluble in water and decomposes when heated to 150° C. Soaking the roots in water and cutting and heating them all aid in removal of this toxin (Moran 1975:178).

The question whether this mode of processing was developed by the Pacific Islanders or was introduced by the Spanish and Portuguese, who were familiar with cassava and grain products, remains to be answered. Arrowroot flour was made throughout the northwest, central, and eastern Pacific, where it appears to have been used for at least two hundred years. It is one of the foodstuffs of Tahiti listed in the 1770s by Morrison (1790).

Commercial exploitation of *Tacca* arrowroot was attempted in the Cook Islands and Societies by missionaries in the mid-1800s, as the flour product had long been known in Europe to have medicinal properties for stomach ailments (Seemann 1862). One of the reasons for the failure of this commercial enterprise was the amount of work involved.

Only a small amount of cassava/manioc is processed into starch. Its use is much more recent in the Pacific. It is reported mainly in the southern Cook Islands, though it was probably made elsewhere on a casual rather than a regular basis. In Tonga in 1982, the nutritionist at the hospital obtained five sugar sacks of flour that had been made from cassava roots remaining after Hurricane Oscar (NJP fieldnotes, Tonga 1982). In Rarotonga cassava flour in 2-kilo sacks was available for sale in a supermarket. This was used for making *poke,* a much favored Rarotongan dish of cassava flour mixed with mashed bananas and baked in the earth oven (NJP fieldnotes, Rarotonga 1982). But making flour from cassava root in a household was considered too much work. The product was not as desirable to local residents, except on special occasions, as it was to missionaries looking for something from which to make bread (Pollock n.d.*a*) and also to starch their clothes.

Use of the Polynesian term *pia* for the starch made from both *Tacca* arrowroot and cassava has led to some confusion. In Rarotonga, *Tacca* arrowroot is known in full as *pia Maori* but is often referred to only as *pia;* cassava is also referred to as *pia,* although the term *maniota* is also used at times. Missionaries in Samoa found the sexual connotations of the term *pia* offensive, so that there and in other Polynesian languages the term *masoa* or *mahoa* was substituted. Subsequently the term has come to mean any starchy flour—e.g., *masoa palagi* for white flour. Whether *pia* originally referred to the plant or to the starchy flour produced from the plant, or both, is now open to debate.

To grate the starch, the raw tubers were rubbed over a rough shell, or later, over a piece of metal with a series of holes punched in it. Water was poured over the grated cassava to leach out the cyanide. The remaining starch was left to dry before being mixed into puddings (see Chapter 4). The dry flour could be stored for long periods, which made it a suitable product to carry between islands on a sailing canoe.

EXTENDED BAKING FOR PRESERVATION

Baking large amounts of breadfruit for long periods of time in the earth oven was another means of processing breadfruit for future use. Ripe breadfruit were baked whole for two or three days and left in the oven to be used as needed. This practice was known in Tahiti as an *opi'o* bake (Ellis 1831:42). Buck described a similar process for Aitutaki in the Cooks, where it was known as *kuru hopiko;* it extended the availability of breadfruit by four to six months (1927:61). No tests or reports are available that indicate whether the process involved fermentation. Buck makes no mention of any considerations of flavor.

Another form of extended baking was practiced in the Marquesas. Breadfruit was cooked in long trenches for two to three days, leaving a jamlike product. Willowdean Handy gives a detailed account of the processing steps (Handy and Handy 1923). This appears to have been done only occasionally, depending perhaps on the amount of excess breadfruit available and people's own whims.

Large roots of *Cordyline terminalis,* known as *ti* in many parts of the Pacific but particularly in the east, were also baked for two or three days to produce a sweet, fibrous delicacy which kept well for several months. Pieces were broken off as needed, much the way sugar cane is eaten in its raw state. The process is not entirely forgotten, as in 1982 Futa Helu offered me a piece of *ti* root that had been baked for a special occasion for the King of Tonga (NJP fieldnotes, Tonga 1982). For a discussion of the *ti* bake, see Chapter 4.

NON-HARVESTING AS MEANS OF PRESERVATION

Some root crops such as *Dioscorea* yams, *Cyrtosperma,* or swamp, taro and the recently introduced cassava were left in the ground because these plants had no period of dormancy of growth (Yen 1975:74). Thus these crops could be used when needed rather than immediately on maturity. In fact, *Dioscorea* yams were sometimes left in the ground to grow very large, mainly as prestige items to be contributed at special occasions to enhance a man's social status, particularly in Pohnpei and Tonga (Bascom 1965; Maude 1971). However, neither of these authors notes whether these large yams were edible or whether they became so enlarged and woody that they were merely presentation items. Other yams found growing wild, such as *D. pentaphylla* and *D. nummularia,* were harvested as needed or left in the ground if more preferred foods were available.

Cyrtosperma taro is the slowest growing of the aroids and can be left in its swamp pit for two, six, or even ten years. It was grown in Yap and in the Gilberts (now Kiribati) where it was a particularly prestigeful food crop (Lingenfelter 1979:418; Untaman 1982:99; Luomala 1974; Catala 1957; Vickers 1982). It does not appear to have been widely used as a foodstuff elsewhere in the Pacific, though at times it might have been a secondary source of food (Wilder 1928:27 for Rarotonga; NJP fieldnotes, Fiji 1982, particularly Rewa delta).

The flavor of certain varieties of *Cyrtosperma (babai)* on Butaritari in Kiribati was preferred over others. The *katutu* variety was the mainstay of the diet outside the breadfruit season; the preferred size was a tuber about a beer bottle's length or half the length from fingers to mid-forearm (Sewell 1977:39). Presumably a corm of this size was not too woody and was thus palatable. But there it was an exception.

Cyrtosperma taro may have been a more important stand-by crop before European contact. Its consumption could be delayed by leaving the corms growing in the pit until needed. I suggest that it may have preceded *Colocasia* taro, or it may have been used more commonly in marshy areas, as both plants like an edaphic environment in which to grow. Probably because *Colocasia* taro, including new and better varieties, matured more quickly than *Cyrtosperma,* more of it was grown, particularly when efficient irrigation systems were developed. Furthermore, preference for *Cyrtosperma* diminished, and therefore less was grown, because it took up more space, took longer to mature, and was less acceptable to the taste. But in sacrificing *Cyrtosperma* for *Colocasia* taro a storable crop was lost.

Cassava can also be left in the ground until needed. This South American root crop has only recently found favor in the islands of the South Pacific, even though it has been known and planted on a limited scale for some one hundred years. Its tolerance of poor soils led to its use at the end of the shifting cultivation cycle when the taros, yams, and sweet potatoes have taken most of the nutrients from the soil. Cassava could then be left in the plot if the roots were not needed immediately. The root does become fibrous after the first year of growth and is eaten only if all other foods are not available (Moran 1975). However, plantations of cassava have increased markedly in size and number since the 1960s; they are widespread particularly on the islands of the southern Cooks (NJP fieldnotes 1982) and are seen intermittently in Tonga.

Storage by non-harvest was suited only to a limited number of crops of the Pacific region. Yet it has persisted on this limited scale to the present day. It was a very practical way of holding a food reserve, but also in the case of yams it was a means of building up a supply of prestige items.

SUMMARY

Each island of the Pacific set aside at least one crop of one food for delayed consumption. That crop was processed in one of several ways— by fermentation, by extended baking, or by processing into flour. Each of these processes required considerable work that involved the whole community, not just separate households, so making fermented breadfruit paste or a *ti* bake became occasions for socializing and merrymaking as much as for laying up a store of food. The processed food might be eaten within a couple of weeks or a couple of years; it might be intended for daily use or as a store for the future.

An important attribute of the processed food was the taste. For example, processing caused breadfruit and *Colocasia* taro to become quite acidic, a taste that was not normally present in Pacific Island diets until citrus fruits were introduced. It may be that the fermented paste products were not even considered the same food as the original.

6

Feasts and Ceremonial Presentations

FEASTS are an extremely visible part of Pacific Island life. Not only is the display of food eye-catching and stimulating to other senses, but these are times when several households get together to join enthusiastically in the spirit of the event. They are occasions as much for the joy of getting together to prepare the setting and cook for the guests as for sharing in the vast amounts of food needed to make them a success.

The sheer volume of food and the amount of work involved caught the attention of many early visitors from Europe (see Figure 21). They were astounded at the 15-foot-high walls of yams topped off with pigs in Fiji, or the riot of color and variety in a Tongan *pola* (a stretcher of food brought to a feast). However, those writers offered little explanation of such feasts, either because they considered them as wasteful of what the Europeans saw as a precious commodity, or because they failed to appreciate the significance of the place of food, and feasts in particular, in the social system.

Feasts are still a prominent part of life in the Pacific. Special persons and visitors are likely to be regaled with a table laden with local fare either for a specific occasion, such as a wedding, or as part of a major celebration, such as the investiture of the Crown Prince in Tonga during the 1975 Constitution centenary (NJP fieldnotes 1975). Much of the food for these occasions is usually cooked in the earth oven and includes many of the traditional foods—taros, yams, pork, and fish. Western foods like the canned corned beef in Samoan *palusami,* or steak, or beer and orange drink have been added, but do not alter the particular island flavor of the occasion. That feasts have persisted despite Western intrusions is one indication of their social importance. Those staged for tourists demonstrate the particular identity of Pacific Island foods.

The structure of a feast is similar to that for household food events, only it is more elaborate. Starches are dominant in volume, but the

Figure 21. Marriage feast. Tonga, c. 1915. Photo by W. S. Sherwill, courtesy Bishop Museum

accompaniments are more elaborate than for household fare. They should include items such as pork, cooked fish (served whole), raw fish, turtle, other seafoods, and chop suey as well as several mixed dishes such as Samoan *palusami, taufolo,* and other puddings. By examining the various types of feasts we can gain some indications of the bases on which people make decisions about what to contribute to a particular festive occasion. Feasts also help to round out the picture of the place of food in the system of social relations and are one indication of how this sharing of food beyond the kin group may be seen within a broader picture of symbolic communication. We can see this picture more clearly if we first describe the main forms of feast activities in several societies.

CASE STUDIES

Namu, Marshall Islands

When I landed on Namu atoll in February 1968 in the company of the paramount chief, I only had time to put down my bags before I was taken to a house where a funeral was in progress. I was taken into the place where the body was lying, surrounded by people weeping and others sitting in groups. I was offered some rice and a drink of tea, as were all the other visitors in the house. There was a continuous though small supply of this food available throughout the day. It was eaten on the spot. The man was buried the following day, and a "large" funeral feast was held that evening—large because everyone in the village attended, not because there was much food to offer them. Because the ship that had brought the paramount chief and myself brought also long-awaited food supplies, the family was saved the embarrassment of having very little food to offer. But the amount of rice and canned corned beef, just off the ship, was very small relative to what the family felt they should offer. January and February are lean periods on Namu: Breadfruit is in its second season and thus in short supply, the pandanus season is over, and fishing is not good (Pollock 1970). Thus they had to offer *ribelle* (foreign) food, which was all they had. Of local fare there was just a little breadfruit and some coconuts to drink. But the family did their best to fulfill their obligations to those joining them in the mourning.

The next day I heard singing gradually drawing closer to the chief's house in which I had a room. I learned that a *kamlo* (party) was about to take place. A line of women, some children, and men, each bearing a small coconut-leaf basket at shoulder height, arrived at the chief's house to welcome him. They were bringing him gifts, mainly of coconuts together with one or two breadfruit and some fish. All of this was placed in the "kitchen" of the house, where pots of rice were being cooked. The singing was accompanied by jocularity once the people got to the house. Members of all the households in the community were there, seated on the ground around the chief's house. Speeches of welcome were made and followed by more singing. Each household group received from the chief a coconut basket full of cooked rice topped with the contents of a can of corned beef. Individuals ate a little and sent the rest back to their own households to be eaten later.

A week or so later another feast was called; this time I was the host, supposedly, as this feast was for the completion of "my" office, a small two-roomed house made of coconut poles and pandanus thatch. I was expected to provide the feast for the men who had worked on the house. The trouble was that I had brought only 25 pounds of rice with me, thinking that would be more than ample for my own needs for a couple of months until the next ship brought supplies. Ten pounds of the rice were used for that feast; the village people supplied coconuts. I was able to provide some packets of orange drink, which, reconstituted, were a great hit.

On an atoll such events take a major toll of the food supply, particularly in the lean months, and I was well initiated into the shortage of food and the kinds of irregular demands made on whatever food people did have. A small gesture (small by *ribelle*, or outsider, standards) such as a can of corned beef or some orange drink "made" these festive occasions.

More important was the getting together, the chance to laugh together, to do something different, and the feeling that the right thing had been done—the dead person had been farewelled, "his spirit sent on its way"; the chief had been welcomed; the builders of the office had received the appropriate recognition for their work and complying with the chief's wishes. Respect and generosity, within the meager bounds possible, had been duly displayed.

The funeral feast and the house-building feast may not seem very feastlike to an outsider, but to the people at the time they were very lively and most welcome. The food was a necessary expression of a social event. The small amount of food was not important because it could not be helped. It was not the material aspects of food that were important but rather the social goodwill and respect for the event that was expressed.

Pohnpei (Formerly Ponape)

On Pohnpei, a high island in Micronesia, feasts were much more elaborate than on Namu, because of its wider range of food resources. Shimizu has examined the role of food in these celebrations, which he sees as dominated by the notion of respect (wahu) not only throughout the political system of which feasts are such an important part, but also in Pohnpeians' views of space. Social life in Pohnpei revolves around "works of honor," which include obligations and voluntary contributions to chiefs (Shimizu 1982:158). Drawing on the Pohnpeian customary code, tiahk, he discusses in detail the first fruits ceremonies for yams and breadfruit that are given to the Nahnmwarki, the senior chief. The list of foods included in the works of honor is very specific and is more restricted than the list of everyday foods (Shimizu 1982:162–165). Not all Pohnpeians strive for high status in the political system by means of food giving, but if they don't they are considered lazy (Shimizu 1982:161).

Of the many types of feasts, the largest, known as kamatipw, involved cooking in the uhmw (earth oven), joint preparation of food by the several participant groups, presentation of the cooked food to the main guest, and redistribution of the food and communal eating. A kamatipw was organized to honor a chief or high-ranking person. At these feasts several other social events were celebrated, such as hospitality when traveling, weddings, and other life-cycle celebrations. Gifts appropriate to the occasions were given; they always included food but sometimes also fabric, oil, or (today) money. Other kinds of feasts celebrated the peak of the yam harvest, the beginning and end of house-building, the coronation of chiefs, and other celebratory occasions.

Bascom (1965) claims that on Pohnpei feasts took priority over everything else. Fischer and Fischer say that feasts were a way to win the favor of senior chiefs and thus to gain prominence through outstanding contributions of food (1957:252). Riesenberg sees the major role of these feasts as prestige competition from which individuals obtained promotion in part by bringing to feasts "larger and better and more frequent food offerings than other men, thus demonstrating industry, ability, loyalty, and affection toward the chiefs. But more important than presentations at feasts are the direct offerings of first fruits *(nohpwei)* and the occasional gifts of food between first fruits *(kaiak* or *unmw en kaiak)*. All of these types of presentation are known as service *(uhpa,* literally 'to stand underneath')" (1968:76). This strong sense of competition comes through clearly in the writings on Pohnpei. Each individual sought to outdo his rival either in the size of yam he brought or in the quantity of contribution, the former being more important. The men who consistently brought the largest yams were most eligible for promotion to higher rank or to be appointed to fill titled positions in each section or district: "Success in competition may thus win actual status as well as prestige and praise," notes Bascom (1965:32), likening these large feasts to the Northwest Coast Indian potlatch because of their strong competitive base.

Yams *(kap)* and breadfruit *(mar)* were the two most common central foods, though no large feast could be given without kava *(sakau)* and a pig; Shimizu includes also dog (1982:186). Hughes suggests that the essential food elements were yams, pigs, and *sakau;* other foods were used but were secondary. Breadfruit was a close second to yams as the main food. Uncooked yams were a major contribution but were regarded more as a contribution or gift than as food; these could be kept by the chiefs and replanted (Hughes 1968:16). The use of the possessive form for food as distinct from alienable objects in the Pohnpeian language, as discussed in Chapter 2, is evidence of this subtle distinction. The feasts occurred mainly during the season of yam harvest, after yams had been given to the chiefs as first fruits.

Allocation of contributions to a feast was discussed ahead of time by members of a group. Each person offered to bring what he could afford. Those who had more than one pig might offer to bring two or more and gain prestige accordingly. "The size of a pig, the length of its tusks and the number of kava plants consumed at a feast bring prestige to the host and donor" (Bascom 1965). These were over and above the prestige derived from bringing the largest yam. Large yams were never used at home for food. They were too important in the feasting game (Bascom 1965:33).

Pit breadfruit *(mar)* was also an important contribution and a basis of competition. One or two persons could bring some *mar.* Its age was more important than the amount contributed; it should be at least ten years old.

Despite what ethnographers such as Shimizu and Bascom have labeled as competitive spirit, those contributing to a feast were expected to be modest about their contributions, for they feared ridicule by being shown up in the future. Bascom notes that gaining prestige was a factor fundamental to Pohnpeian motivations and attitudes toward work.

Attending feasts was one of the most frequent activities of the Nahnmwarki, the primary ruler of the kingdom. The nobles and leaders of individual sections of Pohnpei offered the Nahnmwarki a continual cycle of prescribed feasts of tribute, and they in turn received food from the lesser-ranked people. The Nahnken, the secular ruler of the kingdom, had a special titleholder, the Nahlaim, who was responsible for food distribution; his rank was second in the Nahnken's line. It was his job to indicate what portion should be given to each person at a feast and to make sure those of rank received their due measure of food. He divided the food into baskets and called out the highest titles. It was not the amount but the allocation of a particular pile of food apportioned to the appropriate titled person that was so important a part of the protocol. The nobles and high-ranking people got their allocated shares; "the commoners could take what was left when the distribution was completed—and that was usually very little" (Hughes 1968:16).

First fruit offerings, known in Pohnpei as *nohpwoai,* were an important part of the custom of respect, or works of honor. Shimizu distinguishes seasonal first fruits for breadfruit, yam, pandanus, and mango from "instrumental" first fruits for *sakau,* sugar cane, banana, and *Cyrtosperma* and *Colocasia* taro. He lists seven types of tribute for breadfruit and six types for yams and indicates those rarely made today (Shimizu 1982:163–164). The seasonal tributes must be given every year, but the instrumental tributes were given to the chief only when new lands were cleared; these are rarely given today. Bascom tells us that for district chiefs two special feasts were necessary each year, the first to mark the beginning of the yam harvest and the second when yams were becoming scarce. Between these two special feasts, lesser ones were held. The two major ones were very large; at one in Kiti twenty large pigs, twenty very large yams each requiring eight or twelve men to carry them, five large pit breadfruits, and one hundred kava plants were used. The entire feast house was filled with twelve stone [earth] ovens (Bascom 1965:76).

In addition, on eighteen separate occasions each year tribute was given to the "working for the chiefs." Among these were several kinds of first fruits, such as first yams, first breadfruit, and first fermented breadfruit. First fruits from each farmstead were presented to the section chief; he in turn presented first fruits to the district chief who owned the land. Then the people were free to eat yams or breadfruit until the following season (Bascom 1965:76).

Each tenant gave whatever number of yams or breadfruit he wished to the section chief and the district chiefs. Choice of variety was also up to the donor. Many other forms of produce were given as first fruits, but not the more recently introduced foods or animals or domestic fowls (Bascom 1965:76). It is not surprising, as Bascom suggests, that with such a continuous series of feasts in the old days, it was unnecessary for high-ranking Pohnpeians to do any farming or manual labor (1965:30).

The *kamatipw* given for visitors was also part of customary obligation; the host would be shamed if he did not make a feast for such a visitor. Yams, breadfruit, and other food were contributed by neighbors and relatives, but the host must provide at least one pig and some kava and must later repay the contributions of his neighbors.

"The distribution of food to take home is characteristic of Ponapean feasts. Frequently less is consumed at the feast than is given away to be taken home" (Bascom 1965:73). The main structural elements of the feast were the drinking of kava and the distribution of food.

Samoa

In Samoa also, a complex pattern of feast-giving was part of the way of life, with sharing food as an integral feature. Grattan (1948) identified two main types, the *sua* and the *ta'alolo*. The *sua* was a formal presentation of a specially prepared and cooked pig as a mark of respect for an honored guest, such as a visitor or a chief, by a family group (Milner 1966:217), while the *ta'alolo* was a more formal presentation made to a more respected and larger group.

The main elements of a *sua* were the exchanging of food and fine mats and barkcloth worn by the *taupou* (chief young girl of the village). The food items included at least one cooked pig, a cooked fowl, a coconut with one eye-hole pierced, and a taro or yam cut in pieces and cooked in banana and breadfruit leaves. The fine mats and barkcloth worn by the *taupou* were subject to comment by those present as to their appropriateness for the occasion. All these items were laid before the honored guest on behalf of the people of the village. The food items were announced by the host chief to the assembled company in front of the house in which the presentation was taking place. The honored guest received the gifts seated either inside a house or on a *malae* (meeting area) during the day, or on a *malae* at night. The coconut was drunk by the orator, making loud sucking noises. He also acknowledged receipt of the gifts by calling the name of the donor loudly three times with a peculiar intonation. There were no formal speeches (Grattan 1948).

This form of tribute expressed respect for a high-status member of the chief's immediate family. It could be given when a *matai* (chief) assumed an important title, or as an election feast, or when a *matai* entered hospital. The chief's immediate family must reciprocate by providing good food. Strictly speaking, *sua* is the customary term for any meal of a high chief (Grattan 1948:98–100). The *sua* draws public attention to some event in the family's life. It is an offering of respect from family members to their *matai*.

A *ta'alolo* was a much larger affair put on by an entire village, or even a district, to show respect to distinguished visitors. Turtles and cooked pigs, chicken and live fowls, and coconuts were presented to the guests (Grattan 1948:90). No taro or yams were mentioned by Grattan. On special occasions fine mats and barkcloth were included. The gifts were carried by a crowd of people led by a *taupou, manaia* (chief's son), or chiefs wearing special headdresses and all singing appropriate songs. It always took place during the hours of daylight and in the open, never within a house. Speeches were made both by those giving and by those receiving. A *ta'alolo* might be presented by men or women, and by titled or untitled people.

Another ceremony, known as *laulautasi,* was performed in Samoa by the chiefs and orators of the village, usually on the day before visitors were due to depart. Every family brought cooked food such as chicken, taro, fish, small fish wrapped in leaves, or tinned meat or fish. The orators sometimes made humorous references and derisive comments on the nature of the food. A *laulautasi* could be conducted either outside on the *malae* or within the house (Grattan 1948:92). Its main mark was that the presentation was made by high-ranking people. A *laulautasi* was a smaller feast that could form part of the larger event, the *ta'alolo*. Both involved large groups of people not necessarily related.

In Samoa these *ta'alolo* and *laulautasi* formed part of the custom of *malaga,* journeys or organized visiting between villages. One village would send a message to another that they were coming to visit, either to repay a former visit or because they were running low on food. A *malaga* would be greeted by a *ta'alolo* or a *laulautasi* and further presentations would continue throughout the visitors' stay. Grattan describes such *malaga* for government officials visiting outlying villages (1948: ch. 3).

The food received in the course of these ceremonial presentations was duly distributed. Visitors received amounts according to both custom and the exigencies of the day. The portions into which the pig or fish were divided were designated by custom and were named, each cut having its appropriate status: The *tuala,* the prime portion from the back or loins of the pig, was given to the highest chiefs present. The other portions were likewise assigned with due regard to rank (Grattan 1948:104, 105). Small amounts were eaten at the feast and the rest taken home to be distributed among several households.

It is clear that these ceremonial presentations are more than just eating events. They are expressions of respect and carry a strong message symbolizing the relationships between the hosts and the guests, the givers and the receivers. The boundaries of acceptability are clearly understood. Failure to give food of acceptable standards would be an affront and the hosts would lose face.

Tonga

In Tonga presentations of food accompanied most large social occasions and still do. Ceremonial presentations involved a number of households and/or villages, and thus included the largest number of people. In addition there were many smaller occasions on which food was presented to a chief or high-ranking person, either by the extended family or those united under one noble, or by the village as a whole.

The kava ceremony *(faikava)* has become the best known feast event in Tonga. At this ceremony an infusion made from the pounded root of *Piper methysticum* is drunk. Food may be served at the *faikava* or may follow: It "generally consists of yams, ripe bananas, or plantains in sufficient quantity that each in the superior circle may have a small portion to eat after his dish of cava. . . . Sometimes a baked pig is brought, in which case the liver and a yam" are presented to the chief (Mariner 1831: 338, 340).

The largest celebration, known in Tongan as *'inasi* (literally, "your share"; Tevita Finau, pers. comm. 1988), involved all the islands in the Tonga group. It was held wherever the Tui Tonga (head chief) was residing just before the yams (all species) reached maturity; it celebrated the imminent readiness of the first crop of yams of the season. Yams were considered the one special eatable that should be offered to the gods through the person of the divine chief Tui Tonga. "The object of this offering is to insure the protection of the gods, that their favour may be extended to the welfare of the nation generally, and in particular to the productions of the earth, of which yams are the most important" (Mariner 1831:342). The species of yams known locally as *kahokaho* was always used for this ceremony.

Yams for the ceremony were dug up and each one ornamented with ribands made from the pandanus leaf and dyed red. Each decorated yam was tied to a pole 8 or 9 feet long, which was carried by two men, fore and aft, the yam hanging between them. These poles were placed in front of the assembled chiefs. The chiefs and *matapule*s (second-ranking chiefs) sat in a circle around the yams. "Other articles that form part of the *Inachi* are next brought forward. These are dried fish, *mahoá,* mats, *gnatoo,* and bundles of *mellacoola,* which, together with the yams, (although not cooked), are shared out by one of the matabooles of Tooitonga" (Mariner 1831:345). Of all these articles, about one-fourth was allotted to the gods—and was appropriated by the priests. About one-half was allotted to the head chief, and the remainder was taken away by the Tui Tonga's servants (Mariner 1831:344–345). There followed a regular kava party. The quantity of provisions shared out was incredible, according to Mariner. The people looked upon it as a very heavy tribute, even though the controllers of the plantations (chiefs, *matapules*, etc.) bore the expense. Much more was provided than was eaten, so it aggravated the scarcity if the crops had not been abundant; "but it is so much the custom at Tonga to make liberal and profuse presents, that the people generally either feast or starve" (Mariner 1831: 345). One way to prevent this serious consequence was to place a tabu or prohibition on several kinds of food before the time for the feast arrived (see below).

One very particular first fruits celebration has been under close scrutiny. The *'inasi* that Cook saw, which he called *natche*, did not follow the usual pattern (Beaglehole 1967). Bott (1982) has offered her explanation as to why Cook's *'inasi* (or *natche*) was so different from that described by Mariner and others. The one Cook participated in was held in July rather than in October when it was usually held, though he was told there would be a much bigger *'inasi* later. The timing may account for Cook's observation that small sticks were tied to the carrying pole, not yams (Bott 1982:41). Bott suggests that what Cook saw was a special ceremony held to initiate Pau's son into certain privileges, that is, to change the status of an individual rather than to benefit the nation as a whole. And possibly because it was held three months early, there were not enough mature yams available, so the small sticks were used as substitutes. According to Queen Salote, it was a perversion of the true meaning and intent of the *'inasi* (Bott 1982:47). The fact that the ceremony has not been carried out for a very long time—not since Mariner's time, probably 180 years, according to Bott (1982:39)—means that much of the detail has been lost and our understanding is unclear.

Tributes of yams, mats, *ngatu (tapa),* dried fish, live birds, and so forth were "levied on every man's property in proportion as he can spare. The quantity is sometimes determined by the chief of each district," though in practice "generally by the will of each individual, who will always take care to send quite as much as he can well afford, lest the superior chief should be offended with him, and deprive him of all that he has." A family would be publicly shamed if its contribution was considered inadequate. This tribute was "paid twice a year; once at the ceremony of *Inachi,* or offering the first fruits of the season to the gods, in or about the beginning of October; and again at some other time of the year, when the tributary chief may think proper." Mariner further comments that the paying of tribute at the time of the *'inasi* was "general and absolute"; that which was paid on the other occasion came more in the form of a present and was based on respect *('ofa)*. In this it resembles the first fruits exchanges in Pohnpei. These presents were given frequently from common people to their lesser chiefs, in a chainlike effect right up to the higher class of chiefs. The latter generally made a present of hogs and yams to the king about once a fortnight (Mariner 1831:147).

A temporary tabu that was sometimes put on several kinds of food to prevent scarcity associated with feasting was later removed by a ceremony called *fakalahi*. This term was also used for the period of duration of the tabu itself (Mariner 1831:354). The tabu at the time of the death of the Tui Tonga in 1806, just before Mariner arrived, lasted about eight months during which time hogs, fowls, and coconuts could not be used for food except by great chiefs. To lift this tabu, a *fakalahi* was held at two *malae* (meeting grounds) and at the grave of the Tui Tonga. Four poles about 18 feet tall were set up about 4 feet from each other and smaller poles lashed across. This structure was filled with yams, and two more upright sets of poles were added to make the whole structure some 50 or 60 feet in height. A cold baked pig was placed across the top. Some 300 or 400 hogs were killed and half baked and carried to the king's *malae* together with several "cases" of yams each holding about 500 (Mariner 1831:90, 94). People assembled from all quarters. The numbers of pigs, as well as cases and piles of yams, were announced. Mariner describes how these masses of food were divided up: The greatest quantity went to the most important chiefs, one-quarter to the gods, and another to the new Tui Tonga for his numerous household, so that "every man in the island gets at least a mouthful of pork and yam" (1831:94). The whole ceremony was concluded with a kava party.

In another ceremony, "Tow Tow," yams, coconuts, and other vegetable products were offered to A'lo A'lo, the god of weather, to ensure a continuation of favorable weather and consequent good harvest. It was performed in early November and repeated every ten days for seven or eight times. Each district provided a certain quantity of yams, coconuts, sugar cane, bananas, plantains, and so forth, bearing them to the *malae* tied on poles. Wrestling and boxing matches took place, the god was supplicated, and food was shared out. One pile was marked for A'lo A'lo, the remaining two piles were marked for different principal chiefs and sent to their houses. The pile for the gods was taken in a free-for-all. "All that choose make a sudden dash at the pile appropriated to the gods, and each man secures as much as he can, to the great amusement of the spectators, though many of the scramblers come off with wounded heads, and sometimes with fractured limbs" (Mariner 1831:347). Another great pugilistic contest followed.

Fiji

Feasts in Fiji, known as *magiti,* were also held for many major social occasions. They were among the greatest spectacles recorded in the Pacific. Deane (1921) lists a number of the categories of *magiti* told him by Fijian informants. At these feasts much food was consumed. Derrick refers to *magiti* as occasions of "prodigal abundance" (1946:13) as can be seen in Figure 22.

The main foods at a Fijian feast were and are various root crops, fruits, fish, and whole carcasses of pork and beef; special importance is attached to the fish, pork, and beef. Turtles are a very special feast food in Fiji. Of the starches, yam is still highly regarded but rarely seen at cere-

Figure 22. A wall of food. Fiji, 1870s. Photo courtesy Fiji Museum

monies today, according to Ravuvu (1983:42). So *dalo* (taro) is the most frequently used main food of most *magiti,* together with breadfruit and *vudi* (plantains). *Tavioka* (cassava) forms the main part of the *magiti* only when the other starches are not available. All these starches were cooked whole as "whole yams and dalo are much more presentable at a feast than small chopped up pieces" (Ravuvu 1983:25).

Again the *kakana dina* (true food) was a main part of these food events, but should be accompanied by fish or pork, together with puddings *(vakalolo),* also as an important part of a feast (Wallis 1858:133). This custom of making puddings for feasts still persists. For a meeting of the Great Council of Chiefs at Bau in 1982, a range of special puddings had to be made in honor of those high-ranking people; such puddings were a particular honor for chiefs of that status and not made at other times (Adi Mae Ganilau, pers. comm. 1982). The foods should always be the best and the most one can afford. Such a feast is part of all ceremonials in Fiji. As Ravuvu observes, "No ceremonial function is considered complete without a presentation of food or *magiti.* A function is considered good, apart from other things, if there is more than enough food for everyone attending" (1983:41–42).

The wedding or marriage feast was witnessed by several authors. According to the ethnographer Quain, "the true marriage feast," as distinct from the Wesleyan ceremony, "always falls in April or May, the time when yam and taro gardens were yielding their fullest" (1948:333). Announcing an impending marriage well in advance gave the relatives time to plant sufficient crops and to amass the marriage gifts such as pigs and whales' teeth, mats and *sulu* (loin cloths). The bridal party brought a few pigs baked whole and many basketfuls of cooked food, while the groom's party cooked a large oven full of pigs and yams. The pigs should by custom come from the groom's family. They may conceal whales' teeth inside the pigs presented. "Above all," Quain commented, "it is important that the bride's family and their guests be well fed by the ovens of the groom" (1948:336). When such a feast is impending, access to particular special plots of taro and yams may have been restricted by the chiefs to ensure the necessary abundance for a liberal feast (Williams 1858:146).

The ritual offering of newly harvested yams constituted the *i sevu,* annual first fruits ceremony (Turner 1984:133). Turner observed two *i sevu* in 1976, the traditional one in February or March, and the Christian one. In the first ceremony the yams were presented to the *i taukei* (people of the land, or hosts) after a period of prohibition against digging them up to ensure a sufficient quantity. *Yaqona* (kava) was drunk throughout the whole celebration by the elders of the *i taukei* as the main participants, and they were fed by the community. The yams were presented first to the ancestral spirit, then to the chief, and then the women presented *kaile,* a type of wild yam, to the elders. This whole ceremony was deemed vital to the health and prosperity of the community.

In his endeavor to understand this ceremony, Turner questions why yams had such high ritual significance when they made only a small contribution to the total diet. He concludes that "it would almost appear that, rather than the rite being celebrated to promote the growth of yams, yams are grown in order to hold the rite" (Turner 1984:136). Furthermore, he suggests there are several levels of meaning to this first fruits ceremony. Initially, he examines a sexual significance but prefers to explain the ceremony as a statement through ritual of political bonds between the chief and *i taukei* as representatives of community as a whole. The *i taukei* are the transmitters of the offering to the ancestors; the ceremony thus "both requires and reinforces cooperation and communal identity" (Turner 1984:138, 139). He also assesses the ceremony as a ritual of increase, an appeal for health, well-being, and prosperity; as it expresses concern with the renewal of the fertility of both gardens and forest, "yams can serve as a metonym for both the natural and cultural domains in a way that taro cannot, for the latter is strictly a cultigen" (Turner 1984:142).

The meaning that Turner assigns to this ceremony needs to be questioned on two counts. First, it is not clear whether Fijians accept his mode of reasoning to explain the significance of such an important event in their way of life. And second, we need assurance that Turner's levels of meaning for this particular ceremony fit well with the meaning of other cultural features in Fiji society. In seeking the meaning of food use on a wider scale, we are drawn into such issues.

Vast quantities of food were a notable feature of Fijian feasts and caught the attention of many authors. Miss Constance Gordon Cumming noted a pudding on a gigantic scale, 10 feet by 5 feet, as well as turtles and pigs and a wall of fish 5 feet by 60 feet (1885:163). A row of cooked taro 33 yards long and 2 feet square was recorded by missionary Calvert (1858:14, 124), and Seemann noted a large yam hill (1862:211). Derrick used the epithet "prodigal abundance" for the ten thousand yams, thirty large turtles, forty *yaqona* roots, and hundreds of native puddings (1946:13). As missionary Williams noted, "The food [was] prepared by each tribe and family" according to orders issued by the king (1858:148). This included making the ovens, men's work, "sometimes eight or ten feet deep, and fifty feet in circumference," and "the baking of all kinds of food, and the making of all kinds of puddings" (Williams 1858:147). These gifts were counted and reported by the Tui Rara, the master of the feast, then placed in a public area in front of the chief temple.

> A floor of clean leaves is laid, eight or twelve feet in diameter; on this . . . is placed a layer of cocoa nuts, on which are heaped up the baked taro and yams, to the amount of several tons. The next tier is formed of *vakalolo*, . . . native puddings. . . . Surmounting this pedestal of food are two or three hogs, baked whole, and lying on their bellies. . . . When every thing is ready, all is publicly offered to the gods, to whom a share is voted, the rest being reserved for the visitors. On these occasions profusion is always aimed at. . . . At one public feast, I saw two hundred men employed for nearly six hours in collecting and piling cooked food. (Williams 1858:148)

The food is divided by the Tui Rara, Williams continues. "A Chief is honoured or slighted according to the quantity or quality of the food set before him." The food is "divided into as many portions as there are tribes," who subdivide it "until no one is left without a portion. . . . The males eat in the open air, sending the women's share to their houses." Visitors also received a portion—very likely enough for twenty men would be given to them. Williams assessed this sharing of food partly as hospitality, and partly as fear "lest by withholding any part, or by something in their manner of eating, they should give offence" (Williams 1858:149, 150, 151).

With the strong impact of missionaries on Fijian society since the early 1800s, additional occasions have become incorporated into the calendar, such as feasts for children on the first Sunday in April and a feast to honor parents on an early Sunday in May, the equivalent of Mother's Day. For a church marriage the feast is small compared with that for a traditional marriage feast.

The establishment of colonial government added another group of persons to be feasted when they visited the districts. Each village took turns to provide the feast and, according to Quain, tried to outdo the other villages. Each group of families within that village shared in making up the joint contribution. The women's oven contained fish and yams. The men's contribution consisted of pigs, yams, and taro. The chiefly group prepared the third oven to welcome the guests (Quain 1948:73).

THEMES COMMON TO ISLAND FEASTS

There were so many types of feasts that it is not surprising investigators seek to characterize them in order to simplify their presentation. One set of categories was based on the events for which they were held (see Deane's 1921 list for Fiji). A simple classification of this sort could be the following:

Tribute to chiefs
  first fruits
  planting
  other
Tribute to visitors
Life cycle events
  first birthday
  marriage
  death
  hair-cutting
Inauguration of chiefs
Opening of a new public building

Shimizu's types for Pohnpei are among those most closely derived from local concepts, so they should offer a useful basis from which to begin our comparisons. He makes several distinctions in his analysis of Pohnpeian feasts. A major one is that between the obligatory occasions and those when the contributions were voluntary (see his analysis chart, Shimizu 1982:159). Another is that between feasts *(kamatipw)* as a general category and some of the special occasions on which they occur, such as presentations of first fruits and other forms of tribute to chiefs or high-ranking persons. These involved foodstuffs and other items, with particular foodstuffs having higher significance than others. Other features such as the relative importance of cooked and uncooked foods, the variety, and the division of the large mounds of food were also characteristic of this type of event.

The main feature of all these Pacific Island feasts was that they were occasions for food sharing that brought together different sections of the community to participate in a mutually significant event. The sharing extended from the contributions made by each household to the event, through the cooking and entertainment phases, to the final distribution of the items contributed. Thus the feast was more than just a food event, but the food itself as the common denominator was extremely important. It was the cultural highlight without which a feast was not a feast. The food was the marker of the event and thus its central symbol.

The yam was the most commonly featured food and had major significance in the feasts of the high-island societies we have looked at. It was not part of feasts in Namu because yams do not grow there. On Pohnpei and Tonga, Fiji and Tikopia, the yam was not only a food but was used as a symbol of wider social links (Shimizu 1982 for Pohnpei; Bott 1982 for Tonga; Turner 1984 for Fiji; Firth 1967 for Tikopia). It represented strong ties between those who worked together for social provisioning and those ancestors/gods who were also so involved. "The Work of the

Yams" in Tikopia is thus evidence, expressed ritually, of the continuity of life (Firth 1967).

In addition to its ritual significance, yam production in these societies was surrounded with secrecy, for it was the subject of considerable competition. Each man strived to produce the biggest yam to be presented at a feast, and thereby to derive tremendous prestige. *Babai* (*Cyrtosperma* taro) on atolls of Kiribati was similarly associated with this ritual to produce the biggest root at a feast (Luomala 1974). Perhaps it took the place of yams, which do not grow well on atolls.

Other starches such as cassava, *Alocasia* taro, *Xanthosoma* taro, sweet potatoes, and bananas were not normally part of a feast, as they were predominantly household fare, and used only in emergency situations. However, arrowroot and more recently cassava starch are used as a main ingredient in some of the puddings that are a notable feature of feasts, particularly as food for the chief or honored guests.

One common principle of feasts was that they included as rich a variety of foods as was feasible. We saw in Namu how this was difficult where food was short. Within the group of main feast foods, variety was attained by including different varieties of taro or yam, though one variety such as *kahokaho* in Tonga was the most favored. Puddings (see Chapter 4) also added variety since these were not part of the normal household daily fare. A range of puddings was in fact expected, such as the *vakalolo* in Fiji. Of course, such variety was dependent on the resources available. On atolls where climatic and soil restrictions prevailed, the range of feast foods was inevitably limited.

Abundance of food was also a major mark of a feast. As Williams noted in Fiji, a chief could feel offended if the quality or quantity did not meet his expectations. Ravuvu (1983) tells us that each Fijian was expected to contribute as much as he could, and that a host felt duty bound to make a feast for a guest that was marked by the abundance of food. Such was the local meaning of generosity. European observers too were struck by the vast quantities of food, which they deemed to be in excess of people's needs and thus wasteful. They could not understand in their terms why so much food was brought and presented. What was adequate and appropriate for the occasion in Pacific Island terms was considered excessive and wasteful in outsider's terms.

The distinction between cooked and raw food is a marked characteristic of feasting. Most feasts required that the food be cooked, that is, taro or yam baked in the earth oven and pig or fish. In fact the term for feast in Pohnpei was synonymous with the term for stone (earth) oven cooking (Shimizu 1982:160). Thus feasts were associated with large *umu,* as Williams has described for Fiji (1858:147).

Because of the large scale of the feasts, the cooking involved a greater amount of social activity than household cooking. It too was bound by certain principles. Men were more likely to do most of the work of cooking feast food, except where custom necessitated separate women's ovens, as for the Fiji marriage feast. Large ovens may have been set aside especially for feasts, as distinct from household ovens.

For some food presentations at feasts, items such as yams, taros, pigs, and *yaqona* were presented uncooked in addition to the cooked food. These live items could be used to yield more produce at a later date rather than just being consumed at or after the feast. Such items were part of the tribute to a chief. After the festive occasion, he could either raise them on his own lands or farm them out to his people, and draw on their products at a later date. This was particularly common with live pigs, which constituted one type of "raw" element in the feasts. Another was the raw fish that might be one of the dishes to accompany the starches.

The cooked food had to be presented and divided out before any of it was eaten. The divider, as we have seen for Pohnpei and Fiji, held an important social position. His (it seems to have usually been a male) job was to assure that honor was done. He recorded and, where appropriate, acclaimed those providing the food, but his main job was to divide the food appropriately. This included allotting the piles or towers of food. Four main divisions of food seem to have been common to several societies: one share for the gods, one share for the priests/intermediaries, one or two shares for the chiefs and their people. The amount in each pile was not the significant feature; rather it was the appropriateness of the food to the rank of the recipients.

Another important aspect of the feast was that a significant portion was taken home afterward by the participants. The amount actually eaten in the large group setting was surprisingly small—almost a symbolic pecking at the food, except in the cases of some chiefs and visitors, particularly in Tahiti, where Cook recorded their eating a prodigious amount at both "normal" eating events and special occasions.

We have no way of knowing how often feasts were held in pre-European times. It becomes apparent from reading missionary and travelers' reports that Europeans introduced two new status categories that had to be honored with feasts—the government officials and the missionaries. Once their presence was established in the islands, they were the expected guests. But throughout the nineteenth century the people of the islands had learned to cope with the demands of explorers to provision their ships and the toll this took on the local food supply, local firewood, and fresh water supplies. The pork trade grew noticeably as a result of the demands of these occasional visitors and, later, the development of the pork trade to Sydney (Maude 1968). The toll on local supplies or motivation to increase production can only be guessed at.

Within each island community feasts inevitably took a considerable toll on the food resources. The amounts demanded by the participants for the many feasts that were held used up large amounts of foodstuffs. But, as I pointed out in Chapter 5, this can be seen as a kind of social "investment" of that food with the expectation of reciprocation by the receiving group. And fluctuations in population size (McArthur 1967) also meant that demands on resources and on the land from which those resources were produced could vary greatly over time.

This fitted with what Europeans have labeled an irregular food pattern. When there was plenty of food, as after a feast, it was eaten; when there was not much food, people tightened their belts until food was available. It is clear both from the literature and from contemporary ethnographic evidence that one way around this problem was to plan ahead and plant an ample supply of yams and taros for an impending marriage feast, or hair-cutting in Niue or the Cooks (Pollock 1979b; Loomis 1983). Holding marriage feasts at a time of year when food was in good supply, as in Fiji, was another strategy. Yet another means of conserving the supply was the imposition of a tabu, or *rahui,* on these foods for a period before the feast was to be held (Firth 1967). Preserved food such as *poi* in Hawai'i or fermented breadfruit in Namu might be used if there was no other food to offer at a feast. None of these strategies helped to make availability of food any more regular, but that is a Western value. Rather, the differences between periods of abundance and periods of scarcity became more pronounced.

If we add the problem of lack of means of conserving any excess at the time of a feast, we can see that a prudent strategy was to eat one's fill when there was plenty of food and get by when there was none or little. Some feasts such as those associated with the *ti* ovens and with *opi'o* bakes in Tahiti focused on the technique of conserving by long baking. Since these were successfully stopped some 150 years ago because the missionaries condemned them, it is hard to know whether the food side or the social side of these occasions was the more important.

The view that these feasts drew on a surplus (Friedman 1982; Kirch 1984) can be contended. The huge mounds of food described by early visitors such as Cook, Mariner, and Cumming give credence to the view that excess was drawn off from the community at these feasting times. The question has been raised whether this excess was extracted by chiefs or contributed willingly by the producers. Establishing whether the excess was a true surplus or a calculated part of productive activities is more difficult.

Shimizu makes a distinction between two kinds of surplus in his discussion of Pohnpeian feasts (1985:41). A social surplus was derived from social generosity as distinct from a natural surplus derived from seasonal crops. But the social generosity was based on the natural productivity of those crops used. These two principles were put into action in different kinds of ways according to the social occasion. Shimizu shows how, in the different types of feasts, the natural surplus is given to the people, thereby maintaining the society while also maintaining links with the ancestors and total solidarity.

That distinction is useful, particularly where breadfruit was used as a significant contribution to feasts, as in Micronesia. It produced a crop seasonally, and a group's contribution depended on the number of trees extended families had on their land and whether or not they had suffered storm damage. But where the yam was the significant contribution, different principles applied. Yams could be left in the ground to continue growth. Is that surplus, if the crop is not harvested and left for another time? Decisions were made to plant a certain amount of a crop knowing full well there would be some feast occasions that would draw on that crop. Similarly, the decision whether or not to harvest was made on the basis of the social commitment to make a contribution. A chief might make explicit demands for contributions that could well be considered exploitative in the Marxist sense. But where those demands were less explicit and called on the overall principle of generosity in Pacific societies, surplus would seem to be an inappropriate term.

Food sharing was a very notable part of these feasting events. But it may not have been the most important part. It seems likely that the food part of feasts was a means of expression of relationships and a social commitment, works of honor as Shimizu expresses it for Pohnpei (1982, 1985). It was an enlargement of the social involvement in the earth oven that was so much a mark of these feasts. Thus, despite the large amounts of food in evidence at feasts, this food was only a small part of the total rite, as Turner (1984) notes for the rites he observed in Fiji. Emphasizing the food element in feasts may be a distortion of the way Pacific Island people saw them. The food is a symbol of that community's social well-being.

The strong persistence of feasts into the modern era suggests that this symbolism still carries its message today. The character of feasts has changed somewhat, with bread and beef and salads featuring in the food selection. But taro, pork, and fish are still there. And the earth oven is still made with all the elaborate preparation; it is still men's work but the whole community is involved in preparing the foods to put in the oven.

To the traditional occasions celebrated by feasts have been added modern purposes such as political events and for tourist groups. The ensurance of allegiance of kinsmen and other followers has been linked with getting votes in several recent elections. Hot dog give-aways in

Hawai'i and Guam rank alongside the onions given away by a hopeful congressman visiting the outer islands of the Marshalls in 1969. Similarly, in Samoa much media coverage was given to the feasts before elections, at which food and alcoholic beverages were given away by *matai* vying for office. The concept of "treating" has taken on connotations of bribery in the new setting, so that the Western Samoan *fono* (governing body) ruled that no *matai* who was a candidate for office could give a feast or a party for two weeks preceding the elections (AhMu 1983; Pollock 1983a).

MEANINGS EXPRESSED IN FEASTING

In the anthropological literature feasts have been most frequently treated as one component of rituals (e.g., see Schefold 1982:64 for use of food in a Southeast Asian ritual context). Anthropologists are concerned with what a group of people are expressing by their conceptual and ritual system. In the Tikopian rite "Work of the Yams" (Firth 1967), feasting is included in the wider aspects of this ritual performance. The formalized behavior with "an objective beyond the immediate implications of the set of physical acts involved . . . may also involve a system of signals to convey what cannot be expressed in more articulate precise form" (Firth 1970:199). How we read those signals is of key importance.

There has been a tendency to see feasts as an extended part of economic activity. Firth himself included feasts under a chapter headed "Economic Functions of the Chiefs in Tikopia" (1936:222). Sahlins, in his ethnographic work on Fiji, distinguished those rites characterized by pooling of food from those rites that involved reciprocal exchange in food and goods between kindred sides. He argues that "economic reciprocity, while it established harmony and sets the pattern for future material aid, is less sociable than pooling because it inevitably implies a duality of parties, a separation of interests" (Sahlins 1976:145). Similarly, Tiffany (1975) has examined Samoan feasts as an example of chiefly redistribution activities by means of transactional relations. This mode of analysis does begin to break away from a focus on the material elements of ritual, of which the feast is the most outstanding. But we perhaps need to distance it a little more. By breaking out of our materialist mold we may be able to extend our thinking about food in ritual.

The evidence is strong that there was a social compulsion to participate in feasts, but the degree of compulsion on each household group in each society varied. There are indications of a high level of competition in the growing of yams in Pohnpei and *babai* in the Gilberts, but the reward was not so much a personal one as one that reflected positively on the wider group, such as the extended family. A feast was an occasion at which a family could demonstrate their food contributions to the society by way of the yam, as a symbolic demonstration of carrying out their social responsibilities.

The idea of feasts as occasions for chiefs to demonstrate a control over surplus fits in with our Western individualistic values, but it doesn't fit so well with more communally oriented value systems. Whether chiefs demanded contributions from their subjects, or whether all contributions were given as the participants were able and deemed appropriate to their circumstances, is a question in need of closer examination. Given the consensus approach noted in the literature, particularly for Samoa (Tiffany 1975), it seems more likely that people gave as they were able, but they might be encouraged to extend that liberality while seeking higher status or particular favors. Thus the degree of extractive force or control over resources in Marxist terms does not appear to have been a major issue where consensus politics existed.

The feast in Pacific Island societies appears to have been a major ritual occasion at which the sharing of food contributed to achievement of the overall purpose, whether celebrating a marriage, welcoming a visitor, or celebrating first fruits. Various interpretations of these rituals have failed to note the importance of the food event embedded in the overall range of events. I suggest that the social importance was at least as great as any economic importance, and that food channeled through a feast was more satisfying than food eaten in the household. The question of the meaning of removal of surplus food from household production for feasts needs further consideration.

SUMMARY

The two major issues raised by consideration of the place of food in feasts and ritual are the amount of social commitment entailed and whether the large amounts of food mobilized can be called a surplus. I have argued that the part that food plays in these feasts is more than a matter of just the food itself; its role is largely symbolic. Food is a central feature at all feasts. The manner of cooking and the sharing out after the event are governed by clearly established rules. Because the food is not necessarily eaten there, but much of it taken home, the focus is more on the sharing of community resources than on members of the community eating together.

But more important, the event represents a manifestation of relationships between sectors of the community, a social commitment. Through that commitment there is recognition of the difference in status of those involved. A feast is a highly elaborated form of exchange (for want of a better term) with clearly established rules—but they are flexible rules and have been adapted to include new social groups such as church members and government officials. In so doing the principles have not changed. The traditional foods are still the centerpiece and the mode of cooking has persisted despite new technology, but the setting is sometimes very different, such as tourist occasions. It would appear then that the earth oven is a key feature of feast events that links them to household food preparation. But more important, it embodies and carries in large part the symbolism of what feasts are for. Feasts draw in contributions of food and other gifts from the wide community of related people and become shared festive occasions. Thus they can be said to renew the group's identity and express social solidarity while also providing welcome breaks in the daily round of life.

The matching concepts of respect (as in Pohnpeians' works of honor) and generosity predominated over any notion of surplus. Feasts involved the whole community, both living and dead. This type of food event was a mobilization of people and resources within an accepted structure. Feasts were part of a ritual that used food as a means of conveying messages about the distinctiveness of the community. Feasts were thus special occasions where identity and particular social values were highlighted in the midst of the whole extravaganza.

7

Food Production and Land Tenure

Food and the land are deeply intertwined concepts in Pacific societies. Land is seen as the basis of life, of both present and past generations. It is both spirit and place. Among its many attributes is its ability to produce food crops. Activities connected with production form an important means of ordering life; crops must be planted when they will thrive best. Similarly one dimension of the concept of land involves the kind of foods that it will grow, while others are a place to live, a symbol of bonds of identity, and so forth. Here I will look at the ways societies in the Pacific have ordered their thinking about land and its uses, as well as the ways they have variously codified access to land. These codes include definite principles of control and the means of acquiring access to new land. In recent times there has been a marked movement away from so-called traditional/communal landholding principles toward more individualized landholding. This is bringing about new modes of access as well as new regulatory principles; the courts have become the forum in which these issues are commonly raised.

LAND USE: ANTHROPOLOGICAL STUDIES

Several anthropologists have recorded the local system of classifying land and its uses in the course of their ethnographic reports. The system of the Hanunóo in the Philippines was one of the first recorded and has remained a classic citation. Conklin used the ethnosemantic approach to understand local reasoning about their agricultural system. The Hanunóo practiced shifting agriculture to produce the rice that was their main foodstuff. Even though no swiddens were planted solely in rice or any other single crop, the term for swidden, *parayan,* was derived from the local term for the rice plant. Hanunóo people saw a close link between rice, their main starch food, and the mode in which it was grown. Furthermore the growing cycle of rice and of corn and other crops was a crucial consideration in determining their activities; "the organization of the agricultural year is directly determined by activities connected with the cultivation of those cultigens providing the most desirable foods" (Conklin 1957:29–31). Unfortunately, only a handful of anthropologists have followed Conklin's lead in identifying indigenous features used in classifying production of food crops and considering the close association between the main food plants and the land.

The !Kung, an African hunter society, is another example of a society that makes distinctions among desirable plants from which they derive their food. Lee identified four classes of food, with an additional class of rare foods (nineteen species). These are further classified as strong or weak, according to desirability. There is also a class of supplementary foods that are eaten when the more desirable foods become locally exhausted. The people start by eating out the most desirable species within a range of walking distance from their residences, and then they turn to the less desirable ones (Lee 1984:44). Thus their concept of their environment as a source of food is based on their preferences rather than other criteria such as location and energy expenditure.

The Wola, a New Guinea Highland society, have a discrete set of terms they use when making the decision where to plant a new garden and what to put in it. Their classification is a very pragmatic one, with a strong base in their social commitments. "The Wola do not simply name and classify crops, they cultivate and consume them too" (Sillitoe 1983:260).

Barrau's comprehensive ethnobotanical studies of plant uses throughout the various regions of the Pacific (1958, 1961, 1965a, 1965b; Massal and Barrau 1956) have provided us with an excellent data base from which to examine more closely local production systems and the foods they produce. In addition, the work of Coursey on yams (1967, 1972) and of Yen on sweet potatoes (1974) and on subsistence agricultural systems in prehistory (1980a) have all increased our understanding of these local systems of land use. Chandra (1979a, 1979b) and Sivan (1980a) for Fiji, together with Dharmarju and others working at Alafua, the University of the South Pacific's agricultural research institution in Western Samoa, are also helping to amplify that data base and point up specific local issues.

Other work on agricultural production in the Pacific uses Western concepts rather than local ones. The South Pacific Commission handbook edited by Lambert (1982) brings together recent information on cultivation techniques for the main root crops (see Table 10), as well as their diseases. Also, an agricultural survey conducted under the auspices of the Asian Development Bank (Ward and Proctor 1980) has raised issues concerning the viable size of landholdings in the six Pacific nations

surveyed. These issues have been strongly debated between those supporting smallholder production (Hardaker, Fleming, and Harris 1984)
and those who proposed plantation production as more economically
viable (Ward and Proctor 1980).

To achieve better understanding and implementation of new agricultural programs, indigenous concepts need to be taken into account
alongside the Western concepts that have been promulgated for so long.
Thus I would endorse a plea by the economist Fisk that "we should try
once more to understand the values and excellences of the indigenous
agriculture and landholding systems" (1976:14).

LAND USE AND FOOD PRODUCTION: LOCAL CONCEPTS

Growing successfully the starch and tree crops that have been the mainstay of island Pacific societies has depended on knowing what to plant
when and the different kinds of microclimates most suitable to particular
crops. Local timetables have been developed and important distinctions
have been drawn between types of land suitable for particular crops.

A major part of local knowledge is the indigenous system of classifying
land. Some of these systems have been recorded by anthropologists for
certain Pacific societies. By understanding the local divisions of land we
can improve our understanding of connections between mode of production, the ultimate food crops, and their different uses. Similarly, local
ways of ordering activities connected with production—which we term
calendars—reveal certain principles that throw a new light on the links
between production and consumption of food.

Living in a particular environment for several hundreds, perhaps thou-
sands, of years, Pacific peoples have built up local expertise that is passed
on to each succeeding generation. Knowledge of plant growth cycles,
seasonal changes in weather, and ritual demands on production are but
some aspects of this local heritage. It has resulted in a careful selection of
plant species that suit a particular locale, whether high volcanic island or
low atoll.

Most of the root and tree crops must be reproduced vegetatively, each
requiring a carefully followed set of techniques if the plant is to produce a
crop. The exact mode of reproduction for each of the starchy foods considered here is detailed in Appendix A. Planting of certain plants requires
very careful timing if they are to grow satisfactorily. They thus dominate
the link local people have established between time and the food production cycle.

Calendars

A concept of an established sequence of planting activities is to be found
in many Pacific societies. Such calendars—to use the Western term—have

been noted both in the past by missionaries and other visitors and in the present by ethnographers.

For Tonga the missionary West recorded the important steps in yam cultivation; this calendar set down the appropriate times at which the land should be cleared, how long it should be left before the seed tubers were planted, and the steps toward harvesting (West 1865:35–37). The Uvean calendar as recorded by Kirch (1975) closely resembles the Tongan one. This is not surprising since the islands are geographically and culturally fairly close.

In Fiji also, the activity schedule connected with the yam was important, as shown in the Fijian calendar recorded by both Wilkes (1845) and Seemann (1862). The Fijian calendar began with the *vula i were were*—the month for clearing—and reflected the important points in the growing of the yams (see Table 9). The clearly recognized seasons when the yams must be planted and later harvested may have been a reason that it was the focus of their calendar. Or its importance as a highly favored crop both for ritual and consumption purposes may have led to its domination of the ordering of activities.

Patterns of growing cycles showing the various stages of several crops in any one annual cycle are also helpful (see Christiansen 1975 for Bellona; Aoyagi 1982 for Palau; Pollock 1970 for Namu). They give us an indication of the kind of work activities necessary to maintain the supply of foodstuffs as nearly as possible throughout the year. They also give us an indication that life on an island was not as easy as some early reporters seemed to think from their brief stays.

Varieties of breadfruit and pandanus with different ripening times were obtained from other islands in order to extend the season of harvest. These varieties had to be planted at the right times and in the right places to ensure that there was not overabundance one month and nothing the next.

The modes of planting of the different crops in particular parts of Fiji have been well documented. The methods used depended on location (see Rutz 1976). On Moala yams were the first crop planted in newly made clearings; such a yam garden was called a *weri*. Once the yams had started growing, other, subsidiary crops such as cabbages, *bele (Hibiscus manihot)*, and so forth, were planted among the mounds. When the yams had been dug, sweet potatoes, followed by manioc and some *Xanthosoma* taro, were planted. This garden of mixed starches was known as *teitei*. The cultivation period of an average plot was about three to four years, followed by a rest period for that plot of, Moalans say, five to seven years, though that period could be longer (Sahlins 1962:39–43).

On Namu the calendar was based on two seasonal changes in the wind patterns. The normal direction of the wind was from the northeast; this period could be marked by severe storms and big blows. When the wind

TABLE 9. Fijian Planting Calendar: Two Versions from the
Mid-Nineteenth Century

According to Seemann	According to Wilkes
1. *Vula i werewere* = June, July, clearing month; when the land is cleared of weeds and trees.	1. *Vulai were were*, weeding month.
2. *Vula i cukicuki* = August; when the yam-fields are dug and planted.	2. *Vulai lou lou*, digging ground and planting.
3. *Vula i vavakadi* = September; putting reeds to yams to enable them to climb up.	3. *Vulai Kawawaka.*
4. *Vula i Balolo lailai* = October; when the balolo (*Palolo viridis*, Gray), a remarkable Annelidan animal, first makes its appearance in small numbers.	4. *Bololo vava konde.*
5. *Vula i Balolo levu* = November; when the balolo (*Palolo viridis*, Gray) is seen in great numbers; the 25th of November generally is the day when most of these animals are caught.	5. *Bololo lieb.*
6. *Vula i nuqa laįlai* = December; a fish called "nuqa" comes in in isolated numbers.	6. *Numa lieb*, or *Nuga lailai.*
7. *Vula i nuqa levu* = January; when the nuqa fish arrives in great numbers.	7. *Vulai songa sou tombe sou*, or *Nuga levu;* reed blossoms.
8. *Vula ni sevu* = February; when offerings of the first dug yams (ai sevu) are made to the priests.	8. *Vulai songa sou seselieb*, build yam-houses.
9. *Vula i Kelikeli* = March; digging yams and storing them in sheds.	9. *Vulai Matua*, or *Endoye doye;* yams ripe. [N.B.—Vulai Endoye doye, probably is meant for Vula i doi; the Doi is a tree (*Alphitonia zizyphoides*, A. Gray), B. Seemann.]
10. *Vula i gasau* = April; reeds (gasau) begin to sprout out afresh.	10. *Vulai mbota mbota.*
11. *Vula i doi* = May; the Doi (*Alphitonia zizyphoides*, A. Gray), a tree plentiful in Fiji, flowers.	11. *Vulai kelekele*, or *Vulai mayo mayo;* digging yams.

Sources: Seemann 1862:298–299; Wilkes 1845, 3:341.

turned to the west or southwest, there were periods of calm, known as *rak*. These were the best times to make voyages to other atolls to visit kin and to venture farther a-sea for fishing. Namuans and other Marshallese were very avid seafarers (Krämer and Nevermann 1938).

Namu's calendar also revolved around the availability of breadfruit. Some species produced three crops a year, but one of these was more prolific and longer lasting and so was considered the main crop. This crop began in late April and May and lasted through June. Any left on the trees in June became very soft and sweet. They were picked before they were too soft and made into *bwiru* (fermented breadfruit), which was stored in pits to be eaten later in the year. Pandanus was also a seasonal food plant, but of lesser significance than the breadfruit. Even so, Namu people had acquired twenty-four varieties on Majkin islet alone in order to diversify the range of fruit types and their season of availability. Even when taro had been grown, it seems likely that breadfruit was still the key factor in ordering Namu people's lives. On other Marshallese atolls where taro and breadfruit were more in balance, the people would have had slightly different modes of ordering their food-producing activities.

It is clear from those calendar systems that have been described that the yam dominated the production cycle on high islands where it was important, and breadfruit dominated the harvesting cycle on other islands, particularly those in the central and northwest Pacific. These patterns of ordering were not just for purposes of regulating work patterns and production. They had strong bearing on rituals and were a symbolic summary of the link between food production and the uses of those foods. Calendars depicted the cycle of work, not merely for material needs, but also for rites honoring the ancestors. Firth's book *The Work of the Gods in Tikopia* illustrates well this link between the foodstuff and its wider social implications (1967).

Land Types: Local Classifications

The two major categories of land according to many Pacific societies are garden land and bush land; in some places bush land includes woodland and forest, while in others forest is a separate category. As a general distinction, on garden lands food crops are grown, whereas on bush land or woodland areas, food is gathered. Within the cultivated land category we can distinguish land used in shifting cultivation from irrigated or wetland areas where such crops as *Colocasia* taro are grown. Yet another set of distinctions can be made between land used for root plants and that used for trees.

In Tikopia, gardens are open clearings known as *vao*, where annual crops are grown. The woodland areas are known as *tofi* (Firth 1936: 331). The gardens and woodland areas were generally adjacent (Kirch and Yen 1982:40). Tikopians also distinguish several other categories of land, such as the *mara* where the major root crops are ceremonially planted, and the *roka*, or swampy areas for growing *pulaka* (*Cyrtosperma* taro), as distinct from *pera*, which were swampy areas on the lakeshore for growing *Colocasia* taro.

On Bellona, another Polynesian outlier, food crops are of two types, depending on the source. One is *utunga 'umanga*, the term they use for food from the gardens, including cultivated vine crops such as yams and also non-vine crops such as *Colocasia* taro, *kape* (*Alocasia* taro), banana, and *pueraria*. The other, *utunga mai mouku*, is the term for food from the bush and forests, including trees with edible fruits, vines, and wild plants with tubers—that is, food-bearing plants that are not annuals (Christiansen 1975).

On Futuna and Alofi and Wallis, the yam-aroid swiddens are known as *mouku*, which is the dominant type of shifting cultivation. This is contrasted with *toafa*, the barren bush (Kirch 1975:73). "The aroids, yams, bananas and breadfruit are the four starches that make up more than 90% of staple starches, magiti" (Kirch 1975:107).

On Hawai'i Island the whole island was divided into districts called *moku*, and these were subdivided into smaller sections known as *ahupua'a*, which ran from the top of the mountains to the sea. Within these divisions Hawaiians distinguished tracts for intensive cultivation as taro swamp known as *mo'o'aina*, while *pauku'aina* were garden plots used for growing bananas, sweet potatoes, sugar cane, and paper mulberry (Meller and Herwitz 1971:27). Hawaiians also distinguished the taro they grew on irrigated land from the upland taro, which did not make such good *poi* (Handy and Handy 1972).

In Palau, forests *(chereomel)* were distinguished from savanna *(ked)*, which was dominated by grasses and shrubs. These were distinct from two types of agricultural lands *(sers* and *mesei)* and from mangrove swamp *(keburs)*. *Sers* is the term used for upland gardens for cassava, sweet potato, banana, and other crops, while *mesei* is a swampy field devoted to taro cultivation; both are located near villages (Akimichi 1980:596).

In a number of societies across the Pacific the areas for growing root and tree crops and those areas where food items could be gathered in season provided the staple and supplementary subsistence foods accounting for 85 percent of the food consumed (Barrau 1958:26, 35). Other edibles could be obtained from a variety of locations. As Hipsley and Kirk noted, in the two New Guinea villages they studied the villagers set apart the areas for sweet potatoes from the areas for some twenty other complementary and supplementary food plants in use there (1965:61–67).

MODES OF FOOD PRODUCTION

The four land types discussed below designate particular kinds of cultivation patterns (see Table 10). For details of when different root crops are planted and harvested, their diseases, toxicity, and nutritional value, see Appendix A. What I call gardens here are usually irregularly shaped plots of land on which crops are grown in rotation using shifting cultivation methods, with a rest period during which the soil is allowed to regenerate.

Shifting Cultivation

Shifting cultivation has been closely examined on a worldwide scale (see Harris 1977 for a summary) following Conklin's seminal work on Hanunóo agriculture in the Philippines. In that study he documented closely the local Hanunóo concepts used in the process of cultivating their crops. Hanunóo divide their (swidden) cycle into ten normal, three subsidiary, and two disjunctive stages. The sequence of most swidden activities is geared to cultivation of rice, as the preferred food crop, though other crops were also grown (Conklin 1957:30–31).

In Pacific societies several stages of cultivation have been identified. First, land to be cleared is selected; then it is cleared, usually by cutting down the smaller growth and burning, both to provide ash and to remove debris (Crocombe 1971:293–294). Only a small area may be cleared at one time, sufficient for four or five contiguous lots. This ensures that the soil does not become too dried out or leached of nutrients. Planting follows; it may consist of as few as twenty setts of taro; other setts will be planted in two or three months' time on the contiguous cleared areas. At the time of harvesting taro, yams, or sweet potatoes

TABLE 10. Chief Forms of Production of Food Crops, by Island Societies

Form of Production	Island Societies
Dryland taro	Tahiti, Tonga, Niue, Samoa, Tuvalu, Rapa, Guam, Palau, Hawai'i
Irrigated taro	Hawai'i, Rapa, Tahiti, Rarotonga, Wallis, Futuna, Palau, Fiji, Vanuatu
Swamp taro	Kiribati, Yap, Tuvalu, Fiji (Rewa), Tuamotus
Shifting cultivation; mixed cropping	Niue, Tonga, Samoa, Fiji, So. Cooks, Pohnpei, Kosrae, Palau
Tree crops	Palau, Truk, Pohnpei, Kosrae, Marshalls, Tokelau, Kiribati, Tuvalu, Tahiti, Marquesas, Nauru, Kapingamarangi, Futuna, Fiji, Samoa, Tonga

some of the produce will be used as planting material. Once these roots have been harvested, cassava or *Xanthosoma* taro will be planted in the land they vacated. Then the land is left to rest, the fallow stage—on Niue, for anywhere from three to fifteen years (NJP fieldnotes 1976).

Shifting agriculture in the Pacific differed significantly as a mode of production from European field agriculture. The plots cultivated were irregular in shape, and planted only with as much taro or cassava as the family felt they would need in the next year. Furthermore, once the roots had been harvested the land was either left fallow or one crop of cassava might be planted before the rest period. In general in the Pacific, the fallow period might be anywhere from three to thirty years, depending on the demand for further cropping. Resting was necessary to regenerate the soil, with accumulation of natural humus rather than applying fertilizer. Bananas or breadfruit or pandanus trees might be planted close to these garden areas to provide shelter and easy access to the fruit.

At any one time a household is likely to have four or five plots at different stages of production. Mainly hand-tools such as the digging stick are still used, making this a very labor intensive mode of production. As the population grows people have to travel some distance from their villages to tend these plots (NJP fieldnotes, Niue 1976).

In Tonga cultivation is usually a multicropping system. A six-year rotation is generally followed in this sequence: yam and giant taro → sweet potato → taro → cassava → fallow, followed by bush fallow of two to three years (Thaman 1976). The period of fallow here as elsewhere is being shortened as food from the land is in greater and greater demand. Pressure on the fallow system and thus on regeneration of the land comes both from population increase and from cash cropping (Maude and Sevele 1987).

When assessing land use a shifting cultivation plot may appear to be only partly in use. Or it may contain taros, yams, sweet potatoes, and cassava all at different stages of growth. Large trees will still be growing in these plots unless killed during burn-off. Any one plot is likely to be ringed with banana and papaya and possibly a breadfruit tree or two for shade and for food. Commercial crops such as tomatoes and pineapples are also grown in these plots today, particularly in Tonga and Niue.

Because of the different stages of maturity and different lengths of fallow, it is very hard to calculate exact areas of land in use as shifting cultivation gardens at any one time (Ward and Proctor 1980:84). However, in Fiji, census data for 1978–1980 showed that taro was grown in pure stands on 1,535 hectares and in mixed stands on 1,340 hectares. Chandra and Sivan reported that 22,933 farmers were engaged in this form of agriculture, of whom 75 percent were indigenous Fijians (1981).

Cultivation of these shifting agriculture plots requires considerable

Figure 23. Sweet potato: leaves; stems; planting stem cuttings; edible tuber. Drawing by Tim Galloway

labor. On Niue the whole (extended) family may spend two or three Saturdays clearing one plot; young and old alike can do their share. Crops are planted by hand on Niue because of the rocky soil. In Fiji and parts of Tonga, horses pulling a small disc-plough are used to make the furrows; family members follow behind, planting. The crops must be weeded four

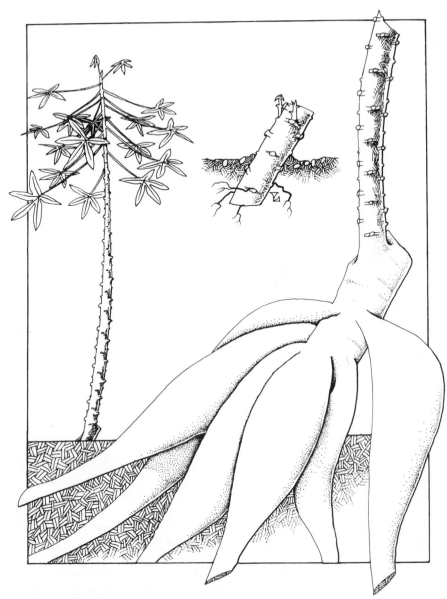

Figure 24. Cassava (manioc): stem and leaves, planting material (cutting from stem), edible root. Drawing by Tim Galloway

or five times before maturity; the extent of the weed problem depends on rainfall. In the islands of the southern Pacific where gardens are grown, both women and men do the weeding. But on Kosrae only the men culti-vate and weed the subsistence crops (Peoples 1986:106).

It appeared to early visitors that this was an easy mode of production because all they saw was a member of the household going to the field, pulling up three or four taro corms for the day's meal, and carrying them home. But this represented only the end point of the cultivation cycle. And what they saw as land lying idle with lots of "wild" growth was part of the natural process of regeneration. Producing food crops by shifting cultivation was an entirely different agricultural process from any that Europeans were familiar with for growing wheat and grains. It required a different conceptual approach.

Pondfield or Irrigated Crops

Some *Colocasia* taro was grown in the shifting cultivation gardens on unirrigated land. But some was grown in irrigated fields. Both *Cyrto-sperma* taro and *Colocasia* taro grow best in a moist environment. *Colocasia* taro needs to have sufficient moisture in the early part of its growing cycle if it is to produce a corm of reasonable size. Irrigated taro is said to have a better taste than the dryland one (Handy and Handy 1972).

Colocasia taro was grown in irrigated plots in Hawai'i and Raro-tonga, Rapa, Palau, and also in Tahiti and the Marquesas on a lesser scale, as well as in parts of Melanesia (Spriggs 1982). Spriggs has care-fully documented modern-day practices of growing irrigated taro in Aneityum, Vanuatu, as part of his endeavor to establish the place of irri-gated taro in subsistence cultivation in the early settlement of the Pacific. He also makes a plea for its regeneration (Spriggs 1981:95–123).

The water must be fresh to brackish and must be flowing. Thus this taro tends to be planted in valleys, run-off areas, and along stream banks or on leveled terraces with irrigation channels. The terrace location was the most preferred though it must have been the most labor intensive. Wet taro was also grown on mounds in Hawai'i (Handy and Handy 1972:97). In Rarotonga taro beds irrigated by streams are located near the stream mouth on the flat areas behind the shoreline, as well as in smaller water-fed terraces alongside many streams. These beds range from 6 to 20 feet square at the largest. The larger beds are subject to an extended family's control, while the smaller ones these days are culti-vated by individual households (NJP fieldnotes 1982).

The young plants grow in 2 to 4 inches of water for the first three to four months. They must be well weeded and also protected from the hot sun. Thus smaller plots are better because they make use of natural or cultivated shade trees. In Rarotonga the beds with young taro plants are covered with coconut palm fronds, which act as a protective cover.

Some *Colocasia* taro has been grown in pits on atolls such as Kapingamarangi and Arno in the Marshalls, but it did less well than *Cyrtosperma* taro, which can better tolerate a degree of salinity in the water (Wiens 1962:378). Some evidence of growing *Colocasia* taro in pits in previous times can still be seen just behind the lagoon shoreline of some islets such as the main one on Takapoto in the Tuamotus. Cyclones, predation by roaming pigs, and the work involved were cited as the main reasons for discontinuing cultivation. In 1968 only three small pits were cultivated on Majkin islet, Namu, mainly to provide for one of the paramount chiefs (NJP fieldnotes 1968–1969).

Since only nine societies of island Oceania used the irrigated method of growing their main foodstuff (see Table 10), it would appear that the importance of this one mode of cultivation has either declined markedly since Western contact or that it has been overrated as typical of Pacific Island cropping patterns.

The second form of wetland cultivation was used for growing *Cyrtosperma* taro. This plant prefers static rather than flowing water and can tolerate brackish water that may occur in the water table on an atoll. It is grown in large pits up to 20 meters long by 10 meters wide that are dug down 2 to 3 meters to reach the freshwater lens (Vickers 1982). It was cultivated more extensively on atolls than on high islands. Wiens claimed that *Cyrtosperma* cultivation has never been as important in the Marshalls as in the Carolines and has "shown a high degree of abandonment in the Marshalls and also in the Tuamotus" (1962:378). To illustrate this he compared land use on Arno atoll in the southern Marshalls with that on Kapingamarangi, a Polynesian outlier south of Pohnpei, and found that 0.2 percent of land area on Arno was devoted to cultivation of *Colocasia* and *Cyrtosperma* taro but 9 percent of the land area of Kapingamarangi was so cultivated (Wiens 1962:378). *Cyrtosperma* taro is no longer grown on Raroia, Tuamotus, but Danielsson recorded Te Iho's account of how every family used to grow taro *(fakea)* in deep ditches. But these taro fields were abandoned after the cyclone in 1903 (Danielsson 1956). On the high island of Tikopia, *Cyrtosperma (pulaka)* was also cultivated (Raymond Firth 1939:166) using the edge of the Ropera swamp (Kirch and Yen 1982:40). These authors indicate that by more regular planting of *pulaka,* production could be increased, but their informants suggested that it was not necessary (Kirch and Yen 1982:62).

In the northern Gilberts/Kiribati the plant is grown in a bottomless basket of woven pandanus or coconut fronds. This basket is kept filled with chopped leaves and soil, which provides the nutrients for the young growing plant. The particular formula of the compost/mulch mixture is a matter of individual choice, each planter following his own knowledge and family lore. Cultivation strategy is a matter of extreme secrecy and ritual particular to the planter's family (see Luomala 1953, 1974, and Geddes 1981 for Tabiteua North; Sewell 1977 for Butaritari and Makin).

In Fiji, where some *Cyrtosperma* was grown, the low-lying areas of the Rewa river delta provided ideal conditions. In some pockets the plant is still grown there today, mainly to provide variety in the diet (NJP fieldnotes 1982). The young plants are mulched and carefully fed by adding more humus around the stem, but the process is not surrounded with the same ritual as Luomala has recorded for the Gilberts.

Tree Crops

Tree crops included breadfruit, bananas, pandanus, pawpaw (papaya), and sago, but the most important was the breadfruit (Figure 25). Breadfruit tree production has been labeled arboriculture (Yen 1980b). The trees may be included as a tree or a forest resource, as in the Marquesas. They may be planted in or near the village, or near the plantations, or even some distance away. They were often planted in groves.

In Tahiti and the Marquesas breadfruit trees grow over the upland slopes (Handy and Handy 1923; Linton 1939). Elsewhere, as in Tonga and Truk and on atolls, they are generally planted around a house site, where they are not only handy for picking the fruit but also provide a broad umbrella of shade. Replanting is vegetative, that is, a shoot taken from the root and planted will bear fruit in about five years. Breadfruit trees are generally owned by the family that planted them and inherited by the heirs collectively. Thus individuals can have use rights to breadfruit trees over a wide area. Rights to the trees are often separate from the land on which they grow.

The breadfruit tree has been described in more detail than the other plants found by the early European explorers because it apparently fascinated them (see de Quiros 1904:28). Not only did it produce edible fruits that were the closest thing these visitors could find in the Pacific to the bread which they lived on at home, but it also produced that breadlike substance with ease. A Tahitian had only to raise a stick and pick several fruits and he had the basis of a meal. To make bread in Europe necessitated many steps, from planting the seeds and harvesting the wheat grains to kneading the dough and baking it, before a loaf of bread was ready to eat. It is no wonder then that Banks, writing in 1769, commented on the ease of procuring breadlike substance in Tahiti:

Figure 25. Breadfruit: tree, fruit, and picker. Drawing by Tim Galloway

In the article of food these happy people may almost be said to be exempt from the curse of our forefathers; scarcely can it be said that they earn their bread by the sweat of their brow, when their chief sustenance, breadfruit, is procured with no more trouble than that of climbing a tree and pulling it down. Not that the trees grew here spontaneously, but, if a man in the course of his life planted ten such trees (which, if well done, might take the labour of an hour or thereabouts), he would as completely fulfil his duty to his own as well as future generations, as we, natives of less temperate climates, can do by toiling in the cold of winter to sow, and in the heat of summer to reap, the annual produce of our soil; which, when once gathered into the barn, must again be re-sowed and re-reaped as often as the colds of winter or the heats of summer return to make such labour disagreeable. (1769:134–135)

On Pohnpei and Kosrae the breadfruit was a mainstay of household diet as well as being a major item of tribute to chiefs. We have seen how on Pohnpei breadfruit was a seasonal crop associated with *nansapw*, humanized land (Shimizu 1982:179). Similarly on Truk the breadfruit tree was an important source of first fruits, and it was an important producer of the main foodstuff, both in the ripe-fruit form and in its preserved form (see Ragone 1988 for details of use on atolls).

Seemann provided a synopsis of thirteen types of breadfruit trees he found cultivated in Fiji in 1858. He recorded their local names and also grouped them by leaf shape; he noted that the names were different in different districts. He also reported that breadfruit was seen in natural forests, and that there were both seeded *(uto sore)* and unseeded types (Seemann 1862:314–315).

In Samoa also breadfruit was an important foodstuff; it stayed in season for about six months and bore two crops (Setchell 1924:100). It was also the mainstay of the Tahitians; the botanist Wilder identified thirty-two varieties and obtained twenty-seven others (Wilder 1928). Three varieties were grown specially for chiefs. Each Tahitian had several breadfruit trees in the family enclosure (Wilder 1928:8). The trees had spread away from cultivated areas in both Tahiti and the Marquesas, but elsewhere they were grown around house sites or in the sheltered middle areas of atolls. Breadfruit's seasonality and that of wild yams meant that these foodstuffs could be harvested only during certain portions of the year, though they could be obtained then with minimal work.

The main use of the breadfruit tree was for its edible fruits, but it also had other useful attributes. The gum was used for caulking, its leaves to cover the earth oven, and its trunk was sometimes sacrificed to make a canoe. It also provided ample shade under its broad spreading canopy and thus was used as a gathering place.

Pandanus was another important tree crop, mainly on atolls of the Marshalls (Spoehr 1949; Bryan 1972), Nauru (Kayser 1934), and the Gilberts (Grimble 1933). Special cultivars were selected for the type of fruit that they bore, sweetness, and time of ripening. On Namu pandanus was in season from November through the end of December (NJP fieldnotes 1968–1969). Other varieties were cultivated for their leaves,

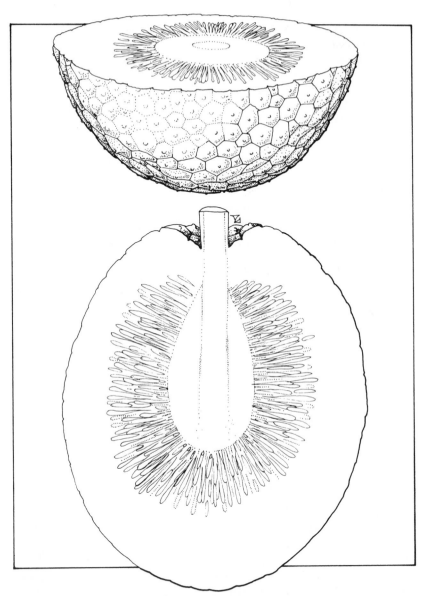

Figure 26. Cross-section of a breadfruit. Drawing by Tim Galloway, after Ellis 1777:2

which were (and are) extensively used in making roof thatch, mats, and other handicrafts.

Bananas, though sometimes classified as a tree crop, were planted mainly with the garden crops. On Niue old shifting cultivation sites could be identified by the banana plants that were still bearing where they had been planted around the edges (NJP fieldnotes 1976; Sykes, pers. comm. 1978). The *feʻi* bananas of Tahiti were grown mainly in sheltered valleys.

Forest Sources of Food

On high islands throughout the Pacific, forests have been a source of wild fruits and roots; these are sometimes referred to as forest or bush foods. Wild yams (*Dioscorea pentaphylla* and other species) were used when other food crops were exhausted or damaged by storm. Similarly *ivi* or Polynesian chestnut *(Inocarpus edulis)*, *vi* or Kafika apple *(Spondia dulcis)*, *dawa (Pommetia pinnata)*, and perhaps mango and oranges were all to be found in the forests of Fiji, Samoa, and Rarotonga. All of these may have been planted a long time ago, perhaps when populations were larger. People are still harvesting the oranges planted years ago by European settlers that now grow wild in the interior of Tahiti and Rarotonga (NJP fieldnotes 1984). Foods from the forest have never been the main source of supply but rather have served as an emergency food source when the cultivated crops and tree crops have been damaged by hurricanes or tidal waves.

The area of land designated as bush or forest land is usually located in the interior, mountainous parts of high islands and the so-called unused areas of low islands. The term "forest" may not represent the kind of vegetation but rather the kind of access rights that people have to that land. Pohnpeians called this forest area *nanwoal,* which Shimizu translates as "wild forests" (1982:163). Forest land is land to which specific lineage rights are not usually applicable.

Also the margins between forest land and shifting cultivation areas are not clear cut. As population sizes have changed over time, more or less land has been needed to feed those people. If secondary growth on a recuperating agricultural plot is left for fifteen to twenty years it becomes harder to distinguish old shifting agricultural plots from forest areas (Sykes, pers. comm. 1976). When population increases, the forest boundary may be pushed back to plant more gardens (Pollock 1986b).

Forests and agricultural sites merge into one another as sources of food. They must be considered as parts of one system when looking at how a society has used its land to maintain itself over time (Pollock 1986b). Too often only one aspect has been examined—the potential for increased production and for cash return—and the wider social obligations have been ignored or relegated as less important than the economic potential. However, it is just these flexible boundaries between gardens and bush or forest that have enabled island populations to feed themselves, expanding the gardens when they needed more food and leaving the secondary growth to regenerate when they needed less.

LANDHOLDING SYSTEMS

Access to land use in most societies is controlled by membership in kin groups. That membership allows particular persons to make particular use of their group's holdings. Sometimes those lands are specifically named. Membership in kin groups holding land confers both use rights and rights of inheritance. Access to land may also be transferred by gift or grant from a chief or other persons in that society. A third mode of access is by sale or lease, or by deed of registration. Thus kinship ties and links between various stratified groups in a society are two important factors governing access to land.

Land rights are used as a means of classification indicating the association between named persons and named lands. Studies of French Polynesian land rights have shown that a major distinction exists between rights of use and rights of control. Rights of use include the right to construct a *fare* on family land and right of residence, the right to cultivate some living plants, and the right to share in fruits of plants such as coconuts and coffee. These rights are held in common by a group of brothers and sisters and their descendants (Ravault 1979:28, 21) and are thus controlled mainly by genealogical heritage, under the chief of the area. The same distinction is found in other parts of the Pacific (see Crocombe 1971, 1987; Lundsgaarde 1974).

Namu

Every Namu person is born into a matrilineage and thereby by birth has rights to use the designated plots belonging to the matrilineal kin group. They share those rights with their sisters and brothers and their mother, and her sisters and brothers. If a woman wants to change residence she has several places she can consider, as long as the land is controlled by her matrilineage. She and her spouse and children can then take up residence with another set of kin.

Similarly, if she wants to make copra to earn some extra cash, she can do so on certain named plots belonging to her lineage. Another choice might be to use the spouse's matrilineal land, though that may not be acceptable to his kin if they already have a large group using the land. Population increase has meant that some large sibling sets are putting considerable pressure on Namu's restricted land resources.

Pohnpei

Pohnpeians' classification of land has been discussed by Bascom (1965), Riesenberg (1968), Hughes (1968), and Shimizu (1982). Shimizu emphasizes the local system within wider aspects of their world view. He demonstrates the links that Pohnpeians make between food concepts, concepts of space, and the social order. He shows how this world view is based on a customary code that is shared by all Pohnpeians and that incorporates ties of respect, honor, and authority between the people and their political leaders. This code is demonstrated in the kinds of work that are necessary in order to make contributions to a feast or present tribute to a chief. Shimizu contrasts three kinds of work a Pohnpeian is expected to perform—domestic work, subsistence work, and works of honor (1982:159). These three kinds of work yield different kinds of foods. By means of these categories he provides us with "an analysis of this selective usage of various plants and animals in the Ponapean lifestyle" (Shimizu 1982:162).

In their view Pohnpeians get food from two distinct areas of their island, the mountainous areas, abandoned land, and wild forests as distinct from the flat areas near the shore where the cultivated land is found. From the mountains and forests they can get certain foods such as wild yams but these can be used only for domestic food—they should not be given at feasts or as tribute to a chief. They rely on these foods in the season when cultivated foods are scarce (Shimizu 1982:170). From the cultivated land near the shore they get most of their foods by means of subsistence work. But cultivated foods are destined both for subsistence and tribute; that is, first fruits of both breadfruit and yams are given to the chiefs. In addition first fruits of pandanus and mango are presented as seasonal tributes. A second class of tribute includes a portion of the first crops of a new harvest of *Colocasia* taro, *Cyrtosperma* taro, banana, sugar cane, and kava. Thus respect and social commitment are shown by making a public presentation of the first of whatever was grown on subsistence land; no such presentation was necessary for food gathered wild in the mountains or forest. Shimizu's interpretation is that "among traditionally utilized plants and animals, the Ponapean culture . . . has found a sharp contrast between the wild and the domesticated" (1982:168). Only the latter has honor value.

Shimizu also describes another Pohnpeian contrast, that between the wild forests or *nanwoal* and the humanized areas (subsistence land), *nansapw* (1982:168) The seasonal crops are more evident on *nansapw* (Shimizu 1982:179). In the rainy months there is a plentiful supply of fruit, especially breadfruit, on which the people can live almost exclusively. But in the dry months some of the daily domestic food supply may come from the wild forests, as well as from the yams. The term for the dry season, *rahk,* means "abundant food" or vast amounts of a plant (Shimizu 1982:173). (In Marshallese it also means the "good" season, that is, plenty of starch foods and plenty of fish [NJP fieldnotes 1968–1969].)

Thus both for day-to-day living and for tributes and feasts Pohnpeians make use of their cultivated land. They plant their breadfruit, mango, and pandanus trees in the cultivated areas and use these mainly in the *rahk* season of plenty. Yam, swamp taro, *Colocasia* taro (irrigated), kava, sugar cane, and banana are also planted in those cultivated areas (Shimizu 1982:179). Only the yam is heavily used for both home consumption and for tribute and feasts. Work is concentrated on the cultivated land; the amount of work needed to produce food is much greater for the root crops than the tree crops.

It is clear from Shimizu's description that Pohnpeians view their land as representing links between themselves and other parts of their social system. Their land is more than just a place that produces good things to eat and things to present as tribute. It plays an important part in their total view of life. He shows how yams and breadfruit are the most socially valued foodstuffs, mainly for their ceremonial (that is, political) meaning, though they are also the main constituents of subsistence diet. He says: "We have hitherto proceeded, just as the Ponapeans do, in a centripetal way to search for what is politically evaluated as higher and/or highest. We should consider in a centrifugal way the political significance of what is more or less excluded from the already analysed political usage" (Shimizu 1982:196). He follows this with an analysis of mankind, gods, and the land. He concludes his study by contrasting the tributes of yams to chiefs as one mode of exploitation of nature with that of food tributes to the gods as another mode of exploitation; he shows similar parallels for the breadfruit. One point of difference is the amount of work involved.

Mo'orea

On the island of Mo'orea in French Polynesia, Robineau has made a careful study of the social and economic uses of land. The village of Ma'atea is interesting because it has been studied at a crucial point in time, between 1966–1967 and 1974. "Ma'atea illustrates an economic organization on the threshold of which is mingled traditional elements and modern elements" (NJP translation of Robineau 1984, 1:338). Change in this village has come about through what he terms autochthonous thinking and the local people's constructs (Robineau 1984, 1:33).

He distinguishes three parts to the village: the village site, the coconut littoral, and the valley, together with the lagoon and sea as a fourth part. The people of Ma'atea use their village sites mainly for their houses and courtyards; these are surrounded by ornamental plants, breadfruit and citrus trees, and some coconuts. Taro fields are placed on the edge of the village in the bed of the river. The coconut area is dominated by three or four large sections (about 78 hectares) belonging now to "demis" (people who are part Tahitian and part French), and 40 hectares is in small holdings. Not much copra is made today (Robineau 1984, 1:271). In the valley sites, evidence of former cultivation is visible as well as remains of vanilla and coffee plantations and remains of *marae* and carved *tiki* images, but use of this area has declined as the population has diminished (Robineau 1984, 1:272). The valley is an important area from which households obtain supplementary supplies.

In his analysis Robineau distinguishes the subsistence level from the salaried level of the village economy. The subsistence level ("auto-consommation") has stayed dominant, somewhat surprisingly, despite the opportunities offered for salaried jobs mainly associated with the setting up of the CEP (Centre d'Experimentation Pacifique) nuclear testing program. The sibling group, *'opu ho'e,* was the main group concerned with rules of land division and allocation of resources. Exchanges between households were an important part of these "relations of subsistence."

Six factors in Polynesian economic ideology apply to household use of land and resources here on Mo'orea: *arofa* or respect for others, *tauturu* or mutual aid, *feti'i* or kinship sentiment, *'opu ho'e* or relations between kin, strict reciprocity, and prestige (Robineau 1984, 1:322). He suggests that these principles are still operating, even now that the economy is based on a mixture of traditional agriculture, salaried work, and tourism (Robineau 1984, 1:447). Thus the land is still very important to these people, but for new ends.

These three case studies serve to demonstrate that land may be classified either explicitly or implicitly, but that those divisions are closely linked to the means of obtaining food and its wider social uses. They help us in understanding the symbolic importance of food in the social system. The Pohnpeian case study shows how spatial organization is deeply imbedded in their world view.

The importance of control over land use has been much discussed in the literature. But Western views of land, starting from the individual's rights and looking at land as an economic entity only, still fail to take into account the local customs and so miss the symbolic attributes of land and attachments to it.

Social control over land use has been necessary over a considerable time, perhaps since the first settlers arrived on the islands. As a result, the rights of one group to use particular areas have come into conflict with the rights of others. Particularly contentious has been the area behind the shoreline and the lower parts of the valleys that were most heavily used; they were generally the most fertile areas. One form of conflict was whether to use that flat area for building houses or for growing crops. Since these shoreline areas were generally small in acreage, the most desirable spots must have been in high demand. Other conflicts arose between different groups, each believing the right to use those areas belonged to it exclusively. Hence social control of access became necessary.

Access to both residence sites and growing sites throughout the Pacific has been regulated through extended families. The sibling group was the main controlling group, as Schneider has recently shown us in his rethinking of the Yapese *tabinaw*, or extended family. He has reexamined the descent model, which for some thirty years has dominated the anthropological view of kinship, in order to place more emphasis on the sibling set. For him, kinship includes the relations between land and people (Schneider 1984). Robineau too has stressed the importance of the sibling group in the Societies, where the *'opu ho'e* is the main group that controls the land. And on Namu also, access to land is shared with siblings born of the same mother; these rights were formerly designated matrilineage rights (Spoehr 1957; Mason 1951; Tobin 1958). Thus we are now seeing how groups around a sibling set play a key role in linking people to their land.

LAND USE AND CONTROL, PAST AND PRESENT

Use of land was under strict control of designated groups in each society (Table 11). Rights were either inherited or received by designation for services rendered. Alienation of land to anyone outside the specified social groups has been strongly resisted, even down to the present day. In general the rights that any one person held were rights of access rather than rights of outright ownership (Lundsgaarde 1974; Crocombe 1987).

Access rights allowed people to use land in several different ways: (1) village areas, or places where the community has established residences; (2) gardens, forests, and bush areas used as sources of food and firewood; (3) individual trees such as breadfruit and pandanus, rights of access to which are separate from the land on which they stand; (4) irrigated plots or pondfields.

Residence plots have tended to become clustered in village areas either because of the pull of the church or for ease of political administration. In Tonga the designation of a man's right to a residence site was built into an 1885 ordinance, and garden areas were also carefully controlled by

Island(s)	Cultivated Land		Irrigated Fields or Swamp (sw)	Non-Cultivated Land: Forest or Bush/Wild	Source
	Gardens	Trees			
Cooks, No.	nd	c,i	nd	c	Buck 1927
Cooks, So.	c	c,i	c,i	c	Buck 1927
Easter	c	none	none	none	Routledge 1919
Ellice/Tuvalu	nd	c	c(sw)	c	David 1899
Fiji	c	c	c	c	Nayacakalou 1978
Futuna	c	c	c	c	Burrows 1936
Gilberts	nd	c	c(sw)	c	Lambert 1980
Guam	i/c	c	?	nd	Safford 1905
Hawai'i	c	c	c	c	Handy and Handy 1972
Kapingamarangi	nd	c	c(sw)	c	Lieber 1974
Kosrae	c	?	c(sw)	c	Wilson 1968
Mangareva	c	nd	nd	nd	Laval 1938
Marianas	c	c	c	c	Thompson 1945
Marquesas	nd	i	nd	c	Linton 1939
Marshalls	c	c	c(sw)	c	Tobin 1958
Nauru	none	c,i	none	c,i	Kayser 1934
Niue	c	i	nd	c	Loeb 1926
Palau	c	c	c	c	McCutcheon 1985a
Pitcairn	nd	nd	nd	nd	
Pohnpei	c	c,i	c(sw)	c	Bascom 1965
Rapa	c	i	c	c	Hanson 1970
Rotuma	c	c	c	c	Howard 1964
Samoa	c	c	c	c	Shore 1982
Tahiti/ Mo'orea	c	c	c	c	Morrison 1790
Tokelau	nd	h	c	c	Huntsman 1978
Tonga	h	c	nd	c	Maude 1971
Truk and atolls	c	i	c(sw)	c	Mahony 1960
Wallis	c	c	c	c	Burrows 1937
Woleai	c	i	c(sw)	c	Alkire 1965
Yap	c	c	c(sw)	c	Owen ca. 1965

i = Individual holding; c = communal/extended family holding; h = household holding.

specific rights of access; use of forest areas was less rigidly controlled (Maude and Sevele 1987).

Irrigated plots, whether of *Colocasia* taro or *Cyrtosperma* taro, were usually large communal areas and thus more difficult to subdivide. In Makin/Butaritari (Gilberts) where *Cyrtosperma* was grown in swampy pits, each social group had its rights to a portion of the pit; yet the pit as a whole was maintained by the community as a whole (Sewell 1977).

Access rights to trees bearing fruit crops were frequently specifically designated and separately controlled from the land on which they stood. Thus rights to pick breadfruit and pandanus (fruits or leaves) belonged to the descendants of the person(s) who planted them; those rights may be different from the rights to the land on which they stood (Wedgwood 1936 for Nauru; Ravault 1979 for the Societies; Burrows 1936 for Futuna). This became a problem when coconut trees represented a cash income. Bananas were regarded as cultivated crops rather than as trees, as they reproduced annually.

Control over access to these areas of useful land has changed markedly as populations have decreased and increased over time and as new crops such as copra, vanilla, coffee, and cocoa have become lucrative. See Table 12 for land control in recent times. Much of the land on the islands of the Pacific is still held by communal rights, despite pressures to individualize them. Cash crops have competed with subsistence crops for use of the best land, which has led to further contentions within the land-holding system (Crocombe 1987).

Garden plots have probably changed most in size and importance. Shortage of land for shifting agriculture plots has become a problem, particularly in Tonga where a system started in the 1880s of granting 8¼-acre plots to every male reaching his sixteenth birthday has cut across what was probably a more flexible pre-European system. European views of land tenure and how rights should be allocated have tended to restrict the amount of land available.

The locus of control over land is in a set of mutually agreed-upon beliefs and practices shared by members of that society. In some Pacific societies the locus of control appears to be very centralized—in one king as in Tonga, or in three *tui* as in the Samoas, or in four *ariki* in Tikopia. In the Marshalls there were some twelve paramount chiefs, *iroij*, controlling the pieces of land on twenty-six atolls. On Namu four of these chiefs were recognized authorities over named pieces of land. They could demand food from the land as tribute; only one did so in fact. And they received a proportion of the cash received for copra made from coconut trees on their lands.

The nature of the ties between the chief and the people who use the

TABLE 12. Types of Kinship Group and Controlling Authority
in Island Land-Control Systems

Island Group	Kinship Group	Controlling Authority
Cook Islands	bilateral group	*ariki* (chief and head of extended family)
Fiji	*mataqali* (extended family) and *yavusa* (lineage)	*roko tui* (district chief) and *turaga ni koro* (village chief)
French Polynesia	bilateral group	head of extended family
Futuna	bilateral group	head of extended family and king of either Alo or Sigave
Kiribati	*kainga* (family)	*boti* (bilateral extended family)
Kosrae	sons, but matrilineal sibs	lineage head
Marshall Islands	matrilineage	clan under *alab* (land manager)
Nauru	matrilineage	*temonibe* (leaders of extended family)
Pohnpei	matrilineage	clan head
Tonga	males inherit, also daughters	village noble and king
Truk	matrilineage	clan head
Wallis	bilateral group	head of extended family, district chief, and the Lavelua (king)
Western Samoa	*'aiga* (extended family)	*matai* (family chief)

lands may be direct or indirect. In the Marshalls a tie of pseudo-kinship provided the tie between an *iroij* (chief) and his *rijerbal* (workers). They expected him to allocate the land that was the basis of their life—a place to live and bear children, to plant breadfruit, pandanus, and taro, and a place to bury one's kin; thus a place where ancestral spirits live and surround the living (Pollock 1974:100–129). The ties between the people and a chief were built around a total relationship, not just economic or political concerns. He gave and they received. They had needs; he met them.

But any one Marshallese was likely to have access rights to land under the control of more than one chief, as well as to have pieces of different size and productivity. A Marshallese usually inherited land from his or her mother, but could also inherit some from his or her father or other relative, or be given a piece for services to an *iroij* (Pollock 1974). These flexibilities built into the system enabled a small society to manage its land and the products of it for maximum satisfaction.

In Western Samoa the *matai* and the *'aiga* (extended family) that he heads are the key people who manage the land by consensus. This system is still operating today. The family that works the village land selects one of its members to take on the named title specific to its group. A *matai* is usually male, though there are one or two female *matai*. The *matai* is expected to look after the rights of the family members, to defend them against others who may wish to usurp their rights, and today, to make sure some profit is made from their land so that the family meets its desired ends. The *matai* and his *'aiga* thus share a mutual respect, and land is part of that expression. Consolidation may take the form of gifts of food and fine mats to another *'aiga* or village. Those gifts bear the givers' honor and respect. The system is becoming more individualized as separate nuclear families wish to retain cash profits from their labors for themselves (O'Meara 1987). Disputes over rights to particular lands and failure to meet obligations are now referred to the Lands Court; formerly they would have been resolved by consensus of the *matai* in the *fono* (political meeting).

These two examples demonstrate that land use has been carefully structured within the kinship framework but with certain flexibilities that allow for some of the major demographic changes and political turnarounds that have marked these societies over time. The trend toward more individualized ownership, although mainly still within the family group, is a response to modern cash demands as well as to increases in population. Maintaining access to land has persisted as a major concern in all Pacific Island societies, for without land the people have no food.

Land Use Classification: Western Views

Various other distinctions of land use in the Pacific have been made, such as those between agriculture and horticulture (Yen 1980b; Irwin 1980) and between agriculture and gathering (e.g., Hunt 1949). For example, for Samoa, Fox and Cumberland (1962) identified five areas of Samoan village agriculture: (1) village—for breadfruit, coconuts, and occasionally *ta'amu*, or taro; (2) coconut zone; (3) mixed crop zone; (4) taro zone; (5) forest. Only the mixed crop zone and taro zone were cultivated by shifting cultivation. Robineau (1984) has identified four similar areas for the village of Ma'atea on Mo'orea. Yen has used the terms "integral subsistence systems," "mixed subsistence–cash cropping systems," and "the plantation mode" when considering prehistoric land use patterns (1980b:73–74). While these divisions may be useful for comparisons with other geographical areas, they need also to be considered alongside the local distinctions in land use.

The label "agriculture" is particularly problematical when applied to land use where shifting cultivation has been the dominant mode of production. For some the term "agriculture" is applied only to field agriculture and monocropping; it does not include shifting cultivation where the area cropped is constantly changing and a mix of crops is planted. But for others shifting cultivation may be considered an incipient form of agriculture incorporating the techniques of domestication and cultivation.

Hutterer has carefully distinguished domestication from cultivation in his examination of early subsistence patterns in Southeast Asia (1983: 177). He uses the term "domestication" for human manipulation of the gene pool of a food item; "cultivation" is human manipulation of the environment. He argues that *Colocasia* taro and yams have been domesticated into many varieties in the Pacific; in so doing several forms of cultivation have been developed. Gardens, irrigated terraces, and shifting cultivation are all forms of cultivation. They can be contrasted with harvesting tree products and gathering roots and other crops growing wild in the forests.

Other Pacific prehistorians and ethnobotanists have applied their own classifications to subsistence systems. They distinguish arboriculture from horticulture and agriculture. They also place considerable emphasis on the distinction between wetland and dryland systems (Barrau 1965a; Spriggs 1982). Wetland systems tend to leave more evidence in the form of irrigation ditches, as Kirch (1985) and others have shown for Hawai'i. Implicit in this categorization there appears to be a built-in assumption that irrigated systems are technologically more advanced than dryland systems and thus were developed later in time. Thus growing irrigated taro is considered a later and more advanced form of agriculture than dryland production. However, Hunter-Anderson (1981/1984) has shown from her archeological investigations and evaluation of land use in Yap during the twentieth century that these people elected to cultivate dryland taro and to let their irrigation facilities become redundant. And that was despite population regeneration and pressure on food resources.

The relative position in time of wetland to dryland systems raises the issue of whether wet rice cultivation commenced before taro was cultivated as a subsistence crop in the Indo-Pacific region (see Pollock 1983b for other references). Yen has suggested that the people who carried horticulture into the Pacific did so from Southeast Asia prior to the full adoption of a rice-dominant agriculture: "the inference [is] that rice could not have been fully domesticated at that time" based on what we know of New Guinea prehistory (Yen 1980a:141).

Spriggs (1982) has summarized the main lines of argument in the debate as to which came first into Oceania, rice or taro. He concludes from his own fieldwork in Aneityum that techniques of pondfield agriculture for *Colocasia* taro were transferred into the Pacific before rice became a staple in island Southeast Asia. Thus the wetland/dryland distinction is a linking factor between the Pacific and Southeast Asia; it is also important when considering the origins of Pacific food plants. Was *Colocasia* taro domesticated before rice, or were both cultivated in Southeast Asia contemporaneously? Did taro enter the Pacific first, or was it rice?

It is not easy to establish direct evidence because these plants leave little material that lasts. However, in the northwest part of the Pacific, we do know from early Spanish reports that rice was in use in Guam in the sixteenth century. A crew member from Magellan's ship who stayed behind after its 1521 visit later reported seeing rice growing on Saipan (Pollock 1983b). However, we have no evidence as yet that rice was cultivated farther east than the Marianas. Thus at the time of contact both taro and rice were being grown and eaten in this area. It is important then that we look closely at Guam or Palau as a possible entry point for plants from Southeast Asia, an alternative theory to that based on a New Guinea entry point.

Much emphasis is currently being placed on an association between irrigated taro and chiefly control, as prehistorians seek to build models of early (pre-contact) social systems (Kirch 1984; Cordy 1984; Earle and Erikson 1977). Because irrigation or pondfield systems leave more tangible evidence of their existence in the past than do dryland cultivation techniques, I would argue that their importance has been exaggerated. An alternative approach may get around this problem.

By asking the question of how *Colocasia* taro was used in the social system, we can establish its importance among all the starchy foodstuffs in the consumption patterns of each of the various islands under study at various time periods from 1521 to the present. Taro grown on wetlands was of major significance in the food habits of people of only two societies of the Pacific, Hawai'i and Rapa (see Table 10). Some irrigated taro was also grown in Rarotonga, Tahiti, and Wallis and Futuna, and even in northern parts of New Zealand at least in the 1800s (Matthews 1985). Elsewhere, as in Fiji, taro *(dalo)* was important in the diet, but it was not necessarily irrigated. In Wallis and Futuna taro and yams were both important, and only some of the taro was irrigated. Other starches such as yams in Tonga and Pohnpei and breadfruit in Tahiti, Truk, and the Marquesas were predominant in those agricultural systems.

Production systems have also been examined by tracing language changes over time. Linguists have tabulated many of the terms used in Pacific subsistence systems, including plant names and terms for cultivation practices. Using comparative methods they have reconstructed a set of terms associated with subsistence practices for proto-forms of the present-day languages (see Appendix B). These proto-Austronesian and proto-Oceanic forms afford one indication that some of the staples, such as three of the taros, yams, breadfruit, and bananas, have been significant subsistence crops since before contact (French Wright 1983).

Thus we have several tools for assessing the relative importance of what are labeled agricultural or horticultural products. Their part in the daily and ceremonial usage patterns must be considered as part of different production features. These various academic modes of classifying food production are here considered as secondary to those derived from local classification systems because they are based (1) on Western modes of production, emphasizing technology; (2) on a Western concept of food, mainly cereal based, and hence involving field agriculture; (3) on Western views of ecology or environment; and (4) on a fixed form of land use. They take no account of local criteria of food use and production.

The Question of Commercial Uses of Land

Pacific Island farmers today face the dilemma of whether to use their land to supply household needs or to generate cash income (Pollock 1986b). During the 1960s Europeans were pressuring for land to be used more advantageously—that is, to produce export crops. But land is still an important source of food for at least half the population of any Pacific Island nation today, in spite of urbanization (Crocombe 1987).

In the 1980s island governments sought to balance the growing reliance on imported food with more reliance on food self-sufficiency within each island nation. The move is toward more independence from financial burdens and trade imbalances.

In colonial times, much tropical agricultural research was directed at improving the varieties and output of cash crops such as copra, coffee, and cocoa. Consequently the subsistence aspect was neglected (Macnaught 1982). This has meant that new varieties of taros and yams have not been developed (Sivan 1983), nor have the acreages been increased to keep pace with the needs of the increasing number of landless people living in towns. So supply has fallen short of demand and prices have risen. Fisk has pointed out the contrast between the traditional agricultural techniques of production and a Western-type commercial farm model in these terms: "The question is whether it is still necessary, or even desirable, that the traditional institutions evolved for the production of root crops should be replaced with foreign institutions on the purely commercial model, or whether it is possible to adapt what is already there to make a more acceptable alternative that will nevertheless effectively provide the urban food supplies required" (1978:20). These alternative models are being weighed by each of the independent governments.

The South Pacific Agricultural Survey (SPAS), a major study of this problem in six South Pacific countries under the auspices of the Asian Development Bank, has recommended ways to make agriculture more efficient and effective. Its recommendations for increasing size of holdings and improved management systems have reaped a harvest of criticism both from the governments concerned and from academic agricultural specialists. The SPAS report suggested that the plantation mode would be more efficient than the smallholder system and would allow for better management (Ward and Proctor 1980). However, Hardaker, Fleming, and Harris (1984) deny this, saying that smallholders are more responsive to innovations suitable to their needs and aspirations, and that semi-subsistence is resilient and flexible. Further, to replace the smallholder system would impose high social costs. They suggest that a new marketing structure needs to be developed that is more suited to smallholder production. The main concern of these authors is whether communal ownership results in the most efficient use of the land. And that question comes down to whether land should be used for growing food crops such as taro and breadfruit for a society's own consumption, or for growing cash crops such as coffee and cocoa so that the nation can build up its exports and the producers can use the money realized. Land as a basis of people's identity, carrying strong symbolic values and emotional bonds, is not considered among these arguments.

Yen's suggestions as part of the SPAS report state that

> A variety of concerns related to developmental planning of agriculture are at issue. Where there is a shortage of land simply through the physical size of islands or through high population area ratios, the strategies available for import substitution by the cultivation of traditional staples are limited to the intensification of small-scale farming. This may or should include the regeneration of past agronomic practices. However, where environmental constraints can accommodate the requirements of efficient large-scale, machine assisted operation, the nature of the alternative choices for land use in terms of cash/export objectives may raise other questions about the wisdom of export substitution. (1980b:212–213)

Yen further questions whether the economic arguments for profitability of land use should dominate the social issues of identity and traditional ties associated with a variety of uses of land including cash cropping.

Agriculture departments throughout the Pacific are trying to rectify the neglect of subsistence crops, which was based in part on a view that expected imported food to supersede local food. But canned and frozen goods cost too much at both the household and the national level. Now the priorities are being reversed and the call is for efforts to upgrade the root crops program (see Ferrando 1981). The work of tropical agriculturists, such as Sivan (1977), Chandra (1979a, 1979b, 1980) for Fiji, and Coursey (1978) at the Tropical Agriculture Institute in London, is now receiving the recognition it deserves in helping to support the greater development of subsistence agriculture. This discussion reflects the difficulties of assessing the best ways of producing crops such as taro and yams to meet the demands of a cash market. At the consumer end, for a family living in a town such as Suva or Apia, a concern is cost. But behind these economic concerns are also social concerns about the quality of life. The big question is, How can individuals reconcile their lifestyles with the many social obligations with which they are faced? And, What impact does the answer have on future uses of the land?

This decision is based in part on the extent of household needs and in part on the quality and location of the land. For those who have land with good soil close to transport to market centers such as Suva, Tongatapu, Apia, or Avarua, selling those root crops can bring a good return and may be more profitable than growing crops just for household use. But if the land is not very productive, requires fertilizer to give any yield, and if the market connections are distant, irregular and costly, then the land may be better used for home supply. With too many uncertainties, plus the costs of middlemen, the taro farmer could end up paying out rather than gaining a cash return.

The choice between selling one's produce or using it for household consumption depends not only on cash flow and factors such as amounts available and transport facilities, but also on the personal values and preferences of household members. Taro, for instance, can bring A$5 to A$10 per bundle or basket in the market. A 20-kilo sack of rice may cost $16 or $18 and last a household for a week. So if that farmer has plenty of taro to sell, he may prefer to buy some rice and thus vary his diet while also gaining some profit from his taro.

Selection between alternative ways of using the land is a very complex problem and requires a market knowledge that may not be available to the farmer. She or he has to decide between planting traditional food crops such as taro, yams, or sweet potato or planting cash crops such as cocoa, coffee, or sugar cane, of which very little can be used to feed the household. At first glance the cash crops may seem more attractive, since the work looks easier and the financial return is good; farmers can turn the cash realized into a wide range of foodstuffs and other purchases. But they may end up spending more of that cash on food items than they feel they should. With a minimal cash income they are likely to be locked into what Robineau (1984) has termed "alimentary dependency" for the people of a Mo'orea village.

These alternatives, by no means new, have existed for some one hundred years. Only the scale is different, particularly with more need for versatile cash. In early times the produce of the land was in demand by

Western visitors who needed the local foods to provision a ship or maintain a mission family. Such sales on an individual basis seemed very small scale, but as visits by Europeans increased and more people were living in the towns, these sales became a vital part of the way of life. And in the 1980s, as Chandra argues, "root crops offer the best possibility to meet the demands for low-priced food crops from the urban poor" (1979b:79).

Today, the crucial question is how to make the best use of the land and of the labor available to work that land in order to obtain at least a small amount of cash. Desai has argued that commercial crops are grown with labor surplus after subsistence requirements are met (1976:131). But the issue is not that clear cut. Rather, it is a question of the proportion of cash crops to subsistence crops that matters, given the land and labor time available and the market. Desai's study of three districts of Fiji showed that 8 percent of land was used for subsistence only, 23 percent mainly for subsistence, and 59 percent mainly for sales. He concluded that, while root cultivation is an efficient use of land, the returns did not warrant the amount of land being allotted for cash crops. Why, we must ask, have farmers been urged to plant cash/export crops instead of getting support for their subsistence crops?

Labor is a key issue. Agriculture is still the main occupation of a large sector of the population (see Table 14 for the proportion of those active in the non-cash economy), despite increasing urbanization and the growth of the service sector in particular. The degree to which those who state agriculture as their occupation are committed to cash cropping as distinct from producing for home consumption, however, is not widely known. Nor do we have precise figures on the area of land used for subsistence or cash income. Even in Fiji where agricultural economists such as Chandra have been working, "it is unclear exactly what proportion of root crops is marketed for cash" (1979b:79). This kind of data may be difficult to obtain because farmers vary their growing patterns during the year to meet what they know of market demands. The contribution of farmers either to food supply or to the cash income of household economy is very important, but barely quantifiable; however, some economists are now willing to put a cash value on the produce consumed by a household from its own land (Fisk 1978; Duttaroy 1980).

Since in many cases some family members are living in towns or overseas, these families can no longer depend on the regular help of a large number of kin for planting and harvesting. They may be mobilized only for a major clearing job. But the everyday maintenance of weeding and pruning or fertilizing must be done by members of the household. With so many in the 18–40 age group away, all the productive activities fall on the few adults remaining. So when planting, a man has to bear in mind that the number and size of his taros or yams will depend on how much time he or his wife can spend weeding and clearing the plantation.

A fortunate few people, mainly on Niue and Rarotonga, are able to combine their plantation work with a regular salaried position. They can gather a few taros or *kumara* (sweet potatoes) on the way home from work or in the evenings and spend Saturdays with the family clearing and planting (Pollock 1977b). In Tonga one informant told me how he and his father, both of whom have jobs in town, bicycle in the evenings to their plantation and weed or plant or harvest their *kumara,* tomatoes, and capsicums to sell. He says he took up this activity to help lose weight and found it more productive than jogging.

It is only recently that Pacific governments have come to support multicropping. By this system the farmer can plant some coffee trees and some cane, and also grow taro, bananas, or sweet potatoes on the same plot. He may get less cash from his cash crop, but he is assured of some foods for the household. Chandra is of the opinion that "agricultural production systems with tropical root crops as the major staple components should now be receiving more research attention since they offer the better potential gains in energy output and are also capable of releasing more resources, especially land, for the production of cash crops and for high protein crops which can supplement the farmer's diet as well as providing increased cash income" (1980:13). As the population grows Chandra expects indigenous Fijians to continue to utilize root crops as their major staple food and Indians to increase their consumption of root crops (1980:15).

Assistance in agricultural management was one of the major recommendations of the South Pacific Agricultural Survey (Ward and Proctor 1980). Specifically, advice on better marketing of all agricultural products and on growing subsistence crops as well as cash crops were identified as urgent needs if Pacific nations were to make the best use of their land.

With increasing experience in marketing, both buying and selling crops, farmers in the Pacific are overcoming some of the earlier hazards of trying to gain a cash return for their traditional starch food crops. Problems of transport to markets, producing a regular supply, and the cut taken by middlemen are still present but are being overcome. Further assistance with these aspects of marketing has become available only in the last twenty years with the setting up of producer boards and special bodies such as Fiji's National Marketing Authority in 1977. The NMA has buying centers in Suva, Lautoka, and Labasa, and handles eighty-five products, of which taro accounted for 91.4 percent of root crops purchased in 1976. The authority buys for sale to urban areas. The price for taro varies between 11 and 14 Fijian cents per kilo (Baxter 1980).

The poor post-harvest storage life of taro, cassava, and sweet potatoes is yet another problem (Chandra 1979b:79). Those who can plant early-maturing varieties are finding that they can get an edge and thus command high prices before the market is saturated during the regular harvest season. The foresighted planter who plans skillfully can make considerable money with his root crop harvest. But if he sells all of it to reap maximum profit he may have to turn around and use the cash to buy high-priced imported foods, which may take up more of his cash in the long run.

Extension assistance to small farmers in the Pacific is also now available to those practicing multicropping so that they can improve both their subsistence crops (which may be sold) as well as their exportable cash crops (Sivan 1977 for Fiji; Wilson, Opio, and Cable 1984 for Western Samoa). The United Nations Food and Agriculture Organization's Root Crops Program is focusing its attention on this problem by assisting agricultural extension officers to develop programs to improve production of starch crops. The experimental plots at Alafua, Western Samoa, and now at Koronivia, Fiji, are designed to improve varieties of taro, yam, cassava, sweet potato, and *kape* cultigens to meet both production demands and consumption preferences. This assistance in improving production of the root crop starches with a view to meeting market demands is part of an overall program designed to reduce the high level of imports, especially of foodstuffs (see Chapter 8).

With this general move toward greater self-reliance in the area of food supply, the taros and similar crops are coming into their own again. I welcome this attempt to regenerate interest in the traditional starch foods. The South Pacific Commission's publication on taro is one indication of this work (Lambert 1982); Wang's book *Taro* (1983) shows the same lively interest in research on the problem. The research and seminars the FAO Root Crops Program has conducted have also served to draw attention to this neglected area. One of their seminars that I attended in December 1982 brought together those working in agricultural extension and focused only on these root crops, their production methods, diseases, and the potential for new processing techniques.

The work of the National Food and Nutrition Committees in Fiji, Tonga, and eventually in Western Samoa and Cook Islands is also designed to help each of these countries to meet as much of their own food needs from local supply as possible. Such encouragement for the small farmer is an important innovation. It is one indication that production concerns are being treated alongside consumption concerns.

SUMMARY

Land has a strong symbolic base. To people of the Pacific Islands, who are so dependent on their very small land areas, it has a wider significance than simply as a base for food production. It is embued with the spirits of the ancestors, and binds together those who share rights in it. It is the source of life, bringing forth the food that plays such a diverse and important part in these people's lives.

Production of food is only one form of land use. Land is locally conceptualized in terms of a general distinction between cultivated garden lands and bush. Other categories may be constructed locally to incorporate the needs of particular crops of significance, such as pondfields for irrigated taro. But these categories are based on different values from those associated with commercial uses of land.

Peoples' lives are ordered around appropriate planting and harvesting times to assure that crops will be ready when needed, and thus land is fundamental to the whole ritual cycle of life.

Control of access to land has been marked by flexibility. This has been necessary as population sizes have fluctuated over time. Today there is a tendency toward control resting with individual nuclear families, though extended families are still closely bound together for land issues.

Land, food production, and social relationships are closely intertwined.

8

Taro for Sale

PACIFIC ISLAND people living in towns have to buy much of their food because they have only occasional access to a traditional subsistence supply. But selling taro amounts to a breach of custom and borders on immorality, as Morton notes for Tonga (1987:62). Yet how else can those landless people get their traditional foodstuffs, especially if they are on a different island from that of their relatives? And the question arises whether urbanization is causing a move away from the use of local starches, or whether the cultural significance of those local starches will continue to be appreciated and valued in the urban households.

FOOD CHOICES IN TOWNS

Selection of foods by those living in towns is based generally on the same criteria as for those living in rural areas, but the decisions are more complex. The city dweller must decide between local or imported foods, taking into account costs, taste, status, time available, and so forth. All these factors become critical for the city dweller whose money is limited, and yet has many cultural commitments. Also, in town the variety of messages about food may cause confusion and questioning of certain values.

The rapid growth of towns since the 1950s has increased the numbers of people who must be fed, not directly from the land but from cash in the pocket (see Tables 13, 14). As people have moved either into urban areas or to settle overseas, they no longer have land to cultivate. Without land and the labor to produce crops, the supply of indigenous starch foodstuffs is uncertain. Furthermore, in the 1950s and 1960s it was expected that Western foods would become dominant for urban households, and planning tended to follow that thinking.

For ordinary day-to-day fare, those providing for a household must juggle several factors. In the back of their minds is the principle of "real

TABLE 13. Urban Growth in Selected Pacific Islands

Country	Date	Urban Area	Population	Annual Growth Rate (last two censuses)	Urban Percentage
Cook Islands	1976	Avarua	4,533	−3.9	25.0
Fiji	1976	Suva	117,827	3.9	
		Lautoka	28,847	3.1	
		Nadi	12,995	1.4	
		Labasa	12,956	2.9	
		Nausori	12,821	2.9	
		Ba	9,173	1.0	
		Sigatoka*	3,635	4.5	
		Levuka	2,764	−0.6	
		Savusavu	2,295	2.1	
		Vatukoula*	6,425	2.6	
		Rakiraki*	3,755	3.3	
		Navua	2,568	4.9	
		Tavua*	2,144	1.0	
		Korovou	290	−1.3	
		Total	*218,495*	*3.2*	37.2
Kiribati	1978	Urban Tarawa incl. Betio	18,116	4.3	32.0
Nauru	1977	All	7,254	1.7	100.0
Niue	1976	Alofi	960	0.1	26.8
Solomon Islands	1976	Honiara	14,942	4.9	
		Gizo (Is.)	1,847	3.5	
		Auki	1,225	2.9	
		Kirakira	561	—	
		Total	*18,575*	*4.6*	9.4
Samoa	1976	Apia	32,099	1.2	21.1
Tokelau		nil			nil
Tonga	1976	Nuku'alofa	18,312	1.7	
		Havelu Loto	2,243	5.3	
		Mu'a	3,969	1.3	
		Neiafu	3,308	−0.8	
		Total	*27,832*	*1.5*	30.1
Tuvalu	1979	Funafuti	2,191	20.3†	29.8

Source: Adapted from ESCAP 1982:10–11.
* Significant intercensal boundary changes.
† Due largely to repatriation from Kiribati following separation and independence.

TABLE 14. Population Data for Selected Pacific Islands, Late 1970s and Early 1980s

Island(s)	Census Year	Proportion of Population in Age Group (%)			Median age	Economically Active Proportion of Population 15–64 Years				Urban Population	
		0–14	15–64	65+		Total %		Cash economy %		Total %	Main center %
						M	F	M	F		
American Samoa	1980	40.9	56.2	2.9	18.8	69	38	55	31	40	35
Cook Islands	1981	42.7	52.9	4.4	17.7	52	48	32	14	27	27
Federated States of Micronesia	1980	46.4	50.1	3.5	16.7	70	33	33	16	26	8
Fiji	1976	41.1	56.4	2.5	18.6	86	18	nd	nd	37	20
French Polynesia	1983	42.0	55.1	2.9	20.1	75	36	nd	nd	59	57
Guam	1980	34.9	62.3	2.8	22.3	85	52	84	51	91	91
Kiribati	1985	38.9	57.6	3.6	19.7	89	48	30	10	33	33
Marshall Islands	1980	50.5	46.4	3.1	14.8	64	31	46	16	60	38
Nauru	1983	46.5	52.2	1.2	16.6	94	19	94	19	100	100
New Caledonia	1983	36.2	59.7	4.1	21.7	71	41	nd	nd	61	53
Niue	1981	46.1	47.3	6.6	16.6	78	29	60	24	21	21
Northern Mariana Islands	1980	40.6	56.5	2.9	19.7	81	51	80	50	94	87
Palau	1980	39.9	54.8	5.3	18.9	78	71	55	33	63	63
Papua New Guinea	1980	43.0	55.5	1.6	18.5	80	69	52	34	13	4
Pitcairn	1976	21.6	55.4	23.0	nd	nd	nd	nd	nd	none	none
Solomon Islands	1976	47.9	48.7	3.4	16.1	nd	nd	nd	nd	9	8
Tokelau	1981	41.1	51.7	7.3	20.2	69	31	44	18	none	none
Tonga	1976	44.4	52.2	3.3	17.4	72	14	22	7	26	20
Tuvalu	1979	31.8	63.1	5.1	22.2	93	78	38	12	30	30
Vanuatu	1979	45.7	51.5	2.9	17.1	46	41	nd	nd	18	13
Wallis and Futuna	1983	45.8	50.1	4.1	17.0	87	47	22	14	7	7
Western Samoa	1981	44.8	52.7	3.1	17.1	85	15	32	13	21	21

Source: Data from SPC 1987:49.

food" and its accompaniment. But cost is a restraint. And whatever food there is must stretch over three meals a day. So rice or bread and some form of meat, such as *sipi* (mutton flaps in Tongan) or *povi masima* (salt beef or brisket in Samoan), have become the basics for those who can afford them, either in Nuku'alofa and Apia or in New Zealand. Other foods such as cakes and doughnuts or fruit may be bought, but they are less satisfying than a good plateful of taro or yams. There is also the dilemma of status; for some it may be more important to be seen to be eating European foods, at whatever the cost, even to feeling hungry.

Bindon, studying two communities in American Samoa, found that the people of the village in Manu'a, which was what he called "outside the mainstream of modernization," bought 69 percent of the total number of food items used, while 30 percent were produced by the households and 1 percent were received as gifts or in exchanges. On Tutuila (including Pago Pago) he labeled the population more modernized because 85 percent of their food items were purchased, much from supermarkets. By comparison, a sample of the American Samoan community living in Hawai'i was found to use 92 percent purchased food. This study provides a useful list of foods consumed by each community; it is clear that the rural people of Manu'a ate a less varied diet, breadfruit being a main item, than either the Tutuila or Hawai'i populations (Bindon 1982).

Analysis of these data shows that people living in the traditional area ate more carbohydrates and took in more calories than those living in modified or modernized areas. But since most of American Samoa is mountainous with difficult terrain for growing subsistence crops and is considered more urbanized than other parts of the Pacific, this is not a clear case of Westernization of diet. On the contrary it is clear that American Samoans have not lost their love for taro; in the 1970s American Samoa became an importer of taro because its farmers were unable to meet local demand. People who might be farming were working at home for family businesses, so were supported by high wages. Shortage of land was also suggested as a reason, together with drought, in 1974 (Merrick 1977).

Poi made from taro has been marketed in Hawai'i since 1906 to meet the health needs of persons other than Polynesians, as well as to supply those Hawaiians who had no other access to *poi*. Much of the taro for *poi* is now grown on Kaua'i, Maui, and Hawai'i and sold to Hawaiians living on O'ahu. Most of them use it only once a week or less now. When asked about their attitude to *poi,* 88 percent liked it for its good taste and 85 percent regarded it as nutritious (Begley, Spielmann, and Vieth 1981). Its cost was a deterrent to more regular use.

Further information on food habits of Pacific Island populations living in urban centers is carefully documented for the Societies. Robineau's comparison of life in Mo'orea, a virtual suburb of Pape'ete, in 1967–1968 and 1974 notes that in the latter period the people of Ma'atea were eating more foods grown on their own land than purchased food. The reverse had been the case at the earlier period. As he viewed the change: "En dépit de certaines tendences, au niveau des maisonnées a compenser la limitation des dépenses par un recours à l'autoconsommation et aux produits tahitiens" (Robineau 1984, 1:336). So, contrary to expectations, their expenditure on food had not increased. Shortage of income had made them more self-reliant in terms of their own produce. Furthermore, he argues that their "alimentary acculturation" had diminished only a little; that is, they were eating a considerable amount of local food. For a society with a higher degree of dependence on European food than elsewhere in the Pacific, this is an interesting trend.

Producers also had new choices between growing crops for immediate household needs or increasing their crops in order to have some to sell, either through the local market or for export. The price the producer is going to get for taro after all the middlemen have taken their cuts also determines whether producing for the urban market is considered worthwhile. With the increase in size and number of towns, households have a wider range of foodstuffs to choose from, but limited by cost. To the existing inventory of five or more starchy foods, local greens and fruits, and fish, chicken, and pork, several new local crops have been added, such as cassava, *Xanthosoma* taro, and pumpkin. In addition imported foods such as rice, bread, potatoes, and canned and frozen foods can be bought. Decisions about the content of the daily diet are thus complex; they may depend on access to relatives who can supply the root crops, or on the dollars in the household purse.

Cost

The cost factor has tended to override other principles of food choice. A 20-kilo sack of rice may cost US$16 or $18 and last a household for one week. If that household sold a truckload of taro at $5 a bundle, they might realize $100 but then have to live on rice for a month. In five Papua New Guinea towns in 1981, "it cost the urban consumer less to obtain energy by buying rice than by buying domestically produced sweet potato, taro or cooking bananas." Moreover the cost of rice has changed little while the cost of these traditional staples increased significantly between 1971 and 1988 (Spencer and Heywood 1983:43). Thus the person shopping for the household must weigh traditional factors against pragmatic ones.

In Tonga in early 1982, a basket of yams (the most desirable food) cost T$11.50; in November 1985 a basket of yams in the market was marked at $30, and there were only a few baskets available (NJP field-notes 1985). Perhaps growers were holding them back for the Christmas market. In 1982 taro Futuna cost T$5.55 a basket and taro Tonga (*Colocasia* taro) cost $4.60 a basket. Cassava and sweet potatoes were the cheapest roots per kilo (Tu'ifua and Rathey 1982). So it is not surprising that these roots were selling in larger quantities than the others. In part these figures reflect the effects of the cyclone that hit Tonga in March 1982. Prices dropped slightly in the period May to August 1982 due to larger supply. Supply fluctuated not only within the year, but from year to year, as figures for total supply of the seven major root crops show in these market reports (Tu'ifua and Rathey 1982).

These fluctuating costs are hard on households with little cash income. Sometimes they may not be able to afford traditional foods and must settle for less-filling foods. So a major consideration for an urban family in Tonga is whether they can afford the cost of maintaining tradition by eating yams, even just once a week for Sunday lunch. Only the well paid are able to follow the traditional principles, while the poorly paid must eat bread and canned fish—if they are lucky. Taro and yams have become luxury foods.

One reason for the high cost of traditional foods is that farmers have not received support for growing subsistence crops. To meet urban demands for low-priced food crops Chandra recommends that the Fijian farming system, which has a high labor absorption capacity, be further encouraged with greater capital investments and cash inputs (1979a:98).

Amounts

Amounts of food used have also changed with urban living. When families have little cash, they can afford to buy only small amounts, so they have to reduce the amount they put on the table. They are thus experiencing a similar situation to one their ancestors faced when food was in short supply. But the effects of this recent pattern are more marked. If there is little cash, families will cut down the amount they are eating and buy cheap foods that go a long way (Crocombe 1985). They would be embarrassed to ask relatives to assist, as they would have done in former times when food was short. In the present-day situation the shortage of money to buy food may result in poor nutrition and long-term health problems. Cases of malnutrition in children are beginning to appear in some Pacific urban centers (Burgess and Burgess 1976). The feasts of former times are less frequent and so the opportunities for an occasional big feed occur less often.

Another factor affecting the amount eaten is the opppportunity to eat independently of the household. Family members who have a little cash may use it to buy take-aways—fast foods and drinks. Thus the shortfall in "real food" may be made up with snacks and other foods that taste good but don't satisfy. Also, in towns the clock becomes a factor guiding eating habits, rather than activities, as we saw in traditional consumption patterns. What money is available must be stretched to put something on the table three times a day. Furthermore a household may struggle to include meat in at least two of those meals, and that is the most expensive food, mainly because it is imported.

TRADE IN FOODSTUFFS

Trade with European visitors has been going on for some four hundred years. It began when explorers appeared, for example, Magellan on Guam in 1521 and Cook in Tahiti in 1769; they were seeking supplies of fresh food to replenish their depleted stores on board their ships. Pacific Islanders quickly learned they could obtain nails, axes, and other metal goods in return for their pigs, fish, and bananas (Wilkes 1845; Forbes 1875). These newcomers provided a new outlet for local produce and promoted the husbandry of pigs.

As a consequence food took on a new meaning. The local people discovered the advantages of planting just a little extra on their land; and they found they could obtain a good "price" for their goods (see Maude's discussion [1968] of the pork trade in Tahiti, and Ward's discussion of bêche de mer trade in Fiji [1972]). They also found that with repeated visits, these foreigners began to place heavy demands on resources, including firewood. Since those times, the volume of exchange has grown and the Pacific Island producers have lost control of the market. Island people now trade on European terms rather than on their own terms, even though they still control the local food supply.

The sale of taro and other local starches for cash, rather than in exchange for items that Europeans offered, began probably in about the 1850s, though it is hard to find precise amounts and dates of these transactions. The establishment of traders in Fiji, Tonga, and so on led to greater demands for the local produce. So local people sold their taro, sweet potatoes, and breadfruit to beachcombers, missionaries, and any other strangers who had no land of their own from which to support themselves (Grattan 1948). The cash they received in payment was then exchangeable for the new imported goods.

Demands for local foodstuffs increased with the growth of the European population. These newcomers had no alternative but to depend on local foods with which to feed their households, as ships bringing produce from overseas were infrequent. Missionary wives in Fiji wrote of bartering their china and their clothes for such foods as yams to feed their husbands and children. Mrs. Cargill's husband tried to raise foods, but apparently with little success (Cargill 1841). Initially the demands that visitors and newcomers placed on the supply of taro, yams, breadfruit, bananas, and fruits were met fairly readily. If the visitors stayed too long, however, the demands for daily provisions put an enormous strain on the local resources and at times even left the locals with the threat of famine (Ralston 1977:6). New demands arose as the European population increased and indentured laborers from India and elsewhere had to be fed.

These new residents brought with them their own food preferences. To those from temperate northern climates local foods were not as acceptable as food as their flour and beef, but if unobtainable they made do with local produce. Such sales became concentrated in the port towns where these visitors plied their trade. Whaling ports such as Honolulu, Pape'ete, Apia, and islands of Fiji became regular ports of call as places to refresh and refit; thus the demands for local produce were more steady in these places and drew on supplies from the hinterland. Later, in the 1870s, as the copra trade developed, the calls became more regular.

By this time several groups of foreigners had settled in the islands, mainly in the port towns (Force 1963). These included missionaries, officials sent from Europe to establish government systems, and beachcombers. The latter, never numerous, had an important impact because they were living throughout the islands, not just in the port towns, and lived mainly with the local people, for example, Mariner in Tonga. Not only did these new arrivals learn to eat local food, but they made their hosts aware of food preferences other than their own.

This period, then, marked the beginning of a diversification of food supplies. In demand in Fiji were fresh meat (beef), breadstuffs, fruits and vegetables, butter and rice (see Pollock 1989). Not only did these products fulfill the desires of Europeans for "food from home," but they also became an alternative that the local people could add to their menus. Imported foods such as white flour, biscuits, and meat (both fresh and tinned) took on a scarcity value and as such became status foods. Fijian, Tongan, and Tahitian women took cooking lessons from missionary and government administrators' wives, who were pleased to note their "progress" in the adoption of these new foods.

MARKETS

The best place to buy taro if you have none of your own is at the local market (see Figure 27). In fact it is the only place where those in town can get taro and other local starch foods. They are seldom sold at the supermarkets where imported foods predominate. Only once, in Majuro, did I find local food on sale in a supermarket; there, a stack of rolls of *bwiru* (fermented breadfruit paste) was placed at the end of an aisle (NJP fieldnotes 1982). There was a distinct physical separation of local foods and imported foods. The markets sell only locally grown produce.

Today the marketplace in Tahiti, Nuku'alofa, Suva, or Apia is the

Figure 27. Sweet potatoes and other locally grown produce at Talamahu market. Tonga, 1990. Photo by Nancy J. Pollock

place where local people go regularly to buy what local food they can afford. There, people jostle in the narrow aisles inspecting the coconut-leaf baskets of yams, sweet potatoes, and cassava, and the bundles of taro standing three or four tied together. Laid out on the ground or on trestle tables are tomatoes, eggplant, beans, lettuce, and other intro-duced foods. Heaps 6 feet high of pineapples and watermelons when they are in season also catch the eye. People wander about or sit amidst the array. Some are carefully assessing what they will buy for the next couple of days' meals or for the important Sunday fare. Some sit hopefully beside their wares, waiting for a customer. Others wander from stall to stall, drinking in the activity and observing a way of buying and selling that differs markedly from that of the supermarkets of the Western world. In Suva market an additional interest is the smell of rope tobacco and spices provided mainly for the Indian community.

The marketplace is a covered structure that may or may not have sides of metal railings that can be locked at night. Each marketplace is also a terminal for the buses or trucks that bring the customers and some of the food in from the outlying areas and bear them and their purchases back home again. Thus the marketplace is an important center of communica-tion (Pollock 1988). It is the place to bump into relatives and friends, to exchange information, and generally to keep in touch. For those living in the scattered suburbs of the towns the market serves several kinds of needs at one time.

Most of the markets open at 6:00 A.M. six days a week and close about 6:00 P.M., though by late in the day choice of foods may be very limited. The foodstuffs may be brought in by truck or by bus, supplies arriving sometime during the morning, not necessarily first thing. Eager buyers in Apia who know the quality of a certain producer's taro may buy it straight from his pickup before he has had a chance to unload (NJP fieldnotes 1982). Fish continue to arrive at the market during the day as the catch is landed. Information on the proportion of middlemen as sellers to those selling their own produce is not available.

Within the market there are three or four main divisions of produce. The taro, *kumara,* cassava, yams, and so on form one section, which may be located on the outside edges of the market building, as in Suva, or within the market building, as in Pape'ete. In Nuku'alofa these foods are sold within the marketplace, but when there is an abundance the women sit along one outside wall of the market shielding themselves and their produce with large black umbrellas. In Fiji men sell most of these root crops, but elsewhere they may be sold by either sex. Yams, cassava, breadfruit, sweet potatoes, and *Xanthosoma* taro are sold by the (coconut-leaf) basket; each filled basket weighs between 14 and 18 kilos (Tu'ifua and Rathey 1982 for Tonga), which may be enough for a household for two or three days. *Kape* (*Alocasia* taro) is sold by the piece. Green bananas are sold by the bunch. *Colocasia* taro is sold in Fiji, Apia, and Pape'ete tied together in bundles of three or four with some of the tops attached. In Nuku'alofa and Rarotonga they are sold by the basket and minus their tops. This difference in practice has long-term implications; those selling their *Colocasia* taro with tops still attached are also selling planting stock, so they must obtain new planting material to generate their next crop. However, their taro will last longer than that sold without tops. Taro without tops may last for only a couple of days unless the cut portion is chemically treated.

The market section for fish or meat is distinctive because of the slabs on which these items are displayed. The fish are kept cool by trickling water across the sloping slab or by placing them on ice. This fish section is staffed mainly by men. In Pape'ete market it can be locked off from the other sections. In Nuku'alofa fish is sold at a separate market close to where fishing boats dock.

A third section is set aside for selling green vegetables and fruits. Here tomatoes, lettuce, eggplants, mangoes, and ripe bananas are found within the main body of the marketplace, usually in the charge of women. The produce is sold by the heap or by the piece rather than by weight; it is rare to see scales. Pineapples and watermelons are sold singly from large piles; some may be cut up for sale for eating on the spot.

The fourth section of the market contains handicrafts such as baskets, fans, wooden ware, and jewelry. These are sold mainly by women, or in

Suva, by Indian men. With the growth of the handicraft industry separate marketplaces have been established on the waterfront in Suva, and also in Pape'ete and Nuku'alofa. The demands of tourists from cruise ships have stimulated the growth of these special handicraft markets to cater to these short-term visitors.

Three groups use the market today, apparently the same ones that have used the markets since they first were established. First, there are the sellers who can find an outlet for their taros and yams and fruits. Second, there are the buyers, of whom there are two distinct groups, the European settlers who want fresh vegetables and the local people who live in the town and need to buy their starchy food instead of growing it. The third group consists of middlemen who sell for producers.

These markets have been in operation in various forms for some one hundred years (see Figure 28). They have developed as part of the European-introduced cash economy. In the early days, island people did not buy foodstuffs, as that practice reflected badly on the buyer's status as a provider (B. Sewell, pers. comm. 1979). For Tahiti in the 1880s, we have a vivid account of the early stage of commercial activity from the pen of a visitor, Miss Constance Gordon Cumming: "Long before sunrise the pretty native boats arrive from all parts of the isle bringing cargo of fish and fruit for the market which is held in a large building in the town. But as the boats are unloaded their wares are outspread on the grass just

Figure 28. Old Pape'ete Market, 1890s. Photo courtesy M. Piot, Tahiti

below these windows. . . . The fruit supply is brought in large baskets—mangoes, oranges and Abercarder [*sic*] pears. The mainstay of life is the faees or wild banana which here takes the place of the yams and taro of the groups further west" (1880:145). She also describes how "enterprising Chinamen improve the vegetable supply especially in the matter of what I venture to call Christian potatoes, in opposition to the indigenous potato, alias yam" (Cumming 1880:179). Her record is also inscribed in a painting, a copy of which hangs in the Gauguin Museum on Tahiti.

Since the turn of the century, across the Pacific the Chinese have filled the demands of Europeans and others for vegetables, while the local people continued to produce their starchy roots and tree crops and bring a few of these to the markets. By 1880 the Chinese had already begun the process of diversification of local agriculture toward growing more European vegetables. Cumming recorded details of the European foods on sale in the Brander's store in Pape'ete. Also in the 1880s, Rarotongans were buying tinned meat when, as Gilson notes, European foods were already popular (1980:51). It is clear that European presence on a semipermanent basis led to the availability of a much wider range of foodstuffs. We have no records to indicate the degree of involvement of Tahitians and other Polynesians in marketing these "new" foods.

In Fiji at that time, the capital was Levuka on the island of Ovalau, which was subject to transportation problems. Thus a number of market centers developed throughout Fiji. About the same time Apia, Pago Pago, and Nuku'alofa, together with Jaluit in the Marshalls and Kolonia in Pohnpei also established marketplaces. They were places to which the local people brought their crops in the hope of a sale. Not many local people would have been buying at this time; only after World War II did urban areas begin to grow rapidly around government centers (Force 1963), as people came to the towns seeking opportunities for employment and where they learned new kinds of food habits.

Today there are extensive marketplaces in Suva and other main towns in Fiji (Labasa, Lautoka, Nausori, Sigatoka), in Nuku'alofa and Vava'u in Tonga, in Apia and Pago Pago, and two in Pape'ete. There is a small one on the waterfront in Avarua, Rarotonga, and a small one (on Fridays only) in Alofi, Niue. Though these markets are actually about a century old, the present sites are new and some are only recently built, as in the case of Pape'ete's second market, opened in 1977. (For a detailed study of markets in Suva and Pape'ete and the produce flowing through them see Thaman 1976/1977 and Pollock 1988).

THE CUSTOMERS AND WHAT THEY BUY

Another way of looking at the marketplace is to establish who the customers are. Today, taro and other root crops and fish and meat are sold

mainly to local residents, whereas the green vegetables and fruit and particularly the handicrafts are sold mainly to visitors and tourists. European residents are also major customers for the green vegetables and fruit
if they do not have their own gardens. Prices for goods in the food sections of the market are usually fixed, whereas negotiation is possible in
the purchase price of handicrafts.

No processed foods are sold in the markets. Most food is bought to be
taken home and cooked. One or two sellers in Suva and Nausori markets
may sell long rolls or leaf packets of *bila* made of grated cassava, or cubes
of cooked cassava covered in coconut cream and baked in the earth oven
or steamed. But these are not available every day. Presumably, demand
does not warrant the work involved. In Apia market an area is set aside
where some families sell prepared food to stall-holders and others who
frequent the market. In Nuku'alofa, Pape'ete, and Suva, stall-holders can
buy food to be eaten that day at nearby small shops or wheeled carts.

The busiest days in the market are Saturday and Friday, as households
purchase in preparation for the Sunday feast. Judging by Saturday
crowds in Suva, Nuku'alofa, Apia, and Pape'ete, there is still a strong
demand for this local produce. But demand does not have much influence on prices, as Tu'ifua and Rathey noted in their study of the Tonga
market (1982). This may indicate, they suggest, that the demand for root
crops has never been fully satisfied. More studies such as theirs are
needed to give a clearer picture of how strong the demand for root crops
is through the market.

In a study of consumption in one urban and one rural community on
Tongatapu published in 1980, Duttaroy found the urban population
dependent on the market for 57 percent by value of its supply of vegetables and starch roots. Of those household purchases, 42 percent by value
were root crops, 16 percent were vegetables, 6 percent were fruits and
nuts, and 35 percent were animal protein. Outside the urban area the
proportion of purchased food in the diet was much smaller, as one might
expect; 37 percent by value was purchased by rural Tongatapu households and 20 percent by value by outer-island households (Duttaroy
1980:13). "In terms of per capita consumption both in value and quantity, root crops dominate the scene amongst local food. . . . Although
the consumption of root crops both in quantity and value is least in
urban Tongatapu, the proportion of consumption of root crops with
respect to all local products is not less, showing the relative importance
of root crops amongst local products even in the urban diet" (Duttaroy
1980:18). When these consumption patterns were examined in terms of
caloric intake, he found that out of a total of 1,776 calories derived from
local products, root crops accounted for 1,150 calories, vegetables for
168, and fruits for 366; local fish and other marine products added 97

calories per day. Imported food accounted for a further 845 calorie units per capita, mainly cereal and cereal products such as bread and flour. This study is an important indicator of how use of root starches is persisting, and how even urban Tongans have not completely given up their traditional foods.

In Western Samoa another market study showed that *Colocasia* taro was selling at 6 Samoan cents per pound in 1974 and 24 cents per pound in 1975 (Enright 1976). In 1982 it was selling at S$4 for a bundle of three (approximately 27 cents per pound). Taro maintained its relative position in Apia market between 1966, when it formed 62.45 percent of all produce on sale, and 1976, when it was 58.97 percent. Enright also found that taro accounted for 54 percent of all produce bought (1976:10).

In 1982 in Suva and Sigatoka markets bundles of four taros were selling for between F$4 and $6 each. *Kumara* and cassava were selling for $4 for a large (approximately 15-kilo) basket. The proportion of bundles to baskets was about equal.

Thus *Colocasia* taro and yams are still important food items in spite of the rich variety of imported foods available. The best place to buy them is at the markets. Some are available at roadside stalls on islands from Guam to Tahiti. And in some small community shopping centers growing up at strategic spots around the island of Tahiti, small amounts of taro and green vegetables can be bought. However, the customer looking for quality is better served by the market produce.

SUPERMARKETS AND SMALL STORES

Supermarkets are now to be found in all the main centers of the Pacific. From casual observations the clientele, particularly in the South Pacific, is mainly European and certainly the food lines cater to Western tastes. Many of these supermarkets have developed from the refurbishing of old general stores such as Burns Philp and Morris Hedstrom, long familiar in urban centers across the Pacific. Reimers store in Majuro introduced the self-service aisle system in 1967—followed shortly by two of the other major retailing firms in town. These stores have all updated their layout of goods two or three times since then. They have a distinct food section, separate from all the clothing, hardware, white ware, and so on. But the basic range of foodstuffs has not increased. Their food stock is 98 percent imported; exceptions are locally packaged juices in Tahiti and Western Samoa, local dairy products in Fiji, and local coconut in Tonga. Some local beef may also be available but is not easily identifiable.

Small stores selling a limited range of goods are found in most village communities (see Figure 29). They service households wanting a can of fish or some matches or a few ounces of tea for immediate use. As

Figure 29. Store. Wallis Island, 1988. Photo by Nancy J. Pollock

Hau'ofa's study showed, people buy these small amounts for several reasons. Often they have limited cash and lack refrigeration at home; also people know that supplies bought in large amounts and intended to last for a week will disappear in a few days. "Thus small trade stores are neighbourhood pantries to which women and children go several times each day" (Hau'ofa 1979:22). As Hau'ofa found, Tongans dream of owning a store as a way to make money, but 50 percent of these stores close within the first three years of operation (1979:15, 56). They operate on a very narrow margin, and the owners have almost no experience in managing the finances of these stores.

Just over half (54 percent) of all the stores Hau'ofa surveyed dealt almost entirely in food and drink. Tinned meat and fish, flour, sugar, butter, and soft drinks account for the six most commonly bought foods. "Corned beef is a prestigious food item with significant ceremonial value. Every major Tongan meal or feast must have *lupulu,* corned beef with taro leaf and coconut cream wrapped and baked in banana leaf. It is a national delicacy" (Hau'ofa 1979:25). But very few locally produced foodstuffs are sold through these small trade stores in Tonga.

In French Polynesia most communities have one or more small stores, or "mini-superettes" as they are now labeled. They carry a wide range of goods, of which food is a significant part. A main item is breadsticks baked centrally in Pape'ete and delivered each day that have become an integral part of the French-type meal and of eating habits in general. The superettes also carry a variety of canned food, some frozen foods, and some hardware—general store goods. The foods they sell are predominantly imported.

So virtually everything sold in retail stores is imported, and virtually everything sold in the produce market is locally produced (Hau'ofa 1979: 2). This broad generalization applies across the Pacific from Guam to Tahiti and the Tuamotus, though there are exceptions. On Easter Island, in contrast, almost all food is imported through Chile and sold through four or five small stores; this is supplemented by what sweet potatoes the residents can grow and fish they can catch (NJP fieldnotes; Routledge n.d.). On Nauru all food is imported except toddy and some fish (Pollock 1987). People on Guam, too, buy most of their food from the supermarket, supplied from California some seven thousand miles away. A few roadside stalls sell locally grown bananas, sweet potatoes, and local fruits, and a few people still grow their own taro, particularly around Umatac (del Valle 1979). Thus the supermarket is an important source of food supply.

OTHER SOURCES OF LOCAL STARCH FOODS

It is clear from the above reports that the locally grown starches are available today in towns, almost exclusively through the markets. People do buy them but the supply is not sufficient to meet demand. In part demand is constrained by the high prices charged; when yams, for example, are

Figure 30. Children with ice lollies. Wallis Island, 1988. Photo by Nancy J. Pollock

out of season, their price in the market is beyond what most people can afford. But if the occasion is important enough, people will buy these roots that play such an important symbolic role in their lives or find other ways to get them.

Urban Gardens

A few households in Pape'ete, Nuku'alofa, and Suva are able to grow some food like taro, bananas, and tomatoes in urban gardens. Those with even small amounts of land are as likely to plant taros as ornamentals. Often the soil is not as good as bush plots, but even a few small taros are a help to household budgets.

In a study of urban gardens in Fiji, Tonga, and Port Moresby, Thaman found *Colocasia* taro growing in 50 percent of all gardens in Port Moresby and Suva and in 81 percent of gardens in Nuku'alofa. Other species of taro were also grown, though less frequently (Thaman 1982). Many Pape'ete gardens have a breadfruit tree or two as well and also bananas, which are a popular garden crop throughout the Pacific. These provide a readily accessible food supply for those who cannot leave town to cultivate larger gardens. Development of species of taro suited to urban conditions would be a useful part of any government's agricultural extension program.

Exchanges

For those living in towns, another way to obtain local food is by exchanges with or gifts from relatives living in rural areas. From Takapoto in the Tuamotus I noted a regular flow of chilly bins (coolers) on the twice-weekly flights between the Marquesas and Tahiti. The chilly bin would travel to Pape'ete full of fresh fish and pawpaws (papayas) and come back on the next plane full of chicken or meat from the Pape'ete market. Relatives of the Tuamotuans living in Tahiti kept these exchanges going (Pollock 1979a). These exchanges provide those living far from home with an important part of their diet, which may be expensive in town, and at the same time keep alive kinship and other social ties. Food is a facilitator in maintaining social relations, not merely the end product in these exchanges.

IMPORTED FOODS AND FOOD DEPENDENCY

Imported foods are competing so successfully with the local starch foods that in some communities a high percentage of the diet now comes from imports. And the proportion of food imports in the total import bill of many island nations has been around 25 percent (see Table 15). So island governments have taken steps to reduce the amount of food imports and thus to counter what has been labeled "dietary colonialism." Encourag-

TABLE 15. Imports and Per Capita GDP by Island Nation or Territory, 1980–1985

Island(s)	Total (A$000)	Food (A$000)	Beverages (A$000)	GDP Per Capita (A$)
	Imports			GDP
American Samoa	322,807	31,567	8,583	7,336
Cook Islands	23,639	5,052	1,329	972
Federated States of Micronesia	nd	nd	nd	1,372
Fiji	512,614	78,669	3,747	2,028
French Polynesia	606,209	101,239	12,591	9,143
Kiribati	20,877	5,626	1,130	505
Marshall Islands	19,890	5,132	1,854	1,559
Nauru	9,713	2,001	894	nd
New Caledonia	359,706	66,290	12,963	6,281
Niue	2,752	766	224	1,499
Palau	28,501	5,033	2,399	2,799
Papua New Guinea	1,107,309	194,600	12,157	996
Solomon Islands	75,530	11,843	3,375	680
Tokelau	145	56	13	500
Tonga	46,152	10,858	2,589	913
Tuvalu	3,965	982	164	452
Vanuatu	77,892	20,189	3,528	654
Wallis and Futuna	9,234	3,227	nd	13
Western Samoa	44,527	9,498	1,198	729

Source: SPC 1987:4, 30.

ing the production of local food crops and proper marketing of these is one such countermove.

Groups such as the Fiji Food and Nutrition Committee are actively encouraging people to eat more local foods; it will be interesting to see the effects on imports. In Papua New Guinea food imports have continued to rise while subsistence production is stagnant or growing only slightly, despite government attempts to hold down imports. In cost the items that rose most between 1975 and 1983 were meat, dairy products, and fish, while cereals and sugar declined (Goodman 1985:73). Now that Pacific people are buying at least some of their food at supermarkets, meat has become the most expensive item in the household food budget. Cheaper cuts such as mutton flaps and salt beef make up a large part of the meat sector, but they are still among the most costly of food imports.

Dependence on imported food has been slowly building up as more Pacific Islanders move into towns and follow the strong advice offered by missionary wives and other European women as to "the proper way" to look after a Fijian or Tongan household. They taught the Fijian women new recipes and new ways of cooking: Women should bake tarts and serve a roast beef dinner in order to keep their families healthy (Pollock 1989). But ingredients could be obtained only from the metropolitan countries—hence dietary colonialism.

In the face of these introduced ideas of feeding a household, traditional concepts may persist, but as ideals rather than everyday practice. Preparing a big earth oven full of traditional food to be served after church on Sunday fulfills some of those ideals. In Tonga traditional food customs are still very important but not always practical (Hau'ofa 1979). At issue for the 1990s is the level at which reliance on imported foods can be maintained. Tourism is one factor that is encouraging high levels of imports of a variety of Western foods. But with active encouragement of local people to grow the local starch foods, their production can be increased, and the price reduced. The increasing concern about the dependence that follows from heavy reliance on imported foods may lead to greater reliance on the traditional starches.

At the present time the small island states that have become very dependent on metropolitan countries for imported food and have minimal goods to trade are in a difficult bargaining position. They are locked into a situation of dependency.

Several dimensions of food dependency in the Pacific have been outlined by McGee, since "it is clear that governments of the region are becoming increasingly concerned with the problems of food supply for their countries" (1975:1). He suggests what he calls a "simple historical model of the manner in which the problem has arisen" (McGee 1975:4), attributing the dependency to four factors: (1) The development of cash cropping of cotton, coconuts, coffee, and sugar necessitated large-scale operations on a plantation scale that drew emphasis away from the production of local food. (2) The arrival of large numbers of expatriates as missionaries, government officials, and plantation managers created a demand for imported foodstuffs to meet their own customary dietary habits, brought with them from Europe and the United States. (3) The plantation laborers, particularly Indians brought into Fiji in the 1880s, were fed imported food such as rice. And (4), the pattern of economic relations was based on developing exports at the expense of the internal marketing system for indigenous foods. McGee suggests that "it has been easier to avoid the problems of developing these marketing systems by allowing increased use of imported foodstuffs," resulting in dietary colonialism (1975:6, 7).

McGee pinpoints rapid population growth and increasing numbers living in towns as the main factors leading to a rapid rise in food imports during the 1960s and 1970s (1975:9). The consequences have been, he suggests, that these food imports have taken up a large proportion of the trade budget and have led to balance of payments problems, and thus the need for overseas aid. Other consequences he suggests are that this dietary dependence will limit the possibilities for growth of indigenous food production for cash sale and that skills used in traditional food production will be lost. His final concern is that "changes from traditional food consumption to imported food consumption may be seen in part as indicators of the manner in which these societies are incorporated into a dependent relationship with the developed world" (McGee 1975:7).

He offers a three-pronged solution: (1) increased production and variety of locally produced foodstuffs; (2) development of adequate marketing systems so locally produced foodstuffs can reach the population in towns regularly and in good condition; and (3) a careful integration between programs for this increased local production and the existing pattern of food importation and consumption (McGee 1975:14–15).

CASE STUDIES IN FOOD DEPENDENCY
Namu

On Namu, an atoll society that has undergone the effects of the political presence of first the Spanish, then the Germans, then the Japanese, and finally the United States as caretaker of the Trust Territory of the Pacific Islands, the crucial step toward the introduction of purchased food was the beginning of copra-making for export in 1860. When German companies based in Samoa began to buy coconut oil from the Pacific Islands, Marshallese, including the Namu people, for the first time had cash to spend. Some of this fell into the hands of the chiefs, who spent it on behalf of their lineages. But some found its way into the hands of the people, who then were able to buy some of the Western goods that seemed to give these *ri-belle* the power to have large ships and travel around on a larger scale than they, the Marshallese could—and they had always loved to travel (Krämer and Nevermann 1938). These ships brought new kinds of foods for them to buy, a welcome addition to the very limited variety of food on the atoll. The medical advantages that came with this Western life-style helped to overcome certain health problems, and so the population began to increase. Then more food was needed to feed the people.

During Japanese times (1920–1945) trade stores were set up on most of the twenty-six atolls throughout the Marshalls, including Namu. From the store the people were able to buy canned fish and rice, as well as cotton cloth and other goods. But these foods were additions to their diet of breadfruit, pandanus, and fresh fish rather than substitutions because the people recognized the risks inherent in depending on the irregular arrival of ships bringing new supplies (Pollock 1976). That pattern has been going on for a hundred years now. An increasing amount of rice was eaten, but breadfruit was still being used, as well as pandanus in season, in 1969. The Namu people cannot afford to become wholly dependent on rice and flour because they never know when the next ship will appear. Their continued life on the atoll requires them to keep as many options open as possible (Pollock 1976).

Fiji

In Fiji reliance on imported foods started when Wesleyan missionaries took up residence there in the 1830s and 1840s. The missionary wives in particular were strongly committed to raising their families on foods they were used to in Britain. Bread and meat were the two main foodstuffs these women believed they needed on a daily basis to please their husbands and to make their children fit and strong. But wheat flour was very hard to obtain in those times. Their only means of supply were the missionary ships bringing supplies—and more missionaries—from Britain. As missionary Thomas Williams noted in the 1850s: "Could the Triton have come when more needed. We were out of sugar; had flour enough for one loaf and several of the stores were in the same low state. Praise the Lord for His kind oversight of us." And that flour was not always the best. Williams also wrote, "Yesterday I opened a new flour cask and unhappily it contains very indifferent sour flour" (in Henderson 1931b, 2: 357, 321). So the bread and pastries that his wife had planned to make had to wait for the next shipment amid hopes that it would be better.

The meat that these missionaries were used to in Britain was even harder to get. They had to rely on salt beef, also coming from Britain, until the raising of cattle in Australia and New Zealand got underway. Seemann, a government botanist sent from Britain to look at the resources in Fiji, commented: "In the tropics to eat day after day pork and yam, the usual food of Fiji, is not very tempting and we therefore endeavoured to introduce some diversity into our mode of living, by obtaining as many fowls as we could. Eggs were seldom seen. The Fijians consider it babyish to eat them" (1862:37). So the missionary and other settler families were forced to live on local foods; David Cargill even tells us of growing his own taros and yams and pigs. But all of them still longed for bread and fruits, such as apples, and fresh beef.

As part of their husbands' work, the missionary wives also felt duty bound to teach Fijian women about these "good foods" and what they perceived as the best ways to run a household, including use of knives and forks and pots and pans. These new practices also included encouraging women who had joined the church to make a feast each Sunday: "After the conclusion of the morning services, the Christians partook of an abundant repast of baked hogs, yams, fish etc. which their own liberality had provided" (Cargill 1841:189). Such frequent and regular feasting required more gardens to be planted, and probably contributed to increased food intake and obesity. The new practices were expensive and hard to fulfill, however, so Fijian demand for imports was minimal, as far as we can tell.

During the 1860s European settlers were attracted to Fiji to set up cotton plantations when American cotton production was halted by the American Civil War. A medical officer who arrived with these cotton planters commented: "Salt beef, yams and bananas . . . the dinner of 365 days out of the year . . . the food—i.e. such food as a white man can live on continuously—is insufficient and bad. . . . No doubt this state of things will be remedied in time but as it is, anyone who wants to live comfortably in Fiji must import from New Zealand and Australia, a distance of 2000 miles" (Forbes 1875:158). His optimism that imports would solve their woes has led to what we are now labeling food dependency.

After Britain took charge of the administration of Fiji in 1875 an increasing number of government officials arrived from Britain, alone or with their families, to swell the demand for imported food, particularly in Levuka, then capital of Fiji. Single men living with Fijian women also helped to introduce these new-found foodways to the Fijians. Bringing their food habits from Britain and the United States and the strong beliefs on which they were based, these new settlers set up a demand for imported foodstuffs, particularly barrels of flour and biscuits and kegs of salt beef. These demands are reflected clearly in the early import figures (*Fiji Blue Book* 1880:56).

There was no marked improvement in the diet for Westerners, though, even some thirty years after the arrival of the missionaries in the 1840s. Miss Constance Gordon Cumming, who arrived in Fiji with Lady Gordon and the first governor's party in 1875, described the situation.

We have not come to a land flowing with milk and honey in any sense. Daily food is both difficult to obtain and expensive. Fish is scarcely to be had at any price, though the sea swarms with many good kinds. Foreign vegetables are not to be got for love or money. The supply of fruit is very scant, consisting only of indifferent bananas, pineapples and oranges. Milk is 1s. quart, eggs 3s. a dozen. Indifferent meat is about the same price as in England, poultry a good deal dearer. And this is the country to which the Colonial Office sends men at ridiculously small salaries because as they were told ere leaving England, living would cost them nothing, and they would save all their pay. Why a man without a private fortune could hardly live here at all. Of course all imported goods are necessarily expensive having to pay freight first to Sydney and then to Levuka. (Cumming 1885: 28–29)

With the arrival of indentured laborers from India to work the sugar plantations in 1880s rice was added to the list of imported foods. By this time, too, ships were crossing the Pacific on a more regular basis, which helped to stimulate demand still further (see Pollock 1989 for a full discussion of food habits of this early period in Fiji). The amount of local food eaten by these settlers was minimal, mainly because it was considered inferior and not suitable to their palates. Not only did these new arrivals favor their own food, but they actively downgraded the local food. It is not surprising then that they did not see fit to encourage subsistence production or promote the marketing of local foodstuffs.

The ten missionary families in the 1840s brought with them particular food needs that set Fiji on a path of dietary colonialism. From these small beginnings the food import bill grew to some 20 percent of all imports in 1976 (Knapman 1985). This is a major turn-around for a country that had its own abundance of foodstuffs in great variety. We must ask who is consuming all those dollars' worth of imported food. We do not have figures to break down exact consumption within that total, but we can surmise that a large proportion of imported food is consumed mainly by the landless people living in towns. These towns had seen rapid growth in the 1960s. Those living in towns are drawn from all the ethnic groups. Many are employed or seeking employment and therefore are living on a cash income and buying much of their food. In the rural areas some food is bought, such as flour, rice, butter, eggs, and tinned fish and meat. But a series of nutrition and agricultural studies of Naduri village in the Sigatoka valley between 1957 and 1982 show that in 1982 these people were still consuming a high proportion of locally grown foodstuffs. Cassava and sweet potatoes with river shellfish were the basis of two meals a day; breakfast might consist now of bread, or an egg for a child. But Langley's expected trend (1973) toward Westernization of food has not happened.

There certainly had been minimal interest in encouraging the production of local foodstuffs such as taro, yams, and sweet potatoes until the work of Param Sivan and the FAO Root Crops Program (Chandra 1979b). Now Fiji's agricultural research station at Koronivia and other such stations around Fiji have experimental plots designed to improve the quality of these indigenous foodstuffs. And the Health Department is behind this program also. It has assisted in setting up the Fiji Food and Nutrition Committee, drawn from across a wide spectrum of government interests. That committee has a lively program aimed at promoting the consumption of locally grown foods by showing new ways the foods can be prepared, particularly new recipes, and ways of cooking to fit with modern constraints of status and time and tastes (see the committee's newsletters for details of their programs). The committee together with other organizations, such as the marketing and development boards, is overseeing the development of a marketing structure to ensure an adequate supply of local foods in good condition for the towns. Price is a major concern. There is need to ensure that local foods are available at a suitable price for those living on a small cash base.

A better understanding of how foods were used in the past is needed to assist in the reduction of dependence on overseas markets. It will not be eliminated entirely, but in drawing attention to the value of local foods both in the diet and in social life, such programs can be useful.

With Fiji's ethnic balance between Fiji Indians and indigenous Fijians there is a growing awareness that identity matters. This identity image is conveyed in a number of ways, one of which is food. On public occasions, such as Independence Day or World Food Day, Fijian foods and dishes made with them were displayed alongside Fiji Indian dishes (NJP fieldnotes 1982). The hotels, too, are beginning to offer tourists more dishes made from local foods such as *vakalolo* and *kokoda* (raw fish in coconut cream) in addition to the regular foods that Westerners seek to buy anywhere in the world. This effort to stimulate tourist demand helps to put a very positive value on an aspect of Fiji life that has been downgraded or passed over for a hundred years.

LOCAL ISLAND FOOD FOR EMIGRANTS

An increasing market overseas has been developing during the 1980s for taro, yams, cassava, and green bananas. These foods are in high demand in metropolitan countries such as Australia, New Zealand, and West Coast United States, places to which Pacific Islanders have migrated. Sacks of taro and hands of bananas are now to be seen regularly in greengrocers in Auckland, Wellington, Honolulu, San Francisco, and Los Angeles (Thaman 1977:87).

New Zealand is the biggest market for tropical root crops from the islands, according to the plan of the South Pacific Bureau for Economic Cooperation (SPEC); 50 percent come from Western Samoa while Fiji and Tonga supply some 25 percent each (Taleafoa 1977:90). Taro was the second largest export earner for Western Samoa in 1981, bringing that country 20.7 percent of its revenue. The volume of taro exports is increasing in part to meet the demand from the large number of Samoans now living in New Zealand and the United States (Fairbairn 1985:316).

The migrants are using these familiar foods mainly for feasts, though some are used on a household basis. They are most noticeable at the large Sunday dinners for church groups or extended families. These foods are expensive, at least in New Zealand; four taros may cost NZ$12 and coconuts $2.50 each (Pollock et al. 1989). But they are preferred for their taste, they are a means of identifying with a particular island group, and they are also a necessary part of the pattern of respect and reciprocity that has persisted throughout Pacific Island life.

No feast in New Zealand is complete without some taro, a whole fish, some chicken, and chop suey, besides European salads and bread and butter. In fact, the range of island dishes has been increasing over the last ten years (see Pollock et al. 1989 for a discussion of Samoan food consumption in Wellington). This is in large part due to the rapid growth of the Pacific Island population in New Zealand (see Table 16). One-third to one-half of those persons calling themselves Pacific Islanders are now New Zealand born. Their parents find they have to make a conscious effort to keep alive the Samoan or Tongan identity in the strange land. Partly that can be done by making sure the language is spoken in the home; partly it can be done by serving island dishes such as *palusami* (a mixed dish consisting of corned beef with taro leaves and coconut cream), taro, and fish at feasts and other community affairs. And partly it can be done by keeping alive other traditional arts and festivals at which food also features.

The degree to which food operates as part of this identity-maintaining mechanism varies from family to family. In a small study asking Samoans living in the Wellington region about their food preferences, over half the responses from some eighty-two informants indicated that taro was their most preferred food (Pollock et al. 1989). This indicates that the ideology of traditional foods is still maintained despite the fact that Pacific Islanders may have moved away from their island environment and been exposed to a wide range of European-type foods found on the supermarket shelves and in the vegetable shops.

SUMMARY

Taro use continues in urban environments today for important festive occasions, if not in daily practice. It must be bought, however, and that goes against some basic social principles about selling local food. But if having it is more important than qualms about buying it, then local crops are bought and sold. The main deterrent to greater use is cost. Even though local foods are sold through the market with few middlemen, the price of enough taro or yams for daily consumption is beyond the pocket of an ordinary Tongan or Western Samoan. So these roots are used mainly on weekends and special occasions. Cassava is widely used as a substitute during the week because it is cheaper, although it is considered second best.

Imported foods such as rice, flour, canned meat and fish, and sugar (except in Fiji) have taken a high profile. These are often less expensive than local foods and can be cooked more quickly. But they are not as satisfying as root crops.

TABLE 16. Numbers of Pacific Islanders in New Zealand and Overseas, 1976, 1981, 1986

Born	1976			1981			1986		
	NZ	Overseas	Total	NZ	Overseas	Total	NZ	Overseas	Total
Cook Islands	7,043	11,567	18,610	10,100	13,848	23,948	9,309	15,678	24,987
Niue	1,917	3,777	5,694	3,079	5,099	8,178	2,934	5,457	8,391
Samoa	11,584	16,292	27,876	18,000	24,141	42,141	19,662	33,864	53,526
Tonga	794	3,186	3,980	1,700	5,232	6,932	2,394	7,218	9,612
Tokelau	524	1,213	1,737	1,100	1,281	2,381	915	11,320	12,235
Other Polynesian Islands	1,834	1,629	3,463	nd	nd	5,613	114	1,608	1,722
Fiji	332	1,216	1,548	nd	nd	6,372	nd	7,239	7,239
Totals			62,908			95,565			127,908*
Increase over the previous census figures			nd			+46%			+41%

Source: Adapted from New Zealand Dept. of Statistics, Census of Population and Dwellings, 1976, 1981, 1986.
* Includes those of mixed parentage, e.g., part Samoan, part Niuean.

When deciding which foods to buy, taro and breadfruit are only two choices out of a wide range of foods available to those with the cash to buy them. But for those with limited income the range of foods from which to select is much smaller in towns than in rural subsistence areas.

The degree of dependence on imported foods is variable and requires closer study. Hauʻofa's survey (1979) of small stores in Tonga gives us some indications of the narrow range of use of these imported foods. Attempts to build up confidence in and agricultural support for subsistence crops are underway. And market studies are also being conducted. So we can expect to see more local produce for sale, not only in island towns, but also in metropolitan markets. Continuity of appreciation of the values of foods and their role in the culture needs greater recognition and support if dependency on imported foods is to be reduced and each Pacific Island nation is to maintain its chosen degree of autonomy.

9

Food and Health

HEALTH OF ISLANDERS, LATE 1700S AND EARLY 1800S

CAPTAIN COOK and other visitors have left us a broad impression of a populace large in stature and generally healthy. On Tahiti, according to Sir Joseph Banks, "Such articles as the island produceth must be in great plenty as the inhabitants seemed to be both numerous and wellfed; the men here are large and stout, one measured 6 foot 3" (in Beaglehole 1962:317). Cook also noted that the people were "tall, strong, well formed; they were fairer than any other we met"; Tongan men he described as tall, strong and very active, while the women were strong and masculine (quoted in Holmes 1982:54, 36). And he described Hawaiians as robust, with a primitive and warlike appearance. William Anderson, who was with Cook on his second voyage, described "Fatafehi chief of Amsterdam and islands, though not very tall he was of a monstrous size with fat which render'd him very unwieldy and almost shapeless." And of another chief, "Tubou seems about 50, rather corpulent and almost blind." Of Tongan women Anderson commented that "they are destitute of that strong fleshy firmness" (in Beaglehole 1967:880, 892–893, 925).

Thus the general impression that these visitors from distant shores have left us is of people who were taller and fatter than their own European populations. Banks (1769) and others alluded to the ease with which these peoples of the Pacific obtained their food, implying that they did not have to work as hard as their European counterparts; perhaps he was making an association between fatness and the easy life, as he saw it. Whether he and others were referring to the whole population's having these characteristics or just those of chiefly status is not quite clear.

But we must also bear in mind the irregularity of their food supply— that vast amounts were eaten when available, and that abstinence for two or three days was commonplace. So the argument has been made that a store of fat would have enabled those people to survive longer than their thin counterparts. Thin, sickly children would not have been likely to survive long under such a regimen. Neel (1962) has called this view the "thrifty gene hypothesis," with reference to South American populations; Baker (1981), Prior (1977), and Zimmet (1980) have applied this hypothesis to Pacific populations.

Special care was taken throughout much of the Pacific to ensure that chiefs in particular were well fed. We have already seen, from Banks's graphic description, how important it was in Tahiti that a chief should eat prodigious amounts of both root starches and puddings, as well as pork and fish. Yet if Anderson's assessment (in Beaglehole 1967) is correct this does not seem to have shortened their life spans.

We do not have many descriptions of women's physical appearances written at the time apart from the "masculine" Tongan women, so we cannot assess their physical proportions at contact. Cook and others were most concerned about the fact that women were not allowed to eat the same food as men. Missionary John Williams commented even more strongly: "Females at Rarotonga were treated as inferiors. They were neither allowed to eat certain kinds of food which were reserved for the men and the gods, nor to dwell under the same roof with their tyrannical masters, but were compelled to take their scanty meal of inferior provisions at a distance while the 'lords of creation' feasted upon the 'fat of the land' and the 'abundance of the sea' " (1838:180). He is referring here to the tabu on women's eating pork and certain fish; his statement also highlights the difference between European and Pacific food concepts and social organization.

While it may be hard to verify causes of death during this early period, we can question whether malnutrition was a contributing factor to morbidity and mortality in these populations. The local food supply was apparently adequate to support large populations in Tahiti and the Marquesas before contact, even though they were subject to periodic declines due to famine, infanticide, and other causes (McArthur 1967:348).

Opposing views of the severity of declines in Pacific Island populations at contact have been put forward by Moorehead (1967) and Lange (1984). Moorehead has popularized the view that Europeans brought disease and other lethal new factors into the Pacific; and McArthur's work gives close documentation of population declines. Together with famines and irregular diet, according to one argument, these were contributing factors to high mortality. On the other hand, Lange has argued that these declines were not as severe as was first supposed. He provides evidence for the stability of the Cook Islands and eastern Polynesian populations.

McArthur has sifted the estimates by missionaries and other visitors for the pre-censal era to establish the most likely population size. She draws attention to the severe effects of epidemics of influenza, whooping cough, and other diseases brought in from outside, which reduced populations by some 5 percent (McArthur 1967:103). These new ailments, together with the impact of wars and storms that reduced the food supply, contributed markedly to an increase of deaths over births. For example, in Rarotonga missionary Buzacott noted the disastrous effects of a virulent scrofulous disease introduced in the mid-1830s by a native teacher who had come from the Society Islands (Sunderland and Buzacott 1866:104). This gives some indication that diseases other than the recognizable Western ones, such as influenza, contributed to the decrease in population during the nineteenth century (McArthur 1967).

It would appear then that food customs two hundred years ago were sufficient to keep the populations alive and to keep the women fertile. That the food supply was adequate, even on atolls, is evidenced by Wilkes's comment on the Gilbertese (1845, 2:219–221). From my reconstruction of genealogies for the people of Namu in the Marshalls (Pollock 1970; Pollock, Morton, and Lalouel 1972) it is evident that the women of this atoll had had a diet adequate to allow them to produce ten to fifteen children each over several generations, and most of those children lived also to reproduce. Similar evidence of large sibling sets is available for Mokil and Pingelap, atolls close to Pohnpei, whose populations were reduced to three adults in the mid-1700s and have regenerated in the subsequent two-hundred-year period (Morton, Lalouel, and Hurst 1971).

For Tahiti, William Ellis has provided one of the earliest detailed accounts of local diseases and healing practices. He described what appears to have been a bone disease that may have been diet related: "Among the most prevalent and obstinate diseases to which, as a nation, they are exposed is one which terminates in a permanent affection of the spine; it usually appears in early life. . . . The body is reduced almost to a skeleton; and the disease terminates in death, or a large curvature of the spine. . . . Multitudes in every one of the Society Islands are to be seen deformed by this disease, which the natives call *tuapu,* literally projecting" (Ellis 1831:38–39). He suggested that the disease could be hereditary, as "children of such persons are more frequently the subjects of it than others." It also was more prevalent among what he called the lower classes of society, the farmers and the mechanics. He could not recollect any principal chief or person of secondary rank thus afflicted. So he felt that "it may certainly warrant the inference that the meagre living of the [lower classes] exposes them to maladies, from which more generous diet and comfortable modes of life exempt their superiors" (Ellis 1831:39). Blindness was frequently associated with the same disease. Ellis suggested that the denial of pork to the lower classes may have been responsible for this condition, in addition to the genetic factor.

Ellis summarized the general health situation in Polynesia in terms of some of the main categories of disease with which he was familiar:

> The diseases formerly prevailing among the South Sea islanders were comparatively few; those from which they now suffer are principally pulmonary, intermittent and cutaneous. The most fatal are, according to their account, of recent origin. While idolaters, they were accustomed to consider every bodily affliction as the result of the anger of their gods; and the priest was a more important personage in time of sickness than the physician. Native practitioners who were almost invariably priests or sorcerers, were accustomed to apply such healing remedies as the islands afforded. (1831:36).

He added some details of their pharmacopeia in which vegetable products alone were used (Ellis 1831:37). These medicines or *raau* consisted mainly of herbs and roots, some rubbed on or applied externally while others were drunk.

These outside viewpoints on island health have become embedded in the historical record of the Pacific. They need to be considered alongside recent studies of the local concepts of health.

LOCAL CONCEPTS OF FOOD IN RELATION TO HEALTH

Information on local views of health and its associations with diet are sparse. Ellis, who used his own classifications of diseases, is one of the few writers of the early times to tell us the distinctions Society Island people made between infirmities. They distinguished those diseases they believed were of local origin from those that had come from outside. Viala (1909) also noted a similar distinction made by Wallis Island people. The foreign diseases such as influenza and whooping cough were beyond the powers of local healers to cure. But we don't know how these views fitted in with the rest of the beliefs that society held at that time. Ellis implied that socioeconomic or class status had an important bearing on health and that sickness was treated by persons who combined what he saw as religious and medical techniques (1831). Others, such as Feinberg for Anuta (1979), have also noted the role of priests as healers and the close association between sickness and magic, and beliefs in the interventive powers of the supernatural. Food plays a small but important part in this healing process.

Spencer (1941) identified three categories of disease according to Fijians' beliefs in the 1930s. They distinguished *mate vayano*, casual conditions arising from incidental circumstances, from *mate ni vanua*, which included headaches, fevers, sorcery, and offenses against the gods. The latter was the largest category and included anything considered the work of the *vu,* sorcerer. Restitution was brought about by a series of rituals, which Spencer refers to as payments, one of which was in the form of a *magiti,* feast. The third category of illness had no specific label but included illnesses brought about by magical means; these were counteracted by use of medicines of death and medicines of life. None of these illnesses was directly associated with food intake, though their remedies necessitated some intake in the form of potions that were considered medicine, rather than drink or food.

Illness on Ifaluk in the central Carolines was attributed in large part to the work of malevolent ghosts. They were seen as the cause of anxiety and sickness (Spiro 1952). The link between food intake and these illnesses is not made clear.

In both Fiji and the Carolines sickness was not directly attributed to food itself. If food was involved it was because some sorcerer had used it as the medium of malevolence. Thus food itself appears to have had a very positive connotation; it was good for society and was a powerful means of expressing well-being.

The Kiribati concept of health has been noted in an interdisciplinary study by epidemiologists, a nutritionist, and an anthropologist looking at the impact of modernization on the health of a Pacific nation (Zimmet et al. 1982). The study set out to ascertain the prevalence of diabetes, cardiovascular disease, and hypertension, and the relationship between their occurrence and the modernization of life-style occurring in Kiribati. The study of the modernization aspects contrasted life in Betio, a very urbanized island, with the rural environment on Tabiteuea North (Geddes 1982). Geddes has drawn particular attention to the attitudes of cosmopolitan medical practitioners as contrasted with those of the Kiribati medical practitioners, based on their contrastive systems of knowledge.

> By way of summary, we might say that cosmopolitan medical practice is undergirt by cosmopolitan cultural assumptions, and the practitioner exercises power in the practitioner-patient relationship in a way more or less acceptable to those who live in Western industrial societies. Neither the assumptions, nor the exercise of power, fit the Kiribati scene; accordingly cosmopolitan medical expertise has far less impact on the life-styles and health of the Kiribati people than is often imagined. If "social development" is to proceed, cosmopolitan offerings will need to be far more carefully adapted to the social contexts in which they are offered. (Geddes 1982:179)

This assessment of the contrasting approaches to health has applications beyond Kiribati. It highlights the need to assess the social context within which our Western medical assumptions concerning health and dietary concerns are located.

The Maori concept of health has been noted as covering four distinct areas, according to Durie: *te taha wairua,* a spiritual dimension; *te taha hinengaro,* a psychic dimension; *te taha tinana,* a bodily dimension; and *te taha whanau,* a family dimension. The preparation and consumption of food is of particular importance in the rituals observed in association with *te taha tinana.* However, the concern for the family and land brings the four aspects together. "To be a total person, 'in one's own right' is, from a Maori perspective, to be in an unhealthy state. The individual has no validity on his own" (Durie 1985:485). Today Maori elders are very concerned about two aspects of their people's health: the pollution of food resources and the health of children. Durie points out that these are different priorities from those identified by Western health professionals.

Other recent studies, such as those reported in Parsons (1985), also allow us to begin to build up a body of information about non-Western concepts of health in Pacific societies. From these we can begin to understand the local conceptualization of links between food and health.

It is apparent that the idea of health was based on a series of beliefs about both physical and spiritual well-being, with the spiritual aspect perhaps being stronger. These beliefs were a composite of ideas about the "right way" of doing things and "right ways" of behaving to one another. They included two aspects: first, giving a group the right food according to the occasion and to their status—that is, showing respect (Tah. *tauturu,* Pohnpei *wahu,* Wallis *arofa*) through sharing food—and second, a sense of orderliness, doing things in the socially acceptable manner. The exercise of power may have been a significant factor (Geddes 1982 for Kiribati). The right way contributed to a sense of order, as Macdonald (1985) demonstrates through the ideas about health expressed by Tikopians. That order was reassuring; it led to a sense of harmony in relationships among family members, both living and deceased (Parsons 1985:90 for Tonga; Kinloch 1985 for Samoa), and thus to a sense of general well-being. It implied living within appropriate physical and social bounds.

That was the aim even though it may not always have been possible in the circumstances, as we saw with the food for a Namu funeral. Attempts to do the right thing may not always be possible, so a compromise is acceptable. Thus if the main principles that ensured order were observed as well as possible, then people were reassured and felt a sense of rightness. One outcome was that people felt healthy because they believed the right steps had been followed to ensure their health. It is clear that health was more a group concept than an individual one.

This sense of order included the concept of food and how it should be used. Conceptual boundaries demarcated food from drink and other edibles, as well as between "real food" and its accompaniments and set apart puddings, refreshments, fruits, and so on (as we saw in Chapter 2). Drinkables included sugar cane and medicines. We saw in Chapter 6 how particular foods were designated for particular ceremonials. Not only were these appropriate, but their use brought a sense of well-being to all the participants, knowing they had contributed their right share of the food. The well-being extended also between the living and the ancestors.

The planting calendar was yet another aspect of this ordering. As we have seen, the planting of yams was the most significant event that regulated the agricultural cycle and thus the food supply. The seasonality of the yams and of the breadfruit enabled the cultural rhythm to be set in time with the natural rhythm of the seasons. The totality formed a pattern for a healthy society.

Large stature and a well-covered frame were also integral to the local view of a healthy individual. In Polynesian societies particularly, a well-covered individual was a good representative of his/her society. Namu women would pinch me in the arm and calf to warn me that people in Hawai'i would not think well of them if they sent me back too thin. This belief in what we would term fatness or even obesity as a sign of well-being and health was strongly held throughout the Pacific, particularly with regard to chiefs; the state of the chief's body was a representation of the health of the people he led. In Tikopia it is believed that " 'the body of the chief is the body of the land.' An aged and decrepit *ariki* is thought to mean that land will bear poorly, reflecting the lack of vigor of its chief." The *ariki* is the "symbolic body of his clan," so if he becomes thin or weak the clan as a whole will suffer (Macdonald 1985:69). If an old chief or commoner did become sickly he was placed in a temporary hut and various remedies were administered. If he or she did not respond, then the sufferer was abandoned. According to Ellis it is possible that many elderly died as much from starvation as from disease (1831:48).

The very positive value placed on large physical stature is in direct opposition to the negative value put on obesity by Western health professionals and others in the latter part of the twentieth century. Some use the term "obesity" strictly in the medical sense, but when read by a wider audience the value judgment is taken. While epidemiologists and others have noted the significance of large stature in social terms (e.g., Prior 1977), they also include it as part of the etiology of other diseases. For example, Pawson and Janes, in their study of obesity in Samoans living in Hawai'i in the 1970s, note that "the cultural beliefs that determine attitudes to food and obesity are currently unknown, but may be of prime importance in understanding the etiology of obesity in this population"

(1981:512). I have set out those main cultural beliefs here so that obesity and other diseases associated with it in the modern era may be understood from two cultural dimensions. It is important that both Western and local concepts of health be given serious consideration if the whole person and not just the symptoms are to be treated.

In Pukapuka in the 1930s a clear association was made between food and health. Diet, blood, and weather were said to affect the people's susceptibility to disease (Beaglehole and Beaglehole 1938:99). The basic precept of Pukapuka diet was expressed by the questions, "Are you full? Have you had enough to eat?" But that did not refer to just any food; it had to be the right foods. Eating enough food, particularly *Cyrtosperma* taro *(pulaka)*, was thought to ensure sufficient blood—and that was important to health. The minimum number of coconuts was ten a day for a man in good health (Hecht 1985:152–153). These food beliefs set some of the physical boundaries of Pukapuka healthy living, but there were also social boundaries. Hecht notes that components of this belief system continue to affect contemporary attitudes and behavior (1985:155).

Thus the value placed on food was of major significance to the Pukapuka sense of well-being. It was a tangible demonstration that an event had been carried out in a culturally appropriate way, and it also provided the spiritual sense of "right action." People felt a sense of health and well-being through these food activities and the sense of good social relations expressed in the appropriate manner (Hecht 1985). We don't have enough data as yet to know whether this high value of food has continued alongside introduced nutritional and medical beliefs.

What is evident is that this local concern for health was based on a shared sense of well-being rather than an individual one. Little concern was expressed about how an individual felt. An individual's sickness was often attributed to sorcery or the fact that the gods were displeased. By making offerings to the local gods, usually of food, that difficulty was put right and the person was reestablished in the social order. So food was a tangible indicator of that order, as well as a means of maintaining it—and the bountiful displays at feasts were a clear message of the well-being of the group.

These concepts show how all encompassing was the early view of what we call health. It included incidents that we might label sorcery, or accidents, or ill health; skin diseases that Western medics would label ailments were considered a necessary part of growing up. Eating the right food, namely plenty of starch and its accompanying dish, was a key factor in the early Pacific view of health. It is obvious that we need more data on belief systems that indicate how health was conceptualized and the part food played in that conceptualization.

FOOD HABITS OVER TIME

Research on food habits is growing and being undertaken from a wide range of approaches. Nutritionists and epidemiologists are asking questions similar to those the anthropologist asks (see Chapter 10). Similar interest is being expressed by some social historians (Rotberg and Rabb 1985) and sociologists. Primatologists have examined closely whether early primate groups were omnivorous or carnivorous (Harding and Teleki 1981), while others have devoted their attention to the question of whether protein was an important part of the human diet (Young 1980; Harris 1986). The degree to which early man was a meat eater is important for understanding modern dietary patterns and biological needs, as are the processes of adaptation to new foods. Such processes incorporate both the biological and cultural aspects of human groups over time (Ritenbaugh 1978:111–120). Thus all of these researchers are interested in determining how present-day health issues may be accounted for by past food habits. The result should be a better-rounded view of total food consumption over a long period of time.

Subsistence patterns in times past have been of major concern to archeologists. Working from the material evidence available in the Pacific, they have attempted to reconstruct both the production systems and the botanical inventory on which these relied (e.g., Kirch 1979). Whether rice preceded taro cultivation in Southeast Asia and the Pacific is but one of the questions for which they are seeking evidence (Pollock 1983b). The nature of the intensification of production is another. Hunter-Anderson has examined the early use of *Cyrtosperma* taro in Yap to show that it was first used as a security food and later became a staple (1981/1984).

Another major area of endeavor is to establish the subsistence patterns associated with Lapita culture, a highly significant cultural system that spread about 1500 B.C. from the southwest New Britain area to the islands to the east and north (Green 1979; Aoyagi 1982). A clearer picture is emerging of what foodstuffs were grown and of some processing methods associated with their consumption, such as pottery, stone ovens, and pits for fermentation (Irwin 1981; Y. Marshall 1985).

Skeletal material excavated by archeologists can also provide additional clues about diet and health. Measurements of the long bones indicate similarities between particular populations (Howells 1979; Katayama 1985 for Gilberts; Pietrusewsky 1977). Houghton, Leach, and Sutton (1975) have suggested, from their study of stature of prehistoric Polynesians in New Zealand, that a change in limb and body proportions marks eastern Polynesian populations from those of western Polynesia. This may imply both a dietary and a genetic change.

Linguists are also helping to rediscover the subsistence patterns of times past and thus to aid in our understanding of food and health in the Pacific Islands. The lead in this field of historical linguistics has been taken by Pawley, who suggests that "terms for taro, yam, sugar cane, sago palm, coconut, breadfruit, banana and a number of other familiar Indo-Pacific root and tree crops are not only reconstructible for PAN [Proto-Austronesian] but are continued by many contemporary languages of Melanesia. These retentions can only be accounted for, in their mass and in their regularity of sound change, in terms of a continuous tradition of horticulture from PAN times through to the present day Melanesian speech communities" (1981). Prehistorians and linguists are helping to demonstrate the continued use of certain plant species that contributed to the health of early populations of Pacific Island societies. Even though new plants have been added (Barrau 1979), the original food plants have been adapted to enable populations to survive adverse times and to reproduce.

However, it may be argued that continuous use of root and tree starches as the main foods, with minor amounts of protein and of some vitamins, may have led to a biological status that differed significantly from that of European populations. For example, Oomen and Malcolm (1961) found that the individuals in their sample of a Papua New Guinea population were excreting more nitrogen than they were taking in from their food, and speculated on the possibility that their gut flora may be producing nitrogen, a condition not noted before in human populations. Such a situation may have had long-term biological effects. These differences between Western and non-Western populations eating a very local diet, once recognized, would require some rethinking of how European-based nutritional theories apply to Pacific societies.

I am posing an argument that Pacific Island populations may have had a biological background that differs significantly enough from Europeans' biological background that different principles regarding the biological base of human nutrition need further consideration. Despite Finau's reservations (1986b) about Western nutrition principles—that they are unprovable and used by Western medical people to advance their own careers—I consider that the possibility of such distinctions needs to be further explored before they are eliminated. In similar vein to the thrifty gene hypothesis, I am suggesting that to survive: (1) Pacific Island populations had a particular metabolism and had made other adaptations to their digestive systems over a considerable period of time, and this allowed them to live on the roots and tree starches that grew well in the island environment; (2) that the patterns of use have continued over a period of about two thousand years; (3) that this time span may be of sig-

nificance when evaluating the impact of new foodways, such as the introduction of wheat in bread, less fiber, more protein and fat, and more regular overloading of the system; (4) that as new varieties and species of
root and tree crops have been introduced to particular societies, their
incorporation into the dietary regimen depended on their acceptance as
healthy food—that is, that they were culturally acceptable; and (5) that it
is important to take close account of the long history of use of traditional
foods while also evaluating the impact of new foods if we are to understand present-day health patterns.

CONCLUSIONS

Food and health are extensions of a basic idea of the order of society in
many parts of the Pacific. Eating the right foods in the right amounts and
with others made all the participants feel not only satisfied but also
healthy and right with the world. Being full was a key factor in health;
there seems to have been no upper limit to the acceptable amount of
food, but being short of food was less than satisfactory, a state to be tolerated only until better times came along.

In the Pacific, health was a shared sense of well-being, not the individual feeling as Westerners see it. It was built on the basis of sharing food as
a symbol of caring and mutual support. Food and health were thus two
dimensions of the ethos of any society. Sharing food was a means of inte-
grating society, keeping people together. The Marshallese had a saying
about famine: "When we go down we all go down together," indicating
that when food was in short supply it would be handed around the community to make sure everyone had at least a little.

This ethic was a strong part of the ordering process. It was confronted
with new ideological principles when Westerners arrived in the islands.
Many of the changes brought about in two hundred years of contact cannot be undone. Any genetic predisposition for coping with periods of
scarcity may have disappeared. Even the categories in which Pacific people think about their food and their health may be disappearing in favor
of those introduced since the early 1800s. The rate of change is alarming,
as is the expectation that Western views of food and health are better
than local views.

According to local concepts of health, food is a positive, not a negative, part of life. The borders between food and medicine are not clear
cut. Food and health are thus inextricably intertwined in Pacific societies,
but more from a cultural than a biological point of view. They are part of
the overall pattern of order of each society and any maladjustment needs
rectifying. This can be achieved usually by appeal to the gods, the spirits
of the ancestors; healers are an intermediary in this process. Such an

ordering system is holistic in that it incorporates all the different sectors of society and different spheres of activity. Food and health are not as compartmentalized as we have made them in Western thinking. This factor needs greater consideration in attempts to minister to health concerns of Pacific Islanders and to change their eating habits.

10

Evaluating Pacific Diets

In order to understand the biological efficiency of Pacific diets, nutritionists have had to rely until recently on food values for crops as derived from studies in the Caribbean and Southeast Asia, and from the U.S. Department of Agriculture Handbook 8 (1963). The South Pacific Commission, the Fiji National Food and Nutrition Committee, and Fiji School of Medicine have published jointly a set of tables entitled *Food Composition Tables for Use in the Pacific Islands* that gives us a standard set of nutritional values for starch foods grown in the Pacific, based on Pacific samples (see Table 17).

By means of dietary surveys, nutritionists have sought to establish data such as the number of calories, or kilocalories, consumed per day, and the amounts of proteins, fats, carbohydrates, minerals, and vitamins in those diets, in order to be able to assess their adequacy for the communities they have studied. Based on standards such as those set out in the *United States Recommended Dietary Allowances* (1968), the FAO recommended dietary allowances (1972), and the *Metric Composition of Australian Foods* (Thomas and Corden 1977), the South Pacific Commission is recommending a total daily intake of 3,000 kilocalories for adult males and 2,200 kilocalories for adult females, both of whom are moderately active (SPC 1983:32). The detailed breakdown of these recommended allowances is shown in Table 18.

The evaluation of Pacific diets has thus been, and still is, based on Western principles pertaining to the biological value of food. These principles have been derived from certain assumptions integral to Western beliefs about the efficacy of food, such as regular daily intake, balanced diet, the idea that food should be eaten only at meals, and the importance of the protein content. They do not include factors such as tabus, the status value of certain foods, or the inclusion of certain days of high consumption, as at feasts.

203

TABLE 17. Nutritional Value of the Main Starch Foods of the Pacific (all figures based on 100-g samples)

Food	Energy (kcal)	Energy (mega-joules)	Protein (g)	Fat (g)	Carbo-hydrate (g)	Ca (mg)	Iron (mg)	Vit. A (microg)	Thiamin (mg)	Ribo-flavin (mg)	Niacin (mg)	Vit. C (mg)	Waste A.C. (%)
Arrowroot flour	340	1.42	0.2	*	85.0	7	1.0	0	*	0.00	0.0	0	0
Breadfruit pulp (raw, mature)	113	0.47	1.5	0.4	26.0	25	1.0	*	0.100	0.06	1.2	20	23
Cassava, fresh	153	0.64	0.7	0.2	37.0	25	1.0	*	0.070	0.03	0.7	30	15
Cassava, flour	342	1.43	1.5	*	84.0	55	2.0	*	0.040	0.04	0.8	0	0
Jackfruit pulp	72	0.30	1.5	0.3	16.0	20	0.5	45	0.030	0.03	0.4	8	72
Plantain (cooking banana)	128	0.54	1.0	0.2	31.0	7	0.5	30	0.050	0.05	0.7	20	33
Potato, European	75	0.31	2.0	*	17.0	10	0.7	*	0.100	0.03	1.5	15	15
Potato, sweet	114	0.48	1.5	0.3	26.0	25	1.0	30†	0.100	0.04	0.7	30	15
Sago, flour	352	1.47	0.5	*	88.0	10	1.0	0	0.010	0.00	0.2	0	0
Tahitian chestnut	240	1.00	4.5	4.5	40.0	-	-	-	0.261	-	-	2	0
Taro, common‡	113	0.47	2.0	*	26.0	25	1.0	*	0.100	0.03	1.0	5	20
Taro, giant†	70	0.29	0.6	0.1	16.9	152	0.5	*	0.104	0.02	0.4	*	-
Taro, swamp‡	122	0.51	0.8	0.2	29.2	577§	1.3	*	0.027	0.11	1.2	*	-
Yam, fresh	104	0.44	2.0	0.2	24.0	10	1.2	6	0.100	0.03	0.4	10	15
Yam, flour	317	1.33	3.5	0.3	75.0	20	10.0	*	0.150	0.10	1.0	0	0

Source: Adapted from SPC 1983:14.

* Trace.

† Large range of values for different varieties.

‡ Common taro = Colocasia esculenta; giant taro = Alocasia macrorrhiza; swamp taro = Cyrtosperma chamissonis.

§ This high content may not be true of all varieties.

Table 18. Recommended Daily Intake of Nutrients

Age	Body Weight (kg)	Energy (mega-joules)	Energy (kcal)	Protein (g)	Vit. A (micrograms)	Vit. D (micrograms)	Thiamin (mg)	Riboflavin (mg)	Niacin (mg)	Folic acid (micrograms)	Vit. B_{12} (micrograms)	Vit. C (mg)	Calcium (g)	Iron (mg)
Children														
0–1	7.3	3.4	820	14	300	10.0	0.3	0.5	5.4	60	0.3	20	0.5–0.6	5–10
1–3	13.4	5.7	1360	16	250	10.0	0.5	0.8	9.0	100	0.9	20	0.4–0.5	5–10
4–6	20.2	7.6	1830	20	300	10.0	0.7	1.1	12.1	100	1.5	20	0.4–0.5	5–10
7–9	28.1	9.2	2190	25	400	2.5	0.9	1.3	14.5	100	1.5	20	0.4–0.5	5–10
Males, adolescents														
10–12	36.9	10.9	2600	30	575	2.5	1.0	1.6	17.2	100	2.0	20	0.6–0.7	5–10
13–15	51.5	12.1	2900	37	725	2.5	1.2	1.7	19.1	200	2.0	30	0.6–0.7	9–18
16–19	62.9	12.8	3070	38	750	2.5	1.2	1.8	20.3	200	2.0	30	0.5–0.6	5–9
Females, adolescents														
10–12	38.0	9.8	2350	29	575	2.5	0.9	1.4	15.5	100	2.0	20	0.6–0.7	5–10
13–15	49.9	10.4	2490	31	725	2.5	1.0	1.5	16.4	200	2.0	30	0.6–0.7	12–24
16–19	54.4	9.7	2310	30	750	2.5	0.9	1.4	15.2	200	2.0	30	0.5–0.6	14–28
Adult man (moderately active)	65.0	12.6	3000	37	750	2.5	1.2	1.8	19.8	200	2.0	30	0.4–0.5	5–9
Adult woman (moderately active)	55.0	9.2	2200	29	750	2.5	0.9	1.3	14.5	200	2.0	30	0.4–0.5	14–28
(pregnancy, later half)		+1.5	+350	38	750	10.0	+0.1	+0.2	+2.3	400	3.0	30	1.0–1.2	
(lactation, first 6 months)		+2.3	+550	46	1200	10.0	+0.2	+0.4	+3.7	300	2.5	30	1.0–1.2	

Source: Adapted from SPC 1983:32, 33.

These different assumptions are reflected in two very different modes of thought about how diet changes. One group has taken the view that Western diets are the best model to follow and that non-Western diets need to be changed to become more like the Western model (Berg 1973). The second group, which is much smaller, takes the view that diets derived from local foods have positive attributes and should be encouraged wherever feasible (Parkinson and Lambert 1982; Spencer and Heywood 1983); they argue that local foods are high in fiber and low in fat and salt, and provide bulk and protein from fish rather than meat. Both these views have had their own kinds of impact on nutrition education. But the basic view has been that "a knowledge of nutrition helps people to make the best use of traditional and modern foods. This in turn provides the basis for good family and community health" (Parkinson and Lambert 1982:2).

NUTRITION STUDIES

The difficulty with these nutrition studies, whichever viewpoint is taken, is that they start from the biological premise, and have not taken into account cultural factors such as the lack of a meal concept, the complementarity of the starch and its accompaniment, and the fact that minimal use has been made in the past of green leafy vegetables. Consideration of the local concepts of food and Pacific peoples' ways of thinking about feeding a household or community would help in understanding why people eat what they do. As I have stressed, food to Pacific Island people has as strong a social component as a material component. Recognition of these differences from European attitudes toward food would result in a more pertinent baseline for nutrition education programs for the region than one drawn from Western biological and medical principles.

Closer attention also needs to be paid to cultural determinants of who can eat what and when. The range of foods eaten varies according to age, sex, and status. We have seen how certain foods such as turtles, pork, and birds were reserved for men in Tahiti, and tabu for women and menstruating girls. Old men in Yap had a different diet from the young active males and thus received a different nutrient intake. Commoners ate less than chiefs, particularly puddings. Since the value of nutrient intake is likely to differ for different sectors of the community, these variations need consideration when evaluating total intake.

Jelliffe and Jelliffe, authorities on child nutrition worldwide, have drawn attention to the need to integrate Western ideas with what they term "bio-traditional cultures." They highlight the difference between the two sets of ideas by categorizing Western approaches as linear and bio-traditional cultures as curved.

It seems increasingly apparent that there is an urgent need for scientific consideration of the values and advantages, the hazards and limitations of different traditional health systems on a world wide basis. . . . The need is to try to evaluate scientifically, and without prior commitment or bias, the efficacy of different methods and practices, and to strive to assess how much has a wide (or universal) application, how much is culture bound, and how much represents alternatives. . . . Fundamentally, the real need is to develop the conceptual flexibility to be able to search for curvilinear compromises—for syntheses between the best of Western medicine and other healing systems, and between the direct linear technological and the improved curved bio-traditional. (Jelliffe and Jelliffe 1977:333)

While they are talking about health systems in general their point applies to nutrition, where there is a need to integrate traditional beliefs with Western beliefs about the kinds of foods appropriate to good health. A question such as "What did you eat today?" is more appropriate than one that asks about what was eaten at a particular meal, as the concept of "meal" does not occur in Pacific thinking (though the idea has been introduced). Thus it is inappropriate to suggest pawpaw (papaya) as a good breakfast food—not only is it considered as food mainly for pigs, but "breakfast" is not easily translated into Pacific languages.

Diet in Relation to Disease

Having measured the total caloric intake per day, a major concern has been to assess the prevalence of certain nutritionally related diseases such as diabetes, obesity, ischaemic heart disease, and dental caries in particular Pacific populations. The incidence of these conditions has generally been found to be higher in urban than in rural groups. Thus certain remedial actions have been suggested, including attempts to provide nutrition education (see Coyne, Badcock, and Taylor 1984 for a comprehensive review of nutritionally related studies in the Pacific).

A large proportion of the dietary studies in the Pacific Islands have been undertaken by nutritionists working for the South Pacific Commission in the 1950s and 1960s (e.g., Oomen and Malcolm 1961; Malcolm 1955; Hipsley and Kirk 1965; McKee 1957). Other studies—such as those by Miller (1927, 1929) in Hawai'i; Murai, Pen, and Miller (1958) in the Marshalls and Pohnpei; Hankin et al. (1970) for Palau and Guam; Holmes (1956) for the Solomons and (1953) for the Gilberts—were also conducted under the aegis of public health schemes. In Rarotonga, Neave (1969) looked at certain sectors of the population, particularly children and pregnant women, that may be at risk for diet-associated diseases such as diabetes, tuberculosis, and coronary heart disease.

In a study of Micronesian children, Malcolm (1955) weighed and measured them to assess their development in comparison with the Australian standard of child development. She found that the birth weight of Micronesian children was below that of the average for Australian children but that their weight increased rapidly during the first seven months. From the eighth to thirteenth month, weight gain was nil. She suggested that this period of no weight gain correlated with weaning and with the introduction of supplementary foods. By one year of age the child was eating a diet similar in composition to that of adults. As these children developed, their health deteriorated because traditional infant feeding practices were no longer being used.

One Pacific society, Nauru, has featured strongly in developing this link between modern diet and disease owing to findings of a very high level of non–insulin dependent diabetes mellitus in the population (Zimmet 1981; Pargeter, King, and Zimmet 1984). All food is imported from Melbourne. From a nutrition study of 70 individuals out of a total Nauruan population of about 4,500 it was found that respondents had an average intake of 7,200 calories per day, that is, more than twice the recommended dietary allowance. The study also found that one-third of respondents were diabetic, and another group showed a high level of glucose intolerance and were thus likely to become diabetic (Zimmet 1981). The series of studies conducted on Nauru has led to much publicity with headlines such as "Nauruans Dying of Wealth" (*Pacific Islands Monthly*, September 1987). A close association is being drawn here between their income from phosphate royalties and a very Westernized diet, as an example of the effects of modernization leading to obesity and a very high incidence of diabetes in a population. The Nauruans are concerned about the negative image of themselves that is being disseminated worldwide (NJP fieldnotes, August 1987).

However, we cannot claim Nauruan obesity and high caloric intake as an example of the effect of dietary change without examining their former diet. Nauruans never had the range of foods used in the rest of the Pacific because of the limestone structure of their island and the lack of good soil; the abundant phosphate is unusable by plants until it has been treated and converted into superphosphate. Their local diet consisted entirely of fish, coconut, and pandanus, but there were considerable periods of drought when food was scarce or unavailable (Delaporte 1920; Wedgwood 1936). Now that food is readily available, their caloric intake has increased at the same time their work has become more sedentary, and they use cars and motorbikes to get around the island instead of walking.

As yet there has been no intensive study of the social factors associated with diet and health to give a well-rounded picture of the place of food in Nauruans' life today and in the past. During a brief visit (NJP fieldnotes,

August 1987) it became very apparent from observations and talking with Nauruans that food has maintained its importance in their social life. There is still fluctuation in intake as a result of feasts and shortages, from time to time. An analysis of the patterns of food use over a year, including feasts, together with a study of the meaning of food to Nauruans and their activity patterns would give us a useful comparison with what we can reconstruct of food use in the days before phosphate export brought the ability to buy imported food. Ethnographic reports indicate that the population was small in numbers then, but healthy (Ellis 1936: 12). Such a comparison would give us a clearer picture of non-biological factors that might be associated with the high incidence of obesity and diabetes on Nauru.

In Kiribati several studies have been conducted over the last thirty years to show the degree to which imported foods have been incorporated in the diet (Turbott 1949; Holmes 1953; Jansen 1977; Franks and Jurgensen 1985). The Jansen study drew comparisons between an outer island, Tabiteuea, and urban Tarawa, while the Franks and Jurgensen study concentrated on one-year-old children on the outer island of Abemama.

Another study in Kiribati is the result of close collaboration among epidemiologists, a nutritionist, and an anthropologist (Zimmet et al. 1982). They combined their approaches to ascertain the prevalence of diabetes, cardiovascular disease, and hypertension; to assess the relationship between the prevalence of these diseases and the modernization of life-style; and to advise the government on intervention programs to prevent further escalation of these diseases. They found no marked difference in nutritional levels between rural and urban populations, but some interesting differences in consumption patterns (Geddes 1982:156). "In the case of many people brought up on a work island [e.g., Betio] store foods have formed their usual diet throughout their lives. . . . However it was found that people who had spent some years on work islands reverted to local foods quite readily when returning to their home island communities." (Geddes 1982:291). Modernization is considered a risk, particularly in regard to diabetes and hypertension. "Even the rural areas may be suffering from some of the consequences of non-traditional living" (Zimmet et al. 1982). In contrast, in earlier times when traditional foods were all that was available, the people had other concerns than these diseases and the cost of food and how long it takes to prepare it. The issue of modernization here seems to be a medical one.

Other studies of particular communities, such as Tokelau (Prior 1977), Samoa (Baker, Hanna, and Baker 1986), Wallis Island (Taylor, Bennett, and Zimmet 1984), and Nauru (Zimmet 1981), have yielded a wealth of information on diabetes, heart disease, and hypertension and their associations with obesity. But the degree to which these associations can be attributed to change, or Westernization, is open to question. The diet on a Tokelau atoll or in Western Samoa is not strictly "traditional" because the people in those communities are undergoing different kinds of changes from those experienced in the past. They don't suffer the same irregularities in food supply that their ancestors did, and today they eat doughnuts and sweet biscuits and canned meat in addition to their fish and coconuts or fish and taro. We need to examine more closely how strictly interpreted traditional diets from earlier times may affect consumption and disease patterns today. Unfortunately we do not have skinfold measurements, urinalysis, or measures of blood pressure for populations in those times past. We have only some indications of height and body build to correlate with dietary amounts and frequency.

Another example of the dilemmas of modernization has been reported for Western Samoa. Schoeffel's study shows that the most extensively documented health problems have been associated with nutritional deterioration there. Moreover she links that deterioration to a decline in the traditional staple diet and an increased use of imported foods. She attributes this to what she terms "well intentioned health education programmes emphasizing 'balanced diets' and the 'three food groups' (vitamin foods, carbohydrate foods and protein foods) [that] have reinforced the notion that imported foods are superior to local foods, and that traditional diet is nutritionally inadequate." Today, bought foods, particularly canned, have been given higher status than local foods: "The consumption of store-bought food is prestigious in a culture which attaches greater prestige to consumption than to production" (Schoeffel 1985: 212). Imports and remittances have played a large part in habituating Samoans to new food tastes. These new-found food experiences have been a contributing factor in the decreasing use of traditional starch foods, particularly in urban and peri-urban areas. But they have not driven them away entirely, as the urban studies might indicate.

Schoeffel's caution as to the inappropriateness of Western categorizations of diet underlines the argument that our own Western criteria may be inadequate for a non-Western food system and that we cannot use these alone to measure change. The gap between new Western ideas and their acceptance in non-Western countries must also be taken into account; bottle- rather than breast-feeding is a classic example of changing fashions in the West that are having harmful effects on developing nations (L. Marshall 1985).

The Nauru, Kiribati, and Western Samoa studies all use the idea of modernization as an important criterion of the seriousness of changes in diet leading to high incidence of non-communicable diseases such as diabetes and heart disease. But the term "modernization" has no foundation as few studies on diet were conducted in any of these communities before the 1950s. Thus these studies have resorted to comparing present-day urban consumption patterns with present-day rural consumption, and then extrapolating as if these rural patterns are the same as or similar to "traditional" consumption patterns from times past. Let us look more closely at what have been called traditional consumption patterns.

"TRADITIONAL" DIETS

The term "traditional diet" has been used by Western scientists to mean either food habits from times past or, more loosely, to mean diets derived from locally produced foods. I will use the term here to mean pre-1945 diets on the grounds that World War II brought major changes to the Pacific, and after that time urbanization began to increase (Schuster 1979).

One difficulty is that pre-1945 diets have not been subject to close scrutiny, so there are few firm data to use as a baseline. From ethnographic and missionary reports we have some descriptions of what foods were eaten and variations due to status, sex, and irregularities of supply. We know also that locally produced foods comprised the diets of indigenous Pacific Islanders, but that new foods grown locally were being introduced, such as *Xanthosoma* taro, cassava, and sweet potato. We know also that indigenous people were under increasing pressure to adopt imported foods on the grounds that they would improve their health (Pollock 1989). So the best we can do is make a guestimate.

Built into the idea of traditional diets is the expectation by some that these were "better" than present-day diets (Coyne, Badcock, and Taylor 1984), and that "traditional" somehow implies stable and unchanging. When the term is used in this way, the claims for the degree of change in diet and health become artificially inflated.

One result of using the assumptions of what constitutes a traditional diet is that diseases are being attributed to changes away from these idealized diets. If, however, a reconstructed value of a traditional diet is used as a baseline, if a year's cycle of diet is built into the thinking, and if cultural factors are also included, we will have a better starting point from which to assess the degree to which modern diets and health differ from those of times past. The concept of traditional diets should include not just the foods eaten but also the mode of cooking, the degree of irregularity of food availability, the persistence of tabus, and changes in status foods—factors that have already been discussed. It is hard to reconstruct all these factors as they have affected Pacific societies variously, but if we take into account these main points, we can calculate an estimated average diet, based on the nutritional value of the so-called traditional foods.

Nutritional Value of Local Starch Foods

Those nutritionists who have looked at Pacific foods closely are generally agreed that the traditional diets of these populations were adequate and healthy, if irregular (Murai, Pen, and Miller 1958; Standal 1983). Some nutritionists imply that those former benefits of a traditional diet are being lost with modernization, and that loss is leading to high incidence of diseases such as hypertension and diabetes (Coyne, Badcock, and Taylor 1984). But if we attempt to quantify those traditional diets we can develop a clearer picture of nutritional status at an earlier period in order to establish whether or not it was beneficial.

Up until the 1950s roots and fruits formed four-fifths of the caloric intake (Massal and Barrau 1956). The predominant nutrient in these foods was carbohydrate. However, this value varied according to the species of taro. *Xanthosoma* taro has 133 kilocalories per 100 grams, while *Alocasia* taro has only 70. The amount of protein in these taros is low, varying from 2.9 grams in *Xanthosoma* to 0.59 in *Alocasia* (Standal 1982). Splittstoesser, Martin, and Rhoades (1973) found that some cultivars of *Colocasia* taro had as much as 7 grams of protein per 100 grams, but we don't know how widely available those cultivars were. *Alocasia* and *Cyrtosperma* taros had much the greater amounts of calcium, and *Xanthosoma* had the greater vitamin C content. *Colocasia* corms were found to be rich in potassium (Standal 1982:126–129). "Taro corms can thus serve as a dietary source of carbohydrates and potassium for all ages and as a major protein source for adults who depend on taro as their staple foods" (Standal 1982:142). The recently introduced *Xanthosoma* is more nutritious than the older three types of taro, so where it is eaten regularly the diet may have improved.

A particular attribute of taro is that its starch granules are easily digested. The size of the taro grain is one-tenth that of potato, thus making it easier to assimilate for those with digestive problems. This property has been recognized commercially; taro flour is now manufactured for infant formulae in the United States and is especially useful for those allergic to cereals or to milk. Also, those who eat taro have been found to be less subject to tooth decay and acute infection of the gums (Wang 1983:4).

The nutritive value of *poi,* taro paste that may be eaten either fresh or fermented, has also been widely acclaimed. It too is an excellent food for people with certain health problems and is recommended for patients with food allergies to certain grains. It was the mainstay food of Hawaiians at the time of contact for whom "it must have furnished the organic acids to the diet of the Hawaiians as fruit furnishes it in the diet of other peoples. . . . The stimulating effect upon the appetite of organic acids of fruits and vegetables is well known" (Miller 1927:8). She notes that 5 pounds of *poi* per day was the average amount for a man or woman, but that oldtime Hawaiians might eat 10 or 15 pounds a day depending on the work they were doing and the abundance of supply (Miller 1927:17). From this excellent carbohydrate food they would have gained an adequate supply of minerals and vitamins.

A major drawback of these edible aroids is the oxalic acid content. Analysis of a number of different cultivars has revealed a wide range of values. In their examination of the chemistry of tropical root crops, Bradbury and Holloway found that the oxalates were concentrated in the skin of various taros and become more concentrated in conditions of drought or poor soil (1988:114–117). The presence of oxalic acid and oxalates can render dietary calcium unabsorbable and therefore unavailable to the human body, according to Standal (1982:129); however, she considered it unlikely that amounts large enough to trigger this action would be consumed. It has been assumed that highly toxic cultivars have been gradually eliminated from cultivation, but it may also be that such toxicity has been increasing with more intensive cultivation practices. Long processing in the earth oven helped to overcome this toxicity problem.

The other starch foods such as yam, sweet potato, banana, and breadfruit are similar to one another in nutritive value. Cassava is often cited as low in protein relative to its caloric value, but its carbohydrate value and a high potassium count give it some positive attributes in terms of nutritional value. (See Table 17 for nutritional values of the main starch foods.)

The accompanying dishes added important vitamins and minerals as well as protein and fat to the carbohydrate. The root and tree starches provided the same nutrients each day. But the accompaniment tended to vary, so if fish was used, then several grams of protein were added; coconut cream added fat. Taro leaves used to wrap puddings, such as *palusami,* added a relatively high amount of both protein and vitamin A. They were the main form of green vegetables used but were not a regular part of the diet. Drinking coconuts also added some necessary vitamins.

The diet before 1945 was thus high in carbohydrates, high in fiber, and low in sucrose. Such sucrose as was used was obtained mainly from chewing raw sugar cane or roasting the roots of the *ti* plant, *Cordyline terminalis* (see Fankhauser 1986 for New Zealand). The latter was eaten mainly as a feast food in Tahiti, the Cook Islands, and New Zealand. Such fruits as were eaten included Tahitian apple *(vi),* mango, and pawpaw, but they were not eaten regularly and contributed additional vitamins and minerals only occasionally to the dietary intake. Similarly, raw fish was consumed by fishermen and was served at feasts, adding important nutrients—but not on a regular basis.

Estimated Intake of Local Starches

Using the information that Cook and Banks and, later, missionaries and ethnographers have left us, and the modern studies of food composition, along with a few simple calculations, a generalized reconstruction can be made of the nutritional value of diets of Pacific populations some two hundred years ago (bona fide traditional diets):

Assuming that an everyday household diet for an individual consisted of

2½ taros @ 600 calories	or	1,500 cals
an accompaniment (fish)		300 cals
a drinking coconut		30 cals

the individual would consume each day 1,830 calories. If this diet was eaten on 25 days out of 30 each month (assuming 5 days with no food, for whatever reason—sickness, famine, war) and subtracting also 20 days of feasting each year (7 feasts, each lasting about 3 days), our Pacific Islander would eat the "everyday" meal 280 days a year. This would amount to 1,830 × 280 or 512,400 calories per year. Then, for those feasts, he/she might eat

starches	or	1,500 cals
accompaniments (some pork)		700 cals
puddings		1,000 cals
coconut		100 cals

or 3,300 calories per day and so, for 20 days of feasting, a total of 66,000 calories each year. Adding these "feast" calories to the total annual "everyday" calories, we arrive at a grand total of 578,400 calories or an average of about 1,585 a day over a year period. This would be considered a bare minimum for survival by present nutritional standards.

But if we also consider what would be called snacks, that is, foods eaten casually and opportunely such as fruits picked in the bush, or a piece of pandanus or coconut meat, or more taro, yam, or puddings, then another 1,000 calories a day would be possible.

Thus total daily intake from a traditional diet probably ranged between 2,000 and 3,000 calories when averaged over a year cycle. But the range on any one day of the year might have been 1,600 to 4,000 calories for an individual adult.

By evaluating the traditional diet using Western standards of what constitutes good nutrition, we can estimate the health impact of these diets of former times. The caloric value of those early diets was in a range similar to those of today, 2,000 to 3,000 calories. But our reconstructed daily intake was calculated by estimating intake over a year period, taking into account the peaks of high and low consumption during that time. And that range of caloric intake probably lasted for at least 150 years in many parts of the Pacific, until the 1950s. The great variations in diet among today's island communities—for example, the huge amounts eaten on Nauru and by contrast the impoverished eating patterns in some urban settings leading almost to malnutrition—have developed only in the last fifteen to twenty years. This seems a relatively short time period, especially when we can already associate certain disease patterns with these diets. We must consider the possibility that part of the etiology of these diseases may not be food habits per se, but the rapidity with which the change to high fat, low fiber diets plus low activity has taken place.

Evidence suggests that the total intake was not lacking in any vital nutrients by today's standards. There may have been an excess of calories consumed at times, but this was probably a vital adaptation to the variations in supply and availability of some foods. Whether that excess contributed to any diseases leading to death is hard to know.

But we must still ask: How important was the fluctuation in intake, from none on some days to 3,000-plus calories during feasts? What effects did this have on the people's general health and their society's operation? Did it affect the periodicity of childbirth, for instance? What diseases were directly connected with this consumption pattern? How close was that traditional diet to the rural and urban diets of today?

PRESENT-DAY RURAL DIETS

Rural diets today should be distinguished both from urban diets of current times and from diets of earlier times. In rural diets the amount of local starchy foods used varies. For example, Naduri people in Fiji's Sigatoka valley eat sweet potatoes, taro, and breadfruit in season, but they also eat some imported foods such as rice and bread. Also, food intake is fairly regular now. They boil the starches, using the earth oven only for special occasions and weekends. And other foods such as spaghetti have been incorporated into the accompanying dish (NJP fieldnotes 1982). Tea, soft drinks, and beer also form part of the caloric intake in rural societies today. In Western Samoa, however, rural "Samoans still prefer traditional foods, [yet] the convenience and relatively low cost in both cash and labour of imported foods such as rice, flour, sugar, lard, chicken backs, bully beef, and canned pilchards have made these items standard fare in rural diets particularly in the most densely populated, land short, peri-urban areas of north eastern Upolu" (Schoeffel 1985: 212). Schoeffel is pointing up the discrepancy between the ideal or preferred dietary patterns today and the practical realities.

These are but two examples of how rural diets are changing to include Western and imported foods. They also give us an indication of the value still placed on the traditional foods, even when it is not always feasible to serve them. In confusing the time scale so that rural and traditional diets are considered as if they were one and the same, some of the major differences have been overlooked. Not only are the foods available different, because of cropping or marketing or other reasons, but also time has become a more significant consideration, and new status factors have emerged. For example, Coyne, Badcock, and Taylor (1984) provide some extracts from Cook's journals to account for food habits in the days before urbanization and Western influence. But the quotations they give refer only to the starchy component of the diet and they don't really evaluate the place of food in the way of life at the time. Instead, they use Turbott's study of diet on a Gilbertese atoll (1949) as an example of traditional diet to illustrate the changes in caloric intake and the associated disease patterns. But the fact that the Gilbertese diet included some Western foods, which were boiled or fried rather than baked in the earth oven, means that it was not traditional. So we should not confuse rural diets with traditional ones in assessing change.

Since rural households comprise more than two-thirds of most island populations (see Tables 13, 14) we need to get a clearer picture of their consumption patterns today in order to distinguish them from traditional and urban diets. Rural diets are derived mainly from food that is locally grown (NJP fieldnotes, Naduri 1983), and so traditional starches are likely to be used, albeit with some modern imported foods added.

Most of the data on rural food consumption has come from anthropologists and rural sociologists. One of the earliest to focus on diet in the Pacific was Finney, working in French Polynesia. He found that the diet of people on an outer island differed significantly from that of residents of a suburb of Pape'ete. The former ate more local starch while the latter ate more purchased starch, particularly bread. He calculated proportions of food consumption in terms of meal units, not calories (Finney 1965; 1973:59, 72).

Also for French Polynesia, Danielsson compared what he terms "aboriginal culture" with imported food consumption for Raroia atoll (1956). He showed that they too made heavy use of flour in 1950, whereas formerly they had relied on pandanus, *fakea* taro *(Cyrtosperma)*, and purslane for their starches. As his informant noted, "In the olden days we were always hungry on Raroia, and eager to fill up our stomachs. . . . If there was anything to eat an earth oven was prepared once a day, otherwise not at all" (Danielsson 1956:53). My own study of diet on Takapoto, Tuamotus, showed a total intake of 2,650 calories, of which 1,154 were derived from local fish and coconuts, while the balance was obtained from food purchased in the stores or brought by plane from Pape'ete (Pollock 1977).

In a team study of another Tuamotu atoll diet, Delebecque et al. (1982) labeled it as "radically altered," with carbohydrates predominating and a high dependence on outside sources. But they give no indication of prior diet or specific caloric measures of food intake. They note several health effects including hypertension, obesity, and dental caries, as well as observing that "some misunderstanding among the population as to what constitutes a sensible diet" prevails (Delebecque et al. 1982: 102). As they specifically mention a lack of fresh fruit and vegetables, it would seem that that "sensible diet" is assessed by Western rather than local measures.

The study of dietary patterns on the atoll of Namu, Marshall Islands, that I conducted over a thirteen-month period showed heavy reliance on local foods and a daily caloric intake (1,700) that was low by Western standards (Pollock 1970, 1976). In the early 1970s these figures were questioned as unreasonably low and suspect because they showed no use of green vegetables. Dietary studies subsequent to mine also have shown a relatively low caloric intake (Neave 1969; Davidson 1975). One difference between my Namu data and those collected by nutritionists is that my data were collected from every household on one islet—that is, from some two hundred people—for one week out of each of nine months during the total fieldwork period so that the seasonal variation during the year is represented. Unfortunately, I had no means of measuring energy expenditure.

Another kind of longitudinal study has been carried out on the diet of one village community in the Sigatoka valley, Fiji. There, a series of dietary studies covers a thirty-year period; the first, in 1953 by Langley, was followed up in 1963, 1972, and 1982 (Parkinson 1987). That community has continued to make heavy use of their local crops of sweet potato, cassava, breadfruit, and river shellfish, but supplements them with purchased foods such as chicken, rice, bread, and eggs, especially for breakfast. Total calories consumed appear to have increased only slightly. Sugar is the main component whose use has increased.

These studies of rural areas, mostly conducted by anthropologists, have not for the most part been concerned with health issues in the Western sense. Rather, they have shown the social variables impinging on food consumption, such as the effects of the cash economy (Finney 1965), ecological effects (Danielsson 1956), and the social organization of food getting (Pollock 1970). Diet and health issues are raised in other ethnographic contexts where they are shown to be part of a wider set of social values, as we have seen for Pohnpei and for Mo'orea (Shimizu 1985; Robineau 1984).

Nutritional surveys in rural areas or outer islands of the Pacific are sparse. Twenty years ago this was not so much of a problem as there was less distinction between rural and urban life-styles. Today rural people eat different foods and have different activities and concerns from those of their urban kin.

URBAN DIETS

Nutrition studies are more easily conducted in urban centers because facilities and local assistants are more readily available. The logistics of getting a team of researchers to an outer island or rural area may prove difficult and too costly. In addition, the changes in diet and incidence of nutrition-related disease are likely to be less marked in rural areas than in urban areas, judging from the few studies that have been done. So surveys have been made of the populations of such urban centers as Tarawa, Rarotonga, and Apia, as well as of urbanized populations on Guam, Palau, and Fiji (Darnton Hill, Badcock, and Taylor 1985).

One study that has compared rural and urban diets of the same society was conducted in Fiji. Using the twenty-four-hour recall method to ascertain food intake, researchers found that the rural population was eating more carbohydrates than the urban population. There was also a marked difference in total calories consumed per day: Rural males consumed 3,152 and rural females consumed 2,644; for urban males the figure was 2,177 and for urban females, 1,910. Yet it was the urban Melanesians who were more obese than the rural people (Zimmet 1981). This study points up the necessity of such carefully controlled comparisons. The lower caloric intake by both urban males and females is due in large part to the cost of food. But their obesity needs some explanation other than caloric intake.

To put such urban studies in proper context we need to consider the proportion of island populations that lives in urban areas (see Tables 13, 14). Figures from the 1980s show a median of 30 percent of population censused in urban areas (omitting Nauru). In the 1950s this proportion would have been 10 percent or less (Reed 1975). So the number of people living in urban areas is still relatively small. Furthermore, it should be noted that a large proportion of those urban populations has moved into the cities from rural areas or outer islands within the last fifteen years. And apart from Fiji, most islands have only one urban center.

The question of whether Guam and Nauru should be considered urban for purposes of nutritional evaluation is debatable. Guam is much larger than Nauru and its population is scattered over its 549 square kilometers, mainly in coastal areas. About 60 percent of the population has some Chamorro ancestry (1978 census). While they have had a history of introductions to their diet over some four hundred years (Pollock 1986a) and have imported most of their food since World War II, there are still pockets of agriculture. Also, people do not all live in Agana, the main

town. Likewise, Nauru is hardly urban either in terms of outright numbers of people or density of population. Most of the people have some
income. Their diet too is heavily reliant on imported foods, though not
enough credence has been given to the local fish they prefer (NJP fieldnotes 1987). Thus, although most of the food of these two communities
is imported, many other aspects of urbanization in a metropolitan context do not apply: The populations are smaller and life is less stressful
than in Sydney or Bangkok.

Some authors consider that urbanization or modernization brings
greater variety to diets. Pelto and Pelto, for example, have characterized
modern diets as more varied than local diets (1983). But in the Pacific
this cannot be used as an indication of change. Rather, the reverse
appears to be the case; that is, diets have become less varied as urban
dwellers have to depend on a small amount of cash to buy food (see
Bakker-Williksen 1984 for Fiji). In Pape'ete bread and perhaps soup or
tea form the basic diet of urban households with many mouths to feed
and only one small pay packet (Marietta in Crocombe 1985), whereas in
times past there were some six or seven different starchy foods to choose
from as basics and a variety of possible accompanying foods.

In Palau the conscientious movement to promote "buy Palauan" has
assisted the rural farmers to sell more of their locally grown produce to
the urban population in Koror, though this has been achieved only
slowly, as the rural market gardeners experienced major difficulties in
getting the goods into town and in preventing it from rotting when there;
also, marijuana has proved more lucrative to those farmers than the food
crops (McCutcheon 1985b). So diversification and increase in the supply
of local foods is beginning to overcome the narrow range available to
urban populations.

The general findings from nutrition studies are that urban populations
are eating more refined carbohydrates (including sugar), more fat and
salt, and less fiber. And their more refined diet is associated with greater
obesity (measured by skinfold thickness) and higher incidence of cardiovascular disease, hypertension, and diabetes. Instances of malnutrition in
children are beginning to show up in hospitals (Burgess and Burgess
1976), as families find it hard to feed themselves on low or nil wages
where costs of food are high. This syndrome is likely to become more
prevalent if employment opportunities do not increase.

Arguments for dietary change based on an urban sample are misleading because they refer to only a small sector of the total population.
Nutritional studies conducted in these urban centers, or close by, indicate
that these populations show nutritional deficiencies and tendencies
toward modern diseases, but these findings must not be applied to whole
populations. More studies are needed specifically directed at rural popu-

lations, as well as studies that compare rural and urban diets within the same time frame. Then claims for the drastic effects of Westernization of diets on health (e.g., Keith-Reid 1982; Bloom 1987; Lane 1987; *Pacific Islands Monthly,* May 1987) may be found to be justified.

EFFECTS OF WESTERN IDEAS ON FOOD AND HEALTH

We must still ask, What effects have the new Western ideas had on local concepts of food and health? To what extent have the new starches been incorporated with the traditional starches; that is, is rice a substitute for taro? Are these alternatives equally acceptable, or is the use of the imported food just pragmatic—because it is quicker and easier to prepare? The answers to some of these questions need to be openly sought to understand fully the nature of change in urban diets. Only with those data established can we expect to mount successful nutrition education programs that make sense in terms of local thinking about food.

Two kinds of dietary studies, those by nutritionists and those by anthropologists, should be complementary. The two need to be combined in order to broaden our understanding of why people eat what they eat today and of the health problems associated with these dietary patterns. As Clements noted, "Before attempting to change dietary patterns it is essential for the 'adviser' to try to find out the significance attributed to food, food groupings, presence of taboos, etc." (1959:176). This nutritionist takes the view that changes should start from existing food habits and should work toward an accommodation with Western biological concerns: "The foods recommended for inclusion should be those that help balance the diet and should be those that are locally available or can be produced locally and be within the acquisition of the whole population" (Clements 1959:177). As two other nutritionsists observed some twenty-five years ago:

> A dietary study of a group of people whose way of life differs from that of the investigator—and this would include most studies—should commence with a study of the broad pattern of the beliefs and values of that group. If changing beliefs and values are involved—as is likely to be the case under the impact of culture contact, and the impetus of modern innovation— some estimation of the direction and velocity of change should be made. With this background it may be possible to determine how far the goals of this value system are limited by food and diet. (Hipsley and Kirk 1965:128)

And rather than merely trying to assess changes, we would be better equipped to understand why certain dietary patterns continue into the modern era in spite of all the new introductions, and to apply these ideas toward more effective nutrition education programs.

In this study I am focusing heavily on beliefs about food and how these have continued over time, with a lesser emphasis on how they are affected by change. Many of us have been too quick to expect incorporation of our own Western belief systems by others and thus to deny the persistence of food habits and their place in a society's world view. By reexamining societies from a different viewpoint it is becoming evident that peoples of the Pacific did not entirely discard their old beliefs. Even those we label religious beliefs were not discarded completely in the face of the new Christian beliefs that missionaries brought. Old beliefs and practices have persisted in small part through to today and can be seen if we look for them instead of looking for change (Hau'ofa 1985). Food habits also die hard.

Comparisons between the diets of different societies are also helping to draw attention to similarities of concerns in different parts of the world—for example, the effects of deficiency in the lactase enzyme in some populations' ability to digest milk (McCracken 1971). In addition, anthropological studies in rural communities reveal the social context and local belief systems, all of which add new dimensions to our thinking about food and health.

Any evaluation of food intake in terms of calories and nutrients must take into consideration local views of the value of food. As we have seen, recent anthropological studies have drawn attention to some of the major differences between these Western and non-Western views of health and the food habits associated with them (Ritenbaugh 1978:23–35; Colson and Selby 1974; Foster and Anderson 1978). With changing views on the superiority of Western medicine and the recognition of the interrelationships between biocultural factors and disease, a greater exchange of ideas between anthropologists and health professionals is being established. Similar exchanges of ideas between anthropologists and nutritionists are occurring. This should help all of us to develop a clearer longitudinal picture of foodways among Pacific populations.

EPIDEMIOLOGICAL STUDIES

Epidemiologists have increased our awareness over the last twenty years of some of the main medical problems facing the people of the South Pacific. In Western populations they are finding that "nutritional factors contribute in one way or another to a sizeable share of the burden of morbidity and mortality of the American people . . . [but] care is required in drawing conclusions about the relationship between dietary patterns and health outcomes" (McGinnis 1986:75, 77). This association is particularly clear when linking diet to Western diseases such as diabetes and hypertension. The same multifactorial approach that Zimmet (1981) uses for the etiology of diabetes is also needed to evaluate the effects of diet on other diseases.

Too much emphasis on change can be misleading, as we have seen, especially with thin evidence for the period before the present. Nevertheless, epidemiologists are using their evaluation of past diets and disease patterns to underline marked differences between rural and urban populations in the Pacific today: "Diabetes, ischaemic heart disease, hypertension and gout are rare in populations maintaining their traditional lifestyle and mainly appear in their urbanized counterparts" (Zimmet 1981: 61). Here traditional life-style refers to rural populations practicing subsistence agriculture, eating root and tree starches, and surviving on a low cash income.

To provide evidence for diet as a main etiological factor, epidemiologists have measured populations for height, weight, and skinfold thickness, and also conducted their own dietary surveys. Their analysis of their findings suggests several major changes in food habits associated with these diseases, notably increases in intake of energy (calories), sugar, salt, fats of animal origin, and alcohol, and a decrease in fiber intake (Coyne, Badcock, and Taylor 1984:3). These changes, they claim, have had serious health consequences, that is, higher incidence of the diseases mentioned. Although malnutrition occurs in only a few pockets at present, other health problems are increasing with modernization.

Analysis of the etiology of these diet-related diseases is thus based on the idea of change. For example, a comprehensive epidemiological study has compared Samoans living a "traditional" life-style in rural parts of Samoa with Samoans living in Pago Pago or Honolulu, in order to show that Westernization has introduced particular disease patterns and associated nutritional deficiencies (Baker 1981; Bindon 1982; Pawson and Janes 1981).

Where contact with Western society has occurred in the last twenty years, the difference between the rural and traditional life-styles, including diet, may not be very great. Even rural communities on the same island may differ markedly. In New Guinea, for example, it is interesting to note a marked distinction between two groups of rural communities, one Austronesian speaking and the other non–Austronesian speaking peoples, the latter showing very little glucose intolerance (Heywood 1987). But elsewhere in the Pacific use of the term "traditional" as synonymous with rural does not provide an adequate base from which to argue the degree of change in the modern era, because rural populations have also changed their traditional food habits.

Obesity

Obesity has been identified as a common factor in these epidemiological studies of modern populations. The term as used by Western observers refers to body build, based on both measurements and health status. Obesity occurs widely throughout the Pacific and is generally seen as an indicator of Westernization. As was noted in the first Marshall Islands Development Plan (1985–1989), "A rather disturbing development in recent years is the increasing incidence of diseases relating to nutritional imbalance, particularly in the urban areas. Such diseases include hypertension, heart diseases, diabetes and illnesses related to obesity. . . . It is believed that the high incidence of these diseases, which are usually associated with economically advanced countries, is due to the high content of fat, carbohydrate, and sugar combined with sedentary type urban life" (Kent 1986:33). This report does not indicate how obesity has been measured. It seems to be rather subjective and carries negative connotations.

Prior, in his classic paper on the subject of obesity, set out the hypothesis that "there is no evidence that obesity constitutes a health hazard in Pacific people" (1977:2) and proceeded to document the cases he had observed of obesity and the diseases with which it was associated. For those concerned to document the harmful elements in today's diets, obesity can be all too easily pinpointed and blame placed on a food intake high in candy, soft drinks, doughnuts, ice cream, and alcohol.

In contrast, by local Pacific standards, so-called obese people have been highly regarded both in the past and at the present time. They were a walking reminder that their society was a caring one, within which such persons were well provided for. They were positive social symbols to the wider world of their society's well-being. Whether there is a limit to the positive view of well paddedness is not clear. I suggest that someone who can no longer take part in social activities, work, and so forth may not be viewed so positively. One of my informants on Namu became nearly immobile during the latter stages of her pregnancy (at a guess she weighed 250 pounds), and another woman informant later died at the age of twenty-eight, her death attributed by other informants to obesity associated with her status as the consort of a paramount chief, a position that restricted her from partaking in any physical activity beyond his house. As the wife of the paramount chief, her physical grandeur was a mark of the community's care for her, and for him. While neither was strongly condemned by the other women, it was felt that their size was an encumbrance to those individuals, even in a society where being well padded was highly valued.

Current Western standards have spread the message both overtly and covertly that slim build is good and healthy. This "think thin" image is more prevalent among women today than among men, as several authors argue in Kaplan's edited volume, *Women's Conflict*. Beller's chapter entitled "Venus as Endomorph" shows how sexual dimorphism has developed over time so that women who are fatter than the image feel guilty. She calls for a reevaluation of food and body image, to allow a broader cultural interpretation of body build (Beller 1980).

Obesity may also be measured physically. By taking many individuals' skinfold measurements at the back of the upper arm and in the lower back, comparative figures can be established for a whole population (Prior 1977). These may be correlated with height-to-weight ratio for the same population to produce the "body mass index" (Taylor 1984). In a few studies, basal metabolic rate is also used as a measure of physical well-being. These figures have then been evaluated against a standard, such as the Harvard Scale, or an Australian measure (Zimmet 1981). Such measures show only the physical manifestations of fat deposition without taking into account any of the etiology or cultural aspects. Thus they are best used as only one of several possible indicators of what constitutes obesity.

From a biological viewpoint, obesity manifests itself in the capacity to make fat cells from a particular dietary regimen. The part carbohydrates play has been downgraded recently, but the link between obesity and diabetes still holds. But now excessive intake of energy is recognized as a true predisposing factor to obesity (Taylor 1984:38). Beller has shown that this is particularly so in the case of women, for whom estrogen acting in tandem with insulin is known to have an even more potent effect on fat deposition than estrogen alone (1980:552). So women are not only likely to be fatter than men but also more prone to diabetes. This factor shows up in some of the studies of diabetes in the Pacific (e.g., Zimmet 1981; Prior 1977).

From a medical point of view, obesity has been seen as a precursor to diseases such as diabetes and heart disease. It may be stated in the form of high caloric intake or skinfold thickness (high body mass index). Zimmet (1981) includes excessive caloric intake along with reduced physical activity, psychosocial stress, and abnormalities in insulin secretion in his five etiological factors leading to fat deposition and contributing to the high incidence of diabetes, particularly in urban areas of the Pacific. For example, in the case of Nauruans, men's weights averaged 11 kilos above those of a comparable Caucasian population, and women's weights were 19 kilos above this standard (Zimmet et al. 1977). We don't have figures for Nauruans' energy expenditure, so the argument for obesity is based mainly on excessive intake, which is associated with a low level of physical activity. Both factors are associated with a life-style dependent on a cash income.

Genetic factors have also been widely cited as contributing to obesity and its associated diseases. We have seen that a certain degree of body fat was probably essential for survival in times when food intake was irregular and that the thinner members of society would have been less likely to live to reproduce. This may have led to a genetic predisposition to obesity in a particular population. If in addition "fat" women were positively selected, then this genetic predisposition for obesity would have been further enhanced. Thus what Neel (1962) has labeled a "thrifty gene" hypothesis with particular reference to his South American population may have its applications to Pacific Island populations. Neel considers that this heritable trait may have had such positive value that obesity and diabetes traits were (unsuspectingly) selected for. Increase in frequency of this gene by natural selection through many centuries of deprivation or irregular food supply would have increased the prevalence of this "thrifty gene." Zimmet (1981) adds the argument that the manifestations of diabetes may have been dormant until unmasked by recent changes in lifestyle.

Beller has followed a similar line of argument in her discussion of how gender differences in slim and obese body forms have developed over time. She refers to an earlier image when Venus was seen as an endomorph, rather than the slim image she bears today. At that time when food supplies were scarce, Beller argues, genetic selection would have favored women best able to accumulate the most fat (1980:129).

Another dimension of this examination of factors contributing to obesity concerns the link between obesity and taste. The development of preference for bitter substances, as in fermented breadfruit or taro, is an interesting extension of what may be a warning against potentially harmful foods. If, as Rozin and Rozin (1981) have argued, flavor selection is biologically based yet uniquely human, then we must ask whether for the obese the flavor principle is too strong. The strength of the demand for sweet foods may be a significant element here. Controlling flavor may be a means of controlling obesity.

Diabetes

Many epidemiologists argue for a close link between obesity and diabetes in their discussions of diet-related diseases, as in the work of Taylor, Bennett, and Zimmet (1984). The most common form of diabetes in the Pacific is the maturity onset, or non-insulin-dependent (NIDDM), type. Urban populations have been found to have a higher rate of incidence of diabetes than rural or outer-island populations. For example, among Wallis Islanders living in Noumea men had seven times higher prevalence of diabetes and women four times higher prevalence than Wallis Islanders living on their home island (Taylor, Bennett, and Zimmet 1984:8). Similarly, for Cook Islanders living in their home islands, the rate of incidence was markedly lower than that for New Zealand Maoris (Prior et al. 1966). In rural Samoa the rate was 2.7 percent in rural populations compared to 7.9 percent in urban populations. Nauru has shown one of the highest prevalence rates in the world; 30.3 percent of that population was shown to be diabetic in 1975 (Zimmet et al. 1977). It is clear that many more persons living in towns are diabetic than those living in rural environments.

We need to ask what part diet plays in this incidence. In Nauru the diet has been considered the main factor. Nauruans' caloric intake, as measured by Zimmet et al. in the course of their diabetes survey, averaged 6,700 calories per day, or twice the World Health Organization–recommended intake. Alcohol also contributes a significant number of calories.

In Kiribati the prevalence figures for diabetes are much lower (9 percent for urban males and females, compared with 3.2 percent for the rural population). Nevertheless, susceptibility to diabetes (and hypertension) was considered "a substantial problem in Kiribati." Increased body weight, reduced physical activity, and increased consumption of imported foods were associated with increased risk of these diseases (Zimmet et al. 1982:10).

Elsewhere, such as in Samoa, urban diets have been found to include more calories from sugar and fat and more salt than in rural diets. These so-called empty calories are seen by some to contribute significantly to the diabetic condition.

In Papua New Guinea the incidence of diabetes in rural Highland communities has been found to be nil or very low, while it was 8.4 percent in coastal populations such as Port Moresby, where adults were found to be on average 10 kilos heavier than village adults. King et al. (1972) have suggested that this susceptibility to glucose intolerance may have been conferred by Austronesian admixture, that is, a genetic trait marking one sector of the population involved in the early settlement of the Pacific Islands. They make a marked distinction between non-Austronesian populations (the Highland PNG communities) and Austronesian populations and propose that the latter are more likely to suffer from diabetes (Heywood 1987:10).

This suggestion, together with the thrifty gene hypothesis for people of the island Pacific, who are mainly Austronesian, provides interesting areas for further research. Genetic factors plus dietary factors, both past and present, plus the larger body size of Austronesians may combine with a more clock-regulated food intake in modern times to trigger glucose intolerance. Or perhaps diabetes was present in the population before now, but not detected as such.

Thus the picture of diabetes as a consequence of dietary change is not as clear as it would seem. It does seem feasible, despite Finau's (1986b) protestations, that there is a genetic factor influencing its incidence, together with low activity, stress, and alcohol as contributory factors.

However, we need also to note that food consumption patterns, particularly in urban areas, are determined more by the clock than by hunger, thereby inducing people to eat more frequently perhaps than they need and to eat cheaper foods with empty calories. Certainly if the previous dietary patterns have been marked by irregular intake, this regularity of three meals a day may not only increase caloric intake but also affect the rate at which that food intake is metabolized. If we add the temptations of readily accessible food in snacks, candy, and soft drinks as well as beer and alcohol, these all add up to significant caloric intake.

We may also need to consider the effects of eating more cassava (with its effects on calcium assimilation) as another factor that may affect metabolism and availability of certain minerals and vitamins. Protein is also consumed in greater quantities in urban areas than in rural areas. Do we fully understand the biological effects of absorption of these new foods, along with these other dietary changes?

These considerations are important to our understanding of whether diabetes is a recent (that is, post–World War II) disease or whether it was a common sickness in earlier populations of Pacific Islanders, when they were eating large amounts of carbohydrates. We don't really know if they suffered from diabetes as such. Their so-called obesity may have been more muscular than fatty—that is, associated with high energy expenditure either in maintaining their taro gardens, walking into the interior of a high island, taking part in wars, or fishing. It is by no means clear to what extent the obesity/diabetes link is a "modern disease."

Another possible cause of diabetes, Zimmet suggests (1981), is abnormalities in insulin secretion. He notes that Pacific Island populations show higher plasma insulin responses to glucose than Caucasian groups. But this line of thinking has been only partially explored as there is little precedent for it in Caucasian disease patterns. We must, however, consider that there may be significant differences in pancreatic function and release of insulin, which again may be part of this thrifty gene syndrome that tolerated a higher intake of carbohydrates. Perhaps genetic changes have already had an effect, as much as environmental changes. However, there may be some isolated populations still living predominantly on their locally produced starch foods, and with minimal out-marriage, that might provide some measures of the physiological responses to high carbohydrate intakes. Futuna may be one such example (Pollock and Tafili 1988).

For those populations eating a combination of Western and local food, the epidemiological studies also include psychosocial stress from the new way of life as part of the etiology of diabetes (Zimmet 1981). This may not be entirely new, as psychosocial stress is likely to have occurred at the time of wars over territory or when states of disorder were paramount (Spiro 1952 for Ifaluk). Levy has given us one of the most intensive examinations of these stress factors, for Tahitians (1973), but unfortunately he does not correlate them with food intake and any disease patterns.

Heart Disease and Blood Pressure

Dietary excesses are also considered worldwide to be the major factor in the etiology of hypertension and ischaemic heart disease. Obesity is cited as a major debilitating factor of urban populations, and when it is combined with stress of urban life, the incidence of these diseases becomes higher than in rural populations. Prior (1981) has compared blood pressure rates for several populations; he finds a notable elevation in Tokelauans living in New Zealand over those still living on the Tokelau atolls. High intakes of fat, refined sugar, and low fiber are the dietary factors blamed.

If the incidence of these diseases does represent the dramatic change that Coyne, Badcock, and Taylor (1984) and Zimmet claim, and if there is a dietary component, then there is a strong case for finding ways to reinstate the more healthful aspects of the early traditional diets, particularly the root and tree starches, and the work patterns involved in producing them. However, the periods when foods were not available are not likely to be reproducible in the modern age. Also, any genetic predispositions to irregular diet, high carbohydrate intake, abnormal insulin secretion, or even low protein requirements (see Hipsley 1947 for Papua New Guinea) must already have lost much of their survival value as these populations have become dependent on bread, rice, and canned and fatty foods.

NUTRITION EDUCATION

For many reasons, then, far more urgent moves are needed toward reinstating the root and tree starchy foods in the diets of the various Pacific Island societies. For those concerned with bringing about change in food habits I have several suggestions. First, the question needs to be asked: On what terms are the changes deemed necessary? If the answer is in terms of some Western evaluation based on biological criteria, then there should be further investigation as to how a change will affect existing ideas as held locally. Second, care should be taken that omissions or shortfalls in the diet are not identified on the basis of too little information or inadequate questions. Third, information on foods that are drunk as well as those that are eaten should be elicited with the appropriate question. And finally, the status foods need to be noted; a question about what foods are considered appropriate for what occasions will yield some interesting responses that are clues to beliefs about foods for infants, for the sick and elderly, as well as those foods saved for feasts and community events.

Much confusion still exists in the rural Pacific about what constitutes an ideal diet, despite the many attempts at nutrition education. For years the Western ways of eating and living have been set up as a model to which the conscientious Pacific Island housewife should aspire. And yet these same housewives are now being told to "Eat Local Foods" (such is the slogan in Fiji). This new message is doubly confusing; not only does it contradict the earlier messages that European settlers in the Pacific had been propounding over the years, but also it is expensive now that local foods cost more than imported food, as discussed in Chapter 8.

Nutrition education programs need to take cognizance of the local messages about what foods are healthful, and they need to be phrased in terms of local categories. That will not only help to reach those families that may be labeled traditional but may also help to promote those local foods. In addition, agriculture departments' support in the development of subsistence crops, small business support for the marketing of local produce, and the serving of local dishes on the menus of the tourist hotels will all give a more positive image to the local starchy foods and their place in the diet.

SUMMARY

Two contrasting approaches to Pacific diets have been highlighted here. The biological one is used by nutritionists within the medical model, while the cultural one is much closer to the way Pacific Island people evaluate their own food intake. Issues such as obesity must be evaluated from both the cultural and the biological dimensions, if nutrition intervention programs are to be successful. Nutrition education also needs to be more directly attuned to cultural views of food if its message is to be received.

Traditional diets, that is, those that can be reconstructed for pre-1945, were not the same as rural diets today. So the whole issue of modernization of diets needs to be examined much more carefully than it has been. The term "modernization" has been too loosely used for adequate consideration of changes in diets over time. The most well-rounded evaluations of diets have been those studies that combine the work of epidemiologists, nutritionists, and anthropologists. Such a team approach will bridge the contrasting principles behind the medical and the cultural models.

11

Conclusions

IN PACIFIC Island societies food is more than just something to eat. Several dimensions of food and its meaning have been explored to show common themes that are widespread across the island Pacific world. Those themes indicate that food is used to satisfy people's desires, both social and physical. A good feed of taro and fish in the company of family and friends is very satisfying, both mentally and physically. After such a feed members of that group feel that the world is right and they are both satisfied and gratified.

The theme of food as a symbol pervasive throughout Pacific societies has been dealt with by looking at food use in both household and communal settings in order to draw out its wider ramifications. Decisions about food are based on a range of factors, including social demands that are in many ways more dominant than the biological ones.

The approach here has been through examining the local view of food in culture. Through the Pacific peoples' own concepts and relations we can "treat the universe as an ordered system, describing it in terms of space, time, matter and motion and peopling it with gods, humans, animals, etc." (Tambiah 1985:3). Food is part of the matter and the motion, has a locus in time and space, and links humans and animals.

TRADITIONAL FOODS IN THE MODERN WORLD

By examining the classifications that Yapese and Fijians use for food, feasts, health, and land use I have tried to establish a local rationale for food use within their ordered system. The concept of world view has been used to encompass these various categories in order to show that food is a cultural construct and, in Pacific societies, is conceptually bound up with other aspects of the social framework; it is part of what Geertz (1973) calls the web of culture. It has major significance in that web, not only as part of the economy but in its symbolic dimensions that reach into many other areas of culture. These symbols are encoded both in the type of food used, in the ways it is cooked and served, and in the relations of those sharing a food event. Each of these aspects symbolizes relationships between those participating, but each also symbolizes moral issues in the sense of total well-being. Food is power.

The key elements in that code have been laid out. The definition of a food event as a starch with some accompanying dish that has been cooked in the earth oven and is eaten and shared with others is widely found from Easter Island to Palau. Those key characteristics contribute to people's satisfaction in eating, whether within the household or at a feast; in the latter case the fellowship and relationships are drawn from a wider community. The amount and type of food are also important.

Those characteristics have been continually changing over time. We can trace only the more recent changes as reported in the writings of European visitors. But they make it clear that new foods, new ways of cooking, new modes of production, and new feast occasions have been introduced and incorporated into the system. The food pattern even extends to migrant communities in metropolitan countries; but it has to be modified according to what foods can be obtained and restrictions that may be encountered on such activities as digging large earth ovens in the back yard.

The value placed on starch foods has persisted over time despite the many changes and new ideas and the threats to their availability. Pacific Islanders have lived through too many typhoons, hurricanes, occasional tidal waves, droughts, and epidemics of plant diseases not to be aware of the constant risks to their food supply. They find that the foods that they have used throughout their long experience are better risks than the new ones, which may not be available if overseas shipping is curtailed. People are aware of the risks and uncertainties associated with food—at lowest risk are those foods that can be grown in the garden areas and harvested as the occasion demands; at high risk are those that are imported. Food-use patterns have persisted; it is just a matter whether the beholder wishes to see change or continuity.

A deliberate focus on change in food habits has been highlighted in health studies. Health professionals have used diet as a key variable, particularly in the causation of non-infectious diseases such as diabetes and heart disease. To mount intervention programs, health professionals have brought their own world view to the Pacific in assessing how the health of Pacific Islanders matches up with some Western-based standards. They have expected diets to have been "modernized." But we need to bring to bear elements of local world view before reaching that conclusion. This will necessitate going back to some communities to assess their values in the use of local foods.

Associated with the expectation of modernized diets, however covert, is the high status given to Western foods. Thus twenty-four-hour recall dietary records are suspect, as they may include many Western foods just to impress the interviewer. Observation of food habits, preferably over several months, gets around part of this problem.

The value of local foods needs to be continually stated in order to raise people's consciousness of the good value of these foods and to reinforce the positive feelings that continue in some population sectors. Local foods gain even higher value for those living away from their home islands, where the foods have scarcity and novelty value. Western foods are prevalent in urban island societies, not because they are considered more nutritious, but because of their ease of preparation and lower cost. We must not expect that Western foods such as rice and bread will necessarily dominate the food habits of all Pacific Island societies in the near future. Rather, outsiders can assist in building a more positive image of local foods so that they will increase in value and use.

FOOD POLICY AND DEPENDENCY

Issues of food policy have been touched on as they arise from our consideration of food in the local world view. The level of dependency on Western foods and its effects on the import bill as well as health are already matters of great concern. "Eat More Local Food" campaigns draw attention to the possibilities for using the local starchy foods and help to bring their price down.

Attention to means of substituting local foods for imported foods are underway in places such as Fiji, Tonga, and Western Samoa, but such concerns have received less direct attention in the island groups of the northwest and central Pacific. The formation of health and nutrition committees drawing members from a wide range of interests can help to influence the direction that food and health concerns are likely to take in the next twenty years.

There are signs that some societies have reached the limits to which dependency on outside food sources is acceptable and have made moves to reduce consumption of imported foods, not only for reasons of trade balance but also as a means of asserting their distinctive Pacific Island identity—and being proud of it. Their concern in the late 1980s is with the large part (14–30 percent) that foodstuffs play in their already negative trade balance figures. The answer as to how this could be reversed lies in the root and tree starches that grow so well on their own islands.

The road to this dependency began in the nineteenth century when colonizers were interested in developing Pacific Island export crops such as sugar cane and cotton. No support was given to subsistence agricul-

Figure 31. Billboard promoting local foods. Tonga, 1990. Photo by Nancy J. Pollock

ture. These new arrivals brought new values and established the belief that bread and rice were somehow "better" than the local root crops. They encouraged consumption of new imported foods in the name of civilization and progress.

Dependency became established early, but realization of its sinister consequences was not apparent until the 1970s. That timing also coincided with independence movements and the desire of many Pacific Island nations to stand on their own feet. To reduce their dependence on external powers, at least as far as food is concerned, the island governments have taken specific measures to increase their own food production levels. In the main this has meant growing more taro and yams. It has also meant the growth of the marketplace as the point of exchange between producers and consumers. Some island nations, such as Fiji and the Solomon Islands, have developed a significant rice crop. The local fishing industry is also under review.

SUBSTITUTING LOCAL FOODS FOR IMPORTS

Moves to substitute taro and cassava for imported goods such as rice and flour began to pay off in the 1980s. Import bills for foodstuffs are being reduced. At the same time governments are changing their food policies as they move into a new era of support for local starch foods. Taro, yams, sweet potato, and cassava are coming into their own again. With support from agricultural development agencies such as the FAO and the local agricultural research stations such as Koronivia in Fiji and Alafua in Western Samoa, cultivars are being developed to meet new needs, such as shorter growing season and less acridity. Local crops still cost more than imported foods, mainly because the development programs take time to show results. At the moment it is still cheaper to buy imported rice in Fiji than taro. But it is optimistically hoped that taro supplies will increase and the price be trimmed to make it more readily available to those who would like to buy it but cannot afford to do so at present.

Land use is a crucial factor in policies for import substitution. Improved management of land and the crops produced was a particular concern of the South Pacific Agricultural Survey (1980). The pressures of population, particularly on atolls such as in Kiribati, and the needs of tourist hotels mean that landholding is confronted with serious competing values. These are translated in various ways into local systems of tenure. But production of food is essential, both in the Western materialist sense and in the local ideological sense. The Pacific Island people have more control over their land if it is growing crops they can then market than if it is leased to a large multinational tourist corporation.

Coping strategies for self-reliant societies have been examined by Colson (1979) with particular regard to food supplies. She underlines the need for a social mechanism for absorbing losses and sharing them among the community. Devices already in use, such as changing from preferred to less liked foods, reducing family size, and trading for food, are short-term solutions only. She suggests that diversification rather than specialization in particular food crops, storage of foodstuffs, transmission of information on famine foods, conversion of surplus food into durable valuables that could be stored and traded for food in emergency, and cultivation of social relations to allow tapping of food resources of other regions are all longer-term devices that could lead to greater self-reliance.

These are practical and political concerns. The ultimate aim of food policies is not only to meet material needs in terms of an adequate, acceptable, and healthful food supply, but also to meet ideological needs of self-respect, community viability, and a positive image of the future. Perhaps necessarily the former prevail. They are based in a Western ideology that takes little account of the local cultural and symbolic values that are my concern. Food can appear to be a very mundane topic, but in many societies it is strongly symbolic. In the Pacific the messages it carries are particularly powerful. We have to be tuned in to hear them.

FOOD AS AN IDENTITY MARKER

Food viewed in its cultural context may be used as an important symbol of identity. During the colonial period, pride in local foods was overwhelmed by messages about cash crops and the greater efficacy of Western foods. But in the last thirty years, with independence and the move of significant numbers of Pacific Island people to metropolitan centers in New Zealand, the United States, and Australia, the old pride in local foods is finding positive reinforcement. In these multicultural environments, as well as at home, Pacific Island foods are increasingly in demand. For community events it is becoming more and more important to have a plate of taro and some fish, as well as all the *palagi* (foreign) foods, in order to stamp the event with a distinctive Pacific Island flavor. The making of the *umu* is not usually practicable in cold, damp climates and in a rented garden. But as migrant populations increase, there is more and more demand for social occasions to have a distinctive Pacific Island identity.

Food is a powerful tool for invoking that identity. It is a means of stamping a particular occasion as Rarotongan or Samoan for those who share the particular ideas that those cultures associate with particular foods. Food is also a means of conveying messages of identity to outsiders. It can act as one form of boundary marker between ethnic groups. In multicultural societies today, that may be a particularly valuable role.

Food events have been a means of conveying messages within the group of people involved, as well as to outsiders. To understand the many meanings of the food system they must be "dialectically and recursively related to one another and to the larger socio-cultural whole" (Tambiah 1985:13). In the Pacific, respect, honor, and social commitment are expressed through food sharing. Food is thus a significant means of reinforcing identities for those who share the messages.

Food communicates. It sends messages between those who share the images and thus can receive the signals. In the case of the Pacific, food represents a way of talking to people; it stands for respect, identity. It is the means to security through self-sufficiency. It comes from the land that ties the present generations to the past and carries the whole group through to the future. It is one symbol of the importance of that land that can never be taken away. It represents the roots of the society. These roots remain.

Appendix A

Characteristics of Eleven Starch Food Plants of the Pacific

TARO

The word "taro" is used in general parlance to refer to any one of four plants that are members of the Araceae family. In this book they are referred to as *Colocasia* taro, *Alocasia* taro, *Cyrtosperma* taro, and *Xanthosoma* taro. *Colocasia* taro is the plant most commonly meant when the unqualified term "taro" is used, though some reports fail to distinguish between the four kinds and use taro as a generic for all of them. (For distribution of taro in the Pacific, see Appendix C1.)

Colocasia taro

LOCAL NAMES. Taro, *talo, dalo, kalo.*

COMMON NAMES. Taro, true taro, Polynesian taro, Asia taro, red taro. The name is derived from the Malay word *tales* (Burkill 1953:278) and has been generally accepted as the cognate in English for the plant. In Micronesian and Melanesian societies the term for taro is different. But the reconstructed proto-Polynesian *talo* has been suggested as the earliest form of the term (Biggs, Walsh, and Waqa 1972).

Other names in English have also been used. "Dasheen" is used for one particular variety of *Colocasia* taro, a name probably derived from the French *de Chine* (Plucknett 1983:16). "Eddoe" is also used both in the Pacific and in the West Indies for the cultivar *Colocasia esculenta* var. *antiquorum* (Lambert 1982). These plants were not well known to visitors from temperate latitudes in the sixteenth and seventeenth centuries, so we must be cautious in interpreting the records of this plant by travelers and missionaries, some of whom may well have confused identification.

LATIN NAME. *Colocasia esculenta.* In the early literature the name *Colocasia antiquorum* was frequently used, following Schott's nomenclature. In discussing the details of taxonomy, Plucknett suggests that "it is probably best to consider *C. esculenta* (L.) Schott as a single polymorphic species" (1983:14–19). See also Lambert 1982:2. The cytological evidence distinguishes "Polynesian taros" from East Asia taros (Yen and Wheeler 1968).

DESCRIPTION. *Colocasia* taro belongs to the family Araceae but differs from the other taros in the same family in characteristics of its leaf structure and of its starchy corm (see Figures 1, 2). The plant grows to a height of about half a meter. The arrow-shaped leaves are 30 to 40 cm in length and are peltate, the leaf stalk joining the blade of about two-thirds the length of the mid-vein. The leaf hangs downward, in contrast to the *Alocasia* leaf which points upward. The main edible part is the single enlarged underground corm that has only one or two small cormels (Strauss 1983:23–26). A corm on average weighs 1 to 2 kg at maturity. Flowers are uncommon, though Massal and Barrau (1956) show a drawing of an inflorescence. Seeds are rarely found in nature (Plucknett, de la Pena, and Obrero 1970:414). However, seeds were reported in Hawai'i by Handy (1940, cited in Handy and Handy 1972:90).

A large number of cultivars are identified locally on each Pacific island, but these have not been thoroughly studied by botanists. Local people use distinguishing names based on time of maturation, color of skin or flesh, size, coarseness, etc. Handy collected living specimens of more than eighty distinct varieties in Hawai'i, and this at a time when Hawaiian taro planting was believed to be verging on extinction; he had collected 346 names (Handy and Handy 1972:90). Other writers have recorded varietal names for taros they collected (e.g., Seemann 1862 for Fiji; Krämer 1906 for Samoa).

However, correlation of these locally identified cultivars with botanically identified cultivars is almost non-existent. Some work is being done in Hawai'i (Wang 1983); also some by the South Pacific Commission (Lambert 1982) and for nineteenth-century New Zealand (Matthews 1985). More work is needed to establish the characteristics of locally identified cultivars, particularly if taro is to become a major food source again.

ORIGIN. By current estimates, *Colocasia* taro may have been one of the world's first domesticated foods, having provided a source of food starch for some 8,000 years (Golson 1977; Bellwood 1980; Hutterer 1983; Petterson 1977). Its likely center of origin is said to be in the general region of India, from whence it spread into Indonesia (Barrau 1965b) and then into the Pacific (Bellwood 1980:67). Kuk Swamp in highland Papua New Guinea may be the earliest site in Oceania yet known for irrigated *Colocasia* taro (Golson 1977).

Whether the use of taro predated or was subsequent to the development of cereal rice in Southeast Asia is a subject of much debate. Bellwood (1980:68) suggests a first stage of horticulture in Southeast Asia that comprised rice, millet, possibly Job's tears, certain legumes, and possibly yam and taro. Wet taro cultivation, he suggests, was a later development in the fringes of this zone where rainfall was seasonal (Bellwood 1980:69). Hutterer proposes an alternative sequence of development: "The Austronesian expansion took place at a time when rice cultivation had not yet been adapted to dry tropical environments [and the migrants] abandoned the cultivation of rice to rely on tubers and other crops instead" (1983:200). Thus the early uses of *Colocasia* taro in Southeast Asia and the Pacific are under close scrutiny by prehistorians, but its soft vegetable matter does not leave much evidence over time.

Terracing, which is generally associated with wet rice cultivation, is a clue to the possible sequence of these two important starch food crops.

The spread of *Colocasia* taro from its Asian source has been traced around the world to Africa and South America, the United States, the Caribbean, and China. Petterson (1977:65, fig. 3) discusses in detail the diffusion and use of *Colocasia* and the other taros in different parts of the world.

While we are more concerned here with cultivated taro, it should be noted that the wild forms of *Colocasia* taro also had their cultural associations. Wild taro in Hawai'i is discussed by Handy and Handy (1972:86–88). They report that Hawaiians distinguished these taros by name. They are unpigmented plants, found mainly in shady places, and characterized by small corms and long vigorous rhizomes. Handy and Handy associated the presence of wild plants possibly with the fact that "some taros reproduce by producing fertile seeds." Mary Kawena Pukui is quoted as saying, "One thing our old folks taught us was that wild food plants did not belong to the gods" (Handy and Handy 1972:88). Some taro plants were found growing wild in the northern part of the North Island of New Zealand in the 1970s (Matthews 1985; Diamond 1982).

GROWING CONDITIONS. *Colocasia* taro can be grown in a wide range of soil types, but it requires adequate rainfall. In Samoa, September and November are the preferred months for planting (see Wilson, Opio, and Cable 1984 for a detailed review of production and harvesting in Samoa). Upland, or dryland, taro is grown on hillsides in warm, moist environments, as in Hawai'i or Samoa. Wetland taro is usually found in low-lying areas or on terraces where it is irrigated with fresh cool water. Some varieties can tolerate marshy or swampy conditions, and even some salinity. The time for each crop to reach maturity varies according to climatic factors, especially temperature (de la Pena 1983:167, 168).

PLANTING. The sett, or planting material, consists of the upper 1-cm section of the corm and the first 20 to 25 cm of the petiole (de la Pena 1983:172). The setts are obtained by cutting off the upper portion of the corm at the time of harvesting. The tops of larger corms grow better taro plants. In their description of Hawaiian methods of selecting planting material, Handy and Handy note that the cuttings are extremely hardy and if kept in a damp place will remain alive for months (1972:94–97). However, beliefs about the influence of local gods may induce those harvesting taro to replant the sett as soon as possible in order not to anger those deities (Kirch 1985:216). Frequently the setts are planted within a couple of weeks of harvest.

Dryland taro fields may be part of a shifting cultivation pattern (see Chapter 7), a new field being planted after scrub and low vegetation has been burned off and the weeds mulched. The soil should be moist. Recommended distances between plants are 90 × 90 cm or 60 × 60 cm to give the best yields per hectare (FAO 1982). Wetland taro is planted in shallow (5 to 10 cm) water until roots have developed; from then on, the base of the plant is kept submerged until harvest (Plucknett, de la Pena, and Obrero 1970:416). Minimal distances between setts are 30 × 30 cm if fertilizer is used (FAO 1982). A detailed discussion of traditional planting methods, together with local names for the various procedures, is provided for Hawai'i by Handy and Handy (1972).

Taro is planted the year round if rainfall is adequate, but best yields are obtained if planting is done at the beginning of the rainy season (Plucknett, de la Pena, and Obrero 1970:417).

DISEASES AND PESTS. Phytophthora leaf blight is the most serious disease of the crop in the humid tropics (Ooka 1983). It has spread rapidly since its introduction during World War II and is responsible for the loss of the taro crop in the Solomons, which resulted in a change fom taro to sweet potatoes as these people's main food (Connell 1978; Packard 1975). Other diseases such as phythium rot and pests such as the taro beetle require constant vigilance by agriculture personnel to protect the crops (Ooka and Trujillo 1982: 52). For full listings of pests of taro, see Mitchell and Maddison (1983:180–235) and of taro diseases, Ooka (1983:236–237). For pests and diseases in Western Samoa, see Wilson, Opio, and Cable (1984).

HARVESTING. The average growing time is 9 to 14 months, depending on variety and growing conditions. Wetland taro takes 12 to 15 months to mature but can be left in the field for as long as 18 months (de la Pena 1983: 175; Plucknett, de la Pena, and Obrero 1970:418). A digging stick is used to prize out wetland taro corms; dryland taro may be pulled out by hand. The estimated area harvested in Samoa ranges from 3,560 to 4,000 acres; total production is around 20,000 to 25,000 metric tons (see Wilson, Opio, and Cable 1984 for details).

STORAGE. *Colocasia* corms cannot be kept more than 10 days to 2 weeks without some form of preservative. If the tops are cut off for planting, the storage life is only 5+ days (FAO 1982). Many early visitors, including Cook, noted that large supplies of taro decayed rapidly and had to be thrown overboard (Beaglehole 1962).

As more taro is sold, storage and transportation problems have led to significant changes in the preparation of the corms for sale. In Fiji they are sold with the tops still on; this creates a problem for the farmers in finding sources of planting material. In Tonga, Samoa, and the Cook Islands, however, taros are marketed without their tops, these having been saved by the farmer for replanting. Since taro corms do not last well once harvested, particularly if the corm has been damaged by cutting off the petiole, those corms marketed with tops removed are more prone to rot than those marketed with the tops left on. Ways of prolonging the storage life for harvested taro corms, such as the use of a retardant powder, are being developed.

NUTRITIONAL VALUE. The carbohydrate content of *Colocasia* corms ranges from 13 to 29 percent and protein, from 1 to 7 percent (Splittstoesser, Martin, and Rhoades 1973; Wenkam 1983; SPC 1983). Since the starch granules of taro are much smaller than those of potato, they are easier to digest, thus making taro suitable for babies and persons with digestive problems (Wang 1983:4). The young leaves are widely used as food in addition to the corms.

Both the corms and the leaves contain oxalic acid which leaves an unpleasant itchy feeling around the mouth if they are not adequately cooked. Consumption of excessive amounts of oxalic acid may render dietary calcium inabsorbable (Standal 1982:129).

Alocasia Taro

LOCAL NAMES. *Kape, 'ape, ta'amu; biga* in Philippines; *piga* in Guam; *via* in New Caledonia. (Burkill 1935, quoted by Petterson 1977:71)

COMMON NAMES. Giant taro, elephant ear taro.

LATIN NAME. *Alocasia macrorrhiza.*

DESCRIPTION. *Alocasia* taro leaves are large and fleshy and can reach 1 m in length. They stand erect, are not peltate, and have no intramarginal vein. The plant may reach 9 to 10 ft (3 to 4.5 m) in height (Petterson 1977:56) (see Figure 2). The large, coarse tubers grow above the ground and look like a swelling out of which the leaves grow, unlike the globular *Colocasia* corm. They are very acrid when raw and must be very thoroughly cooked to remove the calcium oxalate. The plant is frequently found reproducing itself in abandoned sites throughout the Pacific. It has been much less thoroughly studied than *Colocasia* taro.

ORIGIN. This was probably one of the first root crops to be domesticated, along with *Colocasia,* in the Southeast Asia area. It was commonly cultivated in middle and south China in the late nineteenth century, and also in Japan (Petterson 1977:84, 85), but it seems to have been a secondary or insignificant source of dietary starch in both places. It appears to have spread to Africa with minimal effect on local diets (Petterson 1977).

PLANTING. Planting material consists mostly of suckers, though cormlets are sometimes used in Tonga if there is a shortage of suckers. The suckers are planted in holes 15 to 25 cm deep. *Alocasia* taro is usually intercropped in yam plots. Spacing is 3.5 m × 3.5 m (Holo and Taumoefolau 1982:85). Year-round planting is possible if the temperature and rainfall are suitable, as in Wallis. But June through December are the usual planting months in Tonga and Wallis; traditionally Tongans believed that September was the best month (Holo and Taumoefolau 1982:86 for Tonga; Nozieres 1982:87 for Wallis). In Tonga, *Alocasia* taro is planted at the same time as yams.

DISEASES AND PESTS. There are few (Holo and Taumoefolau 1982:86).

HARVESTING. *Alocasia* taro can be harvested one year after planting, but it may also be left in the ground for up to 2+ years. If left in the ground, the oxalate content may increase (Holo and Taumoefolau 1982:87). The root must be used within a month after harvest, as it rots quickly or may start to regrow.

ACRIDITY. *Alocasia* taro has a very high calcium oxalate content; thus the tuber must be very thoroughly cooked to avoid the itchy, stinging sensation around the mouth and the bitter taste. Tang and Sakai state that individuals differ considerably in their sensory evaluation of the stinging and bitterness

(1983:148–163). Many Pacific Islanders downgrade *Alocasia* taro as food because of these unpleasant sensations, yet in Samoa and Tonga it is a highly favored food. Cooking for a long period of time can remove some of the acridity, but is not 100 percent effective.

NUTRITIONAL VALUE. *Alocasia* has greater amounts of calcium than the other taros.

Cyrtosperma Taro

LOCAL NAMES. *Puraka, pulaka, brak, lak, Via kana, babai* (Kiribati).

COMMON NAME. Giant taro, swamp taro.

LATIN NAME. *Cyrtosperma chamissonis,* occasionally referred to as *Cyrtosperma edulis* (Seemann 1862:304).

DESCRIPTION. This is the largest species of the Araceae family because of the size of the leaves. At maturity the plant may measure more than 4 m in height (see Figure 2). The leaves point upward and the petiole extends from the leaf base to form the median vein (Petterson 1977:53). The tubers of this taro are large, weighing between 20 and 50 kg. The plants are grown in a damp environment and require shade and a more or less continuous supply of water. The seed is not usually viable (Vickers 1982:93).

ORIGIN. This plant is also of Southeast Asian origin and was probably dispersed through Micronesia from Indonesia in pre-European times (Vickers 1982:90). The pits in which the plants were grown and which are still in evidence are the best clue to the importance of the species in early times. Luomala (1974) suggests that *Cyrtosperma* taro, found throughout the Pacific, was part of a complex of root crops that included *Colocasia* and *Alocasia* taros, the whole complex having originated as part of a larger horticultural system that embraced wet taro and wet rice. For mythological associations between *Cyrtosperma* and porpoises in central Micronesia, see Luomala (1974) and Alkire (1968).

PLANTING. Planting procedures in Kiribati are subject to much secrecy and variation; Luomala provides us with the greatest detail, supplied by her Kiribati/Gilbertese informant. The planting material is usually shoots coming from old root stock, or the top of a harvested *Cyrtosperma* corm may be replanted (Luomala 1974:15). Leaf stalks can also be used (Petterson 1977:54).

The planting material is placed in deep beds excavated into the coral to reach the freshwater lens (Wiens 1962) or in natural swamps. On atolls the pits are generally located toward the center of the islet where groundwater is fresher. The pit must be well prepared with compost and soil. In Kiribati, each plant is surrounded by chopped leaves and soil contained in a bottomless basket of woven pandanus or coconut fronds, according to the preference and traditional knowledge of each individual planter. As this material rots, more is added to provide a continuous compost. Gilbertese believe the plant must be fed to grow strong (Luomala 1974). Each variety is treated according to its own special cultivation processes. The elaboration of planting techniques has reached its epitome in Gilberts/Kiribati, where they are accompanied by many ritual and magical activities; for details see Luomala (1974) and Catala (1957) for Gilberts/Kiribati, Labby (1976) for Yap.

Yapese plant *Cyrtosperma* taro whenever they go out to harvest tubers, so there is constant harvesting and replanting (Untaman 1982:98). In Kiribati, the very large pits are planted with new material at various times depending on the elaborate rituals and social preliminaries involved.

DISEASES AND PESTS. A taro beetle that has been attacking the Kiribati *babai* is very hard to eradicate because of the cultivation methods (FAO 1982). The plant does not otherwise appear to be especially susceptible to disease.

HARVESTING. In Kiribati, corms of one variety of *babai,* the *ikaraoi* type, may be harvested after 4 years (Luomala 1970:492), or they may be left in the pit for 10 or 15 years. They may be over a meter long and too fibrous to eat, but they are of great prestige value. Younger corms are harvested for feast occasions. If the corms are not cooked immediately after harvesting, bitter spots begin to form (Petterson 1977:55). For cultural uses of *babai* for contests, exchange, and prestige occasions see Luomala (1970:494–499). *Babai* is never a staple food, though it has been mistakenly labeled as such (Luomala 1970:496).

ACRIDITY. Can be high, but varies.

NUTRITIONAL VALUE. *Cyrtosperma* taro shows very high calcium values (SPC 1983:14).

Xanthosoma Taro

LOCAL NAMES. *Taro futuna, taro tarua, taro tonga,* and local variations. (In the Pacific a name often refers to the place from which planting material was obtained.)

COMMON NAMES. Kong kong taro, American taro, *tannia* or *cocoyam* in Caribbean area.

LATIN NAMES. *Xanthosoma sagittifolium, Xanthosoma atrovirens, Xanthosoma violaceum.*

DESCRIPTION. The *Xanthosoma* taro plant is very similar to *Colocasia* taro; the main distinguishing features are that its leaves are drooping, its leaf stalk joins the leaf at the edge, and the leaf has a very distinct marginal vein (see Figure 2). The principal tuber of *Xanthosoma* is seldom harvested because its flesh is very acrid; only the lateral cormels are harvested. *Xanthosoma* grows with a central elongated tuber surrounded by 8 or 10 cormels, often fairly weakly attached to the main corm (Petterson 1977:42). Two or three cormels weigh about 1 kg.

ORIGIN. *Xanthosoma* is a South American plant that spread through tropical South America and through the isthmus to North America. It was most popular as a food in the West Indies, but nowhere did it ever become the dominant food plant. It remained confined to the Western Hemisphere until after the voyages of Columbus. Then it spread across the Atlantic into West

Africa, where it competed successfully with *Colocasia* taro (Petterson 1977:
4–5). It is a relative newcomer to the Pacific, perhaps carried by missionaries
and others from Spanish posts in South America in the mid-1800s, but it was
not significant as a starchy food in the Pacific until the 1960s.

PLANTING. Cormels are the best planting material, producing a quicker and
higher-yielding crop than do setts from the top of the main plant, but the latter may be used. The tubers grow best if the setts are planted on ridges, with
organic material worked in at the base (Weightman and Moros 1982:
76–78).

GROWING CONDITIONS. *Xanthosoma* is a dryland plant that grows best on
well drained soils, as it can withstand neither waterlogging nor prolonged
drought. It may be planted in partially cleared forest, as it tolerates shade. It
will grow in relatively poor quality soils, though tubers will be smaller, and
also in sandy soil mixed with organic matter, such as is found in central areas
of some atolls (Weightman and Moros 1972:74). It is often interplanted with
yams, bananas, and vegetable crops.

DISEASES AND PESTS. *Xanthosoma* does not appear to be susceptible to any
serious diseases or pests.

HARVESTING. *Xanthosoma* normally matures in 9 to 12 months. The mature
tubers may be left in the ground to be harvested as required. Bruising during
harvesting can cause tubers to spoil in 4 or 5 days.

ACRIDITY. The principal tuber is more toxic than the lateral cormels. These
cormels are most usually eaten.

NUTRITIONAL VALUE. *Xanthosoma* contains more carbohydrate, thus yielding more calories, and more vitamin C than do the other taros (Standal
1982:126).

YAMS

LOCAL NAMES. *Ufi, uhi* (for the main form of yam eaten).

COMMON NAME. Yam, sometimes confused with sweet potatoes in American
concepts.

LATIN NAMES. *Dioscorea* species: *D. alata* (water yam), *D. esculenta* (yam),
D. bulbifera (bitter yam, *hoi*), *D. sativa* (bitter yam, *pi'a*), *D. pentaphylla, D.
nummularia.* For a detailed account of the variety of yams, see Coursey
(1967, 1977:191). For Fiji, see Sivan (1980a, 1980b). For Pohnpei, see Hiyane and Hadley (1977). For Tonga, see Fa'anunu (1977:190).

DESCRIPTION. Species of the genus *Dioscorea* are found throughout the tropical regions of the world. The plants are annuals and grow as living vines with
racemes of inconspicuous white, greenish, or yellow flowers; male flowers
are always separate from female flowers. At the end of the rainy season,
when active growth occurs, the vine dies down and only the dormant tubers
remain. These tubers enable the plant to survive the dry season. In all the edible yams these tubers are renewed annually; in *Dioscorea* species that are not

used as food, the tuber is perennial (Coursey 1977:190). *D. pentaphylla* bears small aerial as well as subterranean tubers (Neal 1965:230).

ORIGINS. No single center of origin of domestication is known for yams, though their spread has been generally from west to east. Some yams were cultivated in the African continent, some in Southeast Asia, and some in pre-Columbian tropical America. Murdock's hypothesis (1960) of a Malaysian origin of yam cultivation is now only partially acceptable. *D. alata* and *D. esculenta,* the yam species most commonly grown in the Pacific, may have been domesticated for several thousand years in the agricultural complex of Southeast Asia (Hutterer 1983:183; Bellwood 1980:64; Coursey 1967). *D. alata* is a true cultigen, unknown in the wild state. Barrau (1965c:65–66) drew attention to the erroneous identification of *D. esculenta* as the sweet potato *(batate)* by the first Spaniards in Guam. No doubt other commentators on the Pacific have also wrongly identified the yam because of inadequate knowledge.

GROWING CONDITIONS. A prolonged dry season is necessary to produce the largest tubers of *D. alata.* Thus yam cultivation tends to be associated with upland rather than littoral or riverine peoples in Southeast Asia (Coursey 1977:192). As a vine it is encouraged to grow on other plant material. To obtain the desired long tubers, the soil must be loosened periodically. The techniques of growing yams are kept as highly secret information in Pohnpei, where the tubers are prized for their size rather than their edibility (Shimizu 1982).

CULTIVATOR. On Pohnpei men cultivate the yams; women are not expected to do this work (Hiyane and Hadley 1977:33)

PLANTING MATERIAL. The tops or heads of tubers are usually used (Coursey and Haynes 1970:262), because they germinate faster and produce larger yields, though pieces from the middle may sometimes be used.

DISEASES AND PESTS. There are few pests and diseases (Hiyane and Hadley 1977:34). In some societies certain rites are practiced to protect the crops (Coursey 1967:193).

HARVESTING. Yams are usually harvested after the dry season, though the tubers may be left in the ground to elongate for ceremonial presentations (Bascom 1965 for Pohnpei). They reach maturity in 9 to 14 months after planting. In some regions the people practice multiple harvesting (Hiyane and Hadley 1977). Digging is done manually with digging sticks or spades to avoid damaging tubers. Field experiments have been conducted with early-maturing and later-maturing varieties, testing several characteristics of acceptability (Sivan 1980a).

STORAGE. Yams may be left in the ground until needed. In some societies, mainly in the southwest Pacific, they are stacked in yam houses. The tubers may also be hung on a horizontal pole (Hiyane and Hadley 1977:31). *D. alata* is best adapted for storage and thus may have been more favored by seagoing people than *D. esculenta* and other varieties. Shade, ventilation, and security against pests are the main conditions required for successful storage (Wilson, Opio, and Cable 1984).

ACRIDITY. The wild yams were more acrid than the cultivated species.

NUTRITIONAL VALUE. Yams contribute mainly starch to the diet, but contain also small amounts of protein and minerals.

BREADFRUIT

LOCAL NAMES. *Mei, uru, ulu,* and others (see Appendix D). In Tahiti the name has been changed from *uru* to *maiore te uru* (Henry 1928).

COMMON NAME. Breadfruit. The name was applied by Dampier or Anson in the 1600s because the fruit was the food item they found that most closely resembled bread.

LATIN NAMES. *Artocarpus altilis, Artocarpus incisus* (see Wilder 1928) (seedless breadfruit); *Artocarpus mariannensis* (seeded breadfruit).

DESCRIPTION. The breadfruit tree stands 30 to 60 ft in height, and has a smooth gray trunk, buttressed at the roots. The leaves, which vary greatly in shape, are large and leathery and cut more or less deeply into several blunt lobes. The fruit is round, covered with a tough warty rind that turns from bright green to brown when ripe. A tree produces fruit two or three times during a year.

There are two distinct species, one bearing seeded fruit, the other bearing seedless fruit. The seeded form is used in Papua New Guinea (Paijmans 1976:123) and is also found growing wild in Guam (Coenen and Barrau 1961). It is widely distributed throughout Micronesia but is not as generally used as the seedless form. On Kapingamarangi, Coenen and Barrau (1966) noted that the seeded varieties present characteristics of the breadfruit varieties of western Micronesia, though the island is a Polynesian outlier. The seedless variety is much more widely cultivated in central and eastern Oceania. See Appendix C2 for a map showing limits of distribution of cultivated breadfruit (after Bellwood 1978:137).

ORIGINS. The breadfruit was probably first domesticated in Vavilov's Indo-Malayan area, though the Melanesian area has been suggested (Purseglove 1972, map). It was domesticated 1,000 to 2,000 years ago in the eastern parts of the Malay archipelago (Barrau 1973:201), and now grows throughout tropical Asia and Oceania. Bligh's ill-fated commission in 1788 to carry breadfruit plants from Tahiti to the Caribbean so that the planters there would have an easily prepared food for their slaves brought this tree into world renown. He succeeded on his second attempt in 1792 (Barrow 1980).

GROWING CONDITIONS. Seedless varieties reproduce vegetatively in tropical environments from the shoreline up to several hundred feet above sea level. The tree cannot tolerate severe drought—that is, rainfall below 50 in. per annum. Because it does not tolerate salt spray well, at sea level it is usually grown behind a shelter belt. The tree does not thrive in cooler temperatures, and thus is not profuse in Hawai'i or in New Zealand. It takes 5 years for the tree to begin to produce fruit. It may continue to bear for another 40 to 50 years. See McKnight (1960) for breadfruit cultivation practices in Palau.

PLANTING MATERIAL. Seeds from the seeded variety can be viable, but quicker reproduction is attained from cuttings and from sprouts rising from the roots. Seedless varieties are reproduced entirely from cuttings or from sprouts.

DISEASES. Pingelap disease caused severe damage to breadfruit trees throughout Micronesia in the 1960s. Fruit rot caused by *Phytophthora palmivora* has been found in Western Samoa (Gerlach and Salavao 1984).

HARVESTING. The fruit is picked as needed and according to taste; Samoans, for example, prefer their fruit not quite ripe. The pulp of the breadfruit becomes sweeter as it ripens. The fruits are picked using a long pole with a small fork at the top. Throughout the Pacific there is one major harvest, plus one or two smaller secondary harvests. By careful selection of planting material, varieties are being developed that give fruit at different times so that some fruit can be harvested all year round.

STORAGE. Once ripe, the fruit will not keep unless treated. Fermentation in pits has long been used as the method of storing the ripe breadfruits (see Pollock 1984b).

USES. The breadfruit tree has many uses besides providing food. Its sap can be used for caulking canoes and as an adhesive in the making of *tapa* cloth. The leaves are used extensively to wrap food, to cover the *umu,* and to line the breadfruit storage pits. The trunk is used for canoes on those atolls where no other large trees grow. The bark of some species is used for making *tapa.*

NUTRITIONAL VALUE. The fruit is mainly carbohydrate but contains a small amount of calcium and iron; it is also a source of riboflavin, niacin, and vitamin C (SPC 1983).

SWEET POTATO

LOCAL NAMES. *Kumala, 'umala, kumara.*

LATIN NAME. *Ipomoea batatas.*

COMMON NAMES. Sweet potato, *batate,* or *patata* (Spanish or Portuguese). See Yen (1974) for a full discussion of the name and the relationship to white *(Solanum)* potato.

DESCRIPTION. A perennial herb with purple stems that spread dark green leaves over the ground. The leaves vary greatly, from heart-shaped to five-lobed or five-angled. Flowers are pinkish lavender in color, tubular below, and spreading out widely. They are abundant if plants are not well cared for (Neal 1965:706). Flowering is common throughout tropic zones to about 25 degrees north and south of the equator. The plant is capable of producing seed in most of the areas in which it is cultivated (Yen 1974:231). Many local varieties have been developed throughout the Pacific area, selected for morphological factors such as shape and size, as well as factors of taste, early maturity, texture, and so forth (Yen 1974:230). The skin of the tuber may be white, yellow, orange, red, purple, or orange brown, while the flesh may be white, orange, red, or purple.

ORIGIN. The origin of this food plant has been the subject of many discussions and papers (see Yen 1974 for the most comprehensive survey; cf. Dixon 1932; Stokes 1932; O'Brien 1972). The place of origin is now firmly established in the Americas, in both Mexico and northern South America (Yen 1974). From there it spread to Polynesia before A.D. 800. An alternative view is that it was carried by Spanish travelers from South America about A.D. 1500 (Yen 1973b:42); Yen uses both cytological and ethnological evidence to establish its origin. Its place in the prehistory of New Guinea has been reviewed by White and O'Connell (1982).

GROWING CONDITIONS. The plant is found growing in a wide range of conditions in islands of the Pacific; for example, from sea level to 3,000 to 7,000 ft above sea level in New Guinea (Yen 1974:108–126). It is fairly tolerant of dry sandy conditions and prefers not too wet conditions. Thus in Fiji it is found growing on the western side of Viti Levu. In New Zealand *kumara* crops are lifted in mid-April to avoid damage from frosts and rain (Yen 1974: 216). The plants are frequently grown in mounds. The sweet potato forms part of complex agricultural systems in highland New Guinea (White and O'Connell 1982:182).

PLANTING MATERIAL. Stem cuttings or shoots arising from seed tubers.

STORAGE. Sweet potatoes can be stored if kept dry. Maori storehouses were often semi-subterranean in pre-European times; they were known as *pataka* (Davidson 1984; Jones and Law 1986).

TOXICITY. Some varieties are slightly toxic.

NUTRITIONAL VALUE. Sweet potatoes are a good source of vegetable protein (0.76 g/100), calcium, phosphate, and iron. Yellow varieties have more vitamin A (see Wenkam 1983:90–92). The leaves can be used to feed pigs and chickens.

CASSAVA

LOCAL NAMES. *Manioke, tavioka, pia* (for starch), or *ufi*.

COMMON NAMES. Cassava, manioc.

LATIN NAMES. *Manihot esculenta, Manihot utilissima*.

DESCRIPTION. A member of the Euphorbiaceae family, this bush herb or shrub stands 3 to 9 ft in height. It is widely grown for its tuberous edible roots, which are long and thin. Some roots are toxic, having a high content of hydrocyanic acid, while others are "sweeter," but this distinction has not proved useful botanically and has been dropped (Moran 1975:173). The leaves are 4 to 8 in. long, palmately divided almost to the base into 3 to 7 narrow pointed divisions. Flowers may not develop. The ovoid fruiting capsules have wings (Neal 1965:513).

ORIGIN. The plant has a homeland in Brazil. It was taken to Africa by Europeans after 1492 (Jones 1957:98) and spread rapidly (Moran 1975:173), aided by the Portuguese because of its value in provisioning their stations (Jones 1957:100). The Spanish took it into the Pacific, but it was not widely used as a food crop until the 1960s (see Dixon 1932 for a discussion of its arrival in Hawai'i).

GROWING CONDITIONS. Cassava is confined to the tropics and cannot tolerate cold; frost can kill the plant. It produces best in areas of abundant rainfall but will survive drought. It grows well in a variety of soils and thrives in all except waterlogged conditions (Moran 1975:179). It is now frequently used as the last crop in a shifting agriculture cycle in Pacific islands such as Tonga (Maude 1971). Sivan (1977), evaluating local cassava varieties in Fiji, has shown that they have a limited yield potential compared with selected hybrids from Colombia and India.

PLANTING. Cassava is readily reproduced from cuttings 6 to 12 in. long taken from the center portion of the main stalk (Moran 1975:179). In the Pacific Islands, three or four cuttings are often placed together in the ground at an angle. The crop is planted year round.

DISEASES AND PESTS. Cassava is relatively pest resistant. Mealybug and green spider mite infestations have been reported in Africa (*Newsweek,* 27 Feb. 1984).

HARVESTING. The long thin edible roots are harvested 7 to 9 months after planting.

YIELD. Yields vary from 5 to 10 tons per hectare using traditional methods and up to 65 tons per hectare using fertilizer (Moran 1975:179). Yields are lower when cassava is intercropped with other root or tree crops, as in much of Pacific shifting agriculture.

NUTRITIONAL VALUE. Cassava plants contain 25–35 percent starch. The fresh root is low in calcium and other minerals, and also low in vitamins; the flour contains some calcium and iron. The leaves, which contain some protein, may be eaten. They may be used as animal fodder.

STORAGE. The roots can be left in the ground unharvested, but they become woody and fibrous. After harvesting, roots deteriorate within a few days unless properly stored. The grated and leached product was stored as a fine powder in cake form, processed in a similar manner to arrowroot. This flourlike product was known as *pia* and was sometimes confused with *pia* flour made from Polynesian arrowroot *(Tacca leontopetaloides).* Cassava was also fermented by storing in pits in Fiji and Tikopia (Seemann 1862; Kirch and Yen 1982). New modes of storage are being developed to preserve cassava both for human use and as animal feed. Storage in moist sawdust bins has been tried in Fiji (Sivan 1977).

TOXICITY. The living cassava plant contains cyanogenetic glucoside, which varies in amounts present; that amount may range from harmless to lethal, though the latter has been found rarely. The cyanogenetic glucoside begins to break down into prussic acid, acetone, and glucose once the plant is harvested (Moran 1975). The plant is labeled "sweet" if it contains less than 50 mg of prussic acid per kg of flesh, and "bitter" if over 100 mg per kg. Differences in prussic acid levels have been found between tubers in the same field (Bilhaus 1952 in Moran 1975:178). Because prussic acid is released in water, crushing and soaking in water help to "sweeten" the foodstuff (Montgomery 1969:151). Furthermore, it is unstable in heat and thus disperses with cooking (Lancaster et al. 1982). Cyanogen is found in all parts of the plant, but is concentrated in the cortex of the root (Montgomery 1969:155).

NUTRITIONAL VALUE. Cassava root provides mainly carbohydrates, being low in protein, calcium, and other minerals, as well as vitamins. It can inhibit thyroid activity (Goodland, Watson, and Ledec 1984). The leaves contain some protein.

PANDANUS

NAMES. Pandanus, *bub, fara, hala.*

LATIN NAME. *Pandanus odoratissimus, Pandanus tectorius* (see Stone 1967).

DESCRIPTION. A stumpy tree with proplike roots and long narrow prickly leaves. The fruit can vary from 3 to 30 lb. Each fruit consists of 50 or more wedge-shape drupes that turn from green to bright yellow/orange when ripe. The outer end of the drupe contains nutlike seeds that may be eaten; the inner part of the fruit consists of fiber holding sugar and starch. In the Pacific Islands, particularly the low islands, it is mainly this inner part that is eaten.

ORIGIN. A possible origin in Southeast Asia, though the fruits are not generally eaten there. Pandanus is widely distributed throughout the Pacific. Another variety (or species) is found in Papua New Guinea.

PLANTING MATERIAL. To obtain a tree that will bear edible fruits, slips from a fruiting variety must be taken. If grown from seed a tree will revert to the wild non-edible variety.

HARVESTING. Pandanus may yield 2 crops a year. The fruit is ready in the Marshalls in October/November through January, depending on cultivar. A tree will live for some 20 years or more, though its fruiting may diminish; the leaves are still used and widely sought.

FOOD VALUE. The main value is as a carbohydrate, though the fruits are rich in vitamin A and ascorbic acid. They contain more calcium than apples and peaches (Murai, Pen, and Miller 1958:67–83).

BANANAS

LOCAL NAMES. *Futi, fusi,* or *mei'a* (for the sweet yellow kind); *fe'i, fehi* (for the green, cooking kind) = plantain.

LATIN NAMES. *Musa paradaisica* = *mei'a, fusi. Musa troglodytarum* = *fe'i, fehi.* According to Simmonds (1976), there are two genera of banana in the Pacific: *Eumusa* (for *mei'a*) and *Australimusa* (for *fe'i*).

ORIGIN. The banana apparently originated in Southeast Asia (Sauer 1952:26). The many varieties are derived from two wild species, *Musa acuminata* and *M. balbisiana,* both native to areas of India and Malaya.

DESCRIPTION. Among the tallest of herbs, the banana plant consists of sheaths, out of which the large leaves grow. It reproduces by shoots from around the base. Each plant bears one inflorescence. Several fingerlike fruits on one stem develop out of dark purple flowers. Most varieties of cooking banana are fat and often bright orange. Some bear seeds. (For a detailed description see Massal and Barrau 1956:10–12.)

GROWING CONDITIONS. The plant needs an adequate freshwater supply, protection from the winds, and warm temperatures. It fruits when 12 months old. The *fehi* banana (plantain) can withstand long dry seasons but produces fruit only with a good supply of moisture.

DISEASES. Bunchy top. The banana is also very prone to wind damage and is thus badly at risk in cyclone areas.

PLANTING MATERIAL. Shoots from the base of the parent plant.

NUTRITIONAL VALUE. The banana contains an easily digestible starch. Ripe (i.e., yellow) *mei'a* fruit contain 20 percent starch, 10 percent protein, and 10 g sugar per 100 g fruit; calcium and phosphorus levels are low. This banana is a good source of vitamin A. The plantain contains more vitamin C than the *mei'a.* The percentage of starch is higher and sugar lower in the *fe'i,* or cooking, banana.

STORAGE. Bananas may be stored in pits, as in Fiji, Anuta, and Futuna. They may be dried, and this process is achieving some commercial viability.

ARROWROOT

LOCAL NAMES. *Pia maori* or *pia, masoa* or *mahoa* or *mahoa'a.*

LATIN NAMES. *Tacca leontopetaloides, Tacca pinnatifida.* It is a member of a small Old World family, Taccaceae, consisting of two genera (Purseglove 1972:517). It is closely related to *Dioscorea* (yams), and is sometimes confused with the true arrowroot, *Maranta arundinacea.*

COMMON NAME. Polynesian arrowroot.

BOTANICAL DESCRIPTION. *Tacca* is a monocotyledonous herb with tall, erect, fluted green stems often 1 m high. The leaves are thrice divided and strikingly lobed. The flowers, borne on separate leafless tall stalks, protrude above the leaves (see Oliver 1974, 1:253 for a reproduction of Parkinson's drawing in 1773 of the leaves and flowers). The fruits are yellowish green, about the size of a small olive, and contain many seeds. The tubers, or creeping rhizomes, are hard and potatolike, with a brown skin and a very white interior. Most are small, from 1 to 2.5 in. (3–7 cm), round to irregular in shape. Longer ones may weigh up to 0.9 kg or 1.75 lb (Purseglove 1972:517–518).

ORIGINS. *Tacca* arrowroot probably had its homeland in Southeast Asia (Massal and Barrau 1956:11), as distinct from an Americas homeland for *Maranta*. It may have preceded man in its arrival on Pacific islands if its seeds were viable after floating in the ocean, as Guppy (1906) suggests.

GROWING CONDITIONS. The plant's natural habitat is in loose sand, well above the limits of normal high tide, and in partial shade, such as under coconut trees (Merrill 1943:35).

PLANTING MATERIAL. *Tacca* reproduces itself annually by seed or by tuber sprout.

HARVESTING. *Tacca* can be harvested for about 1 month each year.

YIELD. Depends on degree of cultivation. Much of the *Tacca* that is currently used grows wild—that is, it is left from previous annual growth.

STORAGE. There were several ways of storing arrowroot. The tubers could be left in the ground to reproduce another year; the flour could be dried, wrapped as cakes in leaves, and suspended from a rafter; or the flour could be stored in jars, as Seemann (1862) reports for Fiji.

USE. Arrowroot is used mainly as a flour prepared by grating and leaching the roots, then rinsing the residue repeatedly in clean water. That flour was mixed with pandanus or taro starch, to be used in the form of puddings. *Poke,* a favorite dish in the Cook Islands, was made from arrowroot flour and pawpaw (papaya) or pumpkin. It was also widely used as a starch for clothes, for which purpose the missionaries tried to establish trade in the 1840s with Sydney (Sunderland and Buzacott 1866).

TOXICITY. The root contains some hydrocyanogens. The water from washing it can be highly toxic; chickens are known to have died drinking it (NJP fieldnotes, Cook Islands 1982). The roots must be thoroughly cooked before eating.

NUTRITIONAL VALUE. The flour is high in energy value and contains some calcium and iron but none of the vitamins. Its value is improved considerably when mixed with pandanus, bananas, or pumpkin (SPC 1983).

Appendix B

Proto-Malayo-Polynesian and Proto-Oceanic Lexical Reconstructions Associated with Edible Plants

GLOSS	PMP	POC
taro	tales	ntalos
yam	qubi	qupi
Alocasia	biRaq	(m)piRaq
Cyrtosperma		
banana	pun(t,T)i	punti
Saccharum edule	—	tampukal
sugar cane	tebuS	(n)topu
coconut	niuR	niuR
sago palm	rumbi(a)	d(a,u)mpia
breadfruit	kuluR	kuluR
citrus	limaw	moli
Terminalia	(t,T)ali(c,s)ay	talinse
Inocarpus	qipil	qipil
Pandanus	panDan	pandan
Areca	bu(q)a	mpua
Casuarina	aRuqu/aRuSu	(y)aRu
Syzygium	—	kapika
Zingiber	leqia	laqia
Cordyline	siRi	nsiRi
Piper methysticum	—	kawa
Pometia	—	(n)tawa
Spondias	—	quRi
Barringtonia	butun	putu
Canarium	kaŋari	kaŋadi
melon/cucumber	timun	tim(o,u)n
breadfruit/		
fermented breadfruit	kama(n)(c,s)i	masi

Source: Extracted from Pawley and Green 1985:167.

Appendix C1

Origin and Distribution of Taro in the Pacific.
(After Bellwood 1978:137)

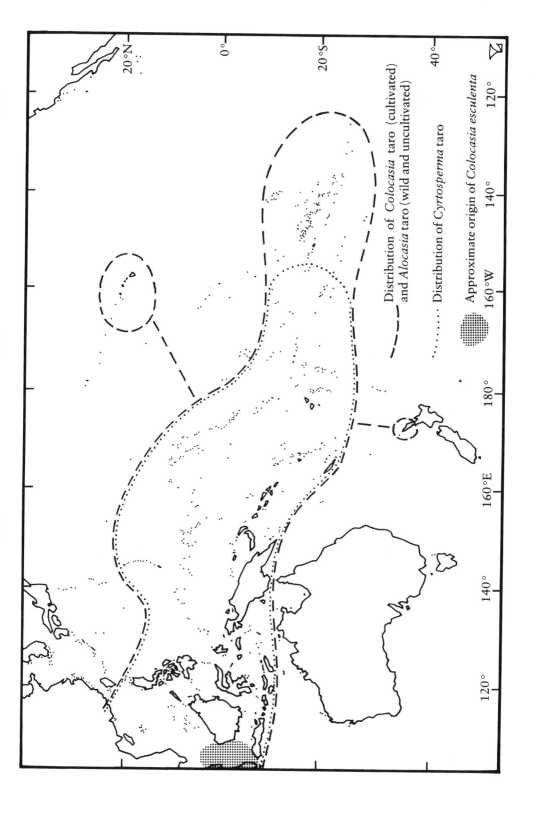

20°N

0°

20°S

40°

Distribution of *Colocasia* taro (cultivated)
and *Alocasia* taro (wild and uncultivated)

Distribution of *Cyrtosperma* taro

Approximate origin of *Colocasia esculenta*

120°   140°   160°W   180°   160°E   140°   120°

Appendix C2

Distribution of Seeded and Seedless Breadfruit
in the Pacific. (After Bellwood 1978:137)

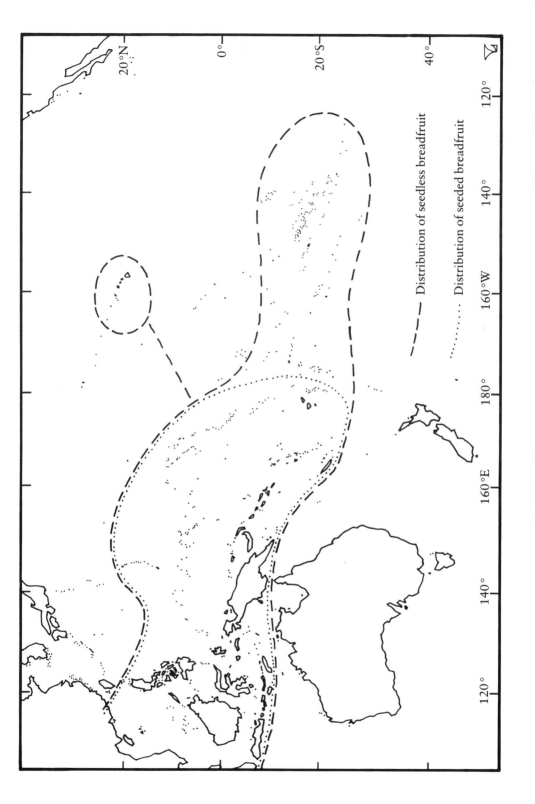

Distribution of seedless breadfruit

Distribution of seeded breadfruit

Appendix D

Breadfruit in the Pacific:
Local Names and Main Season

Island or Island Group	Local Names for Breadfruit — Fresh	Local Names for Breadfruit — Fermented	Main Season	Source
Palau	madu, meduu	nd	nd	Akimichi 1987
Tobi	nd	nd	nd	Black 1981
Ngulu	mafow	mar	nd	Intoh 1981/1984
Yap	thau	bulao	nd	Harmon 1938
Guam	dagdag, lemae	nd	nd	Sproat 1968
Tinian	rima	nd	nd	Sproat 1968
Rota	rima	nd	nd	Sproat 1968
Saipan	rima	nd	nd	Sproat 1968
Ulithi	mae	mar	Jul–Aug	Lessa 1977
Ifaluk	mai	mare	Jun–Nov	Burrows 1953
W. Carolines	mae	nd	brief	none
Puluwat	maajah	mar	Jun–Aug	Steager 1971
Lamotrek	mai	nd	nd	Alkire 1965
Truk	mai	mar	May–Aug	Lebar 1963
Namoluk	mei	nd	nd	Marshall 1975
Pohnpei	mai	mar	Jul–Aug	Bascom 1965
Mokil	mai	nd	nd	Someki 1938
Pingelap	mei	nd	nd	Christian 1970
Nukuoro	kul	nd	nd	Someki 1938
Kapingamarangi	nd	paku kuru	Jul–Sept	Buck 1950
Kosrae	mosse	furo	Jul–Aug	Wilson 1968
Marshalls	me	bwiru	May–Jul	Pollock 1970
Kiribati	temai	te kabuibui	nd	Luomala 1953
Nauru	nd	nd	nd	Pollock 1987
Tuvalu	mei	nd	nd	Kennedy 1931

Island or Island Group	Local Names for Breadfruit		Main Season	Source
	Fresh	Fermented		
Futuna	*mei*	*masi*	Jun–Jul	Burrows 1936
Wallis	*mei*	*mahi*	Jun–Jul	Burrows 1937
Tokelau	*mei**	nd	nd	Macgregor 1937
Rotuma	*ulu*	nd	Oct–Dec	Gardiner 1898
Fiji	*kulu, uto*	*madrai*	nd	Seemann 1862
Tonga	*mei*	*ma Tonga*	Mar–May	Mariner 1831
Niue	*mei*	nd	nd	Cowan 1923b
Samoa	*ulu*	*masi*	Jul–Aug	Grattan 1948
Rarotonga	*kuru*	*mahi*	Jan–Mar	Gill 1876
Aitutaki	*kuru*	*hopiko*	Jan–Mar	Gill 1876
Tahiti	*uru*	*mahi*	May–Aug	J. Ellis 1777
Tuamotus	*ura*	nd	nd	Danielsson 1956
Rurutu	*mai*	*mahi*	nd	Verin 1969
Tubuai	*maiore*	*tio'o*	nd	Aitken 1930
Marquesas	*mei*	*ma*	May–Jun	Linton 1939
Hawai'i	*'ulu*	*poi 'ulu*	Jun–Aug	Handy and Handy 1972
Anuta	*mei*	*ma*	Sep–Oct	Feinberg 1979
Bellona	*mai*	nd	nd	Christiansen 1975
Tikopia	*mei*	nd	Nov–Mar	Firth 1936
Santa Cruz	*mei*	*masi*	nd	Yen 1973b
New Guinea	nd	nd	nd	Powell 1982

*Introduced.

Bibliography

The following abbreviations appear in the Bibliography

ANU	Australian National University
ASAO	Association for Social Anthropology in Oceania
BPBM	Bernice Pauahi Bishop Museum
DSC	Development Studies Centre, Australian National University
FAO	Food and Agriculture Organization, United Nations
HRAF	Human Relations Area Files, Yale University
JPS	*Journal of the Polynesian Society*
JSO	*Journal de la Société des Océanistes*
MARC	Micronesian Area Research Center, University of Guam
ORSTOM	Office de la Recherche Scientifique et Technique d'Outre-Mer
SPC	South Pacific Commission
SPSSA	South Pacific Social Sciences Association
UNESCO	United Nations Educational, Scientific, and Cultural Organization
USP	University of the South Pacific
WHO	World Health Organization, United Nations

Aarlsberg, W. G. L., C. Lovelace, K. Mahoji, and S. Parkinson. 1981. *Davuke,* the traditional Fijian method of pit preservation of staple carbohydrate foods. MS, School of Biological Sciences, USP.

AhMu, Alan. 1983. Food and politics in Western Samoa. Honors paper, Anthropology, Victoria Univ., Wellington.

Aitken, R. 1930. *Ethnology of Tubuai.* BPBM Bull. 70. Honolulu.

Akimichi, T. 1980. A note on Palauan food categories. *Bull. National Museum of Ethnology* 5 (2): 593–610. Osaka, Japan.

———. 1987. Classification and contexts: Food categories in Satawalese culture. In *Cultural uniformity and diversity in Micronesia,* ed. I. Ushijima and K. Sudo. Senri Ethnological Studies 21. Osaka: National Museum of Ethnology.

Alkire, W. H. 1965. *Lamotrek Atoll and inter-island socioeconomic ties.* Illinois Studies in Anthropology 5. Champaign, Ill.: Univ. Illinois Press.

————. 1968. Porpoises and taro. *Ethnology* 7:280–289.

————. 1974. Natural categories of land. In *Land tenure in Oceania. See* Lundsgaarde 1974.

————. 1977. *An introduction to the peoples and cultures of Micronesia.* 2d ed. Newark, N.J.: Cummings.

Allen, J., J. Golson, and R. Jones, eds. 1977. *Sunda and Sahul.* N.Y.: Academic Press.

Alvarado, H. 1978. Medical anthropology and the health professions. In *The anthropology of health. See* Bauwens 1978.

Aoyagi, M. 1982. The geographical recognition of Palauan people. In *Islanders and their outside world,* ed. M. Aoyagi. Tokyo: Committee for Micronesian Research, St. Paul's (Rikkyo) Univ.

Arnott, M., ed. 1975. *Gastronomy.* World Anthropological Series. The Hague: Mouton.

Athens, Stephen. 1987. Early settlement on Kosrae: Where is the pottery? Paper presented at Indo-Pacific Prehistory Association, Micronesian Archeological Conference, Univ. Guam.

Ayres, W. 1983. Prehistoric food production in Micronesia. Paper presented at 15th Pacific Science Congress, Dunedin.

Ayres, W., and A. Haun. 1981. Archeological perspectives on food production in eastern Micronesia. Paper presented at Symposium on Prehistoric Intensive Agriculture in the Tropics, Dept. of Prehistory, ANU, Canberra.

Bailey, K. V. 1968. Composition of New Guinea highland foods. *Tropical Geography and Medicine* 20:141–146.

Baker, Paul. 1981. Modernization and the biological fitness of Samoans. In *Migration, adaptation, and health in the South Pacific. See* Fleming and Prior 1981.

Baker, P., J. M. Hanna, and T. S. Baker. 1986. *The changing Samoans.* N.Y.: Oxford Univ. Press.

Bakker, Solrun, et al. 1986. *Fijians in town.* Suva: Institute of Pacific Studies, USP.

Bakker-Williksen, S. 1984. To do and to be. M.A. thesis, Social Anthropology, Univ. Oslo.

Banks, Joseph. 1769. *Journal of Sir Joseph Banks.* Ed. Sir Joseph Hooker. Reprint. London: Macmillan, 1896.

Barrau, J. 1958. *Subsistence agriculture in Melanesia.* BPBM Bull. 219. Honolulu.

————. 1959. L'Agriculture Polynésienne et les étrangers. *JSO* 15.

————. 1960. The selection, domestication, and cultivation of food plants in tropical Oceania in the pre-European era. In *Symposium on the impact of man on humid tropics vegetation.* Bangkok: UNESCO.

————. 1961. *Subsistence agriculture in Polynesia and Micronesia.* BPBM Bull. 223. Honolulu.

————. 1965a. L'Humide et le sec. *JPS* 74:329–346.

———. 1965b. Witnesses of the past. *Ethnology* 4 (3): 282–294.

———. 1965c. Histoire et prehistoire horticoles de l'oceanie tropicale. *JSO* 21:55–78.

———. 1973. The Oceanians and their food plants. In *Man and his foods,* ed. C. Earle Smith, Jr. University, Ala.: Univ. Alabama Press.

———. 1979. Coping with exotic plants in folk taxonomies. In *Classifications in their social context,* ed. R. Ellen and D. Reason. London and New York: Academic Press.

Barrau, J., and A. Peeters. 1972. Histoire et prehistoire de la préparation des aliments. *JSO* 35:141–152.

Barrow, Sir J. 1980. *The mutiny of the* Bounty. Ed. G. Kennedy. Boston: D. R. Godine.

Barthes, Roland. 1975. Towards a psychosociology of contemporary food consumption. In *European diet from pre-industrial to modern times,* ed. R. I. Forster and O. Ranum. N.Y.: Harper and Row.

Bascom, W. A. 1965. *Ponape, a Pacific economy in transition.* Anthropological Records 22. Berkeley: Univ. California, Berkeley.

Bauwens, Eleanor E., ed. 1978. *The anthropology of health.* St. Louis: C. V. Mosby Co.

Baxter, M. 1980. *Food in Fiji.* DSC Monograph 22. Canberra.

Beaglehole, Ernest, and Pearl Beaglehole. 1938. *Ethnology of Pukapuka.* BPBM Bull. 150. Honolulu. Reprint. N.Y.: Kraus, 1971.

Beaglehole, John, ed. 1955. *The journals of Captain James Cook.* Vol. 1, *The voyage of the* Endeavour *1768–1771.* Cambridge: Cambridge Univ. Press for the Hakluyt Society.

———, ed. 1962. *The* Endeavour *journal of Sir Joseph Banks 1768–1771.* 2 vols. Sydney: Public Library of New South Wales and Angus and Robertson, Australia.

———, ed. 1967. *The journals of Captain James Cook, 1776–1780.* Vol. 3, *The voyages of the* Resolution *and* Discovery. Cambridge: Cambridge Univ. Press for the Hakluyt Society.

Begley, B., H. Spielmann, and G. Vieth. 1981. Poi consumption. Hawaii Institute of Tropical Agriculture and Human Resources, Departmental Paper 54, Univ. Hawaii, Honolulu.

Begley, B., G. Vieth, and R. de la Pena. n.d. Commercial dryland taro in Hawaii. MS, Univ. Hawaii, Dept. of Agricultural and Resource Economics, Honolulu.

Bell, F. S. 1948–1949. The place of food in the social life of the Tanga. *Oceania* 18 (3-4).

Beller, Ann. 1980. Venus as endomorph. In *A woman's conflict,* ed. J. Kaplan. Englewood Cliffs, N.J.: Prentice-Hall.

Bellwood, Peter. 1978. *Man's conquest of the Pacific.* N.Y.: Collins.

———. 1980. Plants, climate, and people. In *Indonesia: Australian perspectives,* ed. J. J. Fox, pp. 57–74. Canberra: Research School of Pacific Studies, ANU.

Bender, Byron. 1969. *Spoken Marshallese.* PALI Language Texts. Honolulu: Univ. Hawaii Press.

Berg, Alan. 1973. *The nutrition factor.* N.Y.: Brookings Institution.

Berlin, B., D. E. Breedlove, and P. Raven. 1973. General principles of classification and nomenclature in folk biology. *American Anthropologist* 75 (1): 214–242.

Berlin, B., and P. Kay. 1969. *Basic color terms.* Berkeley: Univ. California Press.

Biggs, B., D. Walsh, and J. Waqa. 1972. Proto-Polynesian reconstructions with English to Proto-Polynesian finder list. Working papers. Auckland: Dept. of Anthropology, Univ. Auckland.

Bindon, James. 1982. Breadfruit, banana, beef, and beer. *Ecology of Food and Nutrition* 12 (1): 49–60.

Black, Peter. 1981. Fishing for taro. In *Persistence and exchange,* ed. R. Force and B. Bishop. Honolulu: Pacific Science Association.

Bloom, Abby. 1987. Health and nutrition in the Pacific. In *Human resources development in the Pacific,* ed. C. D. Throsby. Pacific Policy Papers 3. Canberra: National Centre for Development Studies, ANU.

Bott, Elizabeth, with Tavi. 1982. *Tongan society at the time of Captain Cook's visits.* Memoir 44. Wellington: Polynesian Society.

Bourdieu, Pierre. 1984. *Distinction—a social critique of the judgment of taste.* Trans. Richard Nice. London: Routledge and Kegan Paul.

Bradbury, J. Howard, and W. D. Holloway. 1988. *Chemistry of tropical root crops: Significance for nutrition and agriculture in the Pacific.* Canberra: Australian Centre for International Agricultural Research.

Brookfield, H. 1972. Intensification and disintensification in Pacific agriculture. *Pacific Viewpoint* 13:30–48.

———. 1984. Intensification revisited. *Pacific Viewpoint* 25 (1).

Brown, George. 1910. *Melanesians and Polynesians.* N.Y.: Macmillan.

Brown, Lester. 1970. *Seeds of change.* N.Y.: Praeger.

Bryan, E. H. 1972. *Life in the Marshall Islands.* Honolulu: Pacific Science Information Center, BPBM.

Buck, Sir Peter. 1927. *The material culture of the Cook Islands (Aitutaki).* Board of Maori Ethnological Research Memoirs, vol. 1. Wellington.

———. 1930. *Samoan material culture.* BPBM Bull. 75. Honolulu.

———. 1934. *Mangaian society.* BPBM Bull. 122. Honolulu.

———. 1950. *Material culture of Kapingamarangi.* BPBM Bull. 200. Honolulu.

Burgess, H. J. L., and Ann P. Burgess. 1976. *Malnutrition in the western Pacific region.* Geneva: WHO.

Burkill, I. H. 1935. *A dictionary of the economic products of the Malay Peninsula.* 2 vols. London.

Burrows, Edwin G. 1936. *Ethnology of Futuna.* BPBM Bull. 138. Honolulu.

———. 1937. *Ethnology of Uvea (Wallis Island).* BPBM Bull. 145. Honolulu.

———. 1953 *An atoll culture.* New Haven: HRAF.

Calvert, James. 1858. *Fiji and the Fijians.* Vol. 2, *Mission history.* Reprint. Suva: Fiji Museum, 1983.

Cambrezy, Luc. 1982. *Problèmes de ravitaillement urbain en Polynésie Française*. Papeʻete: ORSTOM.

Cargill, David. 1841. *Memoirs of Mrs. Margaret Cargill*. London: John Mason.

Catala, R. 1957. *Report on the Gilbert and Ellice Islands*. Atoll Research Bull. 59. Washington, D.C.: National Research Council.

Chandra, S. 1979a. Productive efficiency of Fijian and Indian farming systems in semi-subsistence agriculture. *Fiji Agricultural J.* 39 (1 & 2) and 40 (1).

———. 1979b. Root crops in Fiji. Part 1. *Fiji Agricultural J.* 41 (2): 73–85.

———. 1980. Root crops in Fiji. Part 2. *Fiji Agricultural J.* 42: 11–17.

———. 1981. Food production and consumption on Fijian and Indian farms in the Sigatoka Valley, Fiji. *Fiji Agricultural J.* 43 (1): 33–42.

Chandra, S., and P. Sivan. 1981. Taro production systems studies in Fiji. Paper for International Foods Symposium, regional meeting on edible aroids, Alafua, W. Samoa.

Christian, F. W. 1970. Ponapean superstitions and character. In *Ponape,* ed. F. Morrill. San Francisco: Cadlean Press.

Christiansen, Sofus. 1975. *Subsistence on Bellona Island*. Folia Geographica Danica 13. Copenhagen: C.A. Reitzels.

Churchill, W. S. 1912. *Easter Island: The Rapanui speech and the peopling of south-east Polynesia*. Carnegie Institution, Publication 174. Washington, D.C.

Churchward, W. H. 1887. *My Samoan consulate*. London: Dawsons.

Clark, R. 1979. Language. In *The prehistory of Polynesia. See* Jennings 1979.

Clements, F. 1959. Changing food habits. *South Pacific* 10:173–177.

Clunie, Fergus. 1984. Fijian canoe hearths. *Domodomo* 2 (3): 102–112.

Coenen, J., and J. Barrau. 1961. The breadfruit tree in Micronesia. *SPC Bull.* 11 (4): 37, 39, 65–67.

Colson, A., and H. Selby. 1974. Medical anthropology. In *Annual Review of Anthropology* 3:245–262.

Colson, E. 1979. In good years and bad: Food strategies of self-reliant societies. *J. Anthropological Research* 35:18–39.

Conklin, H. 1957. *Hanunóo agriculture*. FAO Forestry Development Paper 12. Rome.

Connell, John. 1978. The death of taro: Local response to a change of subsistence crops in the northern Solomon Islands. *Mankind* 11: 445–452.

———. 1981. A fatal movement? Migration, urbanisation, nutrition, and health in the South Pacific. Paper for United Nations Development Program/SPC regional meeting, Suva. Copy in SPC Library, Noumea.

Cordy, Ross. 1984. *A study of prehistoric social change*. N.Y.: Academic Press.

Coursey, D. 1967. *Yams*. London: Longmans.

————. 1968. The edible aroids. *World Crops* 20 (4): 25–30.

————. 1972. The civilisation of the yam. *Archeology and Physical Anthropology in Oceania* 7:215–232.

————. 1977. The status of root crops. In *Regional meeting on the production of root crops, 1975. See* SPC 1977.

————. 1978. Some ideological considerations relating to tropical root crop production. In *The adaptation of traditional agriculture,* ed. E. K. Fisk. DSC Monograph 11. Canberra.

Coursey, D., and P. Haynes. 1970. Root crops and their potential as food in the tropics. *World Crops* 22:261–265.

Cowan, J. 1923a. *Maori folk tales.* Auckland: Whitcombe and Tombs.

————. 1923b. The story of Niue. *JPS* 32:238–242.

Cox, Paul. 1980. Masi and Tanuelu. *Pacific Tropical Botanical Garden Bull.* 10 (4): 181–185.

Coyne, T., J. Badcock, and R. Taylor, eds. 1984. *The effect of urbanisation and western diet on the health of Pacific island populations.* SPC Technical Paper 186. Noumea.

Crocombe, R. 1968. Lands policy in the dependencies. In *New Zealand's record in the Pacific in the twentieth century,* ed. A. Ross. N.Y.: Humanities Press.

————, ed. 1971. *Land tenure in Oceania.* London: Oxford Univ. Press.

————, ed. 1985. *Tahiti, the other side.* Suva: SPSSA.

————, ed. 1987. *Land tenure in Oceania.* Rev. ed. Suva: Institute of Pacific Studies, USP.

Cumming, C. F. Gordon. 1880. *A lady's cruise in a French man of war.* N.Y.: Praeger.

————. 1885. *At home in Fiji.* New ed. London: Wm. Blackwood.

Cuzent, Gilbert. 1860. *Archipel de Tahiti.* Reprint, ed. J. Florence et al. Pape'ete: Haere Po No Tahiti, 1983.

Dampier, William. 1697. *A new voyage around the world.* Reprint. London, 1937.

Danielsson, Bengt. 1956. *Work and life in Raroia.* London: Allen and Unwin.

Darnton Hill, R., J. Badcock, and R. Taylor. 1985. Nutrition problems in the Pacific. Paper presented at 2d International Symposium of Clinical Nutrition, Dublin.

Davenport, William H. 1968–1969. The outer reef islands, Santa Cruz. Paper for Conference on Atoll Populations 1971–1972, Honolulu.

David, Mrs. 1899. *Funafuti—or three months on a remote coral island.* London: John Murray.

Davidson, Flora. 1975. The Tokelau Island migrant study—atoll diet. In *Migration and health in New Zealand and the Pacific,* ed. C. Fleming and J. Stanhope, pp. 109–113. Wellington: Wellington Hospital Epidemiology Unit.

Davidson, Janet. 1979. Samoa and Tonga. In *The prehistory of Polynesia. See* Jennings 1979.

————. 1984. *The prehistory of New Zealand.* Auckland: Longman Paul.

Davidson, S., R. Passmore, J. F. Brock, and A. S. Truswell. 1975. *Human nutrition and dietetics.* Edinburgh: Churchill Livingstone.

Deane, Rev. W. 1921. *Fijian society.* London: Macmillan.

de la Pena, R. 1983. Agronomy. In *Taro. See* Wang 1983.

Delaporte, Mrs. Philip A. 1920. The men and women of old Nauru. *Mid Pacific Magazine* 19 (2): 153–156.

Delebecque, K., P. Delebecque, B. Philippe, and J. M. Senehart. 1982. An approach to nutrition and health problems on the Tuamotu Islands. In *Regional technical meeting on atoll cultivation.* SPC Technical Paper 180. Noumea.

del Valle, Theresa. 1979. Social and cultural change in the community of Umatac, Southern Guam. MS, MARC.

Denoon, D., and P. Snowden. 1982. *A time to plant and a time to uproot.* Port Moresby: Institute of Papua New Guinea Studies.

Dentan, Robert. 1968. *The Semai.* N.Y.: Holt, Rinehart and Winston.

de Quiros, Ferdinand. 1904. *The voyages of Pedro Ferdinand de Quiros.* Trans. and ed. Sir Clements Markham. London: Hakluyt.

Derrick, R. A. 1946. *A history of Fiji.* Suva: Printing and Stationers.

Desai, Ashok. 1976. Commercialization of subsistence agriculture. In *Vitian economic policy,* ed. R. Thaman. Parkinson Memorial Lectures. Suva: USP.

Diamond, Jack. 1982. Taro. *New Zealand Archeological Association Newsletter* 25 (3): 195–198.

Dixon, Roland. 1932. The problem of the sweet potato in Oceania. *American Anthropologist* 34 (1): 40–66.

Douglas, M. 1966. *Purity and danger.* Baltimore: Penguin.

———. 1972. Deciphering a meal. *Daedalus* 101:61–81.

———. 1975. *Implicit meanings.* N.Y.: Routledge and Kegan Paul.

———. 1978. *Cultural bias.* London: Royal Anthropological Institute.

———. 1982a. *In the active voice.* London: Routledge and Kegan Paul.

———. 1982b. *Essays in the sociology of perception.* London: Routledge and Kegan Paul.

———. 1984. *Food in the social order.* New York: Russell Sage Foundation.

Drummond, Sir Jack, and Anne Wilbraham. 1939. *The Englishman's food.* London: Jonathan Cape.

Durbin, M. 1973. Cognitive anthropology. In *Handbook of social and cultural anthropology,* ed. J. Honigmann. Chicago: Rand McNally.

Durie, M. 1985. A Maori perspective of health. *Social Science and Medicine* 20 (5): 483–486.

Duttaroy, D. K. 1980. *Report on household consumption and production of crops, livestock, and fish.* Kingdom of Tonga: Ministry of Agriculture, Fisheries, and Forestry.

Dwyer, Peter. 1985. Choice and constraint in a Papua New Guinea food quest. *Human Ecology* 13 (1): 49–70.

Earle, T., and J. Erikson, eds. 1977. *Exchange systems in prehistory.* N.Y.: Academic Press.

Ellen, R. 1979. Introduction. In *Classifications in their social context,* ed. R. Ellen and D. Reason. London and N.Y.: Academic Press.

Ellis, A. F. 1936. *Ocean Island and Nauru.* Melbourne: Angus and Robertson.

Ellis, John. 1777. Extract from a work, entitled, A description of the most delicious of all the fruits in the East Indies. MS copy in Turnbull Library, Wellington.

Ellis, W. H. 1831. *Polynesian researches.* Reprint. Honolulu: Tuttle, 1969.

Emory, Kenneth. 1965. *Kapingamarangi: Social and religious life of a Polynesian atoll.* BPBM Bull. 228. Honolulu.

———. 1975. *Material culture of the Tuamotu Archipelago.* BPBM Pacific Anthropological Records 22. Honolulu.

Enright, H. 1976. Food marketing within Western Samoa—the primary produce component. Mimeo, Dept. of Agriculture, Forestry and Fisheries, Apia.

Epstein, T. Scarlett. 1982. *Urban food marketing and Third World rural development.* London: Croom Helm.

Errington, F. 1984. *Manners and meaning in West Sumatra.* New Haven: Yale Univ. Press.

ESCAP (Economic and Social Commission for Asia and the Pacific). 1982. *Comparative study on migration, urbanization, and development in the ESCAP region.* N.Y.: United Nations.

Fa'anunu, Hanieteli. 1977. Traditional aspects of root crop production in the Kingdom of Tonga. In *Regional meeting on the production of root crops, 1975. See* SPC 1977.

FAO. 1972. *Report of a joint FAO/WHO expert group.* Rome: FAO.

———. 1982. Root crops seminar, 13–17 Dec. Unpublished papers, USP School of Agriculture, Alafua, W. Samoa.

Fairbairn, I. 1985. *Pacific Island economies.* Suva: Institute of Pacific Studies, USP.

Fankhauser, B. 1986. Archeometric studies of *Cordyline (ti)* based on ethnobotanical and archeological research. Ph.D. diss., Univ. Otago.

Feinberg, Richard. 1979. *Anutan concepts of disease: A Polynesian study.* IPS Monograph Series 3. Laie, Hawai'i: Institute for Polynesian Studies.

Ferrando, R. 1981. *Traditional and non-traditional foods.* Rome: FAO.

Fiji Food and Nutrition Committee. various 1981–. *Newsletter.* Suva.

Fiji Blue Book. 1880–1923. Annual. Suva: Government Printer.

Finau, Sitaleki. 1986a. Handling disasters. *Pacific Perspective* 12 (2): 62–68.

———. 1986b. Social policy for health. *Social Science and Economic Development Review* (Fiji) 14:6–9.

Finney, Ben. 1965. Economic change and dietary consequences among the Tahitians. *Micronesica* 2 (1): 1–14.

———. 1973. *Polynesian peasants and proletarians.* N.Y.: Schenkman.

Firth, Raymond. 1936. *We the Tikopia.* Reprint. Chicago: Beacon Press, 1963.

———. 1939. *Primitive Polynesian economy.* Reprint. London: Routledge and Kegan Paul, 1965.

———. 1959. *Social change in Tikopia.* N.Y.: Macmillan.

———. 1967. *The work of the gods in Tikopia.* Melbourne: Melbourne Univ. Press.

———. 1970. *Rank and religion in Tikopia.* London: George Allen and Unwin.

———. 1985. *Tikopia dictionary.* Auckland: Auckland Univ. Press.

Firth, Rosemary. 1939. *Housekeeping among Malay peasants.* London: Athlone Press.

Fischer, John L., and Ann Fischer. 1957. *The Eastern Carolines.* New Haven: HRAF.

Fisk, E. K. 1976. Traditional agriculture as a source of food in a development situation. In *Food production in the South Pacific: R. W. Parkinson Memorial Lectures 1974,* ed. R. Thaman. Suva: USP.

———, ed. 1978. *The adaptation of traditional agriculture.* DSC Monograph 11. Canberra.

Fitzgerald, T. 1978. Migration and reciprocal changes in diet. *South Pacific Bull.,* nos. 3/4: 30–33.

Fleming, C., and I. Prior, eds. 1981. *Migration, adaptation, and health in the South Pacific.* Wellington: Wellington Hospital Epidemiological Unit and Clinical School.

Forbes, Litton. 1875. *Two years in Fiji.* London: Longmans Green.

Force, Roland. 1963. *Pacific port towns.* Honolulu: Bishop Museum Press.

Forster, George R. 1777. *Observations made during a voyage round the world.* London: G. Robinson.

Foster, G., and M. Anderson. 1978. *Medical anthropology.* N.Y.: John Wiley and Sons.

Fox, R., and K. Cumberland. 1962. *Western Samoa—land, life and agriculture.* Wellington: Whitcombe and Tombs.

Franks, A. J., and C. Jurgensen. 1985. Nutrition and health in the first year of life on a Pacific atoll. *Transactions of the Royal Society of Tropical Medicine and Hygiene* 79:681–684.

French Wright, R. 1983. Proto-Oceanic horticultural practices. M.A. thesis, Linguistics, Univ. Auckland.

Freycinet, Louis de. 1960. *Voyage around the world. . . . Book IV, From Guam to the Sandwich Islands* [Ch. 27, pp. 517–622, 1839]. Trans. Ella Wiswell. MS, MARC.

Friedman, J. 1982. Catastrophe and continuity in social evolution. In *Theory and explanation in archeology.* N.Y.: Academic Press.

Fusi, Valerio. 1981. Action and possession in Maori language and culture— a Whorfian approach. *L'Homme* 25 (2): 117–145.

Gardiner, J. Stanley. 1898. The natives of Rotuma. *Royal Anthropological Institute J.* 27.

Geddes, William. 1981. *North Tabiteuea report.* Wellington: Victoria Univ. Gilbert and Ellice Islands Project.

———. 1982. Social and economic change in the Republic of Kiribati. In *The impact of modernization on the health of a Pacific nation 1981. See* Zimmet et al. 1982.

Geertz, Clifford. 1973. *The interpretation of cultures.* N.Y.: Basic Books.

———. 1983. *Local knowledge.* N.Y.: Basic Books.

George, Susan. 1976. *How the other half dies.* N.Y.: Penguin.

George, S., and G. Paige. 1982. *Food for beginners.* San Francisco: Writers and Readers Publishing Coop Society.

Geraghty, Paul. 1983. *The history of the Fijian languages.* Oceanic Linguistics Special Publication 19. Honolulu: Univ. Hawaii Press.

Gerlach, R., and P. Salavao. 1984. Breadfruit. *Alafua Agricultural Bull.,* 1984: 21–26.

Gifford, E. W. 1929. *Tongan society.* BPBM Bull. 61. Honolulu.

Gilbert, Robert I., and James H. Mielke. 1985. *The analysis of prehistoric diets.* N.Y.: Academic Press.

Gill, W. W. 1876. *Life in the southern isles.* London: Religious Tract Society.

———. 1902. *Ocean and isle.* Melbourne: Wm. T. Pater.

Gilson, R. 1980. *The Cook Islands, 1820–1950.* Wellington and Suva: Victoria Univ. and USP.

Gladwin, T., and E. Sarason. 1963. *Truk.* N.Y.: Wenner-Gren Foundation.

Golson, J. 1977. No room at the top. In *Sunda and Sahul,* pp. 600–638. *See* Allen, Golson, and Jones 1977.

Goodenough, W. H., and Hiroshi Sugita. 1980. *Trukese/English dictionary.* Memoir Series, vol. 144. Philadelphia: American Philosophical Society.

Goodland, R., C. Watson, and G. Ledec. 1984. *Environmental management in tropical agriculture.* Chicago: Westview Press.

Goodman, M. 1985. *Women in Asia and the Pacific.* Honolulu: Univ. Hawaii Press for Women's Study Program.

Grattan, F. 1948. *An introduction to Samoan custom.* Apia: Government Printer.

Green, Roger. 1979. Lapita. In *The prehistory of Polynesia. See* Jennings 1979.

Greenwood, Paul J. 1985. *Evolution: Essays in honour of J. Maynard Smith.* N.Y.: Cambridge Univ. Press.

Gregory, C. 1982. *Gifts and commodities.* London: Academic Press.

Grimble, Sir Arthur. 1933. Migrations of a pandanus people. *JPS* 42 (1, 4) and 43 (1).

Grimshaw, Beatrice. 1907a. *From Fiji to the Cannibal Isles.* London: Thomas Nelson and Sons.

———. 1907b. *In the strange South Seas.* London: Hutchinson and Row.

Guiart, Jean. 1982. A Polynesian myth and the invention of Melanesia. *JPS* 91 (1): 139–144.

Guppy, H. B. 1906. *Observations of a naturalist in the Pacific between 1896 and 1899.* Vol. 2, *Plant dispersal.* London: Macmillan.

Hall, E., and K. Pelzer. 1946. *The economy of the Truk Islands.* Honolulu: U.S. Commercial Company, Economic Survey of Micronesia.

Handy, E. S. C., and E. G. Handy, with M. Pukui. 1972. *Native planters in old Hawaii.* BPBM Bull. 233. Honolulu.

Handy, E. S. C., and Willowdean Handy. 1923. *The native culture in the Marquesas.* BPBM Bull. 9. Honolulu.

Handy, E. S. C., and M. K. Pukui. 1933. *Ancient Hawaiian civilization.* Honolulu: The Kamehameha Schools.

———. 1972. *The Polynesian family system in Ka'u.* Rutland, Vt.: Tuttle.

Hankin, J., D. Reed, D. Labarthe, M. Nichaman, and R. Stallones. 1970. Dietary and disease patterns among Micronesians. *American J. Clinical Nutrition* 23 (3): 346–357.

Hanna, J., and R. Severson. 1981. The diet of Samoan migrants to Hawaii. *American J. Physical Anthropology* 54 (2): 229–241.

Hanson, Allen. 1970. *Rapan lifeways.* N.Y.: Little, Brown.

Hardaker, J. B., E. M. Fleming, and G. T. Harris. 1984. Smallholder modes of agricultural production in the South Pacific: Prospects for development. *Pacific Viewpoint* 25 (2).

Harding, R. S. O., and G. Teleki, eds. 1981. *Omnivorous primates: Gathering and hunting in human evolution.* N.Y.: Columbia Univ. Press.

Harmon, Gunner L. McK. 1938. Acho Yap. *The Guam Recorder* 15:8.

Harre, J., ed. 1973. *Living in town.* Suva: SPSSA and Institute of Pacific Studies.

Harris, D. R. 1972. The origins of agriculture in the tropics. *American Scientist* 60:180–193.

———. 1977. Subsistence strategies across Torres Strait. In *Sunda and Sahul. See* Allen, Golson, and Jones 1977.

Harris, M. 1986. *Good to eat.* N.Y.: Simon and Schuster.

Harris, M., and Eric Ross. 1978. How beef became king. *Psychology Today,* Oct., pp. 88–94.

Hau'ofa, Epeli. 1979. *Corned beef and tapioca.* DSC Monograph 19. Canberra.

———. 1982. Anthropology at home: A South Pacific experience. In *Indigenous anthropology in non-western countries,* ed. H. Fahim. Durham, N.C.: Carolina Academic Press.

———. 1985. The future of our past. In *The Pacific Islands in the year 2000,* ed. R. Kiste and R. Herr. Pacific Islands Studies Program Working Paper Series. Honolulu: Univ. Hawaii.

Hawkes, K., and J. O'Connell. 1985. Optimal foraging models and the case of the !Kung. *American Anthropologist* 87 (2): 401–405.

Hecht, Julia. 1985. Physical and social boundaries in Pukapukan theories of disease. In *Healing practices in the South Pacific. See* Parsons 1985.

Hegsted, D. 1985. Nutrition: The changing scene. *Nutrition Reviews* 43 (12): 347–367.

Helu, Futa. 1981. Thinking in Tongan society. In *Thinking, the expanding frontier,* ed. W. Maxwell. San Francisco: L. Erlbaum.

Henderson, G. 1931a. *Fiji and the Fijians.* London: Dawsons.

———. 1931b. *The journal of Thomas Williams, missionary in Fiji 1840–1853.* 2 vols. Australia: Angus and Robertson.

Henry, Teuira. 1928. *Ancient Tahiti.* BPBM Bull. 48. Honolulu.

———. 1893. Te umi-ti, a Raiatean ceremony. *JPS* 2:105–108.

Heywood, Peter. 1987. Food supply in Papua New Guinea: Dependence versus independence. In *Nutrition and health in the tropics,* ed. C. Rae and S. Green. Darwin: Menzies School of Health Research.

Hipsley, E. 1947. *Report of the New Guinea nutrition survey expedition.* Canberra: Dept. of External Territories.

Hipsley, E., and N. Kirk. 1965. *Studies of dietary intake and the expenditure of energy by New Guineans.* SPC Technical Paper 147. Noumea.

Hiyane, J. T., and K. Hadley. 1977. Yam cultivation. In *Regional meeting on the production of root crops, 1975. See* SPC 1977.

Holmes, C. 1982. *Captain Cook's final voyage.* Horsham, Eng.: Caliban.

Holmes, Susan. 1953. Nutrition survey in the Gilbert Islands. Mimeo, South Pacific Health Service, Noumea.

———. 1956. Public health nutrition programmes in the Pacific Islands. SPC *Quarterly Bull.* 6 (2): 13–15.

Holo, F., and S. Taumoefolau. 1982. The cultivation of *kape* in Tonga. In *Taro cultivation in the South Pacific. See* Lambert 1982.

Horne, John. 1881. *A year in Fiji.* London: Eyre and Spottiswoode.

Houghton, P., H. Leach, and D. Sutton. 1975. The estimation of stature of prehistoric Polynesians in New Zealand. *JPS* 84 (3): 325–336.

Howard, A. 1964. Land tenure and social change in Rotuma. *JPS* 73 (1): 26–52.

Howells, W. W. 1979. Physical anthropology. In *The prehistory of Polynesia,* pp. 277–285. *See* Jennings 1979.

Hughes, D. 1968. Democracy in a traditional society—Ponape. Mimeo, Pacific Collection, Hamilton Library, Univ. Hawaii, Honolulu.

Hunn, Eugene. 1977. *Tzeltal folk zoology: The classification of discontinuities in nature.* N.Y.: Academic Press.

———. 1985. The utilitarian factor in folk biological classification. In *Directions in cognitive anthropology,* ed. J. Dougherty. Champaign, Ill.: Univ. Illinois Press.

Hunt, E. E., et al. 1949. *The Micronesians of Yap and their depopulation.* Washington: Pacific Science Board.

Hunt, Terry. 1981. Early horticulture in Fiji. *JPS* 90 (2): 259–266.

Hunter-Anderson, R. 1981/1984. Yapese stone fish traps. *Asian Perspectives* 24 (1).

———. 1983. Recent observations on traditional Yapese settlement patterns. *New Zealand J. Archeology* 6:95–105. Paper presented at 15th Pacific Science Congress, Dunedin.

Huntsman, J. 1978. Tokelau cuisine. Paper prepared for 2d International Symposium of the Art of Oceania, Wellington, Aug.

Hutterer, Karl. 1983. The natural and cultural history of Southeast Asian agriculture. *Anthropos* 78:169–207.

Intoh, Michiko. 1981/1984. Archeological research on Ngulu atoll. *Asian Perspectives* 24 (1): 69–80.

Irwin, Geoff. 1980. The prehistory of Oceania: Colonization and cultural change. In *Cambridge encyclopedia of archeology,* pp. 324–332. Cambridge.

———. 1981. How Lapita lost its pots. *JPS* 90 (2).

Isaacs, Glynn. 1978. Food sharing and human evolution. *J. Anthropological Research* 34:311–325.

Jansen, J. 1977. Malnutrition and child feeding practices among the Gilbertese. *J. Tropical Pediatrics* 22:161–167.

Jelliffe, D., and S. Jelliffe. 1977. The cultural cul de sac of western medicine. *Trans. Royal Society of Tropical Medicine and Hygiene* 77 (4).

Jennings, J., ed. 1979. *The prehistory of Polynesia*. Cambridge: Harvard Univ. Press.

Jerome, N., R. Kandel, and G. Pelto. 1980. *Nutritional anthropology*. N.Y.: Redgrave Publishing.

Jones, Kevin, and Garry Law. 1986. Prehistoric population estimates for the Tolaga Bay vicinity, east coast, North Island, New Zealand. MS, copy in author's possession.

Jones, W. O. 1957. Manioc: An example of innovation in Africa. *Economic Development and Cultural Change* 5 (2): 97–116.

Kahn, Miriam. 1986. *Always hungry, never greedy*. New York: Cambridge Univ. Press.

Katayama, J. 1985. Human skeletal remains from Makin. *Man and culture in Oceania* 1:88–120.

Kayser, P. [Pater A.]. 1934. Der Pandanus auf Nauru. *Anthropos* Band 29, vol. 24: 775–791.

Kearney, M. 1984. *World view*. N.Y.: Sharp and Chandler.

Keith-Reid, Robert. 1982. The eating catastrophe. *Islands Business,* Sept.

Kennedy, D. G. 1931. *Culture of Vaitupu, Ellice Islands*. Memoir 9. Wellington: Polynesian Society.

Kent, George. 1986. Shaping an economy. *Islands Business,* Mar., pp. 33–37.

King, M., F. King, F. Morley, L. Burgess, and M. Burgess. 1972. *Nutrition for developing countries*. London: Oxford Univ. Press.

Kinloch, P. 1985. *Talking health, but doing sickness*. Wellington: Victoria Univ. Press.

Kirch, P. 1975. Cultural adaptation and ecology in western Polynesia. Ph.D. diss., Cultural Anthropology, Yale Univ.

———. 1978. Indigenous agriculture on Uvea (W. Polynesia). *Economic Botany* 32 (2): 157–182.

———. 1979. Subsistence ecology. In *The prehistory of Polynesia. See* Jennings 1979.

———. 1980. Polynesian prehistory: Cultural adaptation in island ecosystems. *American Scientist* 68 (1): 39–48.

———. 1982. Ecology and the adaptation of Polynesian agricultural systems. *Archeology in Oceania* 17:1–6.

———. 1984. *The evolution of the Polynesian chiefdoms*. Cambridge: Cambridge Univ. Press.

———. 1985. *Feathered gods and fishhooks*. Honolulu: Univ. Hawaii Press.

Kirch, P., and D. Yen. 1982. *Tikopia*. BPBM Bull 238. Honolulu.

Knapman, Bruce. 1985. Capitalism's economic impact on colonial Fiji, 1874–1939. *J. Pacific History* 20 (1–2): 66–83.

Krämer, F. Augustin. 1902–1903. *Die Samoa Inseln*. Stuttgart: E. Schweizerbart (E. Nägele).

————. 1906. *Hawaii, Ostmikronesien und Samoa . . . 1897–1899*. Stuttgart: Nägele.

————. 1935. *Inseln um Truk*. Ergebnisse der Südsee Expedition 1908–1910, IIB, ed. G. Thilenius. Hamburg: Friederichsen, de Gruyter.

Krämer, A., and H. Nevermann. 1938. *Ralik Ratak—Die Marshall Inseln*. Ergebnisse der Südsee Expedition 1908–1910, IIB 11, ed. G. Thilenius. Hamburg: Friederichsen, de Gruyter.

Kuipers, J. 1984. Matters of taste in Weyewa. *Anthropological Linguistics* 26 (1): 84–101.

Kurashina, H., Darlene Moore, O. Kataoka, R. Clayshulte, and E. Ray. 1981/1984. Prehistoric and protohistoric cultural occurrences at Tarague, Guam, in Micronesian prehistory. *Asian Perspectives* 24 (1): 57–67.

Labarthe, G., D. Reed, and G. Brody. 1973. Health effects of modernization in Palau. *American J. Epidemiology* 98:161–174.

Labby, David. 1976. *The demystification of Yap*. Chicago: Univ. Chicago Press.

Labillardiere, H. 1800. *Voyage in search of La Perouse*. London: John Stockdale.

Laderman, Carol. 1984. Food ideology and eating behavior. *Social Science and Medicine* 19 (5): 547–559.

Lakoff, George. 1987. *Women, fire, and dangerous things: What categories reveal about the mind*. Chicago: Univ. Chicago Press.

Lambert, Michel, ed. 1980. An overview of agriculture on some Pacific atolls. *South Pacific Bull.*, no. 3: 8–13.

————, ed. 1982. *Taro cultivation in the South Pacific*. SPC Handbook 22. Noumea.

Lancaster, P. A., J. S. Ingram, M. Y. Lim, and D. G. Coursey. 1982. Traditional cassava based foods—survey of processing techniques. *Economic Botany* 36 (1): 12–45.

Lane, M. 1987. Heart disease on the rise in Tonga. *Islands Business*, Mar., p. 48.

Lang, G. 1985. Diabetics and health care in a Sioux community. *Human Organization* 44 (3).

Lange, R. 1984. Plagues and pestilence in Polynesia. *Bull. History of Medicine* 58:325–346.

Langley, D. 1953. Dietary surveys and growth records in a Fijian village, Naduri. South Pacific Health Service. Mimeo, Fiji Food and Nutrition Committee, Suva.

Lappe, F., and G. Collins. 1979. *Food first*. Boston: Houghton Mifflin.

Laval, Hon. Pierre. 1938. *Mangareva—l'histoire ancienne d'un peuple Polynésien*. Paris: Libraire orientaliste, Paul Geuthner.

Lawry, Rev. Walter. 1850. *Friendly and Feejee Islands: A missionary visit*. London.

Leach, H. 1982. Cooking without pots. *New Zealand J. Archeology* 4: 149–156.

————. 1983. Model gardens and the acceptability of new crops to Polynesian horticulturalists. *New Zealand J. Archeology* 5:139–149.

Lebar, F. 1963. The material culture of Truk. MS, HRAF.

Lee, Kee Dong. 1975. *Kusaien reference grammar.* PALI Language Texts. Honolulu: Univ. Press of Hawaii.

Lee, Richard. 1979. *The !Kung San: Men, women, and work in a foraging society.* London: Cambridge Univ. Press.

———. 1984. *The Dobe !Kung.* N.Y.: Holt, Rinehart and Winston.

LeMaitre, Yves. 1972. La hierarchie des termes de nourriture en Tahitien. *Cahier d'ORSTOM Science Humaine* 9 (1): 63–73.

Lessa, William. 1977. Traditional uses of the vascular plants of Ulithi. *Micronesica* 13 (2): 129–190.

Lévi-Strauss, C. 1970. *The raw and the cooked.* London: Jonathan Cape.

———. 1973. *From honey to ashes.* London: Jonathan Cape.

———. 1978. *The origin of table manners.* London: Jonathan Cape.

Levy, Robert. 1973. *Tahitians.* Chicago: Univ. Chicago Press.

———. 1984. Emotion, knowing, and culture. In *Culture theory,* ed. R. Schweder and R. Levine. Cambridge: Cambridge Univ. Press.

Lieber, M. 1974. Land tenure on Kapingamarangi. In *Land tenure in Oceania. See* Lundsgaarde 1974.

Liener, Irvin. 1969. Miscellaneous toxic factors. In *Toxic constituents of plant foodstuffs,* ed. I. Liener. N.Y.: Academic Press.

Lingenfelter, Sherwood. 1975. *Yap: Political leadership and culture change in an island society.* Honolulu: Univ. Press of Hawaii.

———. 1979. Yap eating classes. *JPS* 88 (4): 415–420.

Linton, Ralph. 1939. Marquesan culture. In *The individual and his society,* ed. A. Kardiner. N.Y.: Columbia Univ. Press.

Loeb, E. M. 1926. *History and traditions of Niue.* BPBM Bull. 32. Honolulu.

Loison, G., C. Jardin, and J. Crosnier. 1973. Alimentation et nutrition dans le Pacifique. *Medicine Tropicale* 33 (2–5): 13–63.

———. 1974. Health implications of urbanisation in the South Pacific. *JSO* 30 (42–43): 79–102.

Loomis, Terry. 1983. The Cook Islands haircutting ritual as practised in New Zealand. *JPS* 93 (2): 215–232.

Lundsgaarde, Henry, ed. 1974. *Land tenure in Oceania.* ASAO Monograph 2. Honolulu: Univ. Press of Hawaii.

Luomala, Katharine. 1949. *Maui of a thousand tricks.* BPBM Bull. 198. Honolulu.

———. 1953. *Ethnobotany of the Gilbert Islands.* BPBM Bull. 213. Honolulu.

———. 1970. *Babai (Cyrtosperma chamissonis),* a prestige food in the Gilbert Islands culture. *VII International Congress of Anthropological and Ethnological Sciences, Moscow (1964)* 5:488–499.

———. 1974. The *Cyrtosperma* systemic pattern—aspects of production in the Gilbert Islands. *JPS* 83 (1): 14–34.

Lynch, J. 1982. Towards a theory of the origin of the Oceanic possessive construction. In *Pacific linguistics,* vol. 1, ed. H. Halim et al. Papers from the 3d International Conference on Austronesian Linguistics. Canberra: ANU.

Mahony, F. 1960. Taro cultivation practices and beliefs. Anthropological Working Papers 6, part 2. Office of the Staff Anthropologist, Trust Territory of the Pacific Islands, Guam.

Malcolm, L. 1975. Some biosocial determinants of the growth, health, and nutritional status of Papua New Guinea preschool children. In *Biosocial interrelationships in population adaptation,* ed. G. Lasker. World Anthropology Series. The Hague: Mouton.

Malcolm, S. 1955. *Diet and nutrition in the Trust Territory of the Pacific Islands.* SPC Technical Paper 83. Noumea.

Malinowski, B. 1935. *Coral gardens and their magic.* 2 vols. London: Allen and Unwin.

Manderson, Lenore. 1980. *Women, politics, and change: The Kaum Ibui UNNO, Malaysia 1945–72.* London: Oxford Univ. Press.

———. 1981. Traditional food classifications and humoral medical theory in peninsula Malaya. *Ecology of Food and Nutrition* 11:81–93.

Mariner, W. 1831. *An account of the natives of the Tonga Islands. . . .* Ed. John Martin. Reprint. Tonga: Vava'u Press, 1981.

Marshall, Donald. 1961. *Ra'ivavae.* N.Y.: Doubleday.

Marshall, Leslie. 1985. *Infant care and feeding in the South Pacific.* London: Gordon and Breach.

Marshall, Mac. 1975. *The natural history of Namoluk Atoll, Eastern Caroline Islands.* Atoll Research Bull. 189. Washington, D.C.: Smithsonian Institution.

———. 1979. *Siblingship in Oceania.* ASAO Monograph 8. Ann Arbor: Univ. Michigan Press.

Marshall, Yvonne. 1985. Who made the Lapita pots? *JPS* 94 (3): 205–234.

Marshall Islands. 1985. *Marshall Islands development plan (1985–9).* Majuro.

Mason, L. 1951. Micronesia: Marshalls, Gilberts, Ocean Island, and Nauru. In *Geography of the Pacific,* ed. Otis Freeman. N.Y.: John Wiley and Sons.

Massal, E., and J. Barrau. 1956. *Food plants of the South Sea Islands.* SPC Technical Paper 94. Noumea.

Mathiot, M. 1970. The semantic and cognitive domains of language. In *Cognition,* ed. J. Garvin. N.Y.: Spartan Books.

Matthews, P. 1985. Nga taro o Aotearoa. *JPS* 94 (3): 253–272.

Maude, Alaric. 1971. Tonga: Equality overtaking privilege. In *Land tenure in the Pacific. See* Crocombe 1971.

Maude, Alaric, and F. Sevele. 1987. Tonga: Equality overtaking privilege. In *Land tenure in the Pacific,* rev. ed. *See* Crocombe 1987.

Maude, H. E. 1968. The Tahitian pork trade 1800–1830. In *Of islands and men,* ed. H. Maude. Oxford: Oxford Univ. Press.

May, Ron. 1984. *Kaikai aniani.* Bathurst: Robert Brown Associates.

McArthur, Margaret. 1977. Nutritional research in Melanesia. In *Subsistence and survival,* ed. T. Bayliss-Smith and R. Feachem. N.Y.: Academic Press.

McArthur, Norma. 1967. *Island populations of the Pacific.* Canberra: ANU Press.

McCoy, Patrick. 1978. Stone-lined earth ovens in Easter Island. *Antiquity* 52:204–216.

McCracken, Robert D. 1971. Lactase deficiency. *Current Anthropology* 12: 479–519.

McCutcheon, Mary. 1985a. Fresh fruits and vegetables in Koror, Palau. Paper for ASAO session, The Fresh and the Tinned, Seattle. MS.

———. 1985b. Reading the taro cards—explaining agricultural change in Palau. In *Food energy in tropical ecosystems,* ed. D. Cattle and R. Schwerin. N.Y.: Gordon and Breach.

Macdonald, J. 1985. Contemporary healing practices in Tikopia, Solomon Islands. In *Healing practices in the South Pacific. See* Parsons 1985.

McGee, Terry. 1975. Food dependency in the Pacific: A preliminary statement. DSC Working Papers 2. Canberra.

McGinnis, J. Michael. 1986. Diet and health. *Food, Drug, and Cosmetic Law J.* 41:74–79.

Macgregor, G. 1937. *Ethnology of Tokelau Islands.* BPBM Bull. 146. Honolulu.

McKee, H. S. 1957. *Some food problems in the Pacific Islands.* SPC Technical Paper 106. Noumea.

McKnight, R. 1960. Breadfruit cultivation practices and beliefs in Palau. Anthropological Working Papers 7. Office of the Staff Anthropologist, Trust Territory of the Pacific Islands, Guam.

Macnaught, Timothy. 1982. *The Fijian colonial experience.* Pacific Research Monograph 7. Canberra: DSC.

Mead, Margaret. 1934. How the Papuan plans his dinner. *Natural History* 36, pt. 3.

Meigs, Anna. 1984. *Food, sex, and pollution.* New Brunswick, N.J.: Rutgers Univ. Press.

Meller, N., and G. Herwitz. 1971. Hawaii—themes in land monopoly. In *Land tenure in the Pacific. See* Crocombe 1971.

Mennell, S. 1985. *All manners of food.* London: Blackwell.

Merrick, J. 1977. *Taro variety in American Samoa.* Dept. of Agriculture Booklet 1 (5). Pago Pago.

Merrill, E. E. 1943. *Emergency food plants and poisonous plants of the islands of the Pacific.* War Dept. Technical Manual TM 10–420. Washington: U.S. Government Printing Office.

Messer, Ellen. 1984a. Anthropological perspectives on diet. *Annual Review of Anthropology* 13:205–249.

———. 1984b. Sociocultural aspects of nutrient intake and behavioral responses to nutrition. In *Human nutrition.* Vol. 5, *Nutrition and behavior,* ed. J. Galler, pp. 417–447. N.Y.: Plenum Press.

Miller, Carey. 1927. *Food values of poi, taro, and limu.* BPBM Bull. 37. Honolulu.

———. 1929. *Food values of breadfruit, taro leaves, coconut, and sugar cane.* BPBM Bull. 64. Honolulu.

Milner, G. 1966. *Samoan dictionary.* London: Oxford Univ. Press.

Milner, G., G. Armelagos, and P. Geraghty. 1985. Duivosavosa. *Fiji Museum Bull.* 8. Suva.

Mitchell, Wallace C., and Peter A. Maddison. 1983. Pests of taro. In *Taro.*
    See Wang 1983.
Moerenhout, J. A. 1837. *Voyages aux îles du Grand Océan.* 2 vols. Reprint.
    Paris: A. Bertrand, 1959.
Montgomery, L. D. 1969. Cyanogens. In *Toxic constituents of plant food-*
    stuffs, ed. I. Liener. N.Y.: Academic Press.
Moorehead, Alan. 1967. *The fatal impact.* Harmondsworth, Eng.: Penguin.
Moran, Emile. 1975. Food, development, and man in the tropics. In *Gas-*
    tronomy. See Arnott 1975.
Morrison, James. 1790. *Le journal de James Morrison.* Ed. B. Jaunez.
    Reprint. *JSO,* Publication 16, 1966.
Morton, Keith. 1987. The atomization of Tongan society. *Pacific Studies* 10
    (2): 47–72.
Morton, N., J. Lalouel, and J. Hurst. 1971. Pingelap and Mokil atolls:
    Migration. *American J. Human Genetics* 23:339–349.
Mulloy, G., and S. Rapu. 1977. Possession, dependency, and respect in the
    Rapanui language. *JPS* 86 (1): 7–25.
Murai, M., F. Pen, and C. Miller. 1958. *Some tropical South Pacific island*
    foods. Honolulu: Univ. Hawaii Press.
Murdock, G. P. 1960. *Social structure in South East Asia.* Chicago: Quad-
    rangle Books.
National Research Council. 1980. *Recommended dietary allowances.* Wash-
    ington, D.C.: National Academy of Science.
Navy Handbook. 1949. *Handbook on the Trust Territory of the Pacific*
    Islands. Washington, D.C.: Navy Dept., Office of the Chief of Naval
    Operations.
Nayacakalou, R. 1978. *Tradition and change in the Fijian village.* Suva:
    SPSSA.
Neal, Marie. 1965. *In gardens of Hawaii.* New and rev. ed. Honolulu:
    BPBM Press.
Neave, Margaret. 1969. The nutrition of Polynesian children. *Tropical and*
    Geographical Medicine 21:311–322.
Neel, J. V. 1962. Diabetes mellitus: A "thrifty" genotype rendered detrimen-
    tal by "progress." *American J. Human Genetics* 14:354–362.
Nozieres, F. 1982. The cultivation of *kape* in Wallis. In *Taro cultivation in*
    the South Pacific. See Lambert 1982.
O'Brien, Frederick. 1921. *Mystic isles of the South Seas.* London: Hodder
    and Stoughton.
O'Brien, P. 1972. The sweet potato: Its origin and dispersal. *American*
    Anthropologist 74 (3): 342–365.
Oliver, Douglas. 1974. *Ancient Tahitian society.* Honolulu: Univ. Press of
    Hawaii.
————. 1983. *Two Tahitian villages.* Laie, Hawaiʻi: Institute for Polynesian
    Studies.
O'Meara, Tim. 1987. Samoa—customary individualism. In *Land tenure in*
    the Pacific. See Crocombe 1987.
Ooka, J. J. 1983. Taro diseases. In *Taro. See* Wang 1983.

Ooka, J. J., and E. E. Trujillo. 1982. Taro diseases and their control. In *Taro cultivation in the South Pacific. See* SPC 1982.

Oomen, H. A., and S. Malcolm. 1958. *Nutrition and the Papuan child.* SPC Technical Paper 118. Noumea.

———. 1961. Nutrition situation in Papua New Guinea. In *Tropical and Geographical Medicine* 13:322–355.

Orbell, M. 1985. *The natural world of the Maori.* Auckland: Collins.

O'Reilly, Patrick. 1982. *Tahiti, la vie de chaque jour.* Tahiti: Nouvelles editions Latines.

Orliac, C., and M. Orliac. 1980. Les structures de combustion et leur interpretation archeologique. *JSO* 36 (66–67): 61.

Owen, H. [ca. 1965]. *Eating in the South Seas.* MS in Pacific Collection, Hamilton Library, Univ. Hawaii, Honolulu.

Packard, J. 1975. The Bougainville taro blight. Misc. Work Papers, 1975:1. Honolulu: Pacific Islands Studies Program, Univ. Hawaii, Honolulu.

Paijmans, K. J. 1976. *New Guinea vegetation.* Canberra: ANU Press.

Pargeter, K., H. King, and P. Zimmet. 1984. *Kiribati, a dietary study.* Noumea: SPC.

Parker, Robert Davis. 1967. A field and laboratory study of the storage and preservation of breadfruit in the South Pacific Islands. M.A. thesis, Public Health, Univ. Hawaii.

Parker, R., and H. King. 1981/1984. Recent and current archeological research on Moen Island, Truk. *Asian Perspectives* 24 (1): 11–26.

Parkinson, Susan. 1956. Food conditions in the Gilbert Islands. *Transactions of the Fiji Society,* 1956: 61–68.

———. 1973. Some observations on the cause of malnutrition in Pacific Island urban populations. In *Living in town,* ed. J. Harre. Suva: SPSSA.

———. 1987. A study of the effects of economic development on food consumption and nutrition in a Fijian village 1952–1982. In *Nutrition in the tropics,* ed. C. Rae and S. Green. Darwin: Menzies School of Public Health.

Parkinson, Susan, and J. Lambert. 1982. *The new handbook of South Pacific nutrition.* Suva: Fiji Food and Nutrition Committee.

Parkinson, Sydney. 1784. *A journal of a voyage to the south seas in HMS Endeavour.* Reprint. London: Caliban, 1984.

Parsons, Claire, ed. 1985. *Healing practices in the South Pacific.* Laie, Hawai'i: Institute for Polynesian Studies.

Pawley, A. 1981. Austronesian languages. In *Historical dictionary of Oceania,* ed. R. Craig and F. King, pp. 19–21. Westport, Conn.: Greenwood Press.

Pawley, A., and R. Green. 1985. The Proto-Oceanic language community. In *Out of Asia,* ed. R. Kirk and E. Szathmary, pp. 161–184. Canberra: ANU, Journal of Pacific History.

Pawson, I. G., and C. Janes. 1981. Obesity in a migrant Samoan population. *American J. Public Health* 71 (5): 508–513.

Pelto, P., and G. Pelto. 1983. Diet and delocalization. In *Hunger and his-*

tory, ed. R. I. Rotberg and T. K. Rabb. Studies in Interdisciplinary History. Cambridge: Cambridge Univ. Press.

Peoples, James. 1986. Employment and household economy in a Micronesian village. *Pacific Studies* 9 (2): 103–120.

Peters, F. E. 1958. *Chemical composition of South Pacific foods.* SPC Technical Paper 115. Noumea.

Petterson, Janet. 1977. Dissemination and use of the edible aroids. Ph.D. thesis, Geography, Univ. Florida.

Pietrusewsky, M. 1977. Étude des relations entre les populations du Pacifique. *L'Anthropologie* 81:67–97.

———. 1985. The earliest Lapita skeleton from the Pacific. *JPS* 94 (4): 389–414.

Plucknett, D. L. 1976. Edible aroids. In *Evolution of crop plants,* ed. N. W. Simmonds. London: Longmans Scientific and Technical Publications.

———. 1977. Current outlook for taro and other edible aroids. In *Regional meeting on the production of root crops, 1975. See* SPC 1977.

———. 1983. Taxonomy of the genus *Colocasia.* In *Taro. See* Wang 1983.

Plucknett, D. L., R. de la Pena, and F. Obrero. 1970. Taro *(Colocasia esculenta):* A review. *Field Crop Abstracts* 23 (4): 413–425.

Pollock, Nancy J. 1970. Breadfruit and breadwinning on Namu, a Marshallese atoll. Ph.D. thesis, Anthropology, Univ. Hawaii.

———. 1974. Land holding on Namu atoll. In *Land tenure in Oceania. See* Lundsgaarde 1974.

———. 1975. Risks of dietary choice. In *Gastronomy. See* Arnott 1975.

———. 1977. Takapoto report. Report to French MAB committee. Man and the Biosphere Committee, Musee de l'Homme, Paris.

———. 1979a. Economie des atolls. *Bull. de la Société des Études Océaniennes* No. 207, Tome XVII–No. 8: 463–476.

———. 1979b. Work, wages, and shifting agriculture on Niue. *Pacific Studies* 2 (2): 132–143.

———. 1983a. Food and politics. Paper presented at the 15th Pacific Science Congress, Dunedin.

———. 1983b. The early use of rice in Guam: The evidence from the historic records. *JPS* 92 (4): 509–520.

———. 1984a. Changing food habits in the Pacific. In *Proc. New Zealand Nutrition Society.* Dunedin.

———. 1984b. Breadfruit fermentation. *JSO* 40 (79): 151–164.

———. 1985a. The concept of food in a Pacific society: A Fijian example. *Ecology of Food and Nutrition* 17:195–203.

———. 1985b. On food storage among hunter gatherers in Pacific Island societies. *Current Anthropology* 26 (4): 540–541.

———. 1986a. Food habits in Guam over 500 years. *Pacific Viewpoint* 27 (2): 120–143.

———. 1986b. Taro and timber. In *Shared wealth and symbol,* ed. L. Manderson. Cambridge: Cambridge Univ. Press.

———. 1986c. Food classification in Fiji, Hawaii, and Tahiti. *Ethnology* 25 (2): 107–118.

———. 1987. Nauru report. Report for Commission for Rehabilitation of Nauru. Melbourne.

———. 1988. Markets in French Polynesia. In *French Polynesia, a book of readings,* ed. N. J. Pollock and R. Crocombe. Suva: SPSSA.

———. 1989. The early development of housekeeping and imports in Fiji. *Pacific Studies* 12 (2): 53–82.

———. 1991. Arrowroot. *Ethnobotany* 2 (3 & 4): 1–10.

———. n.d.*a* Pots and pans and earth ovens. MS in author's possession.

———. n.d.*b* Food dependency in Fiji. MS in author's possession.

Pollock, Nancy J., N. E. Morton, and J. Lalouel. 1972. Kinship and inbreeding on Namu. *Human Biology* 44 (3): 459–474.

Pollock, Nancy J., and Malia Tafili. 1988. Futuna and Wallis reports. Reports to Medical Research Council of New Zealand, Auckland.

Pollock, Nancy J., with Alan Ahmu, Sina Asomua, and Arthur Carter. 1989. Food and identity: Food preferences and diet of Samoans in Wellington, New Zealand. In *Publications de l'Université Française du Pacifique.* Vol. 1, *Noumea and Tahiti,* pp. 45–50.

Powell, Jocelyn. 1982. Plant resources and paleobotanical evidence for plant use in the Papua New Guinea Highlands. *Archeology in Oceania* 17 (1): 28–37.

Prior, Ian. 1977. Nutritional problems in Pacific Islanders, New Zealand. *Nutrition Society of New Zealand,* Annual Proceedings.

———. 1981. The Tokelau Island migrant study, morbidity of adults. In *Migration, adaptation, and health in the South Pacific. See* Fleming and Prior 1981.

Prior, I. A., H. P. Harvey, M. Neave, and F. Davidson. 1966. *The health of two groups of Cook Island Maoris.* N.Z. Dept. of Health Report Series 26. Wellington.

Pritchard, W. S. 1866. *Polynesian reminiscences.* Reprint. London: Dawsons, 1968.

Provencher, R. 1979. Orality as a pattern of symbolism. In *The imagination of reality,* ed. R. Becker and A. Yengoyan. Norwood, N.J.: Ablex Publishing.

Pukui, Mary K. 1967. Poi making. In *Polynesian culture history,* ed. G. Highland, R. Force, A. Howard, M. Kelly, and Y. Sinoto. Special Publication 56. Honolulu: BPBM Press.

Pukui, Mary K., and Samuel Elbert. 1965. *Hawaiian-English dictionary.* 3d ed. Honolulu: Univ. Hawaii Press.

Pulu, Tupou. 1981. *Tongan food.* Anchorage: National Bilingual Materials Development Center, Univ. Alaska.

Purseglove, T. 1972. *Tropical crops.* London: Longmans.

Quain, Buell. 1948. *Fijian village.* Chicago: Univ. Chicago Press.

Ragone, Diane. 1988. *Breadfruit varieties in the Pacific atolls.* UNDP Project Series. N.Y.: United Nations Development Program.

Rappaport, Roy A. 1967. *Pigs for the ancestors.* New Haven: Yale Univ. Press.

Ralston, Caroline. 1977. *Grass huts and warehouses.* Canberra: ANU Press.

Ravault, F. 1979. *Le régime foncier de la Polynésie française.* Paris: ORSTOM.

Ravuvu, Asesela. 1983. *Vaka i taukei: The Fijian way of life.* Suva: Institute of Pacific Studies, USP.

Reed, Dwayne. 1975. An ecological approach to urbanization and health in the South Pacific. In *Migration and health in New Zealand and the Pacific,* ed. C. Fleming and J. Stanhope. Wellington: Epidemiology Unit, Wellington Hospital.

Rehg, Ken. 1981. *Ponapean reference grammar.* PALI Language Texts. Honolulu: Univ. Press of Hawaii.

Richards, Audrey. 1939. *Hunger and work amongst the Bemba of northern Rhodesia.* London: Oxford Univ. Press.

Riesenberg, Saul. 1968. *The native polity of Ponape.* Washington, D.C.: Smithsonian Institution.

Ringrose, H., and P. Zimmet. 1979. Nutrient intakes in an urbanized Micronesian population with a high diabetes prevalence. *American J. Clinical Nutrition* 32:1334–1341.

Ritenbaugh, C. 1978. Human foodways. In *The anthropology of health.* See Bauwens 1978.

Roberts, R. G. 1955. Coral atoll cookery. *JPS* 64 (2): 227–232.

Robineau, Claude. 1984. *Du copra à l'atome.* 2 vols. Paris: ORSTOM.

Ross, Eric. 1980. Patterns of diet and forces of production: An economic and ecological history of the ascendancy of beef in the United States diet. In *Beyond the myths of culture,* ed. E. Ross, pp. 188–225. N.Y.: Academic Press.

Rotberg, Robert I., and Theodore Rabb. 1985. *Hunger and history.* Cambridge: Cambridge Univ. Press. Special issue of *J. Interdisciplinary History.*

Roth, G. K. 1953. *Fijian way of life.* Reprint. London: Oxford Univ. Press, 1973.

Routledge, Katherine Scoresby. 1919. *The mystery of Easter Island.* N.Y.: Praed.

———. n.d. Easter Island. MS in Turnbull Library, Wellington.

Rowntree, B. S. 1902. *Poverty: A study of town life.* London: Macmillan.

Rozin, E., and P. Rozin. 1981. Some surprisingly unique characteristics of human food preferences. In *Food in perspective,* ed. O. Fenton and R. Owen. Edinburgh: John Donal.

Rutz, Henry. 1976. The efficiency of traditional agriculture: Phases of development and induced economic change in Waidina Valley, Fiji. In *Development from below,* ed. D. Pitt. The Hague: Mouton.

———. 1977. Individual decisions and functional systems. *American Ethnologist* 4 (1): 156–174.

———. 1981. Material affluence and social time in village Fiji. In *Affluence and cultural survival.* American Ethnological Society Proceedings. Washington, D.C.

Safford, William E. 1905. *The useful plants of the island of Guam.* Washington, D.C.: Smithsonian Institution.

Sahlins, Marshall. 1957. *Social stratification in Polynesia.* Seattle: Univ. Washington Press.

———. 1962. *Moala.* Ann Arbor: Univ. Michigan Press.

———. 1976. *Culture and practical reason.* Chicago: Univ. Chicago Press.

Sakai, William S. 1983. Aroid root crops. In *Handbook of tropical foods,* ed. H. T. Chan, Jr., pp. 29–83. N.Y.: Marcel Dekker.

Sarfert, E. G. *Kusae.* 1919/1920. 2 vols. Ergebnisse der Südsee Expedition 1908–1910. Hamburg: L. Friederichsen.

Sauer, Carl. 1952. *Agricultural origins and dispersals.* Washington D.C.: American Geographical Society.

Schefold, Reimar. 1982. The culinary code in the *Puliaijat* ritual of the Mentawains. *Bijdragen Tot de Taal-, Land- en Volkenkunde* 138 (1): 64–97.

Scheltema, S. 1936. *The food consumption of the native inhabitants of Java and Madura.* Amsterdam: National Council for Netherlands Institute of Pacific Relations.

Schneider, David. 1984. *A critique of the study of kinship.* Ann Arbor: Univ. Michigan Press.

Schoeffel, P. 1985. Dilemmas of modernization in primary health care in Western Samoa. *Social Science and Medicine* 19 (3): 209–216.

Schuster, Donald. 1979. Urbanization in the Pacific. Misc. Work Papers 3. Pacific Islands Studies Program, Univ. Hawaii, Honolulu.

Schütz, A., and P. Geraghty, eds. 1980. *David Cargill's Fijian grammar.* *Bull. Fiji Museum* 6. Suva.

Schwartz, T. 1984. Comment. In *Culture theory,* ed. Richard A. Schweder and R. A. Levine. Cambridge: Cambridge Univ. Press.

Schweder, R., and Robert Levine. 1984. *Culture theory.* Cambridge: Cambridge Univ. Press.

Seemann, Berthold. 1862. *Viti, a government mission.* London: Dawsons of Pall Mall.

Semper, C. 1883. *Die Palau-Inseln.* Leipzig: Brodhaus.

Setchell, William A. 1924. *American Samoa.* Washington D.C.: Dept. of Marine Biology, Carnegie Institute.

Sevele, F. 1981. *South Pacific economies.* Noumea: SPC.

Sewell, Betsy. 1977. *Butaritari report.* Wellington: Victoria Univ. Social Economic Survey.

Shapiro, Harry. 1929. *Descendants of the mutineers of the* Bounty. BPBM Memoirs, vol. 11, no. 1. Honolulu.

Shimizu, Akitoshi. 1982. Chiefdom and the spatial classification of the lifeworld: Everyday life, subsistence, and the political system on Ponape. In *Islanders and their outside world,* ed. M. Aoyagi. Tokyo: Committee for Micronesian Research, St. Paul's (Rikkyo) Univ.

————. 1985. Politics of encounter. In *The 1983–'84 cultural anthropological expedition to Micronesia,* ed. E. Ishikawa, pp. 39–63. Tokyo: Committee for Micronesian Research, St. Paul's (Rikkyo) Univ.

Shore, Bradd. 1982. *Sala'ilua.* N.Y.: Columbia Univ. Press.

Sillitoe, P. 1983. *Roots of the earth.* Dover, N.H.: Manchester Univ. Press.

Simmonds, N. W., ed. 1976. Bananas. In *Evolution of crop plants,* ed. N. W. Simmonds. London: Longmans Scientific and Technical Publications.

Sinnett, Peter F. 1977. Nutritional adaptation among the Enga. In *Subsistence and survival,* ed. T. Bayliss-Smith and R. Feachem. N.Y.: Academic Press.

Sinoto, Y. 1979. The Marquesas. In *The prehistory of Polynesia.* See Jennings 1979.

Sivan, P. 1975. *Technical paper on root crops.* Noumea: SPC.

————. 1976. *Technical paper on atoll cultivation.* Noumea: SPC.

————. 1977. Evaluation of local cassava varieties in Fiji. *Fiji Agricultural J.* 39 (2): 105–109.

————. 1980a. Yams. In *Regional production of root crops.* Noumea: SPC.

————. 1980b. Evaluation of local yam *(D. alata)* varieties in Fiji. *Fiji Agricultural J.* 42 (2): 7–14.

————. 1981. Review of taro research and production. MS, Koronivia, Fiji.

————. 1983. Producing more food crops in the South Pacific. In *Food and national development in the South Pacific: R. W. Parkinson Memorial Lectures, 1982,* ed. R. R. Thaman and W. C. Clarke, pp. 105–112. Suva: USP.

Siwatibau, Suliana. 1981. Energy needs in Fiji. MS, Government Buildings, Suva.

Soderstrom, J. G. K. 1937. Some notes on poi and other preserved vegetables in the Pacific. *Ethnos* (Stockholm) 2:235–242.

Sokal, R. R. 1974. Classification: Purposes, principles, progress, prospects. *Science* 185 (4157): 1115–1118.

Someki, Atsushi. 1938. Ethnographic notes on Stone Money Island (Yap). *Japanese J. Ethnological Studies* 6 (2). (Translated into English by Historical Places Trust, Saipan. Document in MARC.)

SPC. 1977. *Regional meeting on the production of root crops, 1975.* SPC Technical Paper 174. Noumea.

————. 1983. *Food composition tables for use in the Pacific Islands.* Noumea.

————. 1987. *South Pacific economies—statistical summaries.* No. 9. Noumea.

Spencer, Dorothy. 1941. *Disease, religion, and society in the Fiji Islands.* American Ethnological Society Monograph 2. Seattle: Univ. Washington Press.

Spencer, M., and P. Heywood. 1983. Staple foods in Papua New Guinea. *Food and Nutrition Bull.* 5 (3): 40–46.

Spiro, Melford. 1952. Ghosts, Ifaluk, and teleological functionalism. *American Anthropologist* 54:497–503.

Splittstoesser, F. W. Martin, and Ashby Rhoades. 1973. The nutritional value of some tropical root crops. *Horticultural Science* 17: 290–294.

Spoehr, Alexander. 1949. *Majuro*. Fieldiana: Anthropology 39. Chicago: Chicago Natural History Museum. Reprint. N.Y.: Kraus, 1966.

———. 1957. *Marianas prehistory*. Fieldiana: Anthropology 48. Chicago: Field Museum of Natural History.

Spriggs, Matthew. 1981. Vegetable kingdoms: Taro irrigation and Pacific prehistory. Ph.D. diss., Prehistory, ANU.

———. 1982. Taro cropping systems in the South East Asian Pacific region. *Archeology in Oceania* 17 (1): 7–15.

———. 1984. The Lapita cultural complex. *J. Pacific History* 19:202–223.

Sproat, M. N. 1968. *Guide to subsistence agriculture in Micronesia*. Saipan: Trust Territory of the Pacific Islands.

Stahl, Ann. 1984. Hominid dietary selection before fire. *Current Anthropology* 25 (2): 155–168.

Standal, Bluebell. 1982. Nutritional value of edible aroids grown in the South Pacific. In *Taro cultivation in the South Pacific. See* Lambert 1982.

———. 1983. Nutritive value. In *Taro. See* Wang 1983.

Steager, Peter. 1971. Food in its social context on Puluwat, E. Carolines. Ph.D. thesis, Anthropology, Univ. California at Berkeley.

Steinkraus, W. H. 1983. *Handbook of indigenous fermented foods*. N.Y.: Marcel Dekker.

Stokes, J. 1932. Spaniards and the sweet potato in Hawaii, and Hawaiian-American contacts. *American Anthropologist* 34 (4): 594–607.

Stone, B. C. 1967. The genus *Pandanus* in Micronesia. *Micronesica* 3 (2): 105–121.

Strauss, Michael. 1983. Anatomy and morphology of taro, *Colocasia esculenta* (L.) Schott. In *Taro. See* Wang 1983.

Su‘a, To‘aiga. 1987. Polynesian pudding processes in west and east Polynesia. M.A. thesis, Anthropology, Otago Univ., Dunedin.

Sunderland, James, and Aaron Buzacott, eds. 1866. *Mission life in the islands of the Pacific*. London: John Snow.

Takayama, Jun. 1981/1984. Early pottery and population movements in Micronesian prehistory. *Asian Perspectives* 24 (1).

Taleafoa, F. 1977. Marketing of root crops. In *Regional meeting on the production of root crops, 1975. See* SPC 1977.

Tambiah, S. J. 1985. *Culture thought and social action*. Cambridge: Harvard Univ. Press.

Tang, C., and W. Sakai. 1983. Acridity of taro and related plants in Araceae. In *Taro. See* Wang 1983.

Tannahill, Reay. 1975. *Food in history*. N.Y.: Paladin.

Taylor, R. 1984. *Epidemiological studies of cardiovascular disease and diabetes in Polynesia from Rarotonga and Niue*. SPC Technical Paper 185. Noumea.

Taylor, R., J. Bennett, and P. Zimmet. 1984. *Epidemiological studies of dia-*

betes and cardiovascular disease in Wallis Polynesians. SPC Technical Paper 188. Noumea.

Taylor, T. Geoffrey. 1982. *Nutrition and health.* The Institute of Biology's Studies in Biology 141. London: Edward Arnold.

Testart, Alain. 1982. The significance of food storage among hunters and gatherers. *Current Anthropology* 23 (5): 523–537.

Thaman, Randolph. 1976/1977. Plant resources of the Suva municipal market, Fiji. *Ethnomedizin* 4 (1/2): 23–61.

———. 1976. The role of indigenous agriculture systems—Tongan agriculture. In *Food production in the South Pacific: R. W. Parkinson Memorial Lectures 1974,* ed. R. Thaman. Suva: USP.

———. 1977. Urban root crop production in the South West Pacific. In *Regional meeting on the production of root crops, 1975. See* SPC 1977.

———. 1982. Urban taro production in the South Pacific. In *Taro cultivation in the South Pacific. See* Lambert 1982.

Thomas, S., and M. Corden. 1977. *Metric composition of Australian foods.* Canberra: Australian Government Publishing Service.

Thompson, Laura. 1945. *The native cultures of the Marianas Islands.* BPBM Bull. 185. Honolulu.

Thomson, Basil. 1908. *The Fijians.* Reprint. London: Dawsons, 1968.

Tiffany, Sharon. 1975. Giving and receiving—participation in chiefly redistribution activities in Samoa. *Ethnology* 14 (3): 267–286.

Titcomb, M. 1967. The foods of ancient Hawaii. *The Conch Shell* (BPBM) 4 (2).

Tobin, Jack. 1958. *Land tenure in the Marshall Islands.* Part 1, vol. 1 of *Land tenure patterns, Trust Territory of the Pacific Islands: A handbook series.* Guam: Trust Territory of the Pacific Islands.

Tryon, D. 1976. Linguistic subgrouping in the New Hebrides. *Oceanic Linguistics* 12:303–351.

Tu'ifua, H., and R. Rathey. 1982. *Talamahu market report.* Tonga: Planning Unit, Ministry of Agriculture, Forestry, and Fisheries.

Turbott, H. 1949. Diets of the Gilbert and Ellice Islands colony. *JPS* 58: 36–46.

Turner, George. 1841. *Nineteen years in Polynesia.* London: John Snow.

———. 1884. *Samoa a hundred years ago and long before.* London: Macmillan.

Turner, James W. 1984. "True food" and first fruits: rituals of increase. *Ethnology* 23 (2): 133–142.

Ucko, P., and G. Dimbleby, eds. 1969. *The domestication and exploitation of plants and animals.* Chicago: Aldine.

Underwood, J. Hainline. 1983. Population history and the ethnodemography of Guam. Paper presented at the 15th Pacific Science Congress, Dunedin.

United States recommended dietary allowances. 1968. Washington, D.C.: Dept. of Agriculture.

Untaman, Vincent. 1982. The cultivation of giant swamp taro. In *Taro cultivation in the South Pacific. See* Lambert 1982.

Ushijima, I. 1985. The land-holding groups on Mogmog Island, Ulithi Atoll. In *1983–'84 cultural anthropological expedition to Micronesia,* ed. E. Ishikawa, pp. 5–23. Tokyo: Committee for Micronesian Research, St. Paul's (Rikkyo) Univ.

Van Rugge, Eric. 1980. Taro production in Niue. Draft report, Feb.–July 1980. Mimeo, Niue Agriculture Dept.

Vayda, A., and B. McKay. 1975. New directions in ecology and ecological anthropology. *Annual Review of Anthropology* 4:293–306.

Verin, P. 1969. *L'Ancienne civilisation de Rurutu.* Paris: ORSTOM.

Viala, Dr. M. 1909. Les Îles Wallis et Horn. *Annales de medecine de pharmacie coloniales* (also known as *Annales d'hygiène coloniales*) 12: 189–212, 422–448.

Vickers, Maurice. 1982. The agronomy of *Cyrtosperma chamissonis* (Schott) in Kiribati. In *Taro cultivation in the South Pacific. See* Lambert 1982.

Vieth, G., B. Begley, and W. Huang. 1977. *The production of wetland taro in Hawaii.* Honolulu: College of Tropical Agriculture, Univ. Hawaii.

Viviani, Nancy. 1970. *Nauru.* Honolulu: Univ. Hawaii Press.

Wallis, Mrs. Mary (By a Lady). 1858. *Life in Feejee.* Reprint. N.Y.: Gregg Press, 1967.

Wang, J.-K., ed. 1983. *Taro.* Honolulu: Univ. Hawaii Press.

Ward, R. G. 1972. The Pacific bêche-de-mer trade with special reference to Fiji. In *Man in the Pacific Islands.* London: Oxford Univ. Press.

Ward, R. G., and Andrew Proctor, eds. 1980. *South Pacific agricultural survey 1979.* Canberra: ANU and Asian Development Bank.

Waterhouse, Rev. Joseph. 1866. *The king and people of Fiji.* London: Wesleyan Conference Office.

Wedgwood, Camilla. 1936. Notes on fieldwork in Nauru. *Oceania* 6 (4): 359–391; 7 (1): 1–33.

Weightman, B. L., and Ichiro Moros. 1982. The cultivation of taro *Xanthosoma* sp. In *Taro cultivation in the South Pacific. See* Lambert 1982.

Wenkam, Nao. 1983. *Foods of Hawaii and the Pacific Basin.* Vol. 1, *Composition.* Honolulu: Univ. of Hawaii College of Tropical Agriculture.

West, Rev. Thomas. 1865. *Ten years in south central Polynesia.* London: John Snow.

White, P., and J. O'Connell. 1982. *A prehistory of Australia, New Guinea, and Sahul.* N.Y.: Academic Press.

WHO. 1947. Constitution of the WHO. *Chronicle WHO* 1 (1–2).

Wiens, H. 1962. *Atoll environment and ecology.* New Haven: Yale Univ. Press.

Wilder, Gerrit. 1928. *The breadfruit of Tahiti.* BPBM Bull. 50. Honolulu.

Wilkes, Commander Charles. 1845. *Narrative of the United States Exploring Expedition . . . 1838, 1839, 1840, 1841, 1842.* 5 vols. Philadelphia: Lea and Blanchard.

Williams, J. 1838. *A narrative of missionary enterprises in the South Sea Islands.* London: John Snow.

Williams, Thomas. 1858. *Fiji and the Fijians.* Vol. 1, *The islands and their inhabitants.* Reprint. Suva: Fiji Museum, 1982.

——. 1933. *Fiji and the Fijians, 1835–1856.* Ed. G. C. Henderson. Australia: Angus and Robertson.

Williamson, R. W. 1924. *The social and political systems of central Polynesia.* 3 vols. Cambridge: Cambridge Univ. Press.

Wilson, J., F. Opio, and B. Cable. 1984. A review of literature on taro production and marketing in Western Samoa. *Alafua Agricultural Bull.* 9 (1): 72–88.

Wilson, James. 1799. *A missionary voyage to the southern Pacific Ocean in the years 1796, 1797, 1798 in the ship* Duff. London: Chapman.

Wilson, Walter. 1968. Land, activity, and social organization of Lelu, Kusaie. Ph.D. thesis, Anthropology, Univ. Pennsylvania.

Wing, E., and S. Brown. 1980. *Paleonutrition.* N.Y.: Academic Press.

Winterhalder, B., and E. A. Smith. 1981. *Hunter-gatherer foraging strategies.* Chicago: Univ. Chicago Press.

Wirsing, Rolf. 1985. The health of traditional societies and the effects of acculturation. *Current Anthropology* 26 (3): 303–322.

Wolff, R. 1966. Meanings of food. *Tropical and Geographical Medicine* 1: 45–51.

Wright St. Clair, R. 1972. Diet of the Maoris in New Zealand. *Ecology of Food and Nutrition* 1:213–223.

Wu, David. 1979. *Traditional Chinese concepts of food and medicine in Singapore.* Institute of Southeast Asian Studies Occasional Paper 55. Singapore.

Yen, Douglas E. 1971. The development of agriculture in Oceania. In *Studies in Oceanic culture history,* vol. 2. BPBM Pacific Anthropological Records 12. Honolulu.

——. 1973a. Origins of Oceanic agriculture. *Archeology and Physical Anthropology in Oceania* 8:68–85.

——. 1973b. Ethnobotany from the voyages of Mendana and Quiros in the Pacific. *World Archeology* 9.

——. 1974. *The sweet potato and Oceania.* Bishop Museum Bull. 236. Honolulu.

——. 1975. Indigenous food processing in Oceania. In *Gastronomy. See* Arnott 1975.

——. 1980a. The Southeast Asian foundations of Oceanic agriculture. *JSO* 36 (66–67): 140–147.

——. 1980b. Pacific production systems. In *South Pacific agricultural survey 1979. See* Ward and Proctor 1980.

Yen, D., and J. Gordon, eds. 1973. *Anuta.* BPBM Pacific Anthropological Records 21. Honolulu.

Yen, D., and J. Wheeler. 1968. Introduction of taro into the Pacific—chromosome numbers. *Ethnology* 7:250–267.

Young, Michael. 1971. *Fighting with food.* London: Cambridge Univ. Press.

Young, Vernon R. 1980. Animal foods, past, present and future. In *Animals, feed, food, and people,* ed. R. L. Baldwin. American Association for the Advancement of Science Symposium. Colorado: Westview Press.

Zimmet, Paul. 1980. Blood pressure studies in two Pacific populations with varying degrees of modernisation. *New Zealand Medical J.* 657: 249–252.

———. 1981. Diabetes, the paradigm of affluence in response to modernization. In *Migration, adaptation, and health in the South Pacific. See* Fleming and Prior 1981.

Zimmet, P., P. Taft, A. Guinea, W. Guthrie, and K. Thoma. 1977. The high prevalence of diabetes mellitus on a central Pacific island. *Diabetologia* 13:111–115.

Zimmet, P., H. King, R. Taylor, L. R. Rape, B. Balkau, and K. Thoma. 1984. The natural history of impaired glucose tolerance in the Micronesian population of Nauru: A six year follow up study. *Diabetologia* 26 (1): 39–43.

Zimmet, P., R. Taylor, H. King, W. Geddes, and K. Pargeter, eds. 1982. *The impact of modernization on the health of a Pacific nation 1981.* Melbourne: WHO Centre, Royal South Memorial Hospital.

Index

Boldface numbers indicate illustrations.

About the Author

Nancy J. Pollock has worked alongside nutrition educators in the joint endeavor of making food programs more relevant to Pacific cultures. She is Senior Lecturer in Anthropology at Victoria University of Wellington, New Zealand, where she teaches courses on the Pacific, research methodology, and gender issues. Among her many publications she has edited, with Ron Crocombe, *French Polynesia* and contributed to the volume *Gastronomy,* edited by M. L. Arnott.

Production Notes

Composition and paging were done on the
Quadex Composing System and typesetting
on the Compugraphic 8400 by the design
and production staff of University of
Hawaii Press.

The text and display typeface is Sabon.

Offset presswork and binding were done by
The Maple-Vail Book Manufacturing Group.
Text paper is Glatfelter Offset Vellum,
basis 50.

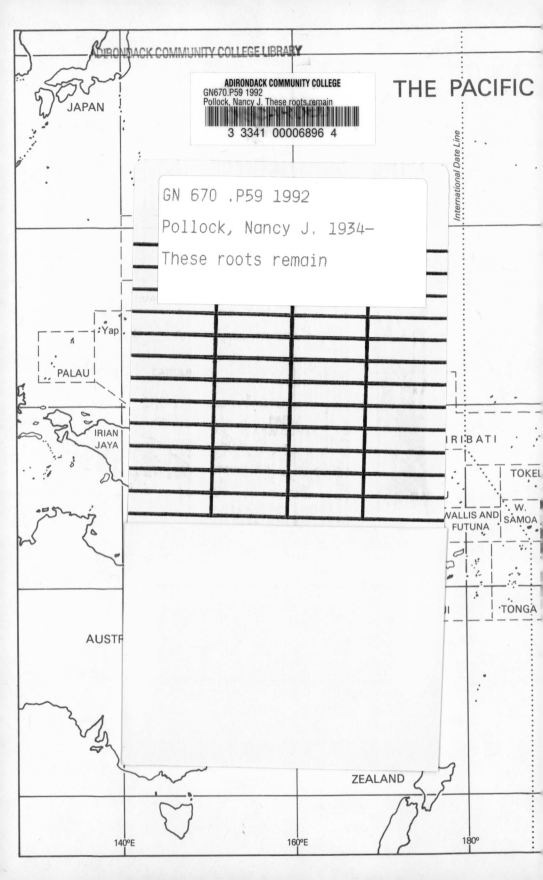

ADIRONDACK COMMUNITY COLLEGE LIBRARY

ADIRONDACK COMMUNITY COLLEGE
GN670.P59 1992
Pollock, Nancy J. These roots remain

3 3341 00006896 4

GN 670 .P59 1992

Pollock, Nancy J. 1934–

These roots remain

THE PACIFIC

JAPAN

International Date Line

Yap

PALAU

IRIAN JAYA

KIRIBATI

TOKEL

WALLIS AND FUTUNA

W. SAMOA

TONGA

AUSTR

ZEALAND

140°E

160°E

180°